S0-BDO-110

Second Edition

COMPENSATION THEORY AND PRACTICE

Marc J. Wallace, Jr.
University of Kentucky

Charles H. Fay
*Institute of Management and Labor Relations
at Rutgers University*

Kent Human Resource Management Series

Series Consulting Editor: Richard W. Beatty
*Institute of Management and Labor Relations
at Rutgers University*

PWS-KENT Publishing Company
Boston, Massachusetts

PWS–KENT
Publishing Company

Editor: Rolf A. Janke
Assistant Editor: Kathleen M. Tibbetts
Production Editor: Susan L. Krikorian
Interior Designer: DeNee Reiton Skipper/Leslie Baker
Cover Designer: Linda Belamarich
Manufacturing Coordinator: Marcia A. Locke

© 1988 by PWS-KENT Publishing Company. All rights reserved. No part of this book may be reproduced, stored in a retrieval system, or transcribed, in any form or by any means, electronic, mechanical, photocopying, recording, or otherwise, without the prior written permission of the publisher, PWS-KENT Publishing Company, 20 Park Plaza, Boston, Massachusetts 02116.

PWS-KENT Publishing Company is a division of Wadsworth, Inc.

Printed in the United States of America

2   3   4   5   6   7   8   9—92   91   90   89

Library of Congress Cataloging-in-Publication Data

Wallace, Marc J.
  Compensation theory and practice / Marc J. Wallace, Jr., Charles
H. Fay—2nd ed.

    p.   cm.   —(Kent human resource management series)
  Includes bibliographies and index.
  1. Compensation management.   I. Fay, Charles H.   II. Title.   III. Series
HF5549.5.C67W35   1988   658.3′2—dc19   88-12609
ISBN 0-534-87198-4

Series Preface

It is with great pleasure that we bring you the revised and expanded Kent Human Resource Management Series from PWS-KENT Publishing Company. The original four books on federal regulation, human resource costing, compensation, and performance appraisal were a great success, as evidenced by both academic and trade sales. We thank you for your support of this series.

The revised series includes strategic purposes and administrative issues in performance appraisal; and significant updating and expansion in federal regulation, human resource costing, and compensation administration. We are currently developing new series entries in executive development, recruitment, and benefits administration—issues long overdue both from an academic and practitioner perspective. We plan to add titles in areas such as international human resource management, human resource information systems, and collective bargaining offerings.

As organizations face the new competition created by global marketing, deregulation, and advancing technology, they are beginning to "resize." Preparing for this new competition raises concerns over the cost of human resources and clear recognition that human resources are indeed an organization's most expensive and least well-managed resource. Certainly, organizations have designed and engineered systems with specific planning and control methods; and tools for material resources, financial resources, information systems, and time management. The new competition, however, recognizes the need for better utilization of human resources. Thus, the issues raised in this series—the costs of human resources, and the function and contribution of each human resource while operating within the domestic legal framework—become more critical as organizations competitively restructure to better utilize their human resources. Ultimately, this series is designed to have an impact upon the practice of human resources in the contemporary economic environment. Implementing these approaches to solving human resource problems will be the ultimate proof of its success.

Many people have helped in the development of this important series. I would like to thank Wayne Barcomb for his faith to initiate and expand it; and Rolf Janke, Diane Miliotes, and Kathleen Tibbetts for their enthusiastic support of the revision and expansion.

Richard W. Beatty

Foreword

The field of compensation is exciting. Part of this excitement stems from the fact that decisions made regarding compensation have a direct bearing on the success or failure of businesses and other organizations. A second factor is that the economy of the 1980s is forcing employers to be more cost conscious than ever before. As labor costs dominate a greater share of the cost of doing business (more than half of this cost for many organizations), people who make compensation decisions will bear the major responsibility for cost control and effectiveness. Third, society has turned its attention to the issue of compensation and, through the legal environment, will hold employers strictly accountable, not only for maintaining employment security for employees, but also for protecting and promoting equal employment opportunity. Finally, compensation is interesting because it affects each of us personally. Most of us have frequently pondered whether or not we are making as much money as we should be, whether what we are making is fair when compared to what others are being paid, or whether we could improve income through a career change, a job change, or harder-nosed bargaining with the boss.

We have written *Compensation Theory and Practice* out of a sense of this excitement and hope to share our enthusiasm with you. You may be preparing for a career in personnel and human resources and may even have a specific interest in a career as a compensation specialist. Or, you may be preparing for a career in line management. Both the line manager and the compensation specialist must be intimately familiar with compensation theory and practice in order to make effective compensation decisions. In most organizations, the responsibility for compensation planning and administration is shared between line and the compensation (or personnel) staff. The line manager is immediately responsible for administration, but relies on the special expertise of the compensation staff officer to design, evaluate, and recommend wage and salary rates and benefit policies. The staff compensation specialist draws on professional expertise in analyzing wage data from external markets, carrying out job evaluation to estimate the internal worth of jobs, and designing merit systems to link pay and performance. The line manager, however, must translate such plans into practice and make them an operational reality that results in bottom-line results for the organization.

How well line managers and compensation specialists manage their relationship will depend in large part on whether they are operating from the same knowledge base. The line manager ignorant of such topics as labor economics, employee behavior, and equity in compensation will probably view the compensation officer as a source of irritation at best, and an obstructionist at worst. The staff compensation officer ignorant of the real world of line production will quickly become tied up in his own little world of compensation theory and will never bother to link his efforts to the broader objectives of the entire organization. The major objective of *Compensation Theory and Practice* is to provide the line and compensation manager with the same knowledge base about compensation.

We believe that effective compensation decisions require a knowledge of both current theory regarding compensation and specific practices. Both theory and practice have changed dramatically in our field during the last ten years. In *Compensation Theory and Practice*, we will analyze these developments and explicitly present the links between theory and practice. In some cases, we will show how specific practices make sense in the light of theory and research. In other cases, we will show how theory and research suggest practical improvements. Finally, we will show how other practices and problems encountered by line managers are calling for additional theory and research.

Marc J. Wallace, Jr.
Charles H. Fay
1983

Foreword to the Second Edition

The field of compensation continues to be challenging and exciting. Events in the 1980s, ranging from continued multinational competition, to the deregulation of many industries, to the emergence of a service economy, have forced organizations to look at their asset bases much more carefully. The conclusions of these evaluations have prompted many organizations to restructure their financial, capital, and human assets; and they have downsized, reorganized, and removed many layers of management. The result is that many organizations have become more concerned with strategy and performance effectiveness than ever before.

As we approach the 1990s, the major strategic vision is in place for most organizations. The challenge will be one of implementation—making business plans happen in renewed and redesigned organizations. Organizations are looking toward compensation as a major vehicle for implementing business strategy and supporting organizational culture. They view compensation practice as a major means for rendering organizations more productive, ensuring product and service quality, and making organizations ever more responsive to customers, employees, and other key constituents.

Compensation Theory and Practice, Second Edition, reflects these developments in our field. We have added chapters on process equity (Chapter 5) and the strategic uses of compensation practice (Chapter 12). In addition, we have updated and revised materials throughout each chapter to reflect the changes that have occurred in the theory and practice of our dynamic field.

We have retained the basic structure of the book, focusing first on theory and then moving into practice, because it has proved to be an effective educational vehicle. Our firm belief that effective compensation decisions require a knowledge of both current theory and practice has motivated us to continue to explore the links between theory and practice, and to show how some practices make sense in the light of theory and how theory continues to lead to improvements in practice.

Acknowledgments

We are indebted to the many researchers and practitioners who have contributed to the current body of knowledge in the study of compensation. We especially acknowledge the research of Thomas Mahoney, of Vanderbilt University, who, more than any other person in our field, has integrated the rather diverse bodies of economic, behavioral, and sociological theory into a richer understanding of compensation phenomena.

Dick Beatty provided the spark that kindled our interest in *Compensation Theory and Practice* and, as consulting editor of the Kent Human Resource Management Series, he has provided us with encouragement throughout the process. Rolf Janke and Kathy Tibbetts of PWS-KENT have provided critical support and the editorial review so necessary to the success of a book of this nature. Fred Crandall is a close friend and professional colleague of long standing. We have frequently relied on him for judgments regarding how compensation is actually practiced in organizations. His insights have helped us in building the links between theory and practice presented in this text. Sandi Jennings, Miami University of Ohio; Tom Mahoney, Vanderbilt University; Robert Malone, Loyola University of Chicago; and Harvey Shore, University of Connecticut, reviewed earlier drafts of this manuscript. The final product is improved because of their constructive criticism.

We thank the College of Business and Economics, University of Kentucky, and the Institute of Management and Labor Relations, Rutgers University, for providing institutional support and the climate that encouraged our efforts. Finally, we thank our families for their support and enthusiasm for our work.

Marc J. Wallace, Jr.
Charles H. Fay
1988

Contents

Money cannot buy happiness, but it will soothe the nerves.
—French proverb

I
Compensation Theory

1

"But It's Not Fair!"

Key Issues and Questions for This Chapter

After you have studied this chapter, you should be able to address the following key issues and questions:

1. What is fair about pay and why is it such a big issue?

2. What is the concept of equity and how can it be used to examine the idea of fairness in compensation?

3. What are the major forms of equity affected by compensation decisions?

4. How might equity be compromised in compensation decisions and what effect will this have?

5. What process should managers follow in order to go about organizing information about compensation in order to better understand the process?

Introduction

No other area of managing relationships with employees is more likely to create problems of achieving fairness than compensation administration — setting wage and salary rates, evaluating jobs, and providing monetary and nonmonetary benefits. *Compensation Theory and Practice* is all about such problems and will show you what basic theory and research tells us about dealing with them. Each of the following cases illustrates quite distinct problems that frequently arise in managing compensation. All of them, however, have a common thread: a norm of equity or fairness has been violated in making a compensation decision: some person or group has been treated unfairly.

Case I   *Tony Dorsett.* Dallas Cowboys football star Tony Dorsett is upset about his salary. He is being paid a $450,000 annual base salary and a benefits package that places his total annual compensation at $700,000.[1] Still, he doesn't think it's fair. *Chicago Tribune* columnist Raymond Coffey agrees and notes that many football fans might also be nodding in agreement with Dorsett.[2]

Dorsett is clearly a football star. He has played with the National Football League's Dallas Cowboys for ten years, he is a Heisman Trophy winner, and, Coffey notes, is well on his way to becoming the second all-time rushing leader in NFL history.

The object of his hurt is the contract Dallas signed with Herschel Walker, who joined the NFL club in 1986 after bailing out of the clearly second-rate and dying U.S. Football League. Walker also has a Heisman Trophy, but has not built the NFL playing record owned by Dorsett. Yet, his contract calls for five years at $1 million per year, making him the highest paid player in NFL history.[3]

Coffey relates that Dorsett is fuming, and notes that the player threatens to be a very disruptive force if he's unhappy. The columnist reflects: "Life isn't fair. But fairness is, nonetheless, one of the most vital, enduring, and widely shared of American values."[4]

Case II   *The Denver Nurses.* Fairness is, indeed, a deep national value and, in compensation practice, it has become a legal issue, as well. Three major lawsuits in recent years illustrate this point: (1) *Lemons et al. v. City and County of Denver* (the Denver nurses case),[5] (2) *International Union of Electrical, Radio, and Machine Workers (IUE) v. Westinghouse Electric Corp.,*[6] and (3) *AFSCME v. State of Washington.*[7] Each of these cases involves charges that wages being paid to women are not fair when compared to those being paid to men employees.

The Denver nurses case is a good illustration of the problem. In 1978, nurses employed by the city of Denver charged in United States District Court that they were being discriminated against because of their sex. They demonstrated that nurses were paid lower wage rates than such craft workers as parking meter repairers, tree trimmers, and sign painters. They argued that the work being done by nurses was at least of equal value (a comparable worth claim that we will discuss more fully) to the work being done by parking meter repairers and other craftsmen. Indeed, they argued that the wage differences did not reflect any difference in the type of work being performed or the value of work being performed but rather society's tendency to pay women less for their work than men. In essence, the nurses argued that nurses are paid less than craft workers because their occupation is dominated by women and craft occupations are dominated by men.

The nurses based their charge of "Unfair!" on two federal statutes: (1) the Equal Pay Act of 1963, an amendment to the Fair Labor Standards Act (FLSA) of 1938, and (2) Title VII of the Civil Rights Act of 1964.[8] The Equal Pay Act establishes a standard of equal pay for equal work that prohibits employers from paying women less than men when they are performing jobs that are essentially equal in terms of content (skill, responsibility, effort, and working conditions).

The Equal Pay Act sets up a very narrow definition of fairness with respect to men's and women's pay. Should a woman's job differ from a man's on any of the job content dimensions cited in the Equal Pay Act (skill, working conditions, effort, and responsibility), the employer will be in compliance with the law if he or she sets different wage rates for men and women. The Denver nurses attempted to broaden that basis for considering the fairness of male-female wage differences by demanding that, beyond pay parity for jobs of equal content, employers should pay equivalent wage rates for jobs of equal value or comparable worth.

The comparable worth argument employed by the nurses is based on Title VII of the 1964 Civil Rights Act, which prohibits any employment action that discriminates against a person because of sex, race, color, religion, or national origin. In this case, the employment action involved setting wage rates, and the violation occurred because jobs dominated by women are paid less than jobs dominated by men even though they are of equal value or comparable worth.

The court agreed with the nurses that occupations dominated by women could historically have been paid less than occupations dominated by men and that such discrimination could in fact lead to a violation of a comparable worth criterion of fairness. The court still found against the nurses, however, by citing a fairness criterion based on the marketplace rather than on comparable worth. In ruling against the nurses, the court commented, "This is a case which is pregnant with the possibility of disrupting the entire economic system of the United States of America . . . . I'm not going to restructure the entire economy of the U.S. Some higher court is going to take that step."[9] The court, in effect, ruled that external market structures are legally acceptable criteria for setting wage rates. Thus, the fact that Denver must pay more to attract parking meter repairers than it does to attract nurses is sufficient reason to pay the former more than the latter.

However, the comparable worth doctrine of fairness is far from dead as a result of the Denver nurses ruling. In a second case, the International Union of Electrical Workers (IUE) charged that Westinghouse historically had established classes of jobs for wage-setting purposes that discriminated against women. Specifically, they demonstrated that Westinghouse historically had segregated "women's" jobs from "men's" jobs and set lower pay rates for women's jobs. The court decided that such a practice discriminated against female employees and was unfair. The practice was ordered stopped.

An equally significant case involving the comparable worth issue is the *American Federation of State, County, and Municipal Employees (AFSCME)* v. *State of Washington.* [10] The case arose as a result of a ten-year campaign by AFSCME to have the state of Washington raise the wages of state employees in traditionally female job classifications. A 1974 study commissioned by the state showed that pay differences existed between job classifications dominated by men and those traditionally dominated by women that were not "due solely to job worth." [11] A subsequent study conducted by the state found that female employees received 20-percent lower pay than men doing work requiring equivalent skill, knowledge, mental demands, accountability, and working conditions. [12]

The state's legislature failed to remedy the disparity even though the pay gaps continued. AFSCME filed suit in federal court against Washington in 1982, charging that this failure to remedy the pay gap constituted a violation of Title VII of the 1964 Civil Rights Act (see Chapter 6). In December 1983, the U.S. District Court agreed with AFSCME and found the state in violation of the law. The court ordered the state immediately to raise the pay of 15,000 employees in predominately female job classifications and give back pay to the employees retroactive to September 1979. Experts estimate that the judgment ultimately will cost the state up to $1 billion.

Cases such as Westinghouse and AFSCME have moved the issue of comparable worth to the forefront of social and legal considerations in compensation. In the wake of these decisions, for example, over one hundred states and cities have undertaken their own comparable worth studies in an effort to avoid Washington's problems. Many states have passed comparable worth statutes demanding that women in public employment be paid the same as men for jobs of comparable worth.

Comparable worth remains a hotly debated issue that does not lend itself readily to solution. [13] Managers confronted with comparable worth demands face uncertainty on the following issues:

1. Is the labor market fair to women? [14]

2. Can job evaluation practices be used to assure that women will be paid as much as men on jobs of comparable worth? [15]

3. What is pay discrimination and what constitutes a violation of the law on an employer's part? [16]

Although we will examine the legal issues and compensation practice more completely in Chapter 6, it is important to note here that the debate underscores the importance our society places on equity and fairness in the pay of women and men. At this writing, the field of compensation has yet to develop an acceptable measure of job worth (fair pay) that is independent of the marketplace.[17] Until such a definition can be developed and accepted, the conflict inherent in the Denver nurses case between market and nonmarket notions of fairness will continue.

Case III   *Quality Stamping, Inc.* Quality Stamping is a highly successful manufacturer of machined parts for office business machines.[18] The company is a major subcontractor to the Information Products Division of International Business Machines (IBM). The company was founded by Richard M. Jackson, who is currently president and chairman of the board. Mr. Jackson worked as a machinist for IBM for ten years before going out on his own as a subcontractor in the 1960s.

Under Jackson's direction, Quality Stamping grew rapidly and expanded its operations. Through the 1970s, sales grew at an annual rate of 15 percent. Having begun in Mr. Jackson's garage, the company now occupies two large buildings and employs forty people including ten mechanics, twenty stamping machine operators, six miscellaneous employees, and three secretaries.

Quality Stamping had never experienced any incident involving employee discontent with personnel policies that had not been resolved to everyone's apparent satisfaction. The company had never been subject to a union organization attempt, nor had any employees expressed a desire to form a union. The employee turnover rate was extremely low: 5 percent, or two employees per year on the average. Even in these cases, exit interviews showed that, for the most part, the employees left for personal reasons unrelated to company policy.

Quality Stamping never had a formal wage and salary program. Mr. Jackson's policy had always been to survey comparable wage rates in the area and offer competitive wage rates to start. He also maintained a policy of strict confidence with respect to wages paid. He firmly believed that it would be an invasion of employee privacy to disclose such information.

But Mr. Jackson's brother, an officer in the company, recently had read an article in the *Harvard Business Review* that ran counter to Jackson's logic regarding wage secrecy. The author of the article, a nationally noted industrial/organizational psychologist, argued on the basis of behavioral principles that wage rates must be known by all employees if they are going to have any effect on employee behavior and performance. Thus, a policy of secrecy would make it impossible for wage rates to act as an incentive for employees. In a classic case of Harvard Business Review Syndrome, the adoption of management ideas read about in a prestigious journal with no thought to their applicability in the current setting, Mr. Jackson decided to switch his policy and make every employee's wage rate public.[19]

He started with the twenty stamping machine operators. A call to the accounting department generated a printout (Exhibit 1.1) that listed each employee, his or her number, number of years employed by Quality Stamping (tenure), and hourly wage rate. Jackson posted the printout in the employee lounge about five minutes before the morning coffee break.

Within a half hour, Mr. Jackson received a call from the stamping machine supervisor. According to him, Marjorie Smith had taken a look at the printout, walked over to Helen Pirenne and Kate Shapiro, and begun a violent verbal argument with them. By the end of the day, twelve of the twenty employees had walked off the job and were picketing the plant. They refused to come back to their jobs until either Joanna Zacher, Marge Shriner, Helen Pirenne, Sylvia Reese, and Barb Kasher were brought down in pay or others were brought up. In addition, a group (led by Marjorie Smith) had contacted the International Association of Machinists (IAM) local in their city for help and advice in forming a local union.

Exhibit 1.1   Quality Stamping's Wage and Salary Printout

Employee	Employee Number	Tenure	Hourly Wage Rate
M. Smith	002	10	$4.45
L. Barth	003	9	4.45
M. Baran	035	5	3.90
M. Boros	037	5	3.80
J. Zacher	040	1/4	4.85
M. Shriner	043	1/4	5.00
E. McConnell	006	10	4.50
D. Edwards	007	10	4.25
R. Kimble	008	8	4.50
D. Grambsch	009	8	4.50
B. Moore	023	6	3.90
D. Dutton	026	6	3.80
S. Reese	038	1/2	4.10
B. Kasher	040	1/2	4.10
H. Pirenne	042	1/8	4.45
K. Shapiro	043	1/8	4.45
M. Lowe	027	6	4.00
H. Breton	029	5	4.00
L. Alquien	033	2	4.40
H. Bernardo	034	2	4.40

Case IV   *Anchor Insurance Corporation.* Anchor Insurance Corporation is among the nation's largest life insurance companies.[20] The company employs a point factor system for job evaluation. Job evaluation is a system for establishing the relative worth of jobs internally to the employer, and the point factor technique (to be explained fully in Chapter 8) represents these value judgments by assigning points to each job. Thus, two jobs that garner 200 points each are considered to be of equal value to the company.

The company's compensation planning committee has a job evaluation problem among their professional and technical series of jobs. The company must pay much higher rates for actuaries and systems analysts than for the other jobs in this series. New graduates in these fields regularly command an annual salary of $38,000 to start. Competition among employers for these people is extremely keen and the supply of qualified actuaries is extremely short. The company not meeting or exceeding the $38,000 rate will not be able to attract qualified people.

The problem arises when the job evaluation results for actuaries and systems analysts are compared with job evaluation results for the other jobs in the professional and technical series (accountant, auditor, and attorney). The data in Exhibit 1.2 display the job evaluation results for these jobs. Pay grades 16 through 20 include all the jobs in this family. A job garnering 100 to 149 points in the job evaluation is assigned to pay grade 16, 150 to 199 points to pay

Exhibit 1.2   Job Evaluation for Professional and Technical Series, Anchor Insurance Corporation

Pay Class	Job Evaluation Points	Job Family			
		Legal	*Accounting*	*Information Systems*	*Actuarial*
20	300–49	Senior Counsel	Senior Accountant	Senior Information Systems Manager	Senior Actuary
19	250–99	General Counsel	General Accountant	Information Systems Manager	
18	200–49	Junior Counsel	Accountant	Systems Analyst II	Actuary II
17	150–99	Attorney II	Auditor II	Systems Analyst I	Actuary I
16	100–49	Attorney I	Auditor I	Programmer/ Analyst	Assistant Actuary

grade 17, and so forth. All jobs in a given pay grade have been judged to have equal value to the company, and a single starting wage rate, midpoint, and maximum rate should be set for all jobs in the pay grade. Thus, for example, the jobs of Attorney I, Auditor I, Programmer/Analyst, and Assistant Actuary should all be set at the same hiring rate, midpoint, and maximum wage rate.

The problem is that Anchor can hire as many Attorney I's and Auditor I's as they need for $28,000 per year, but they have to pay $38,000 for Programmer/Analysts and Assistant Actuaries. How can Anchor resolve this dilemma? There is an internal demand (based on the job evaluation results) to pay each of the jobs in a given pay grade the same. Yet, external market realities force the company to pay actuaries and systems analysts nearly $10,000 more per year than attorneys and other professional and technical workers.

As you will see again and again in this book, there is no single best solution to dilemmas of the type facing Anchor Insurance. The professional compensation planner must consider alternative strategies for dealing with such problems and choose the one that strikes the best compromise among competing objectives. In this situation, many insurance companies have adopted the solution pictured in Exhibit 1.3. In this case, the company has not attempted to stretch the job evalu-

Exhibit 1.3   One Solution to Anchor Insurance's Dilemma

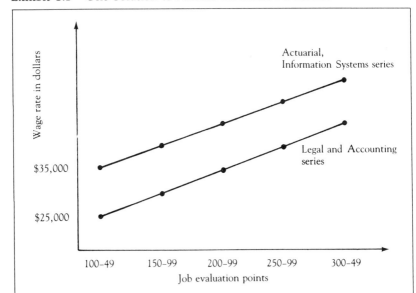

ation system to conform more closely to external market differentials. Instead it has created two separate job series for compensation purposes: (1) a legal and accounting series, and (2) an actuarial and information systems series. Job evaluations are carried out separately within each family, and no job evaluation comparisons are made across series. Thus, an attorney or accountant in the first pay grade (100–149 points) is paid a starting salary of $28,000. An assistant actuary or systems analyst in the same pay grade (100–149 points) starts at $38,000 per year.

You might take a few minutes to think about Anchor's dilemma and the solution we have just presented. What are the strengths of creating two separate classes of jobs for compensation purposes? What else might the company have tried to do? What problems might this solution create?

Case V   *The Insulting Wage Increase.* Mark Williams was extremely unhappy with his 1986 wage increase.[21] He had worked the last two years for General Healthtronics, a manufacturer of high tech medical and health electronic devices, as a patent attorney. He had begun with the company on graduation and was a very eager and hard-working attorney. His superiors were not only pleased with his work but had told him he was the best patent attorney working for the company. In fact, he had just returned from a merit review session with his boss, Steve Mackey, who informed him that he would be given the highest wage increase of the fifteen patent attorneys in his division. He would receive a 6.5-percent increase from $29,960 per year to $31,907, a $1,947 bump.

His new salary sounded pretty good to him until he compared notes with Fred Cadillac, a fellow patent attorney and classmate employed in the same department. Fred was the classic "good ole boy." Never one to work too hard, he came in a few minutes late each day, and was packed and ready to head off for the golf course twenty minutes ahead of quitting time. Extra effort on a particular case was unheard of to Fred, and he had an uncanny skill for riding in on the coattails of others in his group. On cue, at twenty minutes to five, Fred stuck his head into Mark's office and said, "Time to knock off and hit the ball, good buddy! Why don't you join me for a change? I sure can afford to relax a little bit more with the new bread I'll be making next year, thirty-two big ones!"

"How much are you making next year?" asked Mark incredulously. "Actually, I've rounded up a tad," responded Fred, "but I'm slotted in at $31,609. How much have they signed you up for?" Mark replied that he would be making $31,907. "Well, that makes us just about even, doesn't it!" replied Fred, and left for the golf course. Mark fumed in his office. "All that work and I end up making less than $300 more than that goof-off!" He knew that he and Fred had started with General Healthtronics two years earlier at the same salary of $28,000. He had expected to outpace Fred quickly, however, knowing that they would perform at much different levels. Apparently, either the company did not realize this or did not recognize differences in performance when making individual salary adjustments.

After a great deal of thought and agony, Mark approached his supervisor, Steve Mackey. "Steve," he began, "I find this awfully difficult to talk about, but I just can't contain my feelings and I want to have a talk before I leave to find work elsewhere." "What in heaven's name could be so bad?" exclaimed Steve, shaken by the implied threat of losing somebody as valuable as Mark. "The problem is my salary," Mark said. "When you first told me that I would make $31,907 next year, I was really pleased. In fact, I don't even know what I could make on the open market. At any rate, I didn't think anything about it until Fred Cadillac told me he'd be making $31,609 next year. Steve, that's just not fair! You yourself have said in public that Fred is the laziest attorney on board and that he's going to have to shape up in order to make promotion. Also, I did not seek his salary information out; he volunteered it to me and gloated on his way out about how close we are in salary. I guess that's what really burns me!"

"What you're saying, Mark, is that $300 before taxes doesn't accurately reflect the difference between your job performance and Fred's," said Steve. "Darn right!" agreed Mark. "And it's just not fair," he added.

"Mark, I don't have a good answer for you," admitted Steve. "There is no question that you are our best patent attorney and that Fred is our worst. Unfortunately, I'm hamstrung by the company's policy of making external market adjustments across the board so long as an employee's performance is rated acceptable or above. Here, look at this merit matrix for 1986 adjustments" (Exhibit 1.4). He indicated a sheet of paper on his desk. "This is a policy handed down to me by corporate headquarters. I have no options except to assign a 0 percent for someone rated unacceptable, 5.5 percent for acceptable performance, 6 percent for above average, and 6.5 percent for outstanding." "Where did they come up with the 5.5 percent for acceptable?" asked Mark. "The market survey moved 5 percent last year, so the company established an across-the-board market adjustment of 5 percent," explained Steve.

"Here, let me do a little accounting for you on this sheet of paper" (Exhibit 1.5), added Steve. "Both you and Fred started two years ago at $28,000 per year.

Exhibit 1.4   General Healthtronics 1986 Merit Matrix

	Performance Rating			
	Unacceptable	*Acceptable*	*Above Average*	*Outstanding*
Percent Increase:	0%	5.5%	6%	6.5%

Exhibit 1.5 Steve Mackey's Calculations

		1985		1986
Mark	$28,000.00	1984 Base pay	$29,960.00	1985 Base pay
	$ 1,400.00	5% Market adjustment	$ 1,498.00	5% Market adjustment
	$ 560.00	2% Merit increase	$ 499.40	1.5% Merit increase
	$29,960.00	1985 Base pay	$31,907.40	1986 Base pay
	7.0%	Percent increase	6.5%	Percent increase
Fred	$28,000.00	1984 Base pay	$29,820.00	1985 Base pay
	$ 1,400.00	5% Market adjustment	$ 1,491.00	5% Market adjustment
	$ 420.00	1.5% Merit increase	$ 298.20	1% Merit increase
	$29,820.00	1985 Base pay	$31,609.20	1986 Base pay
	6.5%	Percent increase	6.0%	Percent increase

In both years you got the highest performance rating, outstanding, and Fred got the lowest rating short of unacceptable, acceptable. In 1985, you, and everyone else, were given market adjustments of 5 percent, in line with the market survey movement for that year. In addition, you received a 2-percent merit increase on top of that for your outstanding performance. Fred received only a 1.5-percent increase for performance. We did the same thing again this year. Each of you received a 5-percent market adjustment and you received a 1.5-percent increase on top for performance. Again, Fred received only a 1-percent increase for performance."

"That 1.5 percent is actually insulting!" complained Mark. "Why should I work overtime on cases, do extra research at the law library, and generally work my butt off for this outfit when all I get for the effort is $298.20 more than Fred this year on the basis of merit, before taxes! It seems to me that I have only two options: adopt Fred's habits or seek work with a company that actually rewards effort and performance! I think you know what my choice will be, Steve," fumed Mark as he stormed out of Steve's office.

You might take a few minutes to think about the problem faced by Steve and Mark. If you were Mark, what would you do? If you were redesigning General Healthtronic's compensation policies, how might you change them in order not to lose employees like Mark?

The Central Notion of Equity

The cases that opened this chapter raise diverse issues and problems. The Denver nurses case involved what is primarily a legal and economic issue concerning definitions of the worth of a job. The Quality Stamping case was primarily a problem involving fairness of individual wage rates for people doing the same job. Those just beginning employment were coming in at wage rates at or above those being paid to people with several years' experience. Anchor Insurance had a problem very common among employers today: market dislocations. In this case, market conditions were forcing the wages that must be paid actuaries and systems analysts out of line with what internal job evaluation would have suggested. Finally, Tony Dorsett's case, as well as that of the insulting wage increase, showed how a mismanaged merit system can actually create disincentives for performance. In the latter case, the amount of increase given for effective performance was perceived as an insult by the recipient and would probably have led to his quitting the employer.

Each of these cases, however, reflects the critical theme that exists at the center of all compensation theory and practice: equity. You will not become competent in compensation administration until you develop a thorough understanding of this concept.

Equity Defined

Equity is generally defined as anything of value earned through the provision or investment of something of value. An investor, for example, earns equity (ownership) interest in a corporation by providing money (purchasing shares). In compensation, a worker earns equity interest by providing labor on a job.

Fairness is achieved when the return on equity is equivalent to the investment made. For compensation, then, we would define fairness as being achieved when the value of the compensation received is equivalent to the value of the labor performed. Unfairness or inequity occurs when the value of the compensation received does not correspond to the value of the labor performed.

Equity Theory

Research has demonstrated that equity and inequity can create dramatic employee reactions.[22] Indeed, a well-developed body of theory and research has focused on this phenomenon. The belief that one is being treated inequitably (for example, having ten years' experience and being paid less than a newly hired employee, as in the Quality Stamping case) directly affects motivation and therefore influences an employee's behavior and performance.

The work of J. Stacy Adams is most frequently cited as the foundation of equity theory.[23] Specifically, he proposes that employees constantly monitor their exchange relationship with their employer. An exchange relationship is one that involves equity: people exchange things of value. In the setting of compensation, the exchange is one of monetary and nonmonetary compensation for labor. According to equity theory, the principle of *distributive justice* is crucial to the employee. Distributive justice occurs when all parties in an exchange relationship have equal outcome/input ratios. That is, the proportionate relation between outcomes and inputs is equal for all persons in the relationship. Thus, distributive justice defines fairness or equity.

The ratios in Exhibit 1.6 make the notion of distributive justice in equity theory more explicit. The theory proposes that employees evaluate their compensation (as well as all other aspects of their employment) by comparing

Exhibit 1.6 Ratios Defining Equity

$$\frac{O_p}{I_p} = \frac{O_o}{I_o} \text{ , equity}$$

$$\frac{O_p}{I_p} > \frac{O_o}{I_o} \text{ , inequity, overreward}$$

$$\frac{O_p}{I_p} < \frac{O_o}{I_o} \text{ , inequity, underreward}$$

where:

O_p = outcomes for the person
I_p = the person's inputs
O_o = outcomes for other person
I_o = other person's inputs

the ratio of their employment outcomes (O_p) to their inputs (I_p) with a similar ratio for a comparison employee or group (O_o/I_o). Outcomes can include many rewards, including monetary and nonmonetary compensation. Inputs can include performance, effort, skills, experience, responsibility, and working conditions. Distributive justice or equity is achieved when the two ratios in Exhibit 1.6 are equal. If, however, an employee or group of employees perceives an inequality between or among these ratios, inequity will be experienced.

You might take several minutes to analyze each of the cases at the outset of this chapter in terms of the equity ratios in Exhibit 1.6. What would these ratios look like for Tony Dorsett versus Herschel Walker, for nurses versus parking meter repairers in Denver, for M. Smith versus H. Pirenne at Quality Stamping (see Exhibit 1.1), for actuaries versus attorneys at Anchor Insurance, or for Mark Williams versus Fred Cadillac in the case of the insulting wage increase?

Because it has been found that reactions to equity and inequity are strong, they must be considered carefully by compensation managers in making decisions about pay. Indeed, the relative way in which management treats an employee's compensation is at least as important as the absolute level of pay. Perceptions of equity, then, influence the decisions people make about organizations: to accept or reject a job offer, to stay with or leave an organization, and to expend more or less effort on the job. Because these decisions have direct economic consequences for the organization, compensation planners must pay very close attention to equity issues in planning, administering, and auditing compensation practices.

External, Internal, and Individual Equity

Compensation theorists have recognized in recent years that equity is not a simple concept.[24] Indeed, if you tried to create input/outcome ratios in each of the five opening cases to this chapter, you would find a variety of factors. Let's consider inputs as an illustration. An actuary considering the inputs she brings to her work might consider a variety of independent factors. First, she might note that a short supply and strong demand for her occupation make the market tight for her skills, and that she is in a strong position to bid for a higher wage than would be paid for an occupation (for example, elementary schoolteacher) where the market is loose. Economists define the combination (or *intersect*) of what employers are willing to pay (labor demand) and what employees are willing to accept (labor supply) as an *exchange rate*.

The exchange rate or price in the external marketplace for one's occupation is the value that one brings to the job. An employee who compares his or her wage to the wage rate prevailing in the external market for the same occupation is said to be seeking *external equity.*

Instead of looking simply at the external market for one's occupation, an employee may compare the contribution of his or her job to that of another employee's job. Thus, the Denver nurses compared the value of their work as nurses to the city of Denver with the value of the work of Denver parking meter repairers and tree trimmers. They argued that the work of nurses was at least as valuable to the city as the work of the latter. Thus, to pay nurses less violated a norm of *internal equity.*

Finally, employees on the same job frequently count individual effort, performance, and commitment to the employer as a valued input into the ratios in Exhibit 1.6. Thus, in the Quality Stamping case and in the case of the insulting wage increase, the problem centers on individual employee merit (time in grade or tenure and quality of job performance), not on the market rate for jobs or the relative worth of jobs to the employer. This last issue is one of *individual equity.* Let us consider each of these three equity issues in more detail.

External Equity   External equity is a fairness criterion that demands an employer pay a wage rate that corresponds to rates prevailing in external markets for the employee's occupation. Most of us are familiar with the fact that physicians can command higher wages than attorneys, or that business professors can command higher salaries than history professors. These differences have little to do with any differences in the relative worth of these jobs internally to their employers. Rather, they reflect differences in supply and demand across occupational markets. From a purely economic perspective, external equity corresponds to the exchange rates determined by the intersection of the demand for labor (the maximum rates employers are willing to pay) and the supply of labor (the least employees are willing to accept), as in Exhibit 1.7.

Internal Equity   Internal equity is a fairness criterion that requires employers to set wage rates for jobs within their companies that correspond to the relative internal value of each job. That is, theoretically, internal equity as a criterion refers to the value of the work performed on a job to the employer. This value may or may not be tied directly to the marketplace. Empirical research, which will be reviewed in later chapters, suggests that internal and

Exhibit 1.7   Market Definition of External Equity

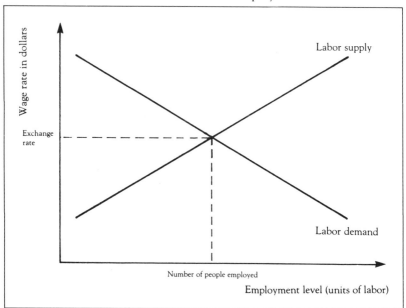

external equity can operate quite independently of each other. We know far less about the roots of internal equity than we do about those of external equity, though. Some have suggested, for example, that a major factor in internal equity is the economic value that the actual work on a job produces for an employer. An alternative concept of internal equity focuses on the value of the labor *itself* that is supplied on a job. The latter basis could include the level of skill a person brings to the job, the level of effort a person must expend on the job, and the amount of training that the job requires. Theory in this area is not yet well-developed and we will discuss the problems employers face in measuring the internal value of jobs in Chapters 3 (job worth) and 8 (job evaluation).

Individual Equity   The individual equity criterion demands that employers pay wage rates to individuals (in the simplest case, workers on the same job) according to variation in individual merit. Better workers should receive higher wages on the same job than poorer workers. Factors contributing to merit may include tenure (how long one has been working for an employer) and job performance. In the Quality Stamping case, a tenure criterion was violated when new people were brought in at wage rates the same or higher than those of long-tenured people. In the case of the insulting wage increase, the wage differences between a high performer and low performer did not adequately reflect actual performance differences.

It is extremely important for managers to keep external, internal, and individual equity issues separate in their thinking about compensation objectives.[25] First, they constitute quite distinct objectives in compensation practices. Thus, for example, Denver might achieve an external equity objective by setting nurses' wage rates equal to those prevailing for nurses in the Denver labor market, yet fail to achieve internal equity when these wage rates are compared to those being paid to parking meter repairers. Indeed, you will find later in this book that external equity, internal equity, and individual equity involve quite different and confusing sets of characteristics or factors. External equity, for example, deals primarily with external economic phenomena involving interactions of supply and demand. Internal equity, in contrast, deals most frequently with job content factors including level of responsibility, education, skills, effort level, and working conditions required by the job. Such factors are not highly correlated with market conditions in most cases. In many cases, external and internal factors will conflict and managers will face the difficult task of finding a compromise between external and internal equity demands.

A second reason for considering external, internal, and individual equity as distinct objectives is that management's success or failure in achieving each of them will have quite different behavioral effects on employees. Thus, for example, an employee's job may be priced competitively with the market for that occupation, but he or she may be dissatisfied because that job is not being paid according to its internal worth to the employer. Or, an employee may perceive that his job is being paid equitably according to the external market and internal value criteria, but may still be dissatisfied because he perceives that his wage does not sufficiently reflect differences in merit between himself and another employee.

Finally, plaintiffs in the comparable worth cases discussed at the outset of this chapter are demanding that the issues of internal and external equity be considered separately in making job value judgments and setting wage rates. Their arguments discredit the idea that an external equity criterion alone is an adequate measure of job value.[26]

_____pensation Is an Important Issue

Although the specifics have varied among the cases we have considered, they all underscore the fact that compensation practice and policy have become much deliberated issues at all levels in our society, ones that will increasingly demand the attention of professionals in personnel and industrial relations.

The Individual

Tony Dorsett's reaction in our opening case and the insulting wage increase in the last case we examined both illustrate how strongly employees react to pay practices. Authorities in the field of compensation have demonstrated that no factor has a greater effect on emotional reactions of employees than perceptions of fairness and equity.[27] The belief that one is being treated unfairly has a direct and dramatic effect on employee behavior and performance. The most frequent sources of such reactions are mistakes made by management in its compensation practices. Management cannot hope to influence employee behavior and performance toward company objectives unless the compensation system is perceived as fair or equitable by employees.

On the positive side, compensation policies can have a dramatic incentive value in influencing employee behavior. Compensation plays many important roles for employees.[28] First, money is instrumental in achieving a number of valued outcomes for a person: security, safety, housing, and sustenance, as well as living standards, vacations, and hobbies. Second, compensation often becomes associated with general levels of anxiety or comfort. Most of us learn to associate a lack of money with events leading to anxiety, and sufficient money with conditions that contribute to feelings of security. Hence, the aphorism at the opening of our book: "Money cannot buy happiness, but it will soothe the nerves." Finally, many employees come to view their level of compensation (relative and absolute) as a symbol of their accomplishment and value to their employer. In sum, compensation is not merely pay for hours worked: it influences employee reactions to their employment in a complex variety of ways.

The Employer

Effective compensation practices are crucial to the employer, as well. Indeed, as labor costs become an increasingly larger part of the total cost of doing business (labor costs constitute the largest proportion of the budget in labor-intensive operations), an employer's economic survival will depend on how effectively it can improve productivity and control costs in its compensation practices. In the 1980s, for example, all major manufacturing industries in the United States have experienced unprecedented multinational competition (including Japanese, Korean, and Chinese). In some instances, manufacturers report offshore competitors selling equipment at retail in the United States for *less than the labor cost* they have in their own products.

In order to stay alive, automobile manufacturers have responded to such competition by reverting from a posture of readily granting wage increases in collective bargaining to seeking wage concessions and the use of two-tier pay plans (new employees coming in at lower wage rates than veterans for the same job).[29]

Employers, in addition, are more conscious than ever of the fair employment legislation liabilities they may run, particularly with respect to sex discrimination. The three comparable worth cases cited earlier underscore the need for employers to ensure that they are not unintentionally discriminating against women in their pay practices. The stakes are high in this arena. The cost to Westinghouse in the *IUE* v. *Westinghouse* case was estimated to be several million dollars in damages and penalties.[30] The cost to the state of Washington has been estimated to exceed $1 billion.

Alternately, companies that have met all the conditions necessary for compensation to influence behavior (see our discussions of these conditions in Chapters 4 and 9) have reported dramatic improvements in their ability to attract qualified employees, to retain valued employees, and to improve work performance and efficiency.[31]

The Society

Compensation practice has become the object of unprecedented attention from a variety of groups and institutions in our society. Advocates of equal employment opportunity for women and minorities are on record as singling out compensation policy as the major target for their efforts and litigation in the 1980s.[32] The U.S. Equal Employment Opportunity Commission, as well as the National Organization of Women, have both forecast that compensation practices will become subject to at least as much enforcement activity, scrutiny, and litigation as testing and selection were during the 1960s and 1970s.[33]

Even those persons who were not previously concerned with economic and legal ramifications are now looking to compensation issues for ways to improve the performance of organizations. The field of organizational development (OD) provides an interesting case in this regard. People in this field are primarily industrial and organizational psychologists interested in improving the effectiveness of organizations through training and development. Most of the techniques that organizational development people have traditionally used have relied heavily on technologies emerging from industrial and organizational psychology. These include group exercises, management by objectives (MBO), brainstorming sessions, sensitivity training, and sociotechnical systems (STS) interventions that focus on changing attitudes and behavior.

We now see the interesting phenomenon of organizational development experts turning their attention to a compensation principle and practice espoused almost eighty years ago by management pioneer F. W. Taylor.[34] Specifically, a recent book, entitled *Pay and Organizational Development*, proposes that pay be used as an organizational development technique.[35] Proponents of the idea have rediscovered Taylor's original proposition that compensation practices can be a powerful tool in creating incentives for employees to change their behavior and performance.[36] Unprecedented attention to pay practices on the individual, employer, and societal levels demands that line and personnel managers look ever more carefully at compensation issues.

Purpose of *Compensation Theory and Practice*

Our purpose in writing *Compensation Theory and Practice* is to provide a thorough introduction to compensation issues and problems challenging compensation managers and the personnel and line managers who depend upon their efforts. We believe that line managers and staff compensation experts must work together closely if compensation practices are to contribute effectively to corporate or organizational objectives.

Our approach in this endeavor is to integrate the rapidly growing body of compensation theory and empirical research into guidelines for practice. Increasing attention is being paid to compensation problems and issues by researchers in a variety of disciplines: personnel and industrial relations, industrial/organizational psychology, labor economics, and labor and employment law. We will review their work relevant to major compensation problems and draw conclusions for administering actual compensation programs.

A final theme supporting *Compensation Theory and Practice* is the crucial need for strategic planning. Compensation objectives must first be elaborated from a consideration of the broader organizational goals to be served. A mission must be established for the compensation program. Compensation practices such as job evaluation, wage surveys, performance appraisal, cost-of-living adjustments, and related techniques must be considered on their merits as alternative strategies. In addition, policies must be established and carried out according to the strategic choices that have been made. Finally, the entire process must be audited for goal achievement and appropriate control steps taken. Frequently, under the pressures of day-to-day business, managers lose sight of these planning steps and come to consider compensation as housekeeping—"something that happens: everyone has to meet a payroll!" A compensation system that operates in such a fashion, without planning, cannot be expected to contribute to the goal achievement of any organization. Indeed, ignoring the compensation program can actually lead to the death of an organization primarily because labor costs rise out of control.

Order of This Book

Compensation Theory and Practice is divided into two parts. Part I deals with compensation issues at a theoretical level. Here, we review and summarize theory and empirical research regarding external equity (Chapter 2), internal equity (Chapter 3), and the achievement of individual equity (Chapter 4). Chapter 5 examines *process equity:* those conditions that must exist for the actual compensation decisions and administration to result in fair outcomes.

In Part II, we translate theory into practice by providing guidelines for compensation policy based on the research literature presented in Part I.

We begin, in Chapter 6, with a consideration of the legal and institutional constraints under which compensation practice operates.

Chapter 7 deals primarily with external equity in a review of practice in pricing jobs. We also discuss the use of wage surveys and how managers should go about organizing and analyzing external market information.

Chapter 8 is concerned with internal equity and, specifically, the practices involved in job evaluation. We present and explain the major techniques of job evaluation and how to design internal structures that satisfy demands for internal and external equity.

Chapter 9 moves directly to the issue of individual equity and discusses practice in setting wage rates for individual employees. Of specific concern is the problem of setting wage rates that create incentives for desired employee behavior and performance. We discuss how to deal with seniority, individual merit, incentives, and pay secrecy policies.

In Chapter 10, we discuss the other third of the compensation program: employee benefits. We focus on the major types of benefits and emphasize the use of benefits to complete the compensation package.

Chapter 11 focuses on the need for managers to audit compensation programs for performance on external, internal, and individual equity criteria. Specific topics covered in this chapter include planning, audit and control statistics, budgeting, and communication.

Chapter 12 presents a view of compensation that has become increasingly attractive to organizations in recent years — the prospect of using compensation practices to implement an organization's strategic plan. We examine what steps an employer must take to use compensation in this fashion and study some of the more frequently employed "alternative" compensation strategies that have been tried in recent years. Finally, we make some forecasts about the shape of compensation programs to come in the 1990s.

Summary

Compensation Theory and Practice has been designed to make you familiar with the process of compensation and how it can support an organization. In order to be successful in this regard, compensation practices must address the objectives of external equity, internal equity, individual equity, and audit and control, as described earlier in this chapter.

Exhibit 1.8 illustrates how this book is organized around these objectives. The model in this exhibit demonstrates that, for each compensation objective (external equity, for example), an organization faces a corresponding problem or challenge (for example, how can we pay our jobs competitively with respect to external markets). *Compensation Theory and Practice* provides an array of solutions to each problem. The model shows where our book treats each of these problems and solutions and should provide a useful guide in organizing your study.

Exhibit 1.8 Model for Studying *Compensation Theory and Practice* (CTP)

Compensation Objective	Compensation Theory Problem	Compensation Practice Solution	CTP Chapters
External Equity	How can an employer set pay for jobs that correspond to pay in external markets?	• Wage and salary surveys • Market definitions • Benchmarks • Salary structure • Statistics	2, 7
Internal Equity	How can an employer set pay for jobs that correspond to their relative internal value to the organization?	• Job analysis • Job families • Job evaluation • Salary structure/ pay grades • Policy lines	3, 8
Individual Equity	How can an employer set individual employee pay according to merit?	• Merit rules • Seniority • Performance appraisal/ evaluation • Maturity curves, piece rates, merit adjustments, bonuses • Benefits	4, 5, 9, 10, 11
Audit and Control	How can an employer achieve effective cost and outcome control over compensation programs?	• Compensation policy • Compensation audits • Structure formation and adjustment • Forecasting budgets • Cash flow models • Communications	6, 11, 12

Notes

[1]This account is based on Raymond Coffey, "All Is Really Not Fair in Love or in War or to Tony Dorsett," *Chicago Tribune*, August 21, 1986.

[2]Ibid.

[3]Ibid.

[4]Ibid.

[5]*Lemons et al.* v. *City and County of Denver*, 17 FEP Cases (BNA) 906 (District Court, Colorado, 1978).

[6]*International Union of Electrical, Radio, and Machine Workers (IUE)* v. *Westinghouse Electric Corporation*, 19 FEP Cases 450 (District Court, New Jersey, 1979).

[7]*AFSCME* v. *State of Washington*, FEP Cases 808 (U.S. District Court, Washington, 1983).

[8]Civil Rights Act of 1964, Title VII.

[9]*Lemons* v. *Denver.*

[10]*AFSCME* v. *Washington.*

[11]Bureau of National Affairs, *Fair Employment Practices*, January 12, 1984, p. 6.

[12]Ibid.

[13]See, for example, Ruth Blumrosen, "Wage Discrimination, Job Segregation, and Women Workers," *Employee Relations Law Journal* (1980): 77–136; H. R. Bloch and R. L. Pennington, "Measuring Discrimination: What Is a Relevant Labor Market?" *Personnel* (July–August 1980): 21–29; R. K. Filer, "Male–Female Wage Differentials: The Importance of Compensating Differentials," *Industrial and Labor Relations Review* (1985): 426–37; H. Hartmann and D. J. Treiman, "Notes on the NAS Study of Equal Pay for Jobs of Equal Value," *Public Personnel Management Journal* (1983): 404–17; L. Thurow, *Generating Inequality* (New York: Basic Books, 1975); A. H. Cook, "Comparable Worth: Recent Developments in Selected States," *Proceedings of the 1983 Spring Meeting of the Industrial Relations Research Association*, Honolulu, pp. 494–504; H. Hartmann (ed.), *Comparable Worth: New Directions for Research* (Washington, D.C.: National Academy Press, 1985); E. R. Livernash (ed.), *Comparable Worth: Issues and Alternatives* (Washington, D.C.: Equal Employment Advisory Council, 1980); T. A. Mahoney, "Approaches to the Definition of Comparable Worth," *Academy of Management Journal* (1983): 14–22; T. A. Mahoney, B. Rosen, and S. Rynes, "Where Do Compensation Specialists Stand on Comparable Worth?" *Compensation Review* (1984): 27–40; G. G. Siniscalco and C. L. Reissler, "Comparable Worth in the Aftermath of *AFSCME* v. *State of Washington*," *Employee Relations Law Journal* (1984): 6–29; H. Remick (ed.), *Comparable Worth and Wage Discrimination: Technical Possibilities* (Philadelphia: Temple University Press, 1984); D. J. Treiman and H. Hartmann (eds.), *Women, Work and Wages: Equal Pay for Jobs of Equal Value* (Washington, D.C.: National Academy Press, 1981).

[14]See, for example, H. Hartmann and D. J. Treiman, "Notes on the NAS Study"; R. D. Arvey, G. A. Davis, S. L. McGowan, and R. L. Dipboye, "Potential Sources of Bias in Job Analytic Processes," *Academy of Management Journal* (1982): 618–29; R. W. Beatty and J. R. Beatty, "Some Problems with Contemporary Job Evaluation Systems," in H. Remick (ed.), *Comparable Worth and Wage Discrimination: Technical Possibilities and Political Realities* (Philadelphia: Temple University Press, 1984), pp. 59–78; A. O. Bellack, M. W. Bates, and D. M. Glasner, "Job Evaluation: Its Role in the Comparable Worth Debate," *Public Personnel Management Journal* (1983): 418–24; D. Doverspike and G. V. Barrett, "An Internal Bias Analysis of a Job Evaluation Instrument," *Journal of Applied Psychology* (1984): 648–62; and R. W.

Fredlund, "Valuing Work: Complications–Contradictions–Compensation," *Public Personnel Management Journal* (1983): 461–66.

[15]Ibid.

[16]Bureau of National Affairs, *Fair Employment Practices*, June 14, 1984, p. 1.

[17]See, for example, Marc J. Wallace, Jr., Charles H. Fay, and Richard W. Beatty, "Pay Equity and Equal Employment Opportunity: An Analysis of the Legal, Research, and Professional Debate," Working paper in management (Lexington, Ky.: University of Kentucky, College of Business and Economics, 1982).

[18]This case was developed by Marc J. Wallace, Jr. The names employed, with the exception of IBM, bear no resemblance to any person or company.

[19]Marc J. Wallace, Jr., N. Fredric Crandall, and Charles H. Fay, *Administering Human Resources* (New York: Random House, 1982), p. 547.

[20]This case was developed by Marc J. Wallace, Jr. The names employed bear no resemblance to any person or company.

[21]This case was developed by Marc J. Wallace, Jr. The names employed bear no resemblance to any person or company.

[22]See, for example, research reviewed in Thomas A. Mahoney, *Compensation and Reward Perspectives* (Homewood, Ill.: Richard D. Irwin, 1979).

[23]J. Stacy Adams, "Towards an Understanding of Inequity," *Journal of Abnormal and Social Psychology* (1963); 422–36.

[24]Elaine Walster, Ellen Berscheid, and William Walster, "New Directions in Equity Research," *Journal of Personality and Social Psychology* (1973); 151–76.

[25]Marc J. Wallace, Jr. and Charles H. Fay, "Labor Markets, Job Evaluation, and Job Worth: Towards a Model of Managerial Judgments of Job Value," Working paper in business administration, BA 74 (Lexington, Ky.: University of Kentucky, College of Business and Economics, 1982).

[26]Ruth G. Blumrosen, "Wage Discrimination, Job Segregation, and Women Workers," *Employee Relations Law Journal* (1980); 77–136.

[27]See, for example, Mahoney, *Compensation and Reward Perspectives.*

[28]R. L. Opsahl and M. D. Dunnette, "The Role of Financial Compensation in Industrial Motivation," *Psychological Bulletin* (1966): 94–118.

[29]See, for example, "1982 Bargaining Schedule: Labor Seeks Less," *Business Week* (December 21, 1981): 82–87.

[30]*IUE* v. *Westinghouse.*

[31]See Edward E. Lawler, III, *Pay and Organization Development* (Reading, Mass.: Addison-Wesley, 1981), Chapter 2 for a full discussion of this issue.

[32]Eleanor Holmes Norton quoted in Bureau of National Affairs, *Fair Employment Practices* 383 (November 8, 1979); Winn Newman, "Pay Equity Emerges as a Top Labor Issue in the 1980s," *Monthly Labor Review* (April 1982): 49–51.

[33]Ibid.

[34]F. W. Taylor, *Shop Management* (New York: Harper, 1903) and *The Principles of Scientific Management* (New York: Norton, 1911).

[35]Lawler, *Pay and Organization Development.*

[36]We are indebted to Thomas Mahoney for pointing out this fact to us. In addition, see Edwin A. Locke, "The Ideas of Frederick W. Taylor: An Evaluation," *Academy of Management Review* (1982): 14–24, for a detailed analysis of Taylor's ideas and contributions.

2

External Equity

Key Issues and Questions for This Chapter

After you have studied this chapter, you should be able to address the following key issues and questions:

1. How would you define external equity?

2. How would you define the market for electrical engineers?

3. How would you define the market for carpenters?

4. Identify four factors one might take into account in defining the external labor market for an occupation.

5. What factors influence an employer's demand for labor?

6. What factors influence the supply of labor faced by a firm?

7. What steps might an employer take to influence the supply of labor he or she faces?

8. How does a union influence the compensation decisions of an employer?

9. What is a wage contour?

10. What factors should an employer consider in defining a wage contour?

Introduction

Managers are acutely aware that they are operating in economic environments. No less an authority than Nobel laureate Herbert A. Simon has noted that even if managers do not always make decisions at the margin, they act as if they do.[1] Managers are sensitive to the marketplace for an evident reason: if they ignore markets, their businesses will eventually fail. In the case of compensation, a company that consistently pays wage rates below those prevailing in the external marketplace will find its ability to attract qualified employees in sufficient numbers and on a timely basis diminished. Eventually, they will be unable to attract any employees. Conversely, most employers who consistently pay more for labor than their competitors will lose a competitive edge and may either price their product out of the market or fail to make sufficient profits. Indeed, the United States District Court's decision in the Denver nurses case (cited in Chapter 1) clearly establishes the legitimacy of the marketplace as a criterion of fairness or equity in setting wage rates: the criterion of external equity. The purpose of this chapter is to examine that criterion in detail. In the process, we will look at forces that determine the demand for labor, the supply of labor, wage rates for labor, and external wage structures. Finally, we will discuss the problems managers must face defining labor markets and obtaining accurate wage information from those markets.

Defining External Equity

Practicing managers quickly become sensitive to the fact that the wages or salaries different kinds of people can command vary in the extreme. Exhibit 2.1 displays U.S. Department of Labor data for the wages of many common occupations in our economy. Notice that tool and die makers averaged $12.80 per hour in December 1985, more than twice the rate of $5.70 earned by key entry operators. How can we explain such a wide variation? To answer this question, we must turn to economics and the subspecialty of labor economics. Labor economists attempt to understand such wage differences as a

Exhibit 2.1   Hourly Earnings[1] of Selected Occupations in Lexington–Fayette, KY, December 1985

Occupation[2]	Number of workers	Hourly earnings (in dollars)[1]			3.35 and under 3.50	3.50 – 4.00	4.00 – 4.50	4.50 – 5.00	5.00 – 5.50	5.50 – 6.00
		Mean	Median	Middle range						
Secretaries	432	9.07	8.43	6.82-11.47	–	–	–	5	22	14
Secretaries I	78	6.61	6.25	5.68- 7.29	–	–	–	5	10	10
Secretaries II	82	7.73	7.18	6.23- 8.26	–	–	–	–	8	3
Secretaries III	205	9.53	9.09	7.93-11.43	–	–	–	–	4	1
Secretaries IV	61	12.34	13.38	10.02-13.98	–	–	–	–	–	–
Word processors	34	6.61	6.96	5.25- 7.56	–	1	1	2	6	2
Word processors I	15	6.09	6.00	5.25- 6.97	–	–	–	1	5	1
Word processors II	19	7.02	7.43	5.72- 8.41	–	1	1	1	1	1
File clerks	47	4.29	4.23	3.62- 4.34	5	11	21	1	2	7
Switchboard operators	58	5.04	4.50	4.19- 5.96	–	4	15	22	1	6
Key entry operators	96	6.03	5.96	5.00- 7.08	–	1	11	6	21	9
Key entry operators I	78	5.70	5.50	5.00- 6.42	–	1	11	6	20	9
Key entry operators II	18	7.44	7.59	7.08- 7.85	–	–	–	–	1	–
Computer operators	131	9.28	8.43	6.73-12.20	–	–	1	–	15	2
Computer operators I	66	6.73	6.81	5.60- 7.56	–	–	1	–	15	2
Computer operators II	30	10.83	11.39	10.39-11.84	–	–	–	–	–	–
Drafters	161	8.64	8.70	7.00-10.45	4	–	4	4	7	–
Drafters II	40	6.98	7.00	6.50- 7.31	–	–	–	–	4	–
Drafters III	56	9.56	9.69	8.10-11.30	–	–	–	–	–	–
Drafters IV	47	10.53	9.50	8.70-12.31	–	–	–	–	–	–
Electronics technicians:										
Electronics technicians III	40	12.32	12.18	11.78-12.18	–	–	–	–	–	–
Maintenance electricians	104	11.72	11.53	10.57-12.39	–	–	–	–	–	–
Maintenance machinists	81	12.43	12.75	9.14-14.38	–	–	–	–	–	–
Maintenance mechanics (machinery)	268	11.87	10.98	10.73-14.20	–	–	–	–	–	–
Motor vehicle mechanics	97	10.32	10.50	7.67-12.66	–	–	–	–	–	–
General maintenance workers	91	5.96	5.14	5.00- 7.20	–	–	6	10	31	9
Tool and die makers	239	12.80	12.82	10.77-14.45	–	–	–	–	–	–
Stationary engineers	10	11.46	11.45	- -	–	–	–	–	–	–
Truckdrivers	611	10.49	10.85	5.85-14.77	–	2	10	70	23	53
Truckdrivers, medium truck	146	12.21	14.64	10.85-14.64	–	–	–	–	–	9
Truckdrivers, tractor-trailer	384	10.96	13.71	7.82-14.77	–	–	8	32	12	30
Material handling laborers	308	8.03	9.16	5.64- 9.70	–	–	24	28	16	18
Forklift operators	395	8.15	8.21	6.61- 9.18	–	16	–	–	25	–
Guards	440	4.27	3.75	3.45- 4.30	114	144	76	17	16	9
Guards I	440	4.27	3.75	3.45- 4.30	114	144	76	17	16	9
Janitors, porters, and cleaners	668	4.12	3.35	3.35- 4.00	371	101	64	43	12	6

[1] Excludes premium pay for overtime and for work on weekends, holidays, and late shifts. Also excluded are performance bonuses and lump-sum payments of the type negotiated in the auto and aerospace industries, as well as profit-sharing payments, attendance bonuses, Christmas or year-end bonuses, and other nonproduction bonuses. Pay increases - but not bonuses - under cost of living allowance clauses and incentive payments, however, are included. Hourly earnings reported for salaried workers are derived from regular salaries divided by the corresponding standard hours of work. The wages of learners, apprentices, and handicapped workers are excluded. The mean is computed for each job by totaling the earnings of all workers and dividing by the number of workers. The median designates position—one-half of the workers receive the

Area Wage Survey: Lexington–Fayette, KY, December 1985 (Washington, D.C.: Bureau of Labor Statistics, February 1986), p. 2.

Number of workers receiving straight-time hourly earnings (in dollars) of —

6.00–6.50	6.50–7.00	7.00–7.50	7.50–8.00	8.00–8.50	8.50–9.00	9.00–9.50	9.50–10.00	10.00–10.50	10.50–11.00	11.00–11.50	11.50–12.00	12.00–13.00	13.00–14.00	14.00–15.00	15.00–16.00	16.00 and over
41	33	39	27	42	26	25	11	8	11	22	34	26	28	8	9	1
21	10	5	3	5	2	4	3	–	–	–	–	–	–	–	–	–
13	14	12	6	8	–	5	–	–	–	2	8	2	1	–	–	–
5	9	21	13	22	23	15	7	6	11	19	24	18	6	1	–	–
–	–	1	5	7	1	1	–	1	–	1	2	6	21	7	8	–
1	11	1	2	7	–	–	–	–	–	–	–	–	–	–	–	–
1	7	–	–	–	–	–	–	–	–	–	–	–	–	–	–	–
–	4	1	2	7	–	–	–	–	–	–	–	–	–	–	–	–
–	–	–	–	–	–	–	–	–	–	–	–	–	–	–	–	–
2	1	2	4	–	1	–	–	–	–	–	–	–	–	–	–	–
15	7	13	8	4	–	–	–	1	–	–	–	–	–	–	–	–
13	6	8	2	2	–	–	–	–	–	–	–	–	–	–	–	–
2	1	5	6	2	–	–	–	1	–	–	–	–	–	–	–	–
12	12	5	15	4	1	1	1	7	3	7	12	19	12	2	–	–
11	11	5	14	3	1	–	1	2	–	–	–	–	–	–	–	–
1	1	–	1	1	–	1	–	5	2	5	9	4	–	–	–	–
5	15	22	2	8	23	12	8	7	2	14	10	4	10	–	–	–
3	6	18	2	5	–	1	–	1	–	–	–	–	–	–	–	–
–	8	4	–	3	11	1	2	6	1	13	7	–	–	–	–	–
–	–	–	–	–	12	10	6	–	1	1	3	4	10	–	–	–
–	–	–	–	–	1	–	1	–	2	2	5	21	5	–	–	3
–	–	4	–	–	–	4	–	12	16	11	27	7	3	17	–	3
–	–	–	–	18	–	4	–	–	–	–	2	18	11	14	5	[3]9
–	–	–	17	–	2	–	44	–	75	7	20	14	6	44	39	–
8	8	5	10	2	–	1	3	10	12	6	–	18	–	14	–	–
9	1	13	3	2	1	1	4	–	–	1	–	–	–	–	–	–
–	–	–	–	–	–	–	6	28	48	10	8	29	49	19	25	17
–	–	–	–	–	–	–	3	–	5	–	1	–	1	–	–	
14	2	4	6	5	–	108	–	2	36	–	–	–	38	238	–	–
–	–	–	–	5	–	20	–	–	34	–	–	–	–	78	–	–
8	2	–	6	–	–	84	–	2	2	–	–	–	38	160	–	–
–	16	22	1	–	2	53	69	59	–	–	–	–	–	–	–	–
24	39	7	52	81	26	48	38	13	–	–	–	26	–	–	–	–
18	31	11	–	–	–	–	–	–	–	–	3	–	1	–	–	–
18	31	11	–	–	–	–	–	–	–	–	3	–	1	–	–	–
13	7	4	2	1	25	7	12	–	–	–	–	–	–	–	–	–

same as or more and one-half receive the same as or less than the rate shown. The middle range is defined by two rates of pay; one-fourth of the workers earn the same as or less than the lower of these rates and one-fourth earn the same as or more than the higher rate.

² For occupations with more than one level, data are included in the overall classification when a subclassification is not shown or information to subclassify is not available.

³ All workers were at $16.00 to $17.00.

function of varying supply and demand conditions across labor markets, a topic we will explore in more detail later. At this point, however, we can define external equity as having been achieved when an employer pays wage rates that correspond to those prevailing in external labor markets (for example, those in Exhibit 2.1). In this sense, the employer is a *price taker* who assigns wages to jobs that correspond to the single price that prevails in the marketplace.

Such a definition, however, is deceptively simple.[2] In reality, most managers quickly run into some thorny problems when they try to translate the external equity criterion into practice. First, no single wage rate prevails in any single labor market. Exhibit 2.1, for example, shows that the hourly earnings for tool and die makers just cited ranged from $10.77 to $14.45, while janitors' hourly earnings varied from $3.35 to $4.00. Employers face a variety of wage rates and a variety of labor markets. The effective compensation planner recognizes this fact and carefully attends to the task of defining external wage rates and external markets as accurately as possible.

As we shall see below, identifying or defining a labor market for the sake of determining the wage that prevails for a job is no simple matter.[3] This fact has been a particular problem in comparable worth cases where the courts have accepted an external equity criterion as a legitimate basis for defending wage differentials. The problem is that two different measurements or definitions of the market for the same job can yield substantially different estimates of the market price for that job.[4] One party's definition of the market can therefore lead to the conclusion that two jobs (one male dominated, the other female) should be paid the same while another party's definition of the same market can lead to the conclusion that they should be paid differently.

Many Markets

Labor economists have long pointed out that there is no such thing as a single, homogenous market for labor.[5] Rather, employers face a series of rather discontinuous or segmented labor markets (early theorists referred to them as Balkanized),[6] in which movement from one market to another is usually quite restricted. It would be quite difficult, for example, for an attorney to become a physician, or for a professor of accounting to become a physicist.

In addition to barriers preventing easy movement from one market to another, supply and demand conditions vary substantially across markets. Economists focus on this fact as the major explanation for wage differences among occupations. Compensation analysts, as a matter of practice, must be sensitive to such wage variation.

Of practical concern to the manager is accurately defining labor markets for compensation planning purposes. The work of labor economists on this problem suggests that the following factors are potentially important in defining the limits of a labor market segment:

geography

education and/or technical background required to perform the job

industry

experience required to do the job

licensing or certification requirements

union membership

Wallace, Crandall, and Fay have pointed out that, quite frequently, a combination of these parameters is used in defining a labor market for a particular job.[7] A company trying to set a wage rate for an electrician, for example, looks at a market largely defined first by the market's geographic proximity to the company's place of business and second by persons who would be willing to accept membership in the union that represents electricians as a condition of their employment (for example, the International Union of Electricians). Few electricians would be willing to commute more than twenty miles from their home to work and, in this case, the company has a union security agreement in their labor contract that requires a new electrician to join the union (a union shop agreement).

In contrast, consider the market faced by a research and development firm, such as Bell Labs, trying to establish market rates for engineering physicists. In this case, geography is not so important a parameter, as the market for such talent is virtually international. Major universities supply such people across the nation, and engineering physicists are far more concerned with job opportunity and prospects than they are with locale. Factors other than geography become crucial, however. The person must hold a Ph.D. in engineering physics (in the extreme case, the market may be defined by a small number of universities specializing in this type of training). In addition, the person may need a specific type of postgraduate experience.

As a strategic matter, employers must define the appropriate market carefully before attempting to get external wage rate information. If they make mistakes in defining the external market, their wage rate estimate will be inappropriate. A compensation planner who defines the market too narrowly may estimate an external wage rate much higher than needed in order to attract adequate labor, driving up costs unnecessarily. On the other hand, too loose a definition of the market's boundaries may result in estimating an external rate below what the company will have to pay in order to attract labor.

An Example

In practice, the task of properly defining a labor market can become quite complicated. The Lexington, Kentucky, labor market for assemblers provides a good example of this point. Geographically, Lexington (and the Bluegrass district) is quite distinct, situated roughly eighty miles south of Cincinnati, Ohio, and eighty miles east of Louisville, Kentucky. In the 1980s, there are approximately thirty divisions of major companies with assembly operations in this market, including IBM's Office Products Division, Square D, Trane Corporation, WABCO (Westinghouse Airbrake), an American Can Company Dixie Cup Division, Clark Equipment Company, Whirlpool, Hobart, and Rockwell International. All of these companies are paying roughly the same starting hourly rate for assembly workers except Rockwell International, which is paying almost twice the rate of the others. The reason for this is that the employees at Rockwell's plant, its truck axle division, are represented by the United Automobile Workers (UAW) and have a labor contract that is negotiated at the industry level and specifies the same wage rate for all employees covered, whether in Detroit, Atlanta, or Lexington, Kentucky. Such a contract is an artificial constraint, not representative of economic conditions in the Bluegrass market. It would be irrational for other employers in this market to set their rates in competition with Rockwell's as long as there are enough assemblers seeking work locally.

Wage and Employment Determination: Understanding the Dynamics of Demand and Supply

Managers will find it fruitful to turn to basic economic theory in an effort to understand why wage rates vary across occupations and labor markets. An economic view of labor markets focuses on the interaction of the demand for labor, or how much employers are willing to pay, and the supply of labor, or how much workers are willing to accept, to answer the following questions:

1. What level will the wage rate be for an occupation?
2. How many people will be employed?

3. How much more will an employer have to pay to attract more employees?

4. How would the number of people a company would employ change if the wage rate were lower? were higher?

Exhibit 2.2 represents a very simple illustration of supply and demand. The vertical axis displays wage rates from $1.00 to $23.00 per hour. The

Exhibit 2.2   The Interaction of Labor Demand and Supply

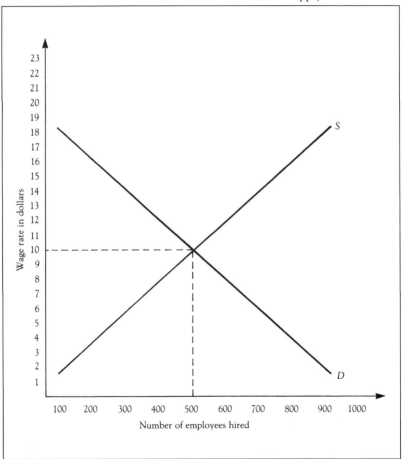

horizontal axis displays the number of employees hired by a company from 100 to 1,000. Economic theory regarding labor demand and labor supply attempts to explain wage rate levels (the vertical axis) and number of people employed (horizontal axis). The major economic theory addressing the question of wage level and employment is called the *marginal revenue product* (MRP) model.[8] At the level of an entire labor market (for example, the market for electrical engineers) the MRP model is a theory of wages, explaining why electrical engineers command wage rates that are different from those of secretaries, for example. At the level of the single employer, MRP is a theory of employment level, explaining, for example, why IBM will employ fifty electrical engineers at its Lexington, Kentucky, division.

Labor Demand

Exhibit 2.3 displays a single employer's demand for labor (line *D*). This line is called the firm's Marginal Revenue Product (MRP) function and represents the *additional revenue product* (product produced multiplied by the price at which the employer can sell the product) that each additional unit of labor (or new employee added) will generate. For the manager, the MRP function (or curve) represents the highest wage a company is willing to pay for various amounts of labor. In our example, for instance, $10.00 is the highest wage rate the company would be willing to pay for 500 employees. The price this company would be willing to pay gets higher with less employment and lower with additional employment.

Theoretically, the labor demand curve (MRP function) could take on any form. In our example, it slopes downward from left to right, indicating that as additional employees are hired, the revenue product generated per employee drops. This is a characteristic slope for companies operating at the margin in many different labor markets for the following two reasons:

1. A firm's demand for labor is a *derived demand*. It is derived from the market demand for the company's product or service. The slope of the demand for the company's product or service will influence the slope of the company's demand for labor. Many companies (especially large firms characteristic of our economy) face downward-sloping demands for their products. The lower the price of an automobile, the more cars will be sold. Thus, we would expect the demand for labor in a typical firm to have a downward slope.

2. Technological and physical limitations come into play in the short run. Most employers cannot add physical plant and equipment continuously.

Exhibit 2.3   The Interaction of Labor Demand and Supply When Supply Is Elastic

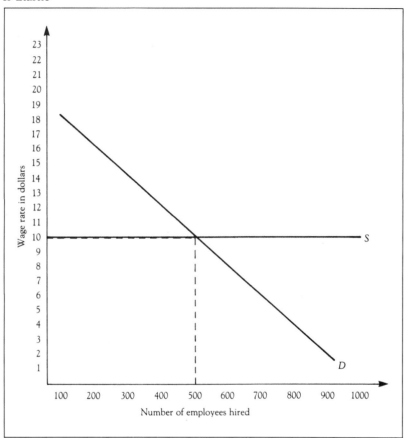

They build a building, outfit it with equipment, and hire employees as needed. At some time in the hiring process the employer will reach what economists call a *point of diminishing returns to scale*. That is, as the number of employees hired begins to approach the physical and technological capacities of the work site, each employee will become less efficient. For this reason, as well, we would expect an employer's demand for labor to slope downward from left to right.

Elasticity of Demand   The concept of *elasticity* helps us to understand the nature of a firm's demand for labor. Technically, elasticity is defined as the proportionate change in the wage an employer is willing to pay given the proportionate change in the number of people he wishes to employ. We have already said that we can expect the sign (or direction) of the elasticity of labor demand to be negative, that is, as the number of people employed increases, we can expect a decrease in the wage the employer is willing to pay each worker (look again at the slope of the demand curve, *D*, in Exhibit 2.2).

Elasticity addresses the question of how much the wage an employer is willing to pay will change proportionately, given a change in the number of people employed. Will the change be extreme (a highly elastic demand) or will it be very slight (a highly inelastic demand)?

Economist Robert Hicks proposed four factors that influence the elasticity of an employer's demand for labor:[9]

1. Elasticity of demand for the employer's product or service

2. Elasticity of substitution, that is, the ease with which the employer can substitute another type of labor or, perhaps, technology for the work being done by the employee

3. Elasticity of the supply of substitutes (other forms of labor or technology)

4. Ratio of that labor's cost to the employer's total operating costs.

Hicks developed a fascinating set of propositions about the above four sources of demand elasticity that bears striking parallels to the realities faced every day by managers. Let's take the example of a group of airline pilots working for a major carrier like United Airlines. From a tactical standpoint, the greater the inelasticity of demand United has for its pilots, the more power the union has to push for hefty wage increases. Thus it's in the union's (and the pilots') best interest to do anything to enhance the inelasticity of United's demand for pilots.

Hicks first proposes that the greater the inelasticity of demand for the employer's product or service, the greater the inelasticity of the employer's demand for labor. A common tactic employed by unions to enhance such inelasticity is to engage in advertising aimed at promoting brand loyalty or the exclusive use of the employer's product or service by customers. Union label campaigns fit into this category. A union label identifies the product as produced by members represented by a union. Thus a tag in a garment or a sign in a restaurant showing that its employees are represented by a union are attempts to induce customers to purchase only those products or services that are union-made and avoid patronizing establishments whose employees are not represented by unions. Similarly, any appeal that creates a segment of customers who continually choose United over a competing airline has the effect of increasing inelasticity of demand for the employer's product or service and, therefore, his demand for labor.

Second, Hicks proposes that the greater the inelasticity of substitution of the employee's labor for other kinds of labor or technology, the greater the inelasticity of the employer's demand for labor. Any rule or policy that limits the number or type of employee who can perform a job decreases management's freedom to substitute other labor or technology and, therefore, contributes to inelasticity of demand for a particular type of labor. In our illustration, for example, the fact that pilots have to be licensed prevents other kinds of employees (for example, flight attendants) from being substituted. Second, certain Federal Aeronautic Administration (FAA) rules severely limit the degree to which airlines can substitute such technology as auto pilots and computer-assisted guidance systems for the work conducted by the pilot. They can be expected to support strongly such limitations not only because of the safety factors but also because they enhance the inelasticity of their employer's demand for their labor.

A particularly vivid illustration of a union's attempting to limit the substitution of technology is the practice of *featherbedding*. Featherbedding is a policy under which an employer retains an employee and pays him for tending to a job that is no longer necessary. In effect, the employer pays a wage for work that is no longer done, adding to the cost of the operation. During the 1940s and 1950s, for example, railroads in the United States phased out steam engines, replacing them with diesel engines. The boiler that created the steam became obsolete and there was no longer a need for the fireman, the person who tended the boiler. Despite this fact, many railroads continued to employ firemen for years after diesels were introduced, paying them for work that was no longer performed.

Third, Hicks points out that the greater the inelasticity of the supply of substitute factors, the greater the inelasticity of demand for labor. If substitutes are easily obtainable (that is, their supply is relatively elastic), management will more easily be able to substitute them for current types of labor. On the other hand, if such substitutes are not easily obtained, management will be less likely to substitute them for current types of labor.

Finally, Hicks proposes that the smaller the ratio of labor's cost to total operating cost, the greater the inelasticity of the employer's demand for labor.

The logic of this proposition may not be immediately evident. Let's examine our airline pilot example for a minute. Currently, most airline pilots who are unionized constitute their own separate union (Airline Pilots Association — ALPA) among airline employees. The other employees may be represented by a union, but not the pilots' union, and they strike their own deals with management. One reason for this pattern is the fact that pilots' salaries taken together represent a far smaller proportion of the employer's operating costs than they would if pooled together with all employees' salaries. Thus, when pilots demand a substantial increase, the cost effect on the employer will be less than if the increases were demanded for all employees. Management, therefore, is more likely to agree to a hefty increase if the number of employees involved is relatively small. This fact explains why many small craft unions (for example, ALPA) strike their own bargains with management and do not broaden membership in their union or bargaining unit (employees covered under the employment contract).

Average Net Revenue Product   Thomas Mahoney has pointed out that when companies are not operating at the margin, marginal revenue product cannot be interpreted as determining the employer's level of demand for labor. In these cases, it is more realistic to view labor demand as determined by the organization's sales forecasts and plans for production. Still, Mahoney argues that an understanding of the concept of *average net revenue product* (the revenue product produced per unit labor minus all production costs other than labor) is of direct relevance in determining wage rates and differences in wage rates employers are willing to pay the same occupation.[10]

If we were to combine the employer's demand for labor (*D* in Exhibit 2.3) with all other employers' demands for labor in the market, we would obtain the aggregate or total demand for labor in that specific market.

Labor Supply

Economic theory is less well developed and less explicit concerning the supply of labor (line *S* in Exhibits 2.2 and 2.3). Technically, labor supply is a function or curve representing the *minimum wage rate* necessary to attract a given number of employees. Classical economic theorists assumed in developing this curve that markets are perfectly competitive (characterized by many small employers and many people seeking employment under conditions of perfect information, mobility, and long-run equilibrium). Under these conditions, we expect the supply function faced by single employers in the market to be perfectly horizontal (see Exhibit 2.3), which implies that employers can hire as many additional employees as they need at a single wage rate ($10.00 per hour in our example). This is probably still true for many small employers in the United States today.

More recent theoretical developments, however, suggest several reasons for expecting large employers to face labor supply functions that slope upward from left to right as illustrated in Exhibit 2.2.[11] Let's examine three of these developments: the work of economist Lloyd Reynolds, the work of economists in the field of human capital theory, and the special case of a labor union.

Lloyd Reynolds   Economist Lloyd Reynolds suggested five conditions under which we could expect an individual employer to face an upward-sloping supply of labor.[12]

1. *Monopsony.* Monopsony is an economic concept describing a market in which one large purchaser dominates the market. Markets dominated by a few large purchasers would approach this condition, as oligopoly approaches monopoly when we think of sellers. In our example, General Motors, Ford, and Chrysler could be considered close to monopsonistic purchasers of labor in the Detroit labor market. Monopsonists find that because of their size they must pay increasingly higher wage rates to attract additional units of labor. Unlike the small competitive employer in classical economic theory, the monopsonist has a significant effect on the entire labor market when expanding or contracting employment.

2. *Employee ignorance of job openings.* It is possible to imagine labor markets in which people have perfect information about all job openings. However, we know that in reality, information is imperfect and often costs resources to obtain. Thus, we might expect an already employed person who is reasonably satisfied with his or her current employment to be unaware of and unaffected by a wage being offered by a competitor for the same job. The only problem with this explanation, as Reynolds points out, is that it proposes that knowledge of a wage rate is a positive function of the level of the rate. Thus, the higher the wage rate, the more people will be aware of and influenced by it. Reynolds (as well as Adam Smith) rejects this logic, but the issue remains unresolved empirically to date.[13]

3. *Variation among workers for monetary and nonmonetary reward combinations.* Compensation experts have pointed out that monetary reward, in the form of a wage rate, is only one element in the total reward structure of interest to a prospective employee. Working conditions, chances for ad-

vancement, flexibility of working hours and job assignment, and interpersonal relationships are just a few nonmonetary conditions that may be of equal concern. Reynolds proposes that different employers represent to employees different combinations of monetary and nonmonetary rewards. For example, employees who are unwilling to face commuting hassles even for higher wage rates may prefer to remain in lower-paying jobs closer to their homes. If we presume that, at any point in time, employed workers have found employment with a satisfactory balance of conditions, then an employer who wants to expand his employment may have to raise wages to compensate new employees for leaving what is for them already a preferred combination of wage and nonwage conditions.

4. *Overcoming risk.* Thomas Mahoney and other compensation theorists have carefully pointed out that a person changes jobs and accepts an offer of employment with a certain amount of personal risk.[14] Consider someone, currently employed by a company as an engineer, who receives an offer of employment from a competitor. She is completely familiar with her current employment situation. She not only knows the rate of her payment but she knows all the positive and negative nonmonetary aspects of her job. She knows what it is like to work for her supervisor and with her coworkers, for example. In contrast, she does not have the same knowledge about the job being offered. All she knows for sure is the wage rate being offered. She has no way to know about things like working conditions, supervision quality, relations with coworkers, and similar conditions until she is actually on the job. Economic theory suggests that the bidding competitor will have to offer an economic premium to make it worth the engineer's while to take on the risk of a job change.

5. *Geographic barriers.* Finally, we know that many occupational markets have geographic constraints. Thus, for example, it is unlikely that the market for assembly workers in Dallas, Texas, extends beyond the immediate environs of that community. Unless faced with unemployment (which unfortunately has been the case in the 1980s), a worker in Detroit would be unlikely to seek work in Dallas.

There is an extremely important warning to managers considering the influence of these five conditions on the supply of labor, and it is especially relevant in the 1980s. Reynolds warns that conditions such as monopsony, employee ignorance, preferences for monetary and nonmonetary combinations of conditions, risk, and geographic barriers hold true only as the *market approaches full employment.* When unemployment sets in and deepens, these conditions do not influence labor supply, and employers find the supply of labor relatively flat and elastic. Thus, in the early 1980s, thousands of workers left the upper Midwest centers of Detroit, Cleveland, Dayton, and similar communities where unemployment rates were the highest since the Great Depression, and moved to Dallas, Houston, Phoenix, and other Sun Belt employment centers, where jobs were more plentiful. Recently, as the oil industry has slowed down, we have seen the same movement *out* of Houston and other oil centers.

Human Capital Theory   A branch of economic theory developed in the 1960s proposed that a person offering his services on the market carries value to the extent that he has had to expend money, time, and other personal resources acquiring skills necessary to perform a job. Thus, a physician invests time and money to acquire the skills employed in the practice of medicine because he expects greater financial gain. Consider, further, the differences between an occupation that requires a substantial outlay in training costs and time (for example, an attorney) and one that requires only minimal costs (for example, an assembly-line job). We would expect, on the basis of training costs alone, that it would be more difficult for a firm to attract additional attorneys than assembly-line workers. Economist Gary Becker provides the most complete analysis of this reasoning.[15] According to this logic, the costs of training and other preparation restrict entry into the occupation and create an upward slope to the supply curve faced by individual employers.

Economist Lester Thurow presents an alternative view of labor supply that would also lead one to expect an upward sloping (inelastic) supply of labor to the firm.[16] Thurow proposes that wage competition does not take place in the labor market, logic that runs contrary to the MRP model presented earlier. According to traditional economic theory, workers compete for wages. Thurow finds reason to doubt this; he believes instead that workers compete for *job openings* or opportunities. Indeed, he hypothesizes that a queue (or waiting line) forms for every job opening that comes onto a market. He believes, further, that the workers in the queue represent varying levels of skills and aptitude relevant to the job. Finally, he argues, the employer orders those in the queue according to these qualities and selects the best prospect. The best prospect will be least costly to train and orient and will be the most productive. Each person farther back in the queue will be more costly to train and will be less productive, even though the same wage is being paid. Thus, the cost of each successive unit in the queue increases, leading to an upward-sloping supply of labor faced by the firm.

The Special Case of a Labor Union   So far in our analysis of labor supply, we have considered only economic factors that would contribute to an upward slope in the supply of labor faced by an employer. Economist Alan Cartter has examined how a labor union also can influence the supply of labor to a firm.[17] Although it is not accurate to consider a union representing a group of employees as a broker of labor (federal law, for example, prohibits agreement by which employers agree to hire only union members in most cases), it is correct to consider the union as the *sole bargaining agent* for a group of employees. The union, then, influences the wage to be paid labor through the process of *collective bargaining.*

Cartter has analyzed the tradeoffs the union must consider between employment levels and wage rates when entering the labor negotiation. His analysis is presented in Exhibit 2.4. The straight lines in the exhibit (N_1 to N_{12}) represent alternative levels of labor demand on the part of the employer

Exhibit 2.4   Union Preferences Between Wages and Employment

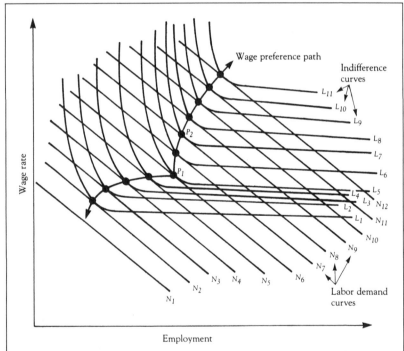

Source: Alan M. Cartter, *Theory of Wages and Employment* (Homewood, Ill.: Richard D. Irwin, 1959), p. 91. Used by permission.

with whom the union is about to bargain. N_6 is the employer's current level of demand, and point P_1 represents the current wage/employment bargain. The kinked lines L_1 to L_{11} are called *indifference curves* and represent points of indifference in tradeoffs between wage rates and employment levels for the union negotiators. Thus, for example, all wage/employment combinations along L_3 are equally valued by the union. The union, however, would prefer to get an agreement that falls on the indifference curve farthest to the upper right in Exhibit 2.4. Thus, for example, L_2 is valued more highly than L_1, L_3 is more valued than L_2, and so forth.

The analysis in Exhibit 2.4 tells us that the union will seek a wage and employment combination that places it on the highest indifference curve, given the employer's demand curve. Thus, if the employer's demand increased from N_6 to N_8 in Exhibit 2.4, we would expect the union to bargain for a wage/employment combination of P_2 because that would place the union on the highest indifference curve (L_7) possible, given labor demand (N_8). Any other combination of wage rate and employment along N_8 would place the union on a lower indifference curve.

The line connecting each of these preferred wage/employment combinations is called a *wage preference path* by Cartter and constitutes the estimate of supply faced by the firm in collective bargaining. The shape of the wage preference path is kinked at point P in Exhibit 2.4 and represents the union's changing interests depending on whether it anticipates an expansion or a decline in labor demand from the present point.

If the union leaders, for example, anticipate an expanding demand for labor, they will pursue increases in wage rates at the expense of employment. Thus, as Cartter points out, the union will emphasize wage issues and play down expansion or even security of employment.[18] If, on the other hand, the union anticipates that labor demand will contract, it will place a priority on maintaining wage rates even at the expense of employment levels. Thus, unions often bargain for seniority as the basis for laying off employees. An exception to this pattern was negotiations between the United Automobile Workers (UAW) and major automobile manufacturers in the early 1980s. In this case, unemployment had become so pervasive that the union was willing to trade wage rates for employment security. In many cases, unions were willing to forego increases in wage rates in order to maintain or increase employment levels.

In summary to this point, it is likely that at least three kinds of factors lead to an upward-sloping supply of labor, which most firms face, at least in the short run: (1) factors creating labor scarcity (monopsony, employee ignorance, preferences for monetary and nonmonetary rewards, risk in changing jobs, and geographic barriers), (2) the varying degrees of human capital represented by people available for employment, and (3) trade union pref-erences in collective bargaining.

Economic theory tells us that at the level of an entire labor market the supply of labor available at various wage rates takes on an upward slope from left to right (as in Exhibit 2.2) in the short run. There are several reasons for this. First, the supply of labor is limited in the short run at the level of the market. If supply is to increase, more people will have to be attracted into the labor market, from nonwork or from other markets. In many oc-cupations, entry to the market is limited or time consuming because of training requirements, certification, union membership requirements, or the need for geographical movement.

The Interaction of Demand and Supply

So far, we have examined labor demand and supply by themselves. In order to understand how forces in external labor markets influence wage and em-ployment levels, we must examine the interaction of labor demand and supply. Refer back, once more, to Exhibits 2.2 and 2.3. Marginal Revenue Product (MRP) theory predicts that the wage level and employment level in a given labor market will be determined by the intersection of the labor demand and supply functions. Thus, at the level of the market, the workers in the oc-cupation whose market is modeled in Exhibit 2.2 make $10.00 per hour because of both demand and supply conditions. Ten dollars is the price that clears the market. It is the price *both* that employers are willing to pay and that employees are willing to accept.

Labor economists refer to the price that clears the labor market as the *exchange rate* of labor; it represents a major basis for considering the value of a job. Indeed, *external equity* is defined as the *exchange rate for labor on a job clearing in the external labor market.*

To answer the question of how much labor will be employed, we must con-sider Exhibits 2.2 and 2.3 at the level of the firm. The MRP model predicts that each firm will continue hiring labor until the last employee hired is equal to its marginal revenue product. At this point, the marginal cost of labor to the employer is exactly equal to the marginal revenue it generates: there is no more profit to be made. If the employer stops hiring short of this point, he is foregoing profit that could be made. If the employer hires beyond this point, he will be incurring losses. Thus, the employer maximizes profit when the MRP of the last employee hired equals its marginal cost.

External Wage Structures

A final task for managers in managing external equity is to become familiar with external wage structures. It is important to recognize (as we pointed out at the beginning of this chapter) that companies face a variety of labor markets in staffing their jobs. Levels of supply and demand vary across these markets and, thus, it is not surprising to find a considerable variation in wage rates across occupations (see, for example, Exhibit 2.1).

Marginal productivity analysis, however, explains only the broad forces that create wage differences. Thus, the MRP model does not predict the actual dollar amount at which a wage will fall but, rather, a range of wage rates within which the actual wage will fall. It is probably more realistic for the practicing compensation manager to consider MRP theory as illustrated in Exhibit 2.5. MRP theory is able to tell us that the likely wage and employment combination will fall somewhere in the shaded area *ABCD*. Within this range, we must turn to structural and institutional considerations in order to understand wage and employment levels. One of the most important concepts in this regard is John Dunlop's notion of the *wage contour.* [19]

Dunlop defines a wage contour as

> a stable group of wage determining units (bargaining units, plants, or firms) which are so linked together by (1) similarity of product markets, (2) resort to similar sources for a labor force, or (3) common market organization (custom) that they have common wage-making characteristics. The wage rates for a particular occupation in a particular firm are not ordinarily independent of all other wage rates; they are more closely related to the wage rates of some firms than to others. A contour for particular occupations is to be defined in terms of both product market and the labor market. A contour, thus, has three dimensions: (1) particular occupations or job clusters, (2) a sector of industry, and (3) a geographical location. [20]

To illustrate the existence of wage contours, Dunlop used the example of beer truck drivers and laundry truck drivers in Boston, who were paid different wage rates. In this case, members of the same occupation were in two different contours (determined by industry) in which two different wage

Exhibit 2.5 Marginal Productivity Theory Predicts Wage and Employment Ranges

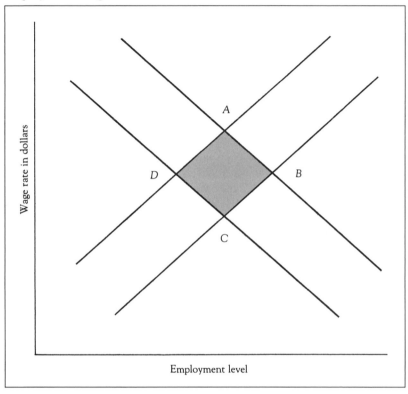

rates prevailed. The compensation manager must pay close attention to external wage contours when trying to bring a company's wage structure into line with the external market. Estimates of market contours must be developed through wage and salary surveys, to be discussed fully in Chapter 7.

Summary

In this chapter, we have been concerned with external equity in compensation practice. External equity refers to setting wage rates for jobs that correspond to those prevailing in external markets — markets from which the employer hires. An employer that ignores the external market will not survive for long.

External equity is a complex and sometimes confusing criterion because employers face a variety of external markets. Care must be taken in choosing the criteria (geography, education, industry, experience, and so forth) used to determine the boundaries of the market. Movement from one market to the next is quite restricted, especially in the short run. Differing supply and demand characteristics across segmented markets lead to differences in wage rates.

In order to understand why wage rates vary across markets, the manager must thoroughly understand the dynamics of supply and demand within a labor market. These dynamics are essential in answering the following questions: (1) What level will the wage rate be for a given job? (2) How many people will be employed? (3) How much more will an employer have to pay in order to attract additional employees? and (4) How will the number of people a company would employ change if the wage rate were lower or higher?

Marginal revenue product (MRP) theory defines a firm's demand for labor as derived from its product demand. Because many firms are faced with downward-sloping demands for their products and because of the principle of diminishing returns to scale, most compensation managers face downward-sloping demands for labor, especially in the short run.

We examined three bodies of theory, Reynolds's notions of labor scarcity, human capital theory, and labor union behavior, which suggest that, in the short run, most firms face upward-sloping labor supply functions. Thus, a firm will have to pay more for additional units of labor or employees.

In order to understand wage and employment levels, we must consider the interaction of labor demand and supply. We concluded that the intersection of labor demand (what employers are willing to pay) and labor supply (what employees are willing to accept) defines the exchange rate of labor and should be considered by the compensation planner as the basis for establishing external equity in setting wage rates for jobs.

Finally, compensation managers should note that a model such as marginal revenue product theory explains only the outer limits of a wage rate. Institutional factors must be considered in addition to supply and demand to get a finer estimate of actual wage rates prevailing in external markets. In this regard, Dunlop's notion of a wage contour is useful. A wage contour is a stable group of wage-determining units (employers) linked by similar product markets and labor markets, and by a common market organization.

Notes

[1]Herbert A. Simon, *Administrative Behavior,* 3rd ed. (New York: The Free Press, 1976), p. xxvii.

[2]Sara L. Rynes and George T. Milkovich, "Wage Surveys: Dispelling Some Myths About the Market Wage:" *Personnel Psychology* (1986): 71–90.

[3]Ibid.

[4]Ibid.; F. Krzystofiak and J. Newman, "Evaluating Employment Outcomes: Availability Models and Measures," *Industrial Relations* (1982): 277–92; M. Rosenblum, "Evolving EEO Decision Law and Applied IR Research," *Industrial Relations* (1982): 34–51.

[5]L. G. Reynolds, "Some Aspects of Labor Market Structure," in R. A. Lester and J. Shister (eds.), *Insights into Labor Issues* (New York: Macmillan, 1949); L. G. Reynolds, *The Structure of Labor Markets* (New York: Harper, 1951); Orme Phelps, "A Structural Model of the U.S. Labor Market," in the President's Committee to Appraise Employment and Unemployment Statistics, *Measuring Employment and Unemployment* (Washington, D.C.: U.S. Government Printing Office, 1962).

[6]Ibid.

[7]Marc J. Wallace, Jr., N. Fredric Crandall, and Charles H. Fay, *Administering Human Resources: An Introduction to the Profession* (New York: Random House, 1982), Chap. 5.

[8]Alan M. Cartter, *Theory of Wages and Employment* (Homewood, Ill.: Richard D. Irwin, 1959).

[9]Robert Hicks, *Theory of Wages* (New York: Macmillan, 1934).

[10]Thomas A. Mahoney, *Compensation and Reward Perspectives* (Homewood, Ill.: Richard D. Irwin, 1979), pp. 118–19.

[11]See Cartter, *Theory of Wages and Employment,* for a more thorough analysis.

[12]Lloyd G. Reynolds, "The Supply of Labor to the Firm," *Quarterly Journal of Economics* 60 (1946): 390–411; Reynolds, *The Structure of Labor Markets.*

[13]Ibid.; Adam Smith, *The Wealth of Nations* (1776; reprint, New York: Random House, 1937, abridged).

[14]Mahoney, *Compensation and Reward Perspectives.*

[15]Gary S. Becker, *Human Capital* (New York: National Bureau for Economic Research, 1964).

[16]Lester C. Thurow, *Generating Inequality* (New York: Basic Books, 1975).

[17]Cartter, *Theory of Wages and Employment.*

[18]Ibid.

[19]John Dunlop, "The Task of Contemporary Wage Theory," in George W. Taylor and Frank C. Pierson (eds.), *New Concepts in Wage Determination* (New York: McGraw-Hill, 1957).

[20]Ibid., p. 131.

3

Internal Equity

Key Issues and Questions for This Chapter

After you have studied this chapter, you should be able to address the following key issues and questions:

1. What is internal equity and how does it differ from external equity?

2. How does job evaluation relate to internal equity?

3. How is the value of a job determined?

4. How might demand-side economic theory provide a basis for valuing jobs?

5. How might supply-side economic theory provide a basis for valuing jobs?

6. What has position in the organization hierarchy got to do with job worth?

7. Is the external exchange or market rate an adequate basis for valuing jobs?

8. What does the comparable worth controversy have to do with the distinction between external and internal equity?

Introduction

The current comparable worth controversy (discussed in Chapter 1) provides a striking example of the need for managers to keep external and internal equity separate in their thinking about job worth or value. Recent pay discrimination cases involving sex (*Lemons et al.* v. *City and County of Denver; International Union of Electrical, Radio, and Machine Workers* v. *Westinghouse Electric Corp.*; and *American Federation of State, County, and Municipal Employees* v. *State of Washington,* cited in Chapter 1) have questioned the adequacy of an external market exchange rate (external equity) as a criterion of job worth.[1] In effect, these cases challenge the legitimacy of external equity as a sole criterion for judging a job's worth, and demand that an internal equity standard be used in judging a job's relative value. In this chapter, we will explore methods for studying job value by examining the criterion of internal equity in detail.

After reading this chapter, you should realize that our knowledge about judging the internal worth of a job is far less developed than our knowledge of external markets. Indeed, a major challenge facing the compensation profession in the 1980s is that of developing both the theory and practice regarding the internal valuing of jobs.

Internal Equity Defined

In Chapter 1, we defined internal equity as the objective of setting wage rates that conform to a job's internal worth to an employer. Indeed, in each of the comparable worth cases, arguments have been made that although the employer may be paying what the job is paid in the marketplace (external equity), women's jobs are still paid less than men's, even though both jobs are of *equal value* or worth to the employer (internal equity).

A number of compensation theorists have long pointed out that the exchange rate, presented in Chapter 2, is not a complete criterion for a job's value. Thomas Mahoney, for example, demonstrated that labor's exchange value (the maximum price employers are willing to pay and the minimum labor is willing to accept) equals its *use value* (the value labor creates for an employer) only if there is: (1) long-run general equilibrium and (2) perfect competition in all markets.[2] These assumptions do not coincide with the real world of segmented labor markets as described in Chapter 2.

Lester Thurow also questions the value of an exchange rate as an adequate definition of a job's value.[3] He reasons that very little wage competition actually takes place in contemporary labor markets. He proposes that external wage rates correspond less to the differences in value to employers than they do to cultural norms about fair or equitable distribution of wage rates and incomes across jobs and occupations — an idea, as you will see, that is very similar to the Just Price doctrine of the Middle Ages (see pp. 55–56). Thus, Thurow's ideas lead to the conclusion that a job's external value lies, not in an exchange rate, but rather in its relative place in a wage contour (described in Chapter 2) reflecting social norms.

Whether we conclude that external equity lies in an exchange rate or in a wage contour defined by society's norms or industry factors, neither criterion defines what value the job is creating for the employer — the central issue in internal equity. Indeed, this is a problem for the compensation profession because we have very little theory and research to guide us in selecting criteria of internal worth.

Is Job Evaluation the Answer?

Some experts have proposed that job evaluation might be a problem.[4] Job evaluation is a formal process by which ma wage rates to jobs according to some preestablished formul such techniques in detail in Chapter 8). Most job ev employ *compensable factors* in assessing job worth. A provides a base for defining the internal worth of a jo employed compensable factors are: (1) responsibi the job, (3) effort required, and (4) working con

Those four compensable factors can be trac Labor Board during World War II.[5] One of th to make sure that women, who were for the fir into industrial jobs vacated by men going same wage as men for work on the "same responsibility, skill, effort, and working venient basis for determining compar became adopted in almost all job e factors were codified in the Equal Pay Act of 1963, a law designed to insure women against sex discrimination in pay. Legal developments subsequent to the Equal Pay Act (to be explored more fully in Chapter 6, pp. 133–34) have set precedents using the four compensable factors to determine pay discrimination against women. Sex-based wage differences have been justified when the jobs in question have been demonstrated to be substantially different on one of these dimensions.

It would appear, then, that job evaluation addressing such compensable factors as skill, responsibility, effort, and working conditions might be an answer to the problem of defining internal equity apart from external equity. In practice, though, job evaluation remains a neutral administrative tool for making job evaluation scores (the value assigned to jobs) conform to *any* definition of worth, internal or external.[6] There is an even more difficult problem in practice, however, and that is forcing the comparable factor data in job evaluation to conform to external wage-rate data. Donald Schwab, and D. J. Treiman and H. I. Hartman, in two recent reviews of job evaluation practices, have concluded that it is common among compensation practitioners to use statistical methods (including multiple linear regression) to force internal job evaluation scores to coincide with external market wage rate distributions.[7] This practice obviously confounds external and internal equity and renders job evaluation a tool merely for bringing internal wage structures into close alignment with external wage structures.[8] Most experts agree, then, that job evaluation, as often practiced, merely reflects external exchange rates and does not adequately define job worth apart from such external rates.

Economist Ruth Blumrosen points out that the problem of not assessing internal equity apart from external equity is compounded for women to the extent that external wages reflect patterns of long-standing sex discrimination and segregation in external markets.[9] She points to instances in which society valued the work of women less than that of men and to how those judgments were reflected in the marketplace for jobs. If she is correct, job evaluation schemes that force internal data into line with external data will only perpetuate sex discrimination in pay. Several pay discrimination cases have advanced this logic. In *Kouba v. Allstate Insurance,* for example, the plaintiff charged that Allstate had engaged in pay discrimination against women insurance sales representatives because it followed a policy of setting initial pay according to the employee's previous earnings.[10] Because women in general earn about 58 percent of what men in general earn, the policy captured this differential and created an earnings gap between men and women sales representatives. Allstate settled the case with the class of plaintiffs.

Unfortunately, then, job evaluation is not, in and of itself, an answer to our field's problem with internal equity. At best, it remains a neutral administrative tool for ensuring consistency in managers' judgments about job worth. At worst, it contributes to problems of pay discrimination by being influenced by biased and/or discriminatory judgments.[11] The field of compensation is just now breaking new ground in a search for bases of job worth internal to the organization. We will examine and integrate several bases in economic and sociological theory for addressing the problem of internal equity in the remainder of this chapter. Such knowledge should prove beneficial for two reasons. First, it will allow us better to explain and understand managers' actual judgments of a job's internal value. Second, it will allow us to ask normative questions about wage setting in organizations. That is, better knowledge about the internal sources of job worth will allow us to ask more readily if specific wage-setting practices achieve the norm of internal equity.

Classical Approaches to Job Value

Society's concern with fairness in pay is not new. As early as the Middle Ages, religious leaders in Europe were concerned with setting wage rates for crafts and trades. In the eighteenth century, Adam Smith, the intellectual father of market analysis, grappled with the problem of determining the value of labor on a job. And in the nineteenth century, Karl Marx, the intellectual father of the Communist ethic, extended Smith's ideas about the value created by labor on a job.

The Just Price Doctrine

During the Middle Ages, the Church in Western Europe decreed that occupations should be paid a just price or wage.[12] According to this doctrine, a just price was one that corresponded to the occupation's station in the social hierarchy. The major proposition in the Just Price doctrine was that a job's value was derived from the status of the occupation in society (an idea, incidentally, that corresponds very closely to Thurow's belief that cultural value, not exchange rates, determines external wage distribution in society).

Strictly speaking, the Just Price doctrine is not a statement of internal equity. It is important in this context, however, because it provides a basis for using social values much broader than an economic exchange for justifying wage differentials. One can see the premises of a just price theory, for example, in the charge that it is unfair to pay nurses less than parking meter repairers. Managers should be aware, therefore, that one major source of equity that goes beyond market criteria is a concern with a job's place in the social pecking order.

The Labor Theory of Value

As articulated by Adam Smith, the labor theory of value directly addressed the worth that labor contributes to a job.[13] Smith proposed that commodities gain value according to the amount of labor necessary to produce them. Thus, value is created through the application of labor.

Smith also reasoned that labor's value is measured not only in simple hours but also as a function of five *job characteristics*: (1) hardship or un-pleasantness, (2) difficulty of learning the job, (3) stability of employment, (4) responsibility or trust inherent in the job, and (5) chances of success or failure inherent in the work. One should be struck by the similarity between these criteria and the compensable factors of skill, responsibility, effort, and working conditions cited earlier.[14] Smith's reasoning, then, specifies that a job's worth is the amount of labor (including the five compensable factors just cited) required to carry it out.

Karl Marx

In nineteenth-century England, Karl Marx extended Adam Smith's labor theory of value to the extreme position that labor was the *sole* source of value in an economy. Using the ideas of earlier economic thinkers Thomas Malthus and David Ricardo, he reasoned that wages in the labor market tend toward subsistence levels and that the difference between such wages and the full value created by labor was a surplus exploited by capitalists in the form of profits. Managers should note the inference that can be drawn from Marx, specifically, that the exchange rate for labor is not an adequate measure of value; it merely reflects a wage at which labor can be sustained.

Contemporary Approaches to Job Value

We will see that contemporary statements of job worth carry over the classical idea that labor on a job creates value. The labor theory of value remains an important legacy of Smith and Marx. We still need, however, to make more explicit what there is about labor that creates value on a job. To accomplish this we must turn to contemporary models of labor demand and supply.

The Need to Distinguish Demand- and Supply-Side Considerations

The marginal revenue product (MRP) model was presented in Chapter 2 as a model of wage and employment levels. The model defines external equity as the exchange value of labor (that is, the intersect of aggregate supply and demand functions in a specific labor market). We have seen that many experts doubt the adequacy of exchange rates as measures of labor value (especially internal equity). Thurow, specifically, believes that external rates have less to do with demand/supply intersects than shared cultural norms, and Mahoney suggests that exchange value is not the same as use value in the real world.

Wallace and Fay have proposed that, to explore internal equity more fully, it is useful to separate demand-side phenomena from supply-side phenomena and address the theory on each side separately.[15] A demand-side perspective focuses on what happens to or for the employer when a job is performed. Such outcomes might be economic (marginal revenue product is created) or administrative (a process is successfully completed, a decision is made, or discretion over resources is exercised). Demand-side models are concerned with making such bases for job worth explicit in understanding a manager's demand for labor on a job.

A supply-side perspective on job worth focuses on the sources of labor supply and any factors that influence such sources, making supply costly to the employer. Such factors include variation in the amount of training that different occupations require, the proportion of training costs borne by the employee and the employer, the ease of entry into an occupation, the differences in quality of members of the same occupation, and any other factor (including geography) that segments a labor market. Such differences may serve as additional bases for judging the internal value of a job to an employer. In effect, a supply-side perspective suggests that jobs can be valued according to the scarcity, the investment value, or the capacity of labor required to perform a job.

Demand-Side Theory

Marginal Revenue Product and Thurow's Job Competition Model In Chapter 2, we examined the MRP model as a theory of wage and employment levels. Economists, however, have judged MRP theory most effective, not as a complete model of wage and employment, but, rather, as a model of labor demand and labor's use value in a job.[16] One does not need to assume long-run general equilibrium and perfect competition in all markets to use MRP's core thesis: labor in a job is worth the additional value it creates for the employer. The model, further, breaks marginal revenue product (MRP) into two components: (1) the *marginal physical product* (MPP) produced by the employee, and (2) the *marginal revenue* (MR) or price per unit generated when the additional product is sold (that is, $MRP = MR \times MPP$).

Managers should carefully consider the internal value implications of marginal revenue and marginal physical product. The marginal revenue component (MR) suggests that the internal worth of a job to a manager is influenced by the revenue or prices the output of the job can command in the employer's product or service market. This leads one to conclude that, in part, the internal value of labor on a job is derived from the product market demand faced by the employer (an idea we made explicit in the course of Chapter 2).

The marginal physical product (MPP) component refers to the productivity of labor, that is, the number of units of product or service the job can be credited with per unit time. We would expect part of the value of a job to a manager to be influenced by productivity.

Again, we mentioned earlier in this chapter that Lester Thurow questions the value of MRP theory as a model of external wage rates, which he claims are set by cultural rather than marginal economic forces. Thurow's job competition model still postulates, however, that job value is derived from the value added (marginal revenue product) through employment. Thurow, in fact, goes so far as to maintain that a job's value lies solely in the job itself, and is quite distinct from any qualities of the individual person filling the job.[17]

Both the MRP model and Thurow's job competition model make important statements about the sources of job value that a manager should consider. Both statements focus the manager's attention on the economic value of job outcomes to the manager or the employer as a basis for determining the internal value or worth of a job. In effect, they tell managers that the bottom line (contribution to profit or other managerial financial objectives) is the appropriate measure of a job's internal worth, and that internal equity is achieved when wages are set according to this contribution.

Time Span of Discretion   Marginal revenue product theory is an economic definition of a job's contribution to an employer. Elliott Jaques provides a noneconomic, administrative definition of use value by capturing the notion of job responsibility in the concept of *time span of discretion,* which is defined by Jaques as "the maximum period of time during which the use of discretion is authorized and expected without review of that discretion by a superior."[18] Jaques's theory is an important alternative statement of job worth for managers to consider. The model implies that the exercise of discretion over resources is an important job outcome that employers purchase, and it provides a basis for valuing the work performed in a job. In effect, time span of discretion is one measure of the level of responsibility on a job.

Supply-Side Theory

We have already examined several models of labor supply (Reynolds theory, human capital theory, and the existence of a labor union) in Chapter 2. We will reexamine them in this chapter for inferences regarding job value that lie, not in the job itself (demand-side theory), but in the character and quality of labor seeking work on the job. These supply-side efforts fall into three major groups: (1) those concentrating on labor's *scarcity value,* (2) those concentrating on labor's *human capital* or *investment value,* and (3) those concentrating on variation in labor's *capacity value.*

Labor's Scarcity Value   As we mentioned in Chapter 2, economist Lloyd G. Reynolds proposed the following as factors contributing to labor scarcity in the short run under conditions approaching full employment:[19]

> the employer's monopsonist influence (when employers in a market are few and large relative to labor supplies)
>
> employees' ignorance of job openings
>
> employees' preferences for monetary and nonmonetary reward combinations
>
> employees' willingness to take on the risk of changing jobs
>
> geographic barriers

Of concern to the compensation manager is that such factors contribute to labor scarcity during periods approaching full employment.

In addition to these factors, union organization contributes to labor scarcity. Alan Cartter's analysis of union leadership preferences in collective bargaining (examined in Chapter 2, pp. 43–46) suggests that union leaders prefer to use increases in labor demand primarily for wage improvements, at the expense of employment, and will resist wage cuts with decreases in labor demand, again at the expense of employment, unless unemployment becomes a long-term and deep problem for the union's membership, as it has in the automobile industry. In most circumstances, then, the result of the union's attempt to place upward pressure on wages is to contribute to labor scarcity.

Labor's Human Capital Value The adaptation of financial capital models to labor supply offers a second major supply-side perspective on job worth. Economist Gary Becker and others have developed models of the economic value created by the investment of resources in the development of skills and knowledge required by various jobs.[20] According to human capital theory, wages are in part a return on the investment of resources in developing skills.

Of key importance to the issues of judging job worth is Becker's distinction between *general* and *specific* training.[21] General training contributes marginal revenue product (MRP) in all employment settings. At the extreme, if training were perfectly general, the results would be equally valuable to all employers bidding in the labor market and MRP would be equal for all employers. Firms providing for or investing in such training could not capture any of the return to such equity.

Specific training (as well as employer-specific recruiting, screening, and orientation costs), in contrast, is an investment that contributes to the marginal revenue product of the employer providing it and not to that of other employers. At the extreme, specific training contributes MRP only to the employer providing it.

Compensation managers should carefully consider the distinction between general and specific training when thinking about the sources of value in a job. In the extreme case of general training, the job applicant pays for all training costs and earns all the equity value of his or her new skills, and employers bid for that value (the wage competition model in Thurow's terms). In this extreme case, value resides solely in the person and not in the job. We would expect, further, that employers would bid for those skills and such value would be an important supply-side basis for valuing a job internally.

In the extreme opposite case of specific training, the employer pays all the development costs and earns the equity in the value created. In fact, this extreme case corresponds to Thurow's job competition model. In this extreme case, labor to a job carries no inherent value and all worth lies in the job itself.

Compensation managers should recognize that in most cases some combination of specific and general training is required to fill a job. Thus, both job factors and individual employee factors become appropriate anchors for making job-worth judgments.

Labor's Capacity Value Human capital theory proposes that job seekers bring valued general skills to the job. In addition, a broad range of research findings suggests that, within a labor or occupational market, people vary widely in their skills. Some accountants are more skilled than others. Some electricians are more competent than others. Lester Thurow proposes the interesting idea that labor queues form for each job opening that appears in the market (an idea we explained in detail in Chapter 2, p. 43).[22] He proposes, further, that the employer orders the job applicants in the queue according to each person's skill, and selects the most skilled applicant available. The best prospect will be least costly to train and will be the most productive. More important, people farther back in the ordered queue will be more expensive to train and less productive, even though the same wage is being paid.

The practicing manager should recognize that attending to differences in labor's capacity value will be extremely important when trying to staff jobs that rely heavily on general training, such as the jobs of engineers, physicians, attorneys, geologists, or computer systems analysts. Concern with variation in labor's capacity value will not be so great for managers when trying to staff jobs that do not rely so heavily on general training, such as materials handling, low-level clerical work, and unskilled assembly jobs. The point is that jobs do vary in the importance of general training. We would expect among those jobs where general training is critical that labor's capacity value would be an important basis for judging the internal worth of those jobs.

Sociological Views of Job Worth

The demand-side and supply-side models of job worth we have just presented provide a rather narrow economic view of the notion of job worth. Several theorists have provided an additional, broader sociological view of job worth of concern to the compensation manager. The most important work in this regard is that of Thomas Mahoney, who has proposed that a job's place in a formal organizational hierarchy alone, apart from any job content elements, is an important determinant of perceived job worth.[23] He reasons that norms exist in our society regarding the power, influence, and status associated with levels in a formal, organizational hierarchy.

Mahoney cites the work in the 1950s of Herbert Simon as the basis for his ideas.[24] Simon proposed that hierarchical level, apart from any other job or organizational characteristic, is a major factor influencing the level of executive compensation. He specified his ideas in the following model:

$$C = Ab^{L-1}$$

where

C = compensation of the chief executive

A = salary for management trainees

b = proportional compensation difference between adjacent hierarchical levels

L = number of levels in the organization.

Mahoney focused on estimating the coefficient b in Simon's model and reported intriguing empirical results. He reported a wide range of data relevant to estimating the coefficient b, including:

United States salary survey data

Canadian salary survey data

judgments of sociology students about what the jobs in a hierarchy should be paid, once the salary of one position is given[25]

similar judgments of business school students[26]

perceived fair pay data according to Jaques's notion of time span of discretion

Mahoney reports that there is a striking degree of agreement between what people perceive to be the appropriate differences in pay for adjacent levels in a job hierarchy and what those differences in pay actually are. The data he cites agree closely that the appropriate difference of one rank over another is 30 to 40 percent. That is, the appropriate pay level for one position should be 1.3 to 1.4 times the level set for the next job down in the hierarchy. Mahoney further points out (in line with Simon's original thinking) that the traditional job content factors that are employed in job evaluation but not associated with hierarchy could not explain these differences.

Mahoney interprets these data as evidence of social norms regarding the power, influence, and status reflected in a job's place in an organizational hierarchy and advises, "Organizational level of a position, whatever it connotes regarding position content, clearly is a significant influence on the worth or status of positions in organizations."[27]

In this chapter and the last, we have reviewed a broad range of economic and sociological theory regarding the determinants of external and internal equity in managers' thinking about job worth. Exhibit 3.1 summarizes these statements. Each theory or model is briefly stated along with its major proposition regarding job worth. The final column states the explicit job-worth inference to be drawn from the proposition. This exhibit will help you organize the information about job worth presented in Chapters 2 and 3.

Exhibit 3.1   Theory Bases for Job Worth

Model	*Proposition*	*Job Worth Implications*
Classical Theory		
1. Just Price	A job's value derives from the relative status of the occupation in society. A just wage therefore is one that corresponds to the status distribution in society and preserves customary relationships among classes of workers.	A job derives value from the place of its occupation in society.
2. Labor Theory of Value		
• Smith	A commodity is worth the amount of labor required to produce it.	Labor on a job creates value.
• Marx	Labor is the sole source of value.	
Demand/Supply Theory		
3. Market Exchange Model	Wage and employment levels are determined by labor demand and labor supply intersects.	A job is worth the exchange rate clearing in the market for labor required to fill it.

Exhibit 3.1   (*continued*)

Model	Proposition	Job Worth Implications
Demand-Side Theory		
4. Marginal Revenue	$MRP = MPP \times MR$ where: MRP = Marginal Revenue Product MPP = Marginal Physical Product MR = Marginal Revenue	A job is worth the marginal revenue product it generates.
5. Thurow's Job Competition Model	Jobs are training opportunities. Marginal product lies solely in the job.	A job is worth the value of the product it generates.
6. Elliott Jaques	Jobs vary in time span of discretion they demand. People share norms regarding equitable pay according to time span of discretion.	Job value is measured by time span of discretion.
Supply-Side Theory		
7. Labor Scarcity Models • Monopsony • Employee preferences for money income and nonmonetary conditions	Additional units of labor become increasingly costly to the employer (upward-sloping supply curve).	Labor to a job (like diamonds) has a scarcity value apart from its use value.

Exhibit 3.1 *(continued)*

Model	Proposition	Job Worth Implications
• Employee preferences for money and risk		
• Collective bargaining		
8. Human Capital Models	Long-run marginal returns to labor will equal the long-run marginal investments made in it.	Wages paid to a job represent, in part, a return on the investments made to develop skills required by a job.
9. Labor Capacity Models	Labor units vary in capacity for carrying out a job.	Labor to a job has value that varies according to capacity.
Sociological Theory		
10. Organizational Hierarchy	Shared norms exist in society regarding the power, influence, and status reflected in a job's place in an organizational hierarchy. Such norms dictate a pay or value differential of between 30 and 40% between adjacent positions.	Organizational level is a determinant of the worth of a job.

Source: Adapted from Marc J. Wallace, Jr. and Charles H. Fay, "Labor Markets, Job Evaluation, and Job Worth: Towards a Model of Managerial Judgements of Job Value," Working paper in business administration, BA 74, University of Kentucky, 1982.

The Need for Further Study

There is little doubt that the field of compensation needs additional research to provide managers with some direction regarding their practices in valuing jobs. Indeed, the two major professional organizations in the field, the American Compensation Association (ACA) and the American Society for Personnel Administration (ASPA) have recently issued a joint policy statement that reflects the dilemma over external equity (Chapter 2) and internal equity (this chapter):

> Regardless of the methodology selected (in job evaluation), pay grades and pay ranges are ultimately determined by:
>
> 1. Market rates for comparable jobs — external competitiveness. This approach is referred to as the "the labor market," or "market supply" approach.
>
> 2. Management's judgments as to the relative internal worth of the job's content — internal equity.
>
> Organizations may place different emphasis on either external competitiveness, internal equity, or a blend of the two depending on their objectives or circumstances. [28]

Clearly this statement reflects the dilemma that currently exists in our field regarding the balance to be struck between external and internal criteria in setting wage rates for jobs in organizations. In light of the comparable worth controversy described in Chapters 1 and 3 (and to be discussed in Chapter 6), two important questions arise: (1) Should external market criteria and internal worth criteria be applied in similar fashion across all jobs within an organization, or should market criteria be paramount among one set of jobs and internal equity among another? In practical terms, should management pay more to fill a job with high training requirements than to fill one with no training requirements, even though there is a plentiful supply of applicants for the former job and a severe shortage of candidates for the latter? (2) Should external market criteria and internal worth criteria be applied consistently across different organizations for the same job?

Unfortunately, compensation theory and practice have not yet reached a stage of development sufficient to provide much direction for the compensation manager in resolving these questions. The economic and sociological theories reviewed in this chapter and Chapter 2 take a first step toward increasing our knowledge about how to assess job worth. There remain, however, three immediate needs for future research in compensation theory and practice:

1. to integrate theory further with respect to the valuation of jobs
2. to study the actual job valuations of managers
3. to build an integrative model of job valuation with theoretical and heuristic implications for compensation practice.

Managerial Judgments of Job Worth: A Model and Propositions for Research

The examination of economic and related theory in this chapter has suggested several major classes of variables that are likely to be used as criteria of job worth. These can be organized into the following general model:

$$V_k = W_k C_k + \sum_{i=1}^{I} W_{ik} R_{ik} + \sum_{j=1}^{J} W_{jk} R_{jk} \qquad (3.1)$$

where

V_k = value placed on job k

W_k = weight placed on the external wage rate for job k

C_k = prevailing external wage rate for job k

W_{ik} = weight placed on demand-side factor i for job k

R_{ik} = judged amount of demand-side factor i held by job k

W_{jk} = weight placed on supply-side factor j for job k

R_{jk} = judged amount of supply-side factor j held by job k

The term $W_k C_k$ in Equation 3.1 is an external equity model, proposing that exchange rates in external markets (C_k) will influence the value placed on a job (V_k). The term $\sum_{i=1}^{I} W_{ik} R_{ik} + \sum_{j=1}^{J} W_{jk} R_{jk}$ in Equation 3.1 is an internal equity model consisting of demand-side and supply-side influences on value judgments. Demand-side factors (R_{ik}) are proposed to reside in the job itself and to influence value judgments (V_k) independently from supply-side factors (R_{jk}). Exhibit 3.2 summarizes the theory bases for job worth organized in our model.

Exhibit 3.2 Alternative Bases for Job Worth Judgments

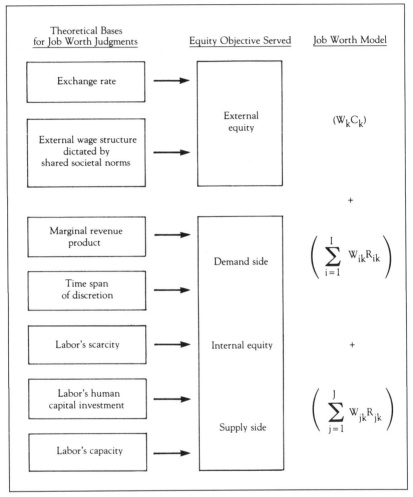

Heuristic Value

What inferences can be drawn from the compensation theories integrated in Chapters 2 and 3 for modeling job worth? A starting place would be to test the descriptive accuracy of the external equity and internal equity models in Equation 3.1 in predicting actual job evaluations. Integration and extension of compensation theory suggests the following empirical propositions for research.

Independence of Internal and External Equity   The model in Equation 3.1 reflects the theoretical proposition that external equity and internal equity involve different classes of phenomena. The theories reviewed here suggest specifically that exchange value is independent of use value and supply-side sources of value. This reasoning leads logically to the hypothesis that external market factors and internal factors have independent effects on managerial estimates of job value.

If subsequent research confirms this proposition, we will have evidence that managers do, indeed, consider nonmarket factors in valuing jobs as suggested in the ACA/ASPA policy statement.

Relative Importance of External and Internal Factors   Compensation theorists have long pointed out that jobs vary in their exposure to external market influences.[29] Entry-level jobs and jobs being used as benchmarks for interfirm pay comparisons, for example, can be expected to provide management with far less latitude in setting wage rates than jobs that are more insulated from the market.

This reasoning implies that the external equity model in Equation 3.1 $(W_k C_k)$ will be more powerful than the internal equity model $(\sum_{i=1}^{I} W_{ik} R_{ik} + \sum_{j=1}^{J} W_{jk} R_{jk})$ in predicting job evaluation outcomes and judgments for jobs tied closely to the market. We could expect the weight W_k to be greater, empirically, than weights W_{ik} or W_{jk}. We expect, conversely, that the internal equity model will be the stronger predictor of job evaluation results among jobs that are insulated from the market. The primary importance of testing this hypothesis, from a comparable worth perspective, will be to confirm or disconfirm empirically whether latitude for making comparable worth judgments independent from the marketplace varies across types of jobs.

Empirical knowledge about the sources of job worth and their influences on actual wage-setting practices will allow compensation theorists to examine compensation policies in the light of pay equity demands. Implicit job valuation policies evident in the weighing of alternative compensable factors can be evaluated, for example, against the fair employment standards of the Equal Pay Act of 1963, Title VII of the Civil Rights Act of 1964, and all other relevant standards of pay equity.

Summary

In this chapter, we have examined the problem of internal equity in setting wage rates within organizations. We have reviewed evidence that suggests that external equity (the exchange rate for jobs clearing in external markets) is, in many cases, different from internal equity and is therefore a poor measure of the internal value of a job.

We have examined a number of theoretical approaches to the definition of a job's internal value. They include the classical principles inherent in the Just Price doctrine of the Middle Ages, and the labor theory of value proposed by Adam Smith and extended by Karl Marx.

Contemporary approaches to the problem of internal worth include the separate examination of demand-side and supply-side influences on job worth. The marginal revenue product (MRP) demand-side model and Thurow's job competition model were examined in this regard. Both theories propose that a job's worth lies in the value created for management when work is performed on the job. Elliott Jaques's concept of time span of discretion was analyzed as a noneconomic, administrative measure of a job's worth.

Three kinds of supply-side theory were examined for propositions regarding a job's worth. These included statements of (1) labor's scarcity value, (2) labor's human capital value, and (3) labor's capacity. In each case, labor to a job was considered to have value, apart from the job itself, that could be considered in establishing the value of the job.

Finally, we examined a sociological view, in which a job's value resides in that job's place in an organizational hierarchy. The premise of this view is that societal norms regarding the power, influence, and status represented by placement in an organization's hierarchy dictate norms regarding fair payment for jobs.

We concluded with the observation that much more research and theory about job worth are needed before practitioners will have any better guides for policy in setting wage rates within organizations.

Notes

[1]*Lemons et al.* v. *City and County of Denver,* 17 FEP Cases (BNA) 906 (District Court, Colorado, 1978); *International Union of Electrical, Radio, and Machine Workers (IUE)* v. *Westinghouse Electric Corporation,* 19 FEP Cases 450 (District Court, New Jersey, 1979); AFSCME v. *State of Washington,* FEP Cases 808 (U.S. District Court, Washington, 1983).

[2]Thomas A. Mahoney, "Justice and Equity: A Recurring Theme in Compensation," *Personnel* 52 (1975): 60–66.

[3]Lester C. Thurow, *Generating Inequality* (New York: Basic Books, 1975).

[4]E. J. McCormick, *Job Analysis: Methods and Applications* (New York: AMACOM, 1979); E. J. McCormick, "Job Analysis," in D. J. Treiman and H. I. Hartmann (eds.), *Women, Work, and Wages: Equal Pay for Jobs of Equal Value* (Washington, D.C.: National Academy Press, 1981).

[5]3 *War Labor Report* 321 (1942); 3 *War Labor Report* 348 (1942); 5 *War Labor Report* 461 (1943); 28 *War Labor Report* 666 (1945).

[6]R. Grams and D. P. Schwab, "An Investigation of Systematic Gender-Related Error in Job Evaluation," *Academy of Management Journal* (1985): 279–90; Nancy B. Johnson and Ronald A. Ash, "Integrating the Labor Market With Job Evaluation: Clearing the Cobwebs," Annual Meeting of the Society for Industrial and Organizational Psychology, Chicago, April 1986; Edward E. Lawler, "What's Wrong With Point-Factor Job Evaluation," *Compensation Review* (1986): 20–28; Robert M. Madigan and David J. Hoover, "Effects of Alternative Job Evaluation Methods on Decisions Involving Pay Equity," *Academy of Management Journal* (1986): 84–100; Donald P. Schwab, "Job Evaluation and Pay Setting: Concepts and Practices," in E. R. Livernash (ed.), *Comparable Worth: Issues and Alternatives* (Washington, D.C.: Equal Employment Advisory Council, 1980); and Marc J. Wallace, Jr. and Charles H. Fay, "Labor Markets, Job Evaluation, and Job Worth: Towards a Model of Managerial Judgments of Job Value," Working paper in business administration, BA 74 (Lexington, Ky.: University of Kentucky, 1982).

[7]Schwab, "Job Evaluation and Pay Setting"; Treiman and Hartman, "Women, Work, and Wages."

[8]Wallace and Fay, "Labor Markets."

[9]Ruth G. Blumrosen, "Wage Discrimination, Job Segregation, and Women Workers," *Employee Relations Law Journal* 6 (1980): 77–136; Blumrosen, "Wage Discrimination, Job Segregation, and Title VII of the Civil Rights Act of 1964," 12 *U. Mich. J.L. Ref.* 397 (1979); see Bruce A. Nelson, Edward M. Opton, Jr., and Thomas E. Wilson, "Wage Discrimination and the Comparable Worth Theory in Perspective," 13 *U. Mich. J.L. Ref.* 231 (1980) for an opposing view.

[10]*Kouba* v. *Allstate Insurance Company,* 691 F.2d 873 (1982).

[11]See, for example, R. D. Arvey, G. A. Davis, S. L. McGowan, and R. L. Dipboye, "Potential Sources of Bias in Job Analytic Processes," *Academy of Management Journal* (1982): 618–29; D. Doverspike and G. Barrett, "An Internal Bias Analysis of a Job Evaluation Instrument," *Journal of Applied Psychology* (1984): 648–62; Grams and Schwab, "An Investigation of Systematic Gender-Related Error"; Lawler, "What's Wrong With Point-Factor Job Evaluation"; *Madigan and Hoover,* "Effects of Alternative Job Evaluation Methods"; Michael K. Mount and Rebecca Ellis, "Impacts of Pay Level, Job Gender and Job Type on Job Evaluation Ratings," Unpublished paper, University of Iowa, 1986; and David J. Thomsen, "Eliminating Pay Discrimination Caused by Job Evaluation," *Compensation Review* (1978): 11–18.

[12]Wallace and Fay, "Labor Markets."

[13]Adam Smith, *The Wealth of Nations* (1776; reprint, New York: Random House, 1937, abridged).

[14]Herbert G. Heneman, Jr. and Dale Yoder, *Labor Economics* (Cincinnati: South-Western Publishing Co., 1965).

[15]Wallace and Fay, "Labor Markets."

[16]Alan M. Cartter, *Theory of Wages and Employment* (Homewood, Ill.: Richard D. Irwin, 1959).

[17]Thurow, *Generating Inequality.*

[18]Elliott Jaques, *Equitable Payment* (New York: John Wiley & Sons, 1961).

[19]Lloyd G. Reynolds, "Some Aspects of Labor Market Structure," in R. A. Lester and J. Shister (eds.), *Insights Into Labor Issues* (New York: Macmillan, 1949); and Reynolds, "The Supply of Labor to the Firm," *Quarterly Journal of Economics* 60 (1946): 390–411.

[20]Gary S. Becker, *Human Capital* (New York: National Bureau of Economic Research, 1964).

[21]Ibid.

[22]Thurow, *Generating Inequality.*

[23]Thomas A. Mahoney, "Organizational Hierarchy and Position Worth," *Academy of Management Journal* (1979): 726–37.

[24]Herbert A. Simon, "The Compensation of Executives," *Sociometry* 20 (1957): 32–35.

[25]James L. Kuethe and Bernard Levinson, "Conceptions of Organizational Worth," *American Journal of Sociology* (November 1964): 342–48.

[26]Fred Champlin, "An Analysis of the Effects of Organizational Structure on Perceptions of Appropriate Pay," Unpublished paper, University of Minnesota, 1976, cited by Mahoney, "Organizational Hierarchy"; Charles A. Lindberg, "An Empirical Study of the Influence of Structural Variables on Conceptions of Position Worth," Unpublished paper, University of Minnesota, 1975, cited by Mahoney, "Organizational Hierarchy."

[27]Mahoney, "Organizational Hierarchy."

[28]American Society for Personnel Administration and American Compensation Association, *Elements of Sound Base Pay Administration* (Scottsdale, Ariz.: American Compensation Association, 1986).

[29]E. R. Livernash, "The Internal Wage Structure," in G. W. Taylor and F. C. Pierson (eds.), *New Concepts in Wage Determination* (New York: McGraw-Hill, 1957), pp. 140–72.

4

Individual Equity

After you have studied this chapter, you should be able to address the following key issues and questions:

1. What is the difference between individual equity as a compensation objective on the one hand, and external and internal equity on the other?

2. Why is equity or fairness such a crucial condition for the success of a compensation program?

3. Why are relative pay comparisons even more important to individuals, in some cases, than absolute pay levels?

4. What are the major sources of or influences on pay equity perceptions?

5. What are the major impacts of pay practices on employee motivation?

6. What major employee decisions made about organizations are influenced by pay?

Introduction

Individual equity has to do with the fairness with which individuals (as opposed to jobs) are paid. It is a concept quite different from either external equity (Chapter 2) or internal equity (Chapter 3) because we are no longer focusing on the job but on the merits of the individual who fills the job. You should think of individual equity as a criterion that requires employers to pay wage rates to individuals — in the simplest case, workers on the same job — according to variation in individual qualities and qualifications. In the equity theory terms we presented in Chapter 1, individual equity is achieved when the input/output ratios for one person and a comparable other person are equal.

This chapter will pursue the notion of individual equity in more detail. We will examine two major issues regarding individual equity. First, we will explore the challenge of influencing motivation. We will show that managers face three tasks in attempting to use compensation to influence employee behavior and performance: (1) managing fairness, (2) managing expectations or beliefs, and (3) managing results. We will summarize this section with a conceptual model of individual behavior that will illustrate exactly the way in which success or failure in achieving these three tasks will influence employee behavior and performance and all other employee decisions made regarding the employer.

Second, we will examine several decisions made by individuals regarding their employers when evaluating their employers against individual equity criteria. Finally, we will show how much pay satisfaction and dissatisfaction affect pay-related individual decisions.

Influencing Motivation

Managing Fairness: Equity Theory

First and foremost, a compensation system must be fair and equitable. Equity is a necessary (although not sufficient) condition for success. Unless it achieves equity, a compensation plan cannot have a positive impact on decisions people make about organizations. The first task for managing compensation, then, is to assure that the results will achieve individual equity. The central models for individual equity are those of J. Stacy Adams and Elliott Jaques.[1] Adams's ideas are represented in Exhibit 4.1. According to this model, individuals constantly monitor the exchange relationship with their employer. An ex-

Exhibit 4.1   Individual Equity Defined

$$\frac{O_p}{I_p} = \frac{O_o}{I_o}$$

where:

O_p = outcomes (rewards) for the person
I_p = the person's inputs
O_o = outcomes (rewards) for a comparison person
I_o = the comparison person's inputs

change relationship (as we pointed out in Chapter 1) involves equity or inequity: people invest inputs (the *I*'s in Exhibit 4.1) and receive outcomes or rewards (the *O*'s). The exchange may or may not be fair.

Of significance to Adams's theory is the concept of distributive justice, an idea originally made formal by sociologist George Homans.[2] This is the condition that is achieved when the ratio of inputs to outcomes for a person is equal to that for some *comparison person*. The comparison person may be another person on the same job, a member of the same occupation, or even a composite of several comparison persons. The experience of inequity is very distressing, according to Adams, and people will try several strategies for bringing the ratios in Exhibit 4.1 back into alignment. Such actions fall into the following categories:

1. adjusting one's outcomes or inputs
2. adjusting the outcomes or inputs of others
3. changing comparison persons
4. leaving the situation.

One of the difficulties of translating equity theory into practice, so far, is confusion over which of these steps a person will take in an actual situation. The employee who experiences inequity, for example, whether over- or under-reward, can behave either overtly to reduce inequity — for example, by asking an employer for a raise to bring his or her salary into line with a comparison person's — or psychologically. The latter form of behavior is much more difficult for the manager to detect. In this case, the employee changes a perception of some element in the ratios displayed in Exhibit 4.1.

He may, for example, perceptually increase or decrease the valuation of inputs and outcomes. An employee who perceives that he is being paid too much when compared to another employee will tend to rationalize the condition by adding to the perceived value of his own relative inputs, rather than go to the employer and ask for an adjustment in pay.

Perhaps the most important revision of Adams's equity theory has been suggested by Walster, Berscheid, and Walster.[3] Their ideas are represented in Exhibit 4.2 and constitute several important departures from Adams's original notions. The main difference from the original equity formulation is that the ratios now have a net return — outcomes or rewards *less* inputs — in the numerator and absolute value of inputs in the denominator. Computationally, the ratios in Exhibit 4.2 redefine equity as a rate of return or profit on the absolute value of inputs. One of the conditions such a revision allows us to consider is an exchange relationship where a person's inputs are actually negative. According to this reformulation, then, equity is achieved when the rate of return from the employment relationship is equal between an individual employee and a comparison person.

Another departure from traditional equity theory made by Walster et al. has to do with the notion of distributive justice. Adams's theory proposed that all people seek distributive justice, equality of the comparison ratios in Exhibit 4.1 and 4.2. Although this proposition makes intuitive sense in those cases where the employee perceives that he or she is underrewarded, it is not so straightforward in the case of overreward. Equity theory predicts that an employee experiencing overreward would be as distressed as he or she would be if underrewarded, and would act to reduce inequity in both cases. Although some limited experimental evidence suggests that this is the case, researchers are still doubtful that employees would act altruistically if they perceived that they were being overrewarded.[4]

The Walster, Berscheid, and Walster revision of equity theory proposes that individuals seek to maximize their individual rates of return [(outcomes − inputs) ÷ inputs] and do so *if unchecked by group and social norms.*

Exhibit 4.2   The Individual Equity Criterion

$$\frac{O_p - I_p}{I_p} = \frac{O_o - I_o}{I_o}$$

Source: Elaine Walster, Ellen Berscheid, and William Walster, "New Directions in Equity Theory," *Journal of Personality and Social Psychology,* 1973, pp. 151–76.

They propose, further, that work groups develop norms regarding equity among outcome/input ratios and censure members who seek to violate such norms.

The form of equity theory we have just examined involves social comparison. Equity is defined in terms of one person's comparisons of his or her welfare with that of some comparison person. Elliott Jaques proposes an alternative mechanism for defining equity that derives from the following propositions:[5]

1. Every worker is endowed with a specific level of capacity for work and expenditure (C). This capacity varies across people.

2. Each job demands a specific level of capacity. Jaques defines the capacity demanded by a job as its time span of discretion (W). Time span is the period of time that elapses between the performance of a task and its review. The longer this span, the greater the capacity demanded by the job. Of course, jobs vary in their time spans of discretion.

3. Any group of individuals will have norms regarding the rate of pay that is fair for each job (Jaques calls this *felt fair pay*); it corresponds to each job's time span of discretion. Surprisingly, strong empirical evidence supports this third proposition.[6]

Exhibit 4.3 presents a sampling of situations that could lead an individual employee to perceive inequity according to Jaques's theory. In the arrays in

Exhibit 4.3   Inequity Defined by Jaques

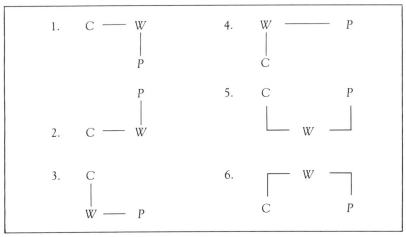

Exhibit 4.3, C is the individual's own capacity for work, W is the level of capacity (time span) demanded by the job, and P is the rate of pay the employer attaches to the job. The cases in Exhibit 4.3 show a variety of ways that inequity can develop. In cases 1 and 2, for example, the link between an individual's capacity and the time span demanded by the job is equitable. The person is perfectly qualified for the job. However, inequity exists because in case 1 the job is underpaid and in case 2 the job is overpaid.

However, inequity can arise not only from over- and underpayment of a job but also from poor job assignments. In cases 3 and 4, for example, the wage set for the job (P) corresponds equitably to the level of work required (W). Inequity develops, however, because the person assigned to the job is either overqualified (case 3) or underqualified (case 4).

Finally, inequity can arise even when a person is paid according to his or her own personal capacity. In case 5, for example, an employee is being paid a wage that corresponds to his own capacity for work, but his work assignment is below both his capacity for work and the wage being paid. In the last case, case 6, inequity exists because a person is assigned to a job that is both above his capacity to perform and above the rate being paid.

Examination of the possibilities in Exhibit 4.3 should demonstrate that Jaques's theory is rich in implications regarding the variety of ways inequity can arise in compensation:

1. People can be assigned to jobs that do not correspond to their capacities.

2. Wages can be set that do not correspond to the level of work the job demands.

3. Wages can be set that correspond to the level of work demanded by a job but not to the individual's capacity for work.

Although there are differences between Adams's and Jaques's notions of equity, research carried out on these two theories so far should convince the manager that the experience of inequity in rewards is a very powerful influence on employee satisfaction and behavior.[7] The compensation planner cannot ignore the issue of equity (defined in Exhibits 4.1–4.3) in setting wage rates for individual employees.

Managing Expectations and Results: Expectancy, Reward, and Goal Setting Theory

We noted earlier that although fairness is a necessary condition for a compensation program to influence people, it is not a sufficient condition. That is, managers may succeed in developing a compensation program that is fair, but still not influence employees. The reason for this is that equity is only the first leg of a three-legged challenge in motivation. In addition to being fair, a compensation plan must also (1) manage expectations or beliefs people have about their pay and (2) manage pay outcomes or results in a way that links up with desired behavior and performance.

Managing Expectations: Expectancy Theory   Expectations are beliefs that people have about the results of their actions. Employees, for example, will behave and perform in directions that they *believe* will result in outcomes or rewards of importance to them. The major theory addressing this problem is expectancy theory, a model that explains that an employee's effort and performance (or any other choice) are determined by expectations — beliefs that the effort and action will result in desired outcomes.[8] Much of expectancy theory can be summarized in two concepts: (1) the expectation or belief that a given level of effort will result in a given level of performance (let's call this an $E \rightarrow P$ belief) and (2) the expectation or belief that the achieved level of performance will result in outcomes that are desired by the employee (including compensation levels) (let's call this a $P \rightarrow O$ belief).

In the context of a job, we can say that $E \rightarrow P$ is the belief that if one puts out the effort, she will succeed in terms of job performance. In the context of a job applicant, $E \rightarrow P$ could be the belief that if one accepts the job offer, he will succeed on that job. The $P \rightarrow O$ belief is different and consists of the belief that if one succeeds in achieving a given level of performance (P), one will be rewarded in the form of higher earnings and other desired rewards, for example, promotion and advancement (O).

What impact can compensation have on $E \rightarrow P$ and $P \rightarrow O$ beliefs? The $E \rightarrow P$ perception entails confidence in one's abilities: "How much confidence do I have that if I really expend the effort on my job I will succeed?" There is little impact, probably, that compensation can have on this belief. Merely paying someone will probably not influence self-confidence all that much. Still, there are some things managers can do to influence a person's confidence indirectly. First, managers can provide employees with the information and skills needed to perform well (through formal and informal training and development efforts, for example.) Second, immediate supervisors can promote confidence through coaching, feedback, and encouragement.

The $P \rightarrow O$ belief is another matter entirely, in that compensation practice should have a direct impact on beliefs about performance outcomes. In fact, the $P \rightarrow O$ perception is where the employee really meets the system: "If I really perform well, will the employer actually deliver the goods in the form of a meaningful reward?"[9] The potential for compensation practice to influence motivation should be obvious. This is one area where management's actions speak much louder than its words.[10] Actual pay outcomes, the way people are really paid, and not policy alone must confirm the belief that if one actually performs well, he will be rewarded. High performers must end up being paid more than average performers. Average performers must end up earning more than low performers.

Confidence that performance will be rewarded, belief in the compensation system, can only be earned. It might take several cycles under a pay-for-performance system for employees to change their perceptions and develop strong $P \rightarrow O$ beliefs.

Expectancy theory leads to two conclusions for compensation management: (1) compensation can only influence effort and performance if people believe that performance will actually result in rewards (for example, higher earnings), and (2) the only way managers can positively influence this belief is through actual practice — making pay contingent upon performance.

Managing Results: Reward Theory   We just said that the only way to influence beliefs about performance and rewards is to make rewards contingent upon performance. This forces managers to gain control over results or incentives. Compensation theory deals with this as a twofold problem: first, finding those rewards that have incentive value (employees desire and seek them) and second, making the achievement of such rewards contingent upon desired performance. Reward theory and goal setting theory help us with these two problems directly.

Reward theory, or *reinforcement theory*, is a body of research that addresses the problem of making rewards contingent upon performance.[11] Research in reward theory clearly demonstrates that rewards that are made contingent upon performance (for example, a sales commission or payment by piece of work completed) are far more effective than other rewards (for example, paying people only for time worked).

Central to reward theory is the principle known as the law of effect.[12] This law states that behaviors that are rewarded will tend to be repeated while behaviors that are not rewarded will not be repeated. Compensation theorists translate the law of effect into a rather stark principle for compensation practice: *employees learn to behave in ways that get rewarded and avoid behavior that does not get rewarded.*[13]

As simple and obvious as this principle seems, managers often fail to take advantage of it in compensation practice and, unwittingly, fall into the trap of allowing the principle to work against them. Paying for time rather than paying for performance is a perfect illustration of this problem.

Many employers still use time-based pay systems, that is, paying straight hourly wage rates. Earnings, therefore, are simply a function of the number of hours of work the person has logged in a week, month, or year. This practice sends a rather clear message to employees: "Stay out of trouble, perform in a way that just meets your boss's demands, and pick up your check." Such a practice merely enforces acceptable performance. There is no incentive to put out more than minimum effort.

In order to motivate higher than acceptable levels of effort and performance, managers must make pay contingent on performance, not time. In other words, those who perform at high levels must end up earning more than those who perform simply at acceptable levels. The research is clear and provides managers interested in motivating with pay a simple guide: where the amount of pay is tied to level of performance (that is, where pay is contingent upon performance), pay influences performance.

Managing Results: Goal Setting Theory   Reward theory shows managers the need to make rewards contingent upon performance. But the rewards or results must have incentive value, that is, they must be valued or sought after by the employee. The challenge is to link performance objectives that are important to the organization with reward outcomes that are valued by employees in order to create a win/win situation. Goal setting theory and research suggests that this can be done through a process of mutual objective setting involving managers and employees.

Goals, according to Craig Pinder, are any outcomes a person may seek to achieve, attain, or accomplish.[14] Goals, therefore, can include a level of performance, meeting a deadline, or spending a certain amount within a budget.[15] Goals can also include earnings levels or other rewards contingent upon performance. A rich body of theory and numerous research studies have developed over the last fifteen years that lead to five important principles for managers to follow in setting goals that will motivate performance:

1. No goal will have an incentive effect on an employee's performance unless he or she accepts that goal as his or her own. Merely setting a goal of selling $5,000 worth of goods for a sales representative, for example, will not assure that she will make the sales. Only if she accepts the goal as her

own and commits to it will it have a motivational impact on her effort and behavior.

2. Once goals are accepted, the higher or more difficult the goal, the higher the resulting performance levels. This finding has been repeated time after time in both laboratory experiments and field studies in actual organizations.[16]

3. Employee participation in setting the goal increases the likelihood that she will accept the goal as her own, and commit to it. This principle explains why management by objectives (MBO) programs have achieved the level of success they have as a management technique.[17] Employee involvement in setting performance goals creates a climate that enhances commitment to them.[18]

4. Research also demonstrates that an employee's acceptance and commitment to performance goals is enhanced when the goal and contingent reward are in monetary form. Thus, attaching specific financial incentives to performance will have a positive impact on effort and performance.

5. Finally, goal setting research confirms that the more specific the goal, the higher the levels of acceptance and subsequent performance. Thus, establishing performance goals in terms of specific units of output, dollars, or deadlines has far greater motivational value than goals like, "Do your best," or "Try to improve."[19]

As mentioned earlier, goal setting has an impressive track record. Extensive empirical investigations in widely different settings confirm the five principles just presented. Why does goal setting work? Experts suggest four reasons.[20]

1. Goals focus attention on specifics. They direct managers and employees to think of performance and rewards in very tangible and explicit terms. Goals are oriented toward action and show the way toward achieving results.

2. Goal setting gets people to think strategically about performance. Thinking about a goal almost inevitably leads to a consideration of the steps that will be necessary to get there. Strategic thinking focuses on behavior and timing. We expect that people who think about performance strategically will become more efficient and productive.

3. Goals require effort. Hard goals elicit higher levels of effort and performance than easy goals. Thus, if a goal is set high and accepted, it will lead to high levels of effort over an extended period of time.

4. Goals require employee participation and involvement. Research shows that employees who are actively involved in performance planning tend to try harder and perform at higher levels than those who are not.[21]

Taken together, reward theory and goal setting theory provide a useful model for structuring compensation practices. Reward (or reinforcement) models tell us that making pay contingent on performance will enhance motivation. Goal setting models show that an effective way to join the interests of the organization and the individual is to tie monetary outcomes to performance objectives and involve employees in the goal setting process.

An Integrative Model of Individual Decisions Influenced by Compensation Practices

Our review of motivation theory suggests that a compensation system must affect three factors in order to have an impact on employees: (1) equity or fairness, (2) beliefs about the system, and (3) rewards or outcomes under the system. The model in Exhibit 4.4 summarizes research and theory in the field of organizational behavior that addresses the above three questions.[22] We have adapted it here to the question of behavior in response to rewards.

The first thing to know about the model in Exhibit 4.4 is that it attempts to explain a variety of decisions people make about employers: (1) the decision to enter an occupation, (2) the decision to accept a job offer, (3) the decision to leave or stay once one has been employed by a company, and (4) the level of performance one tries to achieve.

The model specifies, further, that each of these decisions is *motivated through effort*. The work of theorists March, Cyert, and Simon, especially, suggests that effort in the direction of a decision is not spontaneous but, rather, motivated by a process that begins with *search* and *choice*.[23] According to our model, several mental activities occur during search and choice:

1. Alternative actions are considered and evaluated in terms of the likelihood that each will result in desired outcomes.

2. Outcomes are evaluated in terms of *reward value.*

3. Equity, as defined earlier, is an important component in assessing the reward value of an outcome.

4. The most effort will be expended toward a choice (decision) that maximizes the person's *anticipated satisfaction with rewards.*

Finally, the model in Exhibit 4.4 proposes that the search and choice behavior preceding a person's decision is influenced both by organizational

Exhibit 4.4 Integrative Model of Individual Equity

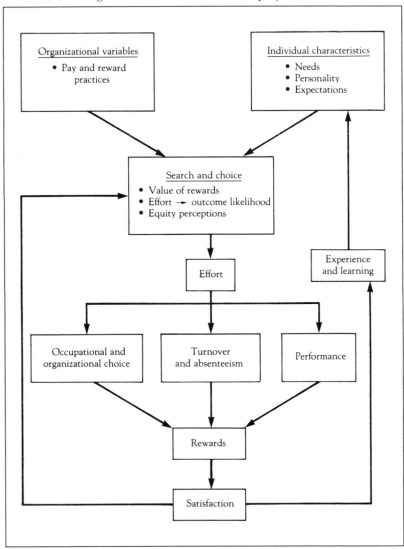

Source: Andrew D. Szilagyi, Jr., and Marc J. Wallace, Jr., *Organizational Behavior and Performance*, 4th ed. (Glenview, Ill.: Scott, Foresman & Company, 1987). Used by permission.

variables, including specific pay and reward practices, and by individual characteristics, including experience, needs related to pay, personality, and expectations about the employers that have been influenced by previous experience and learning.

What are some of the major implications of the model in Exhibit 4.4 about rewarding people? First, the model specifies that employee behavior and choices regarding the employer — for example, the choice of a job, the decision to remain, the decision to perform — are motivated in part by some anticipated satisfaction with rewards. In other words, people will behave and choose in directions that maximize anticipated satisfaction. Second, the way employers reward or fail to reward specific behavior will have a direct influence on actual satisfaction. Third, experienced levels of satisfaction or dissatisfaction will add to an individual's experience and learning. If dissatisfaction with rewards becomes sufficiently intense, we can expect that search and choice behavior will be motivated, and behavior will change.

We should note that satisfaction with compensation plays two extremely important roles in employee behavior. First, anticipated satisfaction with compensation plays an important role in directing a person's current behavior. The actual satisfaction with compensation achieved affects subsequent decisions and adjustments in behavior. Finally, the model predicts that individuals quickly learn the intentional or unintentional reward contingencies that an employer's reward policies imply and behave accordingly. Thus, for example, an employer might not want employees to be sloppy in their work, but may have a piece rate incentive system that rewards only quantity, not quality and cleanliness. As indicated by the model in Exhibit 4.4, it should be no surprise that employees will generally maximize quantity at the expense of quality and cleanliness.

The integrative model in Exhibit 4.4 is general: it addresses all of the possible employee decisions that are influenced by compensation practices. We will see in the next section that such decisions are quite different from each other and should be analyzed separately by compensation practitioners.

Decisions Influenced by Compensation

Compensation theorist Thomas Mahoney has distinguished five decisions that are influenced by compensation policies.[24] He speculates, further, that they occur in the sequence outlined in Exhibit 4.5: (1) the decision to enter the labor force and seek work, (2) the decision to seek work in a given

Exhibit 4.5   The Sequence of Pay-Related Behaviors

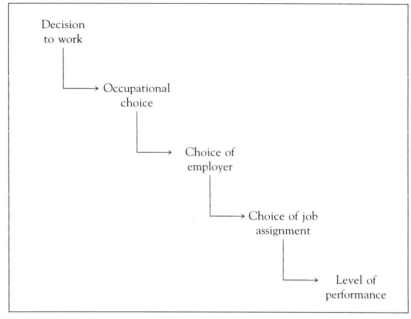

Source: Thomas A. Mahoney, *Compensation and Reward Perspectives* (Homewood, Ill.: Richard D. Irwin, 1979), p. 368. Used by permission.

occupation (that is, vocational choice), (3) the choice of an employer, (4) the choice of a job assignment, and (5) the choice regarding level of performance. Mahoney notes that although some of the decisions in this sequence may be contingent on others (for example, the choice of an occupation might be influenced by employment opportunities already offered in the occupation by specific employers), it is convenient to consider each individually in a sequence that goes from very general (the decision to work) to very specific (the decision to perform at a given level).[25] We will examine here three of the decisions influenced by compensation policy: (1) the decision to accept a job offer, or, from the other side of the coin, (2) the decision to leave or to remain with the employer, and (3) the decision to perform. Decisions (1) and (2) are both aspects of the decision that Mahoney placed third in his sequence. Decision (3), of course, is Mahoney's fifth and most specific, the decision on level of performance.

The Decision to Accept a Job Offer

The decision to accept a job offer is a fairly infrequent one according to Mahoney.[26] Employers compete by offering job opportunities to an external market consisting of applicants for such opportunities. Economists differ in their opinion of how important wage competition is in bringing together job offers with those seeking work. Classical economic theorists would suggest that within broad limits wage competition does take place among employers when bidding for employees, and that the management of a wage offer would directly influence an employer's success in attracting qualified job applicants.[27] Economist Lester Thurow disagrees with this logic, however.[28] He believes that wages are set by social forces rather than by competition among employers. As noted in Chapter 2 on p. 43, Thurow proposes that employers will come to the market with a variety of job opportunities that can be ranked in terms of attractiveness. People in the labor force will compete for these opportunities, forming a queue or line of applicants, and employers will order the members of the queue in terms of their qualifications in a way that will minimize anticipated training and orientation costs. They will offer the opportunity to the most qualified person in the queue.

The model in Exhibit 4.4 suggests that an individual in the labor force will accept the job offer that maximizes anticipated satisfaction with rewards.[29] The rewards will include the wage rate being offered, but may also include the kind of work, working conditions, opportunities for career advancement, and other elements of importance to the job seeker.

The Decision to Remain with or to Leave an Employer

Mahoney makes a significant distinction between an outsider's decision to accept or reject a job offer and an insider's decision to stay with or leave an employer.[30] This distinction parallels that between the external and internal labor market. Mahoney points out that "individuals attracted to join a specific organization are removed from competition in the broader, external marketplace, and subsequent decisions and behavior are more a function of influences within the organization than of competing influences in the external market."[31]

Several implications for compensation managers arise from Mahoney's ideas. First, job competition, or wage competition, in the external market does not have a direct and constant effect on people once they are employed and out of the external market. Information about external job opportunities and competing wage rates takes time and resources to obtain, and these are not expended spontaneously. Indeed, our model in Exhibit 4.4 suggests that the effort involved in considering the decision to leave an employer will be expended only if the employee experiences sufficient levels of dissatisfaction with current employment, not the attraction of alternative employment. What this means as a practical matter for managers is that most employees who leave are rarely attracted away by better job offers but, rather, are driven away by sufficient levels of dissatisfaction with their current employment. Compensation planners should routinely audit all aspects of the compensation package and the way it is administered to determine if any practices provide sufficient grounds for dissatisfaction to encourage a substantial number of valued employees to seek job opportunities in external markets.

It is significant that both the decision to accept a job offer and the decision to seek employment elsewhere are very infrequent. Mahoney, for example, points out that it is unrealistic to believe that typical employees constantly consider whether or not they should seek outside employment opportunities. He notes that mobility within the organization is far greater than mobility between organizations for most employees. The decision to leave an employer is likely to be motivated only when dissatisfaction with current rewards becomes great enough to energize a search for alternative employment in the external labor market. March and Simon, in their analysis of the decision to leave, believe that the likelihood of a person's leaving is a function of not only perceived dissatisfaction with current employment but also the number of perceived job opportunities outside the current employer. General economic conditions, including unemployment rates in the person's occupation and area, influence such perceptions. [32]

The Decision to Perform

Decisions regarding performance levels, in contrast to the two other decisions we have discussed, are far more frequent, and are most likely to be made on a continuous basis as people perform their jobs. Here, we will now use our reward model to analyze the decision to perform.

Mahoney has pointed out that the structure of wage rates, that is, differences in individual pay, influences the equity perceived by a group of employees. An equitable distribution, may well influence pay satisfaction and the desire to stay, but it does not guarantee that employees will perform at high levels: "The provision of an equitable compensation structure is a necessary but not sufficient condition for the motivation of task performance."[33] Theoretically, the connection between compensation and performance should be as simple (see Exhibit 4.4) as the connection with the decision to join and the decision to leave. In practice, however, performance is far more complex and difficult to predict than decisions to join or to leave.

The model in Exhibit 4.4 predicts that an employee's maximum effort is directed at the level of performance that maximizes anticipated satisfaction with rewards. It would appear from this analysis that an employer could maximize performance through the use of wage incentives. If a person's pay could be tied directly to performance level, then we would expect the highest level of effort to be directed toward maximizing performance. Several facts of life in the real world of organizations, however, make this logic difficult to apply in compensation practices:

1. Simply creating equity in a wage distribution does not guarantee high levels of performance. Specific incentives have to be tied to specific levels of performance in order to influence performance.

2. Frequently, rewards, in addition to straight earnings, are important to employees (for example, the opportunity to pursue valued friendships with coworkers). High earnings may conflict with other valued outcomes and prevent an employee from responding to a wage incentive with maximum performance.

3. Work groups have been found to develop informal norms about the "proper" work pace, and to take very painful sanctions against members who are rate busters, that is, people who respond to wage incentives and violate group norms.

4. Although many firms believe that they have tied wages or earnings to performance, they have failed, in fact, to make the connection in their practices.

5. Performance outcomes must be under the direct and individual control of employees if wage incentives can be expected to have an effect. If an employee has to depend on another employee to complete a task, or if events beyond the control of the employee also influence results, a pay system's effect as an incentive toward a high performance is bound to fail.

Each of these factors leads to the conclusion that four conditions must be met in a compensation system if it can be hoped to have any incentive effect on performance:[34]

1. Employees must strongly believe that high performance will lead to high levels of reward.

2. The perceived negative consequences of performing at high levels (for example, fatigue, being labeled a rate buster) must be minimized in the anticipations of the employee.

3. Positively valued outcomes other than money (including praise, promotions, recognition) must also be tied directly to high levels of individual performance.

4. Employees must perceive a direct and independent connection between their efforts and the rewards for their efforts.

When these conditions are met simultaneously, compensation can have an impressive effect on the incentive toward performance. Edward Lawler has summarized the most common forms of compensation in terms of their effect on performance.[35] Exhibit 4.6 contains a classification of major pay plans, including payment by straight salary and bonus. Within each of these types, payment on an individual, group, and organization-wide basis is considered. Each type of plan is examined with respect to (1) the performance measure employed, (2) the type of reward employed, (3) the quality of perceived pay–performance linkage, (4) the quality of minimizing negative side-effects, and (5) the quality of the perceived relationship between other rewards and performance.

Exhibit 4.6 should impress managers with the fact that not all forms of compensation are equally effective in creating incentives for maximizing performance, and most salary systems, the most common form of compensation, are at best fair in tying pay to performance.

Finally, much has been made of the problem of pay secrecy in setting up monetary incentives for performance. Theoretically, pay secrecy would make it impossible for a pay system to act as an incentive, because employees would have no way to evaluate the size of a wage rate relative to individual performance or merit. In addition, research suggests that under conditions of secrecy employees tend to misperceive fellow employees' actual pay rates. One study, for example, found that managers tend to overestimate the salaries of other managers in the organization.[36] Such misperception can lead to intense dissatisfaction with pay and negate the positive influence of any incentive system, no matter how well designed. Pay secrecy, however, is not bad in all cases. We are quick to caution a practicing manager against reading this passage and making public what has been a secret pay structure without auditing that structure for external and internal equity. Secrecy may be the best policy for a structure that grossly deviates from external and internal equity criteria, especially where the problem involves the compression of wages being paid to newly hired people and long-term employees.

The Importance of Pay Satisfaction

Our integrative model of rewards and performance in Exhibit 4.4 points to the great role pay satisfaction or dissatisfaction plays in motivation. Satisfaction is an evaluative reaction, an attitude, that determines the degree of like or dislike for an employer's compensation policies and practices. The research we have reviewed in this chapter suggests that pay satisfaction operates in two major ways. First, motivational theory and research suggest that actual rewards influence satisfaction and thereby provide feedback that inclines employees to adjust their behavior. Thus, we can expect reward practices to influence changes in behavior in performance. Second, the anticipation of reward satisfaction will act as an incentive influencing a number of employment decisions, including decisions to accept a job offer, to remain employed, and to improve performance.

What is pay or reward satisfaction? Research on its content is not very well developed. It is safe to conclude at this point, however, that pay satisfaction has many dimensions. The fact that an organization offers many rewards implies that there are just as many possibilities for satisfaction or dissatisfaction. Thus, for example, an employee may be very happy with his hourly pay rate, but very dissatisfied with his benefit package. Although pay satisfaction is many-faceted, most research shows that equity is one of its more important determinants.

Edward Lawler has recently proposed a model explaining the causes of pay satisfaction or dissatisfaction.[37] His schema is displayed in Exhibit 4.7. According to Lawler's thinking, the immediate cause of satisfaction or dissatisfaction with pay is the distinction between the amount employees think they should receive and the amount they think they are actually receiving relative to others. An equality between these two amounts creates an equitable situation and leads to satisfaction with pay. His model relies on an equity theory framework (see pp. 74–78) to explain why employees think they should receive a certain amount and how they perceive what they actually do earn.

Exhibit 4.6 Classification and Ratings of Various Pay Plans

Type of Pay Plan	Performance Measure	Type of Rewards		Perceived Pay-Performance Linkage	Minimization of Negative Consequences	Perceived Relationship Between Other Rewards and Performance
		Salary Increase	Cash Bonus			
Salary						
For Individuals	Productivity	—	—	—	—	—
	Cost effectiveness	—	—	—	—	—
	Superior's rating	Merit rating	—	Fair	Neutral	Fair
For Group	Productivity	Productivity	—	Fair	Neutral	Fair
	Cost effectiveness	—	—	—	—	—
	Superior's rating	—	—	—	—	—
For Total Organization	Productivity	Productivity	—	Fair	Neutral	Fair
	Cost effectiveness	Bargaining	—	Fair	Neutral	Fair
	Profits	—	—	—	—	—

Type of Pay Plan	Performance Measure	Type of Rewards		Perceived Pay-Performance Linkage	Minimization of Negative Consequences	Perceived Relationship Between Other Rewards and Performance
		Salary Increase	Cash Bonus			
Bonus						
For Individuals	Productivity	—	Piecerate	Excellent	Poor	Neutral
	Cost effectiveness	—	Sales Commission	Excellent	Poor	Neutral
	Superior's rating	—	Lump-Sum Bonus	Good	Neutral	Neutral
For Group	Productivity	—	Group incentive	Good	Neutral	Fair
	Cost effectiveness	—	Group incentive	Good	Neutral	Fair
	Superior's rating	—		—	—	—
For Total Organization	Productivity	—	Improshare, Gainsharing	Good	Neutral	Fair
	Cost effectiveness	—	Scanlon, Rucker	Good	Neutral	Fair
	Profits	—	Profit sharing	Fair	Neutral	Fair

Source: Adapted from Edward E. Lawler, III, *Pay and Organizational Effectiveness* (New York: McGraw-Hill, 1971), pp. 164–65. © by Edward E. Lawler, III. Used by permission.

Exhibit 4.7 Lawler's Model of Pay Satisfaction

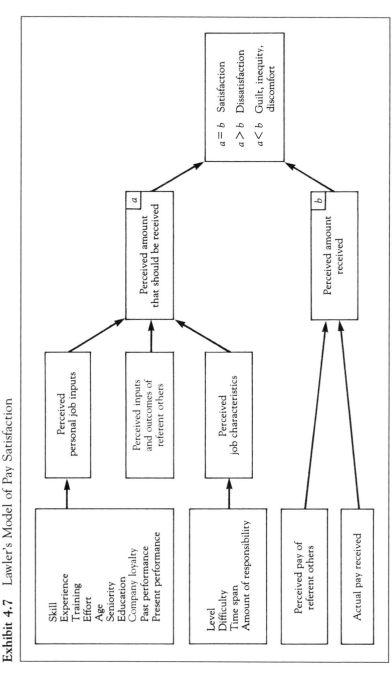

Source: Edward E. Lawler, III, *Pay and Organizational Development,* © 1981, Addison-Wesley Publishing Company, Inc., Reading, Massachusetts. P. 13. Used by permission.

The amount of pay an individual judges that he should be paid depends upon the amount of input he sees himself contributing as compared to the input of another. Perceived inputs include personal characteristics — for example, skills, experience level, age, seniority, and others as shown in Exhibit 4.7 — as well as the demands made by the job: the level of difficulty, the time span of discretion, and the amount of responsibility, for example. Such inputs are not considered alone, according to the model, but in comparison to the inputs being demanded of another person.

The perceived amount of received pay is a relative amount, based on a comparison of the perceived pay of referent others to the actual pay one receives. Actually, Lawler has merely transformed the terms of the ratios in Adams's original formulation, as indicated in Exhibit 4.8. In this case, the ratios defining equity have been transformed into a comparison between an income/outcome ratio (O_p / O_o) and an input/input ratio (I_p / I_o).

Summary

The practicing compensation manager should pay close attention to pay satisfaction in his or her organization, particularly to those dimensions that deal with individual equity. If individual equity is consistently denied, pay dissatisfaction will result, and it will become increasingly difficult for the organization to attract and retain valued employees. In addition, individual equity is a necessary, although not sufficient condition for performance in-

Exhibit 4.8   Adams's Versus Lawler's Conception of Equity

Adams

$$\frac{O_p}{I_p} = \frac{O_o}{I_o}$$

Lawler

$$\frac{O_p}{O_o} = \frac{I_p}{I_o}$$

centives. If individual equity norms are violated, pay incentives cannot have any measurable effects on the decision to perform. Beyond individual equity, however, pay systems actually linking pay to performance and integrating noncompensation rewards must be in place in order for pay to influence performance positively.

Notes

[1]J. Stacy Adams, "Injustice in Social Exchange," in L. Berkowitz (ed.), *Advances in Experimental Social Psychology* (New York: Academic Press, 1965), pp. 267–99; Elliott Jaques, *Equitable Payment* (New York: John Wiley & Sons, 1961); Jaques, "Taking Time Seriously in Evaluating Jobs," *Harvard Business Review* (1979): 124–32.

[2]George C. Homans, *Social Behavior in Its Elementary Forms* (New York: Harcourt, Brace and World, 1961).

[3]Elaine Walster, Ellen Berscheid, and William Walster, "New Directions in Equity Research," *Journal of Personality and Social Psychology* (1973): 151–76.

[4]Robert D. Pritchard, "Equity Theory: A Review and Critique," *Organizational Behavior and Human Performance* (1969): 172–211.

[5]Jaques, *Equitable Payment.*

[6]Roy Richardson, Unpublished Ph.D. dissertation, Industrial Relations Center, University of Minnesota, 1967.

[7]Thomas A. Mahoney, "Towards an Integrated Theory of Compensation," in T. A. Mahoney (ed.), *Compensation and Reward Perspectives* (Homewood, Ill.: Richard D. Irwin, 1979), pp. 367–81.

[8] See, for example, V. Vroom, *Work and Motivation* (New York: John Wiley & Sons, 1964); L. Porter and E. E. Lawler, *Managerial Attitudes and Performance* (Homewood, Ill.: Richard D. Irwin, 1968); T. R. Mitchell, "Expectancy Model of Job Satisfaction, Occupational Preference, and Effort: A Theoretical, Methodological, and Empirical Appraisal," *Psychological Bulletin* (1974): 1053–75; E. E. Lawler, *Pay and Organizational Effectiveness: A Psychological View,* (New York: McGraw-Hill, 1971); and E. E. Lawler, *Pay and Organizational Development* (Reading, Mass.: Addison-Wesley, 1981).

[9]Lawler, 1981, *Pay and Organizational Development.*

[10]Ibid.

[11]B. F. Skinner, *Contingencies of Reinforcement* (New York: Appleton-Century-Crofts, 1969); E. L. Deci, "The Effects of Contingent and Non-Contingent Rewards and Control in Intrinsic Motivation," *Organizational Behavior and Human Performance* (1972): 217–29; W. Clay Hamner, "Reinforcement Theory and Contingency Management in Organizational Settings," in H. L. Tosi and W. C. Hamner (eds.), *Organizational Behavior and Management: A Contingency Approach* (Chicago: St. Clair Press, 1974); and L. Saari and G. Latham, "Employee Reactions to Continuous and Variable Ratio Reinforcement Schedules Involving a Monetary Incentive," *Journal of Applied Psychology* (1982): 506–08.

[12]C. Cofer and M. Appley, *Motivation* (New York: John Wiley & Sons, 1964).

[13]Lawler, *Pay and Organizational Development.*

[14]Craig Pinder, *Motivation in Work Organizations* (Glenview, Ill.: Scott, Foresman, 1984), Chapter 8.

[15]Ibid.

[16]Ibid.; also see, for example, E. Locke, "Towards a Theory of Task Motivation and Incentives," *Organizational Behavior and Human Performance* (1968): 157–89; G. Latham and G. Yukl, "A Review of Research" and "On the Application of Goal Setting in Organizations," *Academy of Management Journal* (1975): 824–45; E. Locke, K. Shaw, L. Saari, and G. Latham, "Goal Setting and Task Performance: 1969–1980," *Psychological Bulletin* (1981): 125–52; G. Latham, T. Mitchell, and L. Dossett, "Importance of Participative Goal Setting and Anticipated Rewards on Goal Difficulty and Job Performance," *Journal of Applied Psychology* (1978): 163–71; M. London and G. Oldham, "Effects of Varying Goal Types and Incentive Systems on Performance and Satisfaction," *Academy of Management Journal* (1976): 537–46; R. Pritchard and D. Curtis, "The Influence of Goal Setting and Financial Incentives on Task Performance," *Organizational Behavior and Human Performance* (1973): 175–83; J. Terborg and H. Miller, "Motivation, Behavior, and Performance: A Closer Examination of Goal Setting and the Monetary Incentives," *Journal of Applied Psychology* (1978): 29–30.

[17]A. J. Szilagyi and M. J. Wallace, Jr., *Organizational Behavior and Performance*, 4th ed. (Glenview, Ill.: Scott, Foresman, 1987).

[18]Ibid.

[19]Ibid.

[20]Pinder, *Motivation*; Locke, et al., "Goal Setting."

[21]Ibid.

[22]Szilagyi and Wallace, *Organizational Behavior and Performance.*

[23]James G. March and Herbert A. Simon, *Organizations* (New York: John Wiley & Sons, 1958); Richard M. Cyert and James G. March, *A Behavioral Theory of the Firm* (Englewood Cliffs, N.J.: Prentice-Hall, 1963); Herbert A. Simon, *Administrative Behavior* (New York: Macmillan, 1957).

[24]Mahoney, "Towards an Integrated Theory."

[25]Ibid.

[26]Ibid.

[27]Alan M. Cartter, *Theory of Wages and Employment* (Homewood, Ill.: Richard D. Irwin, 1959).

[28]Lester Thurow, *Generating Inequality* (New York: Basic Books, 1975).

[29]Donald P. Schwab, "Organizational Recruiting and the Decision to Participate," in K. Rowland and G. Ferris (eds.), *Personnel Management: New Perspectives* (Boston: Allyn and Bacon, 1982); S. L. Rynes, "Recruitment, Organizational Entry, and Early Work Adjustment," in M. D. Dunnette (ed.), *Handbook of Industrial and Organizational Psychology* (Chicago: Rand-McNally, 1987); and D. P. Schwab, S. L. Rynes, and R. J. Aldag, "Theories and Research on Job Search and Choice," in K. Rowland and G. Ferris (eds.), *Research in Personnel and Human Resource Management*, vol. 5 (Greenwich, Ct.: JAI Press, 1987).

[30]Mahoney, "Towards an Integrated Theory."

[31]Ibid., p. 369.

[32]March and Simon, *Organizations.*

[33]Mahoney, "Towards an Integrated Theory."

[34]See, for example, Fred Luthans, Robert Paul, and Douglas Baker, "An Experimental Analysis of the Impact of Contingent Reinforcement on Salesperson's Performance," *Journal of Applied Psychology* (1981):314–23.

[35]Lawler, *Pay and Organizational Effectiveness.*

[36]George T. Milkovich and P. H. Anderson, "Management Compensation and Pay Secrecy Policies," *Personnel Psychology* (1972): 293–302.

[37]Lawler, *Pay and Organizational Development.*

5

Process Equity

After you have studied this chapter, you should be able to address the following key issues and questions:

1. What is process equity?
2. What impact does an organization's culture have on compensation?
3. Why is openness in communication important as a compensation practice?
4. What impact does employee participation have on the effectiveness of compensation programs?
5. What aspects of the compensation program need to be communicated?

Introduction

To this point we have spoken of equity largely in terms of output factors. Thus, an employee may have external equity norms satisfied if the wage received is equivalent to that received for similar jobs in other organizations. Internal equity norm perceptions will depend on the relative pay for different jobs in the same organization, and individual equity norms will be satisfied if salary differentials between individuals holding similar jobs in the same organization mirror performance or other individual contribution differentials. We have noted that organizations utilize market wage surveys to achieve external equity, job evaluation techniques to further internal equity goals, and merit pay systems to achieve individual equity. In all three cases, equity is thought to be achieved if compensation (outcomes) differentials reflect inputs to the job, and if the ratios of inputs and outcomes are equivalent across jobs and across individuals within jobs.

Experience with a wide variety of compensation systems has led us to recognize that this concern for equity of outcomes alone is not sufficient if employees are to perceive the compensation structure to be fair. Perhaps equally important to perceptions of equity is the manner in which those outcomes are reached. Consider two organizations with two different compensation systems.

In organization A, there is a compensation group within the human resource management department. The group evaluates jobs on the basis of job descriptions developed by job analysts in the unit. The basis for internal valuation of jobs is considered proprietary information, and even the factors used (if factors are used) are unknown to employees outside the compensation group. Other information kept secret includes: the salary structure (is there one?); the basis for salary increases; and any information on the compensation program at all, other than that required by law (e.g., ERISA pension reporting requirements). All compensation activities are carried out by the compensation group. Discussion of salary issues is grounds for discipline.

In fact, the compensation group in organization A is an extremely professional group, and the organization's pay policy is extremely competitive. Considerable effort is paid to measurement of performance, and, in most cases, outcome equity norms (whether external, internal, or individual) are maintained or exceeded. At the same time, most employees are not very happy with the compensation system (or most of the organization's other human resource management systems). The company is viewed, at best, as paternalistic and, more seriously, is sometimes thought to have "something to hide."

Organization B, on the other hand, is not very competitive with respect to outcomes, at least for many jobs. Further, its internal job hierarchy is compressed, at best, at least when compared with the hierarchies of similar jobs in other organizations. The opportunity for recognizing merit is highly constrained. Most outside analysts would view organization B as limited in meeting any outcome equity norms.

At the same time, many of its employees view organization B's compensation system as relatively equitable. The basis for determining salary levels for jobs is well known, and many employees participate in the determination process. The actual salary structure is publicized, and the place in that structure of every job in the organization is likewise common knowledge. Committees made up of compensation group members and other employees study various problems thought to exist in the system. Finally, employees who disagree with specific decisions made by administrators may try to get the decisions changed through a formal appeals process. The organization is seen by most of its members as constrained with respect to compensation levels, but relatively equitable in sharing the lack of resources.

Organization B can be readily identified as the federal government. Unfortunately, a large number of corporations fit most of the description characterizing organization A. But if we consider only outcome equity, then organization A would appear to have a much more equitable compensation program than organization B. Many employees in both organizations would disagree over which one has the better compensation system.

In looking at the factors that differentiate organizations A and B, there seem to be five major characteristics that account for most of the differences between them:

1. *Organizational culture.* The compensation system is only one of the human resource management systems in the organization. The total culture of the organization, whether paternalistic, bureaucratic, or democratic, provides the setting for the compensation system.

2. *Openness of the compensation system.* This is a passive characteristic. Those individuals who seek out information about the system can find it.

3. *Communications.* This is an active characteristic. Compensation analysts and other human resource specialists actively seek information from employees and actively communicate aspects of the system to employees.

4. *Participation in compensation system decisions.* This involves a greater role on the part of employees than merely providing information as inputs to the system.

5. *Grievance/appeal systems.* This includes any formal internal process through which an employee who disagrees with any compensation outcome (or part of the process through which the outcome was reached) may seek a reversal of the decision, or adjustment of the outcome.

Clearly, something more than notions of external, internal, and individual equity are at work. In our work with compensation systems in organizations, we have seen again and again how important this "something more" is. Because most employees we have talked with speak of compensation system administration in terms of equity, we describe this setting for achieving outcome equity in terms of *process equity*. Some psychologists doing research in the field refer to *procedural justice* rather than process equity, and much of our initial discussion of the notion of process equity rests on their work.[1]

Studies in Process Equity

A number of early studies on compensation equity took into account the effect of process on perceptions of equity,[2] but these studies were limited with respect to understanding process equity for two reasons. First, because they were not cross-organizational, the studies could only measure the effect of different treatment of employees within organizations by administrators of one compensation system. Second, consideration of process equity was limited to two factors: whether there was a discrepancy between what the system promised ("We have a merit system") and what it delivered ("Everyone got a 6-percent merit increase this year"), and whether there were inconsistencies in administration of the system ("The policy is to give a 10-percent raise with promotions; I didn't get any increase at all even though I was promoted").

More recent work has dealt with the first limitation entirely and with the second to some degree. In one laboratory study, for instance, subject "workers" were told they would share their pay fifty/fifty with an administrator. After two pay periods, the workers discovered the administrator was actually getting two-thirds of the total earned rather than half. The experimenter met with each of the workers to "make sure" the workers understood their job. Half of the workers were allowed to ask questions, and were told the administrator would be reminded of the initial pay split agreement. The one-third/two-thirds split continued for eight more pay periods for both sets of workers. At the end of the experiment, workers were asked to rate outcome equity. Those workers who were allowed to give their opinion (experimenters described this as having a "voice" in the process) saw the outcome as being more equitable than did the workers with no voice, even though the outcomes were equally inequitable in both cases.[3]

A number of other studies, both in the laboratory and in the field, indicate that there is a greater degree of acceptance of outcomes as being equitable when the process associated with the distribution of those outcomes is perceived as being equitable. Procedures seen as giving people process control in the form of voice affect the degree to which the reward allocation process is seen as equitable.[4] Other work suggests that the institutional context, or culture, of the reward system is likely to affect perceptions of process equity; what might be acceptable in the culture of one organization would be seen as less equitable in another.[5]

E. E. Lawler has proposed[6] a new set of assumptions about how compensation systems should be constructed. Included in these assumptions are that people should be "allowed to make up their own pay package, they should have a significant say in how their pay system is designed, and finally they should have open communication with respect to the pay system." While not all compensation experts are ready to accept this approach, portions of it have been tried in a number of situations. In the discussion that follows, we will look at what theory and practice suggest with respect to organizational culture and compensation system congruence, openness of the compensation system, proactive communication between compensation administrators and employees, participation by employees in the design and administration of the compensation system, and the existence of a formal appeals or grievance system for employees.

Organizational Culture and Compensation System Congruence

Organizational culture is a "pattern of basic assumptions — invented, discovered, or developed by a given group as it learns to cope with its problems of external adaptation and internal integration — that has worked well enough to be considered valid and, therefore, to be taught to new members as the correct way to perceive, think, and feel in relation to those problems."[7] There is no one particular culture that is the "correct" one for any organization, but it is important that there be a match between cultural assumptions and environmental realities.[8] Likewise, it is important that there be a match between the culture and the various systems that operate within it.[9] Culture is important because it helps the organization survive in and adapt to its external environment and also helps it to structure its internal processes to help ensure continued survival and adaptability.[10]

A schematic showing the relationship between the organizational culture and the organizational reward systems is shown in Exhibit 5.1. Reward systems, as defined here, include not only the compensation system, but also

Exhibit 5.1   Culture–Reward System Relationship

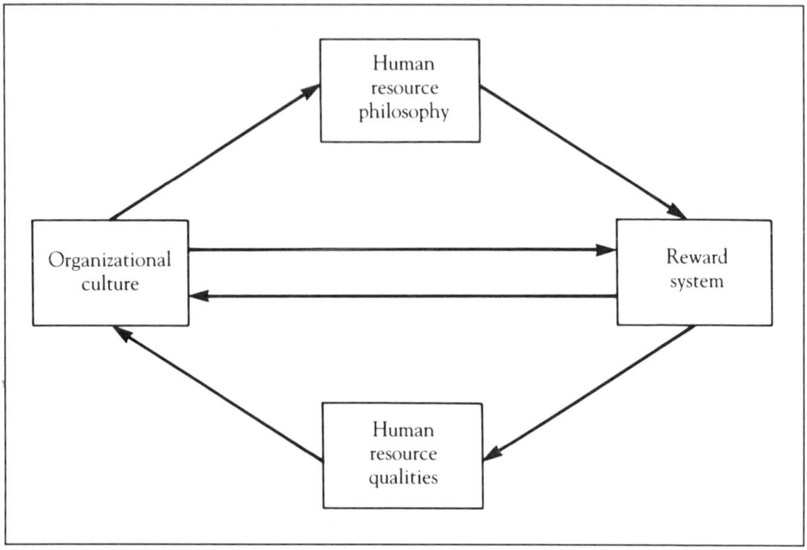

Source: N. K. Sethia and M. A. Von Glinow, "Arriving at Four Cultures by Managing the Reward System," in Ralph Kilmann, Mary Faxton and Roy Serpa (eds.),*Gaining Control of the Corporate Culture* (San Francisco: Jossey-Bass, 1985), p. 405.

job content (challenge, responsibility), career (job security, promotion opportunities), and status (special privileges, titles) systems.[11] The relationship is an interactive one in that the reward system both affects and is affected by the organizational culture. Two other factors also play a role. First, the organizational culture influences the general human resource philosophy, which in turn affects the reward system. Likewise, the reward system, because it attracts and retains employees in accord with its unique characteristics, affects the kinds of employees who are attracted to, and will stay with, the organization. These human resource qualities over time affect the organizational culture.

Four generic types of organizational cultures as they relate to human resources are shown in Exhibit 5.2.[12] The basis for differentiation is the degree to which each culture shows a concern for people and for performance. If the culture of the organization stresses low concern for people and for performance, the human resource culture is said to be *apathetic*. A high concern

Exhibit 5.2 A Framework of Human Resource Cultures

Concern for Performance

	Low	High
High	Caring	Integrative
Low	Apathetic	Exacting

Concern for People

Source: N. K. Sethia and M. A. Von Glinow, "Arriving at Four Cultures by Managing the Reward System," in Ralph Kilman, Mary Faxton, and Roy Serpa (eds.), *Gaining Control of the Corporate Culture* (San Francisco: Jossey-Bass, 1985), p. 409.

for people coupled with a low emphasis on performance results in a *caring* human resource culture, while a reversed emphasis results in what is called an *exacting* human resource culture. When both performance and people are stressed, the human resource culture is said to be *integrative*.

Each different culture calls for different series of reward systems. Exhibit 5.3 shows the characteristics of the reward systems that are thought to be consistent with the four cultures. We shall extend further the framework of the four cultures to process aspects of the reward system after discussing those aspects in more detail.

Openness of the Compensation System

In some organizations, information about its compensation program is readily available. The federal government is an example of such an organization. Most public bodies have open compensation systems, to some degree, because taxpayers are thought to have the right to know how much their public servants are paid. Likewise, in the private sector, government regulation makes it necessary for publicly traded corporations (i.e., those regulated by the SEC) to report top executive salaries. Also, when a union contract is involved, the compensation structure for the bargaining unit is public knowledge.

Just because an organization is not overtly secretive about aspects of compensation, though, it does not mean that it communicates much about

Exhibit 5.3 Reward Systems in Four Cultures

Reward System Dimensions	Human Resource Cultures			
	Apathetic	Caring	Exacting	Integrative
1. Kinds of rewards				
Financial rewards	Poor	Average	Variable	Superior
Job-content rewards	Poor	Average	Good	Superior
Career rewards	Poor	Good	Average	Superior
Status differentiation	High	High	Moderate	Low
2. Criteria for rewards (examples)				
Performance results	Individual success	(Reasonable effort)	Individual success	Group/company success
	Illusory	Day-to-day	Short-term	Long-term
Performance actions and	Manipulation	Compliance	Efficiency	Innovation
behaviors	Politicking	Cooperation	Competition	Independence
Nonperformance	Contract	Membership	Nature of work	Equity
considerations	Patronage	Position	Replaceability	Potential

Source: N. K. Sethia and M. A. Von Glinow, "Arriving at Four Cultures by Managing the Reward System," in Ralph Kilman, Mary Faxton, and Roy Serga (eds.), *Gaining Control of the Corporate Culture* (San Francisco: Jossey-Bass, 1985), p. 410.

its system to its employees. In one public organization we know of, for example, the pay structure is, by law, open to the public, including organizational employees; there are some costs to getting the information, however. An inquirer must submit a written request to a vice president's office specifying the positions for which salaries are wanted. There is a small copying fee. Several days later the information is made available. The atmosphere in the vice president's office is chilly, and one has the feeling that some breach of etiquette has been committed. The president of the organization has been heard to express dismay that anyone would ever get such information. When employees have circulated pay data, mid-level managers have responded with hints of reprisals. It should be noted that this organization generally falls into the apathetic culture category described above, and that the rest of the human resource systems are more successfully secretive. The openness of the pay system is clearly at odds with the rest of this organization's culture.

In fact, most organizations are likely to have more information available about the compensation system than they readily communicate. Organizations vary widely in the amount of information about the compensation system that is available. In addition, the degree to which information is available is likely to differ by hierarchical level of the employee. Such differentiation is likely to be greatest in the apathetic organization; it will probably be least apparent in organizations with an integrative culture.

Communications and the Compensation System

Communications about an organization's compensation program can be either from organization to employee or from employee to organization. Most organizations do seek some information relevant to the compensation program from at least some of their employees, and most organizations do actively communicate some information about their programs to their employees on a voluntary basis. Communications in either case can vary from nearly no information exchange to total information exchange. But, as noted before, just giving employees a voice in the system increases the perceived equity of the system, even if no action is taken because of the input.

Employee Information Input   It is possible for an organization to build a complete compensation system virtually without seeking any information from employees. Consider the following broad categories of information required to construct a typical compensation system:

job information

labor market information

performance information

organizational economic capabilities

legal requirements.

An organization could get all of this information without any input from employees. Job information could come from professional job analysts and from management. Labor market information would be available from external sources. Performance information could come from supervisors, or from some accounting system. And organizational economic capabilities and legal requirements would not be likely to come from employees in any organization. The organization could set up a compensation program without any further considerations, and many have. But an organization may also choose to get much of the information that goes into building the compensation system from employees themselves. The organization may also wish to consider:

compensation expectations of employees

benefits preferences of employees

administrative preferences of employees

employee equity perceptions.

Many organizations get most job information directly from job incumbents. This is sometimes in the form of standardized job descriptions. Some organizations have employees answer questionnaires that cover a variety of compensable factors; the information is then fed directly into the job evaluation or market pricing process. But whether the information is sought in the form of job descriptions or direct input, accuracy is an issue. The information is usually subject to review, either by the incumbents' supervisors or by the compensation analyst. Some organizations use job-evaluation or market-pricing software that employs sophisticated statistical techniques to flag jobs that have unusual compensable factor profiles.

Labor market information can also be collected from current employees. New employees can provide market wage data, and employees who leave sometimes provide information in the exit interview. Employee information can also help define appropriate labor markets (i.e., which organizations, or types of organizations, or geographic areas really constitute competition for labor in selected jobs).

Performance information is the area in which an organization is most likely to seek input from employees. The literature of performance management documents this use, and suggests that employee information input is necessary if the performance appraisal and management systems are to be accurate and effective.[13]

If the organization wishes to ensure that the compensation system attracts, retains, and motivates employees, it will want to collect information from employees that compensation analysts can use in the design of the system to make sure that the system satisfies employee needs. It will also wish to collect information indicating the degree to which employees understand the system and organizational policies with respect to compensation.

The organization may wish to know, for example, what the compensation expectations of different employees are. Such expectations might include employee expectations of the relative roles of seniority and performance in the determination of merit increases. Other expectations of interest include competitive policy with respect to pay levels, organizational commitment to "keep people whole," or the relationship between promotions and raises. It is important that employee expectations be realistic, and that important characteristics of the system and policies relating to compensation are understood. Some studies have shown, for example, that even when compensation system information is available to employees, they may misinterpret it.[14]

Benefits preferences and preferences for salary/benefit splits can help analysts develop programs that will meet employee requirements. Likewise, information on perceptions of the compensation administration process may allow administrators to create systems that do not have unintended side effects.

An example of such a side effect occurs when compensation structures that have been differentiated because of legal requirements or administrative ease become symbols of status differentials. Many organizations (in response to the requirements of the Fair Labor Standards Act to keep records on "time worked" and "overtime payments due nonexempt workers") have set up separate compensation administration systems for exempt and nonexempt workers. Then, to more evenly distribute the workload for payroll, separate paydays for the two systems have been introduced. To ease record-keeping activities, time clocks have been introduced for nonexempts. In a short period of time, elaborate status differentials have been attached to the two systems, and nonexempts clearly have become second-class citizens. If such status differentials are desired by management, then the system is supportive, but it works against an integrative culture, if that is what is desired. If compensation analysts do not seek information on perceptions of the quality of administration of the compensation system, they are unlikely to recognize the source of its dysfunctional side effects.

Communicating the Program to Employees   Organizations have a wide range of options in choosing what to communicate to employees about the compensation program. At the very least, federal law requires that employees receive a W-2 form, which provides information on total taxable salary earned during the year and the amount withheld for FICA (Social Security contributions) and for federal income tax. State and local laws generally require similar disclosure of withholding for state and local taxes. If there is a qualified pension plan, ERISA regulations require that the employee be notified annually of his or her standing with the plan.

At the opposite end of the spectrum, organizations may actively communicate with employees about most aspects of the compensation system. The report of the American Compensation Association/American Society for Personnel Administration Joint Task Force on Compensation has suggested six subjects to include in any well-communicated program dealing with pay: (1) the methods used in job analysis and job evaluation; (2) the organizational policy with respect to matching the market on pay levels; (3) the role of performance and performance appraisal in determining individual pay; (4) the pay increase policy and administration; (5) the effect of governmental and economic constraints on the amount of money available for compensation purposes; and (6) the pay policies and procedures used in compensation administration on a day-to-day basis.[15]

Among the pay policies the task force has suggested be communicated to all employees are:

general pay policy

pay system objectives

pay structure

job descriptions

nondiscrimination in pay

budgeting and control

job evaluation

salary changes — pay for performance

positions within ranges

performance appraisal

system maintenance and audit[16]

These policy statements explain to an employee an organization's basic philosophy in each of these areas. While these policies may be somewhat general, they do communicate to employees where the organization stands with respect to various aspects of the pay program. The sample pay structure policy, for example, provides a foundation for employee understanding of the basis for pay level:

> It is our policy that salaries for individuals be competitive with the external labor market, be internally equitable, and reflect:
>
> > a level of responsibility (grade)
> > a range of value around that grade
> > the length of experience at that level of responsibility
> > individual performance based on objective performance criteria.[17]

The task force recommends actively communicating to employees the methods an organization follows with respect to:

job analysis

job descriptions

market analysis

job content evaluation

changing grades and ranges

adding/changing positions

salary changes

> performance increase
>
> initial increase
>
> promotional increase
>
> geographic transfer
>
> economic and other special adjustments
>
> pay freezes or decreases
>
> approval of salary changes
>
> communication of salary changes

performance appraisal

initial review

periodic review

communications

system maintenance and update

system audit[18]

It also recommends communication of pay system policies and procedures through multiple means:

written policy statements

presentations to employee groups

direct communications between supervisors and employees

written procedure manuals prescribing how the system operates

individualized employee statements

ongoing written communications covering current topics, using news-letters, payroll stuffers, etc.[19]

While the ACA/ASPA task force document does not speak to communication of benefits programs directly, most of its suggestions can be applied in that area as well. One form of communication specific to the benefits area is the employee annual benefits report. Because ERISA requires organizations with qualified (i.e., eligible for favorable tax treatment) plans to report to members of the plan their individual standing in the plan on an annual basis, many organizations have turned a requirement into an opportunity to let employees know not only the value (cost to the organization) of accrued pension rights but also the value of the entire benefits package. An example of such a report is shown in Exhibit 5.4.

Among the benefit policies the organization should consider communicating to employees should be the following:

general benefits policy

benefit system objectives

benefits offered

eligibility for benefits

nondiscrimination in benefits

budgeting and control

coinsurance

Exhibit 5.4 Personal Benefits Statement—IBM

Dear IBMer,

This marks the twenty-fifth consecutive year that we have provided personal benefits statements to all employees. Since that first statement, seven new benefit plans have been established and more than ninety improvements have been made. Our objective now, as it was then, is to provide a comprehensive and balanced program that will continue to serve your needs effectively.

I trust you find this statement a convenient source of information showing how the plans apply to you and that it will be useful in your personal planning.

Sincerely,

In 1981 IBM paid

$30.2 million for Survivors

$292.2 million for Medical/Dental

$551.9 million for Retirement

$347.4 million for Social Security

in addition to payments for other plans such as holidays, vacation, sickness and accident and disability

---

Service

As you look over your *Benefits Statement* there's one number to keep in mind. It's your length of service with IBM. As of December 31, 1981, it was

•

This number is important when figuring several of your benefits, for example, Retirement, Life Insurance, and Vacation.

Time Off

To allow you personal time away from work, IBM provides vacations and holidays. There are 11 holidays each year. In 1982 your vacation will be

•

And if you've deferred any vacation from previous years, those days are additional.

Exhibit 5.4   (continued)

Your Protection Today

Survivors Benefits
(As of 12/31/81)
To help protect your survivors,
the IBM benefit program provides
several coverages.

Group Life Insurance
The beneficiary you named will
receive

●

Periodically review your beneficiary
designation to be sure it is current.

Survivors Income
Your spouse, eligible children or
dependent parents can receive
monthly payments up to a total of

●

This is in addition to your Group
Life Insurance Coverage.

Travel Accident Insurance
If you die accidentally while travel-
ing on company business, the beneficiary you have named will receive

●

This is in addition to your Group
Life Insurance and Survivors
Income Coverage.

**Medical and Disability Income
Benefits** (As of 12/31/81)
When a serious illness or injury
occurs, the combination of medical
expenses and regular living costs
can put a strain on your budget.
The IBM benefit program provides
substantial assistance to help meet
both needs.

Sickness and Accident Income
If you're unable to work due to
sickness or accident, you'll still
continue to receive your regular
salary for up to 52 weeks in a
period of 24 consecutive months.

Exhibit 5.4   (continued)

Your Protection Today

**Total and Permanent
Disability Income**
Once you've been with IBM for five years, if you become totally and permanently disabled, you'll receive monthly, for 18 months, following Sickness and Accident payments.

•

After that, you will receive payments as long as your disability lasts, up to age 65, in the monthly amount of

•

At age 65 you would receive an income from the IBM Retirement Plan. You may also qualify for Social Security Disability Benefits during your disability.

If you have less than 5 years service, you will receive benefits for up to 18 months based on your length of service.

Payments in 1981
During 1981, benefit payments were made on your behalf as indicated:

Sickness and Accident Income Plan

•

Dental Plan

•

Hospitalization Plan

•

Major Medical Plan

•

Surgical Plan

•

Exhibit 5.4   (continued)

Your Retirement Security

The IBM Retirement Plan provides an income, with various options, to help you provide for your financial security.

Your Retirement
If you retire at age
your estimated annual lifetime income will be

•

(assuming your benefits are paid as a single life annuity without adjustment for a Pre-Retirement Spouse Option)

That means payments would begin on

•

Your estimated annual income (on the same basis) at selected earlier retirement ages would be

This amount	Starting At Age
•	

Joint & Survivor Income
At retirement you can choose a joint & survivor income, which means your designated survivor will receive a lifetime income after your death.

If you're married, your retirement payment automatically will be in a 50% joint & survivor form unless you choose otherwise. Here are some estimated amounts at the 50% rate (assuming you and your survivor are the same age and there has been no adjustment for a Pre-Retirement Spouse Option).

If You Retire At This Age	You'd Get This Annual Income	At Your Death, Your Survivor Would Receive
•		

Pre-Retirement Spouse Option (PRSO)
Unless declined, this coverage is automatic at the 50% level with a reduction in your retirement income, if you're married and eligible to retire but remain an active IBM employee. The coverage provides a lifetime income for your surviving spouse if you die before you actually retire.

•

Exhibit 5.4   (continued)

Your Retirement Security

**Group Life Insurance
at Retirement**
If you retire before age 65, you'll
have 50% of your Group Life Insurance coverage until you're 65.
Group Life Insurance for retired employees 65 and over will be $5,000.

Vested Rights
If you leave IBM before retirement
with at least 10 years of service,
you have vested rights to a
retirement income. As of

•

Your estimated annual vested
rights income, payable at age 65
on a single life basis, is

•

If you have 15 years of service,
reduced benefits are available as
early as age 55. With 10-14 years
of service reduced benefits are
available at age 62.

Social Security
Social Security can pay benefits
during retirement, if you're disabled, or at your death. For every
dollar you pay to Social Security,
IBM contributes an equal amount.

Let's consider one of the benefits.
Your estimated annual Social
Security retirement benefit (based
on your 1981 compensation and
current Social Security benefit
computations) will be.

This Amount   Starting At Age

•

IBM ®

Source: Courtesy IBM

copayments

system maintenance and audit

The procedures to be communicated might include:

benefit enrollment

benefit vendor selection

basis for employee status change

system maintenance and update

system audit

Not too long ago the sharing of such communication with employees might have been thought radical. When the structure of organizations was strictly hierarchical, a layered sharing of information about compensation made sense; as Lawler has noted, "it is a matter of picking a position on the continuum from open to secret that is supportive of the overall climate and types of behavior that are needed for organizational effectiveness."[20] But many organizations now are moving toward an increased sharing of information with employees as they become less hierarchical in nature. Even greater and more broad-ranging sharing of information has been proposed as one means of creating a more "productive and engaged work force"; information sharing now is seen as a management technique to "turn around our poor productivity level."[21]

Employee Participation and the Compensation System

Asking employees for information relevant to the compensation system and communicating information about the system to employees can be considered one form of participation. But while communication is certainly a prerequisite to employee participation, it does not mean that employees really have much control over how the system is designed or how it operates.

Participation of employees in various aspects of organizational processes is a subject that can be approached from various starting points. The field of organizational development (OD) has based much of its argument for participation on *moral* imperatives. The Labor movement has generally based its claims for power sharing on *ideological* grounds. A more recent point of view, considered more acceptable to management, is based on *organizational effectiveness,* which is somewhat broadly defined in terms of all the "stakeholders" in the organization, including management, employees, shareholders, and society.[22] The *human resources* of an organization are defined as its "social capital," and related policies must be judged in the light of the effect they have on the commitment and competence of that social capital, as well as the degree to which the policies are cost-effective and promote congruence between the interests of the various stakeholders.[23]

Approached from these points of view, participation is seen as a "checks and balances" system that management "creates over its own decisions in the conviction that checks and balances are needed over their [the organization's] natural tendency to take primarily the shareholder perspective or to emphasize business outcomes at the expense of human outcomes."[24] In Exhibit 5.5, a variety of mechanisms are listed that can be used as checks

Exhibit 5.5   Mechanisms for Employee Voice

1. "Speak up" or feedback programs. Employees may telephone a special number to raise questions or voice concerns, or may write letters to a designated company representative.

2. Special councils where management and/or employees regularly get together to talk about problems. Agendas are submitted by employees and management.

3. "Sensing groups" in which managers meet periodically with small random samples of employees to hear their concerns or suggestions and to communicate company policy and goals.

4. Open-door policy and other formal grievance systems in which employees may complain to a manager who is not their immediate supervisor. Typically, a formal and preplanned process for review of the complaint is part of such a policy.

5. Task forces of employee groups (women or minority caucuses, for example). They can be commissioned to review corporate personnel policies including pay, affirmative action, promotion policies, and the like.

6. Employee relations personnel and ombudsmen located throughout the organization, accessible to employees to deal with grievance or concerns and to expedite their solutions.

7. Attitude surveys conducted by questionnaire or by an employee task force to diagnose problems and make suggestions to management. Management commits to respond publicly.

Source: Michael Beer, Bert Spector, Paul R. Lawrence, D. Quinn Mills, and Richard E. Walton, *Managing Human Assets* (New York: The Free Press, 1984), p. 55.

and balances; some of these are primarily communications programs while others involve employee participation to a greater degree.

Before looking at specific employee participation programs, we should state that the empirical evidence supporting every beneficial aspect of participation is not very strong. Locke and Latham note that, although "organizational theorists have argued that employee participation in decision making is the primary means of increasing employee commitment to productivity and lowering employee resistance to change,"[25] a summary of all available experiments on the effects of motivational techniques on performance indicates relatively low impact on participation. Exhibit 5.6 shows the results of all of the methods compared.[26] Some caution, though, should be used in interpreting these findings: not many studies have been conducted in organizations on the effects of participating in the construction of compensation systems or in their administration.[27] More importantly, even if performance is not greatly increased by participation, there are other outcomes, such as pay satisfaction, that may be. (See below for a discussion of pay satisfaction.)

Participation in the Design of Compensation Systems   There are two ways in which employees can participate in decisions relevant to the compensation program. The first is participation in the design of the program; the second is participation in decisions made within the framework of the system.[28]

Participation in the design of the compensation system can take many forms. At the extreme, the organization can have employees determine the goals of the compensation system itself and the major policies and procedures connected with reaching those goals. On a more limited basis, employees can be asked for input into each policy area.

Exhibit 5.6   Effects of Motivation Techniques on Performance

Motivation Technique	Median Improvement in Performance
Money, individual incentives	30%
Money, group incentives	20
Goal setting	16
Job enrichment	9
Participation	0.5

Source: E. A. Locke and G. P. Latham, *Goal Setting: A Motivational Technique That Works!* (Englewood Cliffs, N.J.: Prentice-Hall, 1984), p. 117. Used by permission.

An example of the development of a compensation system based largely on employee inputs is a salary program developed by the Dade County School System for its administrators. A large task force (over 30 administrators) representing the entire administrative staff defined the goals of the system. Subunits of the task force developed the set of compensable factors that were to be used in evaluating jobs. The task force agreed on which school districts to use as comparisons for market pricing purposes and also suggested other types of organizations for market comparisons. The manner in which performance differences were to determine salary differentials was also discussed by the task force. Finally, the task force selected an outside consultant to handle the actual details of developing the system and to describe the options available at various stages of system development. The consultant also served as a neutral who could make unbiased recommendations.

As the system was developed, reports were made to the entire task force by the consultant. Task force members reported back to other administrators in their units and took their reactions back to task force meetings. When the task force reached consensus on the salary structure, a recommendation was made to the superintendent of the district and to the school board, both of which adopted the new system without change. The fact that this was a public organization and that the system was created only for administrators made participation much more acceptable than it might have been in a traditional corporate structure or if the employees had covered the entire range of the hierarchy. However, reports of other participative projects do exist.

In another study, Lawler and Hackman reported on an incentive plan to reward good attendance on the job.[29] Work groups that participated in the development of the plan had a significant increase in attendance after the plan went into effect. In a follow-up study of the same work groups one year later, attendance was still higher for the one group that had participated in plan development and for which the incentive plan was still in effect. The plan had been discontinued for two groups involved in plan development and their attendance had dropped after plan discontinuance. Attendance in the groups that were still under the plan but that had no part in its development had risen, but it was still lower than in the participative group still in the plan.[30]

In yet another case, Jenkins and Lawler described a participative pay plan development project in a small manufacturing plant.[31] A pay plan developed by a committee was put to a vote of a group of employees, who rejected it. The group itself then developed the outline of a new plan, and the committee developed specific policies and procedures to enact it. This program was approved by the group and set in place. The plan is interesting because it reflected the group's wishes that pay be based on the job holder and not the job. Wages of a worker were set by a committee of two co-workers and a supervisor. Measures of job satisfaction, pay satisfaction, understanding of the pay plan, and trust in management all increased after the plan was established. Payroll, however, increased by about 5 percent, and the average worker's wage increased by nearly 13 percent (the range of increases was from 0 to 26.5 percent); it is difficult to say conclusively whether the increases in satisfaction, understanding, and trust were due to participation in the plan, increases in wages, or some combination of the two.

Still other researchers have recorded their observations: Carey describes a participative job evaluation program used with a number of his clients;[32] French and Hollmann propose a participative approach toward MBO that would remove some of that process's dysfunctional effects when used as a basis for individual or group merit increases.[33] Studies by Bullock[34] and Gabris, Mitchell, and McLemore[35] document the development of merit pay programs through participatory means. *Gainsharing*, described in Chapter 12, is thought by many of its advocates to be inherently participatory in nature.[36] And a more general study of productivity sharing plans conducted by the U.S. General Accounting Office found that half of the firms interviewed had employees vote on productivity plans before the plans were adopted.[37] Indeed, many of the newer forms of performance reward are linked strongly with participatory development procedures.

Participation in Decisions Made Within the Framework of an Existing System   Once the compensation system has been put in place, some organizations allow additional employee participation in operating the system. The decisions in which employees most often are allowed to participate are in the area of benefits. Many organizations have developed "cafeteria," or flexible benefit programs. (A full discussion of flexible benefits programs is beyond the scope of this book; a good source of information is R. M. McCaffery's *Managing the Employee Benefits Program* [Kent, 1987].) Briefly, in a flexible benefits program the employee has some degree of freedom to select some subset of benefits from a larger set made available by the employer. A core set (insurance, etc.) is usually required, but considerable choice is available.

Participation with respect to salary administration is less usual. Generally, this form of participation takes place in the area of individual merit payments.

Lawler, for example, notes that in many plants with skill-based pay, coworkers or team members decide whether a team member has mastered a new skill sufficiently to merit an increase.[38] He also notes that work teams and top-level managers in some companies discuss and make decisions about peers' pay.[39] At Romac Corporation, all workers have their pay openly posted on a plant bulletin board, along with each worker's picture and date of hire. Workers who want a raise post a two-line advertisement explaining why they feel the raise is justified. Five days later, a majority vote on a secret ballot determines whether the raise is granted. About 90 percent of the raises are granted, although some take two or three tries.[40]

It is unlikely that many organizations go to the extreme form of participation that was espoused by the Friedman-Jacobs Co., an appliance retailer. In that organization, an employee (there were fifteen) told the bookkeeper what his or her rate of pay should be. In addition, most workers had access to the cash box, and could take what they wanted if they left a voucher.[41] Ten years after Friedman's practices were published, he was contacted again to see if his compensation practices had paid off. Although the appliance store had been sold, Friedman now owned six microwave oven stores and had ninety franchises. Operating procedures were just the same, including the open cash box; even new employees set their own salaries. He regrets only that he did not try his system sooner.[42]

Grievance/Appeal Systems and the Compensation System

A specific process sometimes lumped together with other participation processes is an employee's ability to appeal or grieve decisions. Yet, even organizations that have little other form of employee participation may have extended formal grievance systems. The most obvious example is the system set up pursuant to the administration of a union contract. However, many organizations whose workers are not unionized have set up grievance systems for their workers, too. In addition, many companies that are unionized have developed grievance systems for their nonunion employees. In one survey of both unionized and nonunionized organizations, for example, it was found that more than three-quarters of the respondents encouraged managers of nonunion employees to "develop and sustain" formal complaint or grievance systems.[43]

At IBM, employees can appeal directly to the president of the corporation if they feel they have been unfairly treated or evaluated.[44] Employees from a different work site investigate the complaint; IBM tracks those who file complaints to make sure their progress in the organization is similar to that of an equivalent group of noncomplainants. The Nucor Corporation, too, has built an "avenue of appeal" into all aspects of the compensation program for those employees who feel they are being treated unfairly.[45] If organizations wish to give employees voice, some form of appeals, complaint, or grievance system is a necessary part of the process.

Culture and Process Equity

Rosabeth Moss Kanter has recently noted that one of the principal dilemmas facing organizations that have developed new workplace practices (employee involvement programs such as quality circles; matrix organization structures; downsizing, particularly by reducing layers of hierarchy; programs to stimulate innovation and entrepreneurship; and flextime, part-time work, and job sharing) is the "impact of greater employee participation on the legitimacy of pay systems."[46] Many of the new programs undertaken by business organizations in this country appear to have a concomitant requirement for greater involvement of employees in the formulation and implementation of compensation programs. Process equity concerns of employees may be one outcome of organizational innovation.

At the same time we cannot recommend that all organizations involve their employees in the design and administration of their pay programs. As noted at the beginning of this chapter, the overall organizational culture provides the setting for employee involvement; process equity programs and organizational cultures should be congruent.[47]

The four generic types of cultures provide a starting point for determining how deeply an organization should concern itself with process equity approaches. Exhibit 5.7 shows which process equity approaches appear consistent with each of the four cultures. (It should be noted that this configuration is not based on research findings, but on a logic of congruency of other cultural characteristics and aspects of the compensation system.)

In the apathetic culture, concern for process equity issues would be low in all areas. This would fit in with the lack of concern for either people or performance in other human resource areas. In the caring organization, there could be a good deal of openness about compensation, but much of it might be illusory because communications concerning compensation might be expected to be medium. Employees of the caring organization would participate in designing the compensation system, but would be unlikely to participate

Exhibit 5.7   Process Equity Concerns in Four Cultures

Process Equity Concern	Type of Culture			
	Apathetic	Caring	Exacting	Integrative
Openness	Low	High#	Medium	High
Communications	Low	Medium	High*	High
Participation in Design	Low	Medium#	High*	High
Participation in Administration	Low	Low	Low	High
Grievance Appeal Procedures	Low	High	Medium	High

#Illusory
*Selected Areas Only

much in its administration; however, a formal grievance/appeals system would fit in well with the rest of the caring organization's culture.

The exacting organization would be likely to place a medium-to-high emphasis on openness, communications, and participation in design aspects of process equity in selected areas. One would expect high emphasis on these factors in so far as they relate to organizational performance expectations, performance–rewards linkages, and development of incentive plans. External equity processes might also be developed with concern paid to process equity issues. A relatively low emphasis on participation in administration of the program would be expected, since the performance culture would utilize "objective" administrative techniques that would reduce the need for administrative judgment. There could be some emphasis on appeal/grievance systems, less because of expected need, though, than because audit processes are expected in performance-oriented cultures.

In the integrative culture, all aspects of process equity should be of concern. Those organizations responding to the demands of the new workplace may find that attention to management practices promoting process equity becomes as important in reaching the goals of attracting, retaining, and motivating the new workforce as does attention to practices promoting external, internal, and individual equity.

Summary

In this chapter, we have shown that fairness or equity in the administration of compensation (process equity) is just as important as the design issues of external, internal, and individual equity. Process equity, then, also has a bearing on the success of a compensation program. We have examined five process issues managers need to consider as part of the ongoing administration of a compensation system. The first of the five issues is organizational culture, which refers to the pattern of values and basic assumptions that pervade an organization. It is critical for a reward system to match up correctly with the culture of an organization. Second, the elements of the compensation system must be open to employees — and they must be readily shared by management. Third, communication of the reward system is crucial. All elements of the system — including ability to pay, merit rules, policies regarding external, internal, and individual equity, job evaluation procedures, and benefits — must be clearly communicated in order to be understood. Fourth, employee participation is a powerful tool for encouraging acceptance and credibility for the compensation program. Finally, the widespread use of appeals procedures in both unionized and nonunionized organizations provides an important opportunity for employees to appeal complaints they may have about compensation decisions. Such systems provide an important avenue for assuring process equity.

Notes

[1]R. L. Cohen, "Procedural Justice and Participation," *Human Relations* 38(7) (1985): 643–63; R. Folger and J. Greenberg, "Procedural Justice: An Interpretive Analysis of Personnel Systems," *Research in Personnel and Human Resources Management* 3 (1985): 141–83.

[2]P. S. Goodman, "An Examination of the Referents Used in the Evaluation of Pay," *Organizational Behavior and Human Performance* 12 (1974): 170–95; M. R. Carrell, "A Longitudinal Field Assessment of Employee Perceptions of Equitable Treatment," *Organizational Behavior and Human Performance* 21 (1978): 108–18.

[3]R. Folger. "Distributive and Procedural Justice: Combined Impact of 'Voice' and Improvement on Experienced Inequity," *Journal of Personality and Social Psychology* 35 (1977): 108–19.

[4]Folger and Greenberg, "Procedural Justices," p. 156.

[5]Cohen, "Procedural Justice and Participation."

[6]E. E. Lawler, III, "Pay and the Quality of Work Life," *ACA 1982 Conference Proceedings* (Scottsdale, Ariz.: American Compensation Association, 1982), p. 6.

[7]E. H. Schein, *Organizational Culture and Leadership* (San Francisco: Jossey-Bass, 1985), p. 9.

[8]Ibid., p. 315.

[9]L. L. Cummings, "Compensation, Culture, and Motivation: A Systems Perspective," *Organizational Dynamics* (Winter 1984): 33–44.

[10] Schein, *Organization Culture*, p. 50.

[11]N. K. Sethia and M. A. Von Glinow, "Arriving at Four Cultures by Managing the Reward System," in R. Kilmann, M. Faxton, and R. Serga, *Gaining Control of the Corporate Culture* (San Francisco: Jossey-Bass, 1985), p. 404.

[12]Ibid., pp. 408–14.

[13]See, for example, H. J. Bernardin and R. W. Beatty, *Performance Appraisal: Assessing Human Behavior at Work* (Boston: Kent, 1984), or S. J. Carroll and C. E. Schneier, *Performance Appraisal and Review Systems* (Glenview, Ill.: Scott, Foresman, 1982), for discussions of this area.

[14]T. A. Mahoney and W. Weitzel, "Secrecy and Managerial Compensation," *Industrial Relations* 17(2) (1978): 245–51.

[15]*Elements of Sound Base Pay Administration* (Scottsdale, Ariz.: American Compensation Association/American Society for Personnel Administration, 1981), p. 18.

[16]Ibid., p. 30.

[17]Ibid.

[18]Ibid., p. 30–31.

[19]Ibid., p. 18.

[20]E. E. Lawler, III, "The Strategic Design of Reward Systems," in C. J. Fombrun, N. M. Tichy, and M. A. Devanna, *Strategic Human Resource Management* (New York: John Wiley & Sons, 1984), p. 143.

[21]*Reward Systems and Productivity: A Final Report for the White House Conference on Productivity* (Houston: American Productivity Center, 1983), p. 4.

[22]Michael Beer, Bert Spector, Paul R. Lawrence, D. Quinn Mills, and Richard E. Walton, *Managing Human Assets* (New York: The Free Press, 1984), p. 11.

[23]Ibid., p. 19.

[24]Ibid., p. 54.

[25]E. A. Locke and G. P. Latham, *Goal Setting: A Motivational Technique That Works!* (Englewood Cliffs, N.J.: Prentice-Hall, 1984), p. 46.

[26]Ibid., p. 116–17.

[27]R. J. Bullock, "Participation and Pay," *Group and Organization Studies* 8(1) (1983): 127–83.

[28]Lawler, "The Strategic Design of Reward Systems," p. 143.

[29]E. E. Lawler, III, and J. R. Hackman, "Impact of Employee Participation in the Development of Pay Incentive Plans: A Field Experiment," *Journal of Applied Psychology* 53(6) (1969): 467–71.

[30]K. C. Scheflen, E. E. Lawler, III, and J. R. Hackman, "Long-Term Impact of Employee Participation in the Development of Pay Incentive Plans: A Field Experiment Revisited," *Journal of Applied Psychology* 55(3) (1971): 182–86.

[31]G. D. Jenkins, Jr. and E. E. Lawler, III, "Impact of Employee Participation in Pay Plan Development," *Organizational Behavior and Human Performance* 28 (1981): 111–28.

[32]J. F. Carey, "Participative Job Evaluation," *Compensation Review* Fourth Quarter (1977): 29–38.

[33]W. L. French and R. W. Hollmann, "Management by Objectives: The Team Approach," *California Management Review* XVII(3) (1975): 13–22.

[34]Bullock, "Participation and Pay."

[35]G. T. Gabris, K. Mitchell, and R. McLemore, "Rewarding Individual and Team Productivity: The Biloxi Merit Bonus Plan," *Public Personnel Management* 14(3) (1985): 231–44.

[36]B. L. Metzger, *Participative Gainsharing* (Evanston, Ill.: Profit Sharing Research Foundation, 1984).

[37]*Productivity Sharing Programs: Can They Contribute to Productivity Improvement?* (Washington, D.C.: U.S. General Accounting Office, 1981), p. 22.

[38]E. E. Lawler, III, *High Involvement Management* (San Francisco: Jossey-Bass, 1986), p. 175.

[39]Ibid., p. 204.

[40]D. O. Stuhaug, "Want a Raise? At Romac You Do a Little Politicking with Your Peers," *Daily Journal of Commerce and Northwest Construction Record,* Seattle, Wash., February 5, 1979, p. 1.

[41]M. Koughan, "Arthur Friedman's Outrage: Employees Decide Their Pay," *The Washington Post,* February 23, 1975, reprinted in F. J. Landy, *Readings in Industrial and Organizational Psychology* (Chicago: The Dorsey Press, 1986), pp. 309–11.

[42]F. J. Landy, "Arthur Friedman: A Decade Later," in his *Readings in Industrial and Organizational Psychology,* p. 312.

[43]A. Freedman, *The New Look in Wage Policy and Employee Relations,* Report No. 865 (New York: The Conference Board, 1985), p. 20.

[44]M. A. Devanna, "The Executive Appraisal," in Fombrun, Tichy, and Devanna, *Strategic Human Resource Management,* p. 107.

[45]A. Freedman, *The New Look,* p. 21.

[46]R. M. Kanter, "The New Workforce Meets the Changing Workplace: Strains, Dilemmas, and Contradictions in Attempts to Implement Participative and Entrepreneurial Management," *Human Resource Management* 25(4) (1986): 515–37.

[47]Schein, *Organizational Culture and Leadership;* Cummings, "Compensation, Culture, and Motivation."

II

Compensation Practice

6

Constraints on Compensation Practice

Key Issues and Questions for This Chapter

After you have studied this chapter, you should be able to address the following key issues and questions:

1. What are the major constraints on compensation practice?
2. What are the major laws and regulations that bear on compensation practice?
3. How do laws and regulations influence compensation practice?
4. What impact do unions and labor contracts have on compensation practice?

Introduction

Although the major determinants of compensation and benefit levels are economic (for example, market forces, value added through job performance,

131

and the organization's ability to pay) as well as sociopsychological (as with felt fair pay and motivational needs), there are also a number of constraints that prevent the organization from responding to shifts in these factors with like adjustments in the compensation program. These constraints are of three major types. The first and most severe constraints are legal. There are major federal laws restricting amount, type, and administration of both salaries and benefits, and additional state laws constrain the compensation administrator.

The second major constraint is found in the various tax laws of the federal and state governments. Though akin to legal constraints, they neither require nor forbid any particular administration, amount, or type of salary or benefit but, rather, make it costly to both employer and employee to follow what might otherwise be a preferred course of action.

The final major constraint (which tends to be more of a short-run problem) arises from the contracts that some employers enter into with unions that represent some or all of their employees. Although contracts can at some point be renegotiated, in the short run, at least, they prevent some kinds of adjustments in the compensation program. And even in the long run, they may provide a barrier to certain changes, desired by the compensation manager.

Compensation Laws

Minimum wage, FICA deductions, comparable worth, garnishment, vesting requirements, overtime, prevailing wage: these are only a few of the words that are part of the compensation analyst's language as a result of the many federal and state laws governing compensation practices. The variety of regulations can be confusing. Many of the major laws deal with several areas of compensation regulation at once; thus, no classification scheme can be entirely satisfactory. In this section, we discuss each of the major laws affecting compensation. We consider only those sections of each law that relate directly to compensation issues. We then conclude with a summary of the different aspects of compensation systems and of which law or laws affect each aspect.

The Fair Labor Standards Act — 1938

The Fair Labor Standards Act (FLSA) contains five major provisions: minimum wage, overtime pay, equal pay (the Equal Pay Act of 1963 is an amendment to FLSA), record-keeping requirements, and child labor laws. All of these except the child labor laws have a major effect on compensation programs.

Minimum Wage   Minimum-wage provisions set a floor on the amount of base pay an employer can offer an employee. The minimum wage was raised to $3.35 per hour starting January 1, 1981; currently (1988), there is no legislation mandating increases in the minimum-wage level.

Almost all employers are covered by minimum-wage requirements. FLSA was made possible by the authority of Congress under the Constitution to regulate interstate commerce; thus, it regulates all employers engaged in interstate commerce, producing goods for interstate commerce, or having employees who handle, sell, or otherwise work on goods or materials produced for or moved in interstate commerce. This has been interpreted to include organizations involved in construction; hospitals or other resident health care institutions; educational institutions, including preschools, elementary and high schools, institutions of higher education, and schools for the mentally or physically handicapped; laundries and cleaners; retail or service establishments with an annual gross (as of January 1, 1982) of $362,500; the federal government; state and local governments (although coverage is not in fact extended to all workers); and employers of domestic workers who receive at least $100 per calendar year from the employer.

However, not all workers are covered by minimum-wage provisions. Some employees are exempt, and the distinction made by personnel managers between exempt and nonexempt employees is based on this fact. Exempt employees include executives, administrative and professional employees (for example, teachers), outside salespersons, fishermen, seasonal employees of amusement or recreational organizations, some farm workers, and casual babysitters and companions.[1] Given permission of the Wage and Hour Division of the Department of Labor, which is responsible for enforcement of FLSA, employers need not pay the minimum wage to apprentices, handicapped workers, or full-time students working in certain retail or service establishments, in agricultural enterprises, or in institutions of higher education. Under some circumstances the value of room, board, or other facilities may be considered part of wages when calculating wages paid for minimum-wage purposes. If employees receive tips in excess of thirty dollars per month, employers may include those tips when calculating the wages paid for minimum wage purposes. However, the amount used in calculations cannot exceed 40 percent of the minimum wage for the period.

Overtime   FLSA overtime provisions do two things: (1) specify a normal workweek and (2) mandate a pay rate of 150 percent of regular pay for all hours worked in excess of the norm. The workweek is defined as a period of 168 hours during seven consecutive 24-hour periods. An employer may arbitrarily decide the day and hour that the workweek begins. An employee may be expected to work 40 hours during the workweek at a regular rate of pay. For every hour in excess of 40 worked the employee must be paid 150 percent of his or her regular wage. Hours cannot be shifted from one week to another by the employer. An exception to this rule is the hospital; hospitals may set up 14-day periods and must pay employees 150 percent of regular wages for all hours worked in excess of 80 in the work period.

Calculating overtime pay is not as easy in all cases as it would seem. For hourly workers the calculations are straightforward. If an employee is ordinarily paid $8.00 per hour and works 48 hours in one workweek, then the pay earned is 40 hours at $8.00 per hour (or $320) plus 8 hours at $12.00 per hour (base rate of $8.00 per hour and overtime of $4.00 per hour, or $96) for a total of $416 for the week.

Things become more complicated, however, when the worker is paid on a piecework basis. In this case, there is no hourly rate. There are two methods of calculating overtime for piecework employees. One is to increase the rate for parts completed during overtime. Thus, if a worker receives $2.00 per piece for parts completed during the regular workweek, he receives $3.00 for any part completed during overtime. A second method of calculating overtime due the piecework employee is to convert the piecerate earned to hourly earnings and base overtime on that. If, for example, an employee works 48 hours in a week and produces enough pieces to earn $400, then her average hourly earnings would be $8.33. Her total pay would then be $400 plus one-half of the hourly rate times the overtime hours worked ($\frac{1}{2} \times 8.33 \times 8 = 33.32$), or $433.32.

Salaried nonexempt employees present similar problems. To calculate overtime for these employees it is necessary to convert monthly salary to weekly salary. This is done by multiplying the monthly rate by 12 to get an annual rate and then dividing by 52 to get a weekly rate. This conversion takes care of differences in length of month. The appropriate overtime rate can then be calculated.

As with the minimum-wage provisions, the overtime provisions of FLSA do not apply to all workers. All employees exempt under minimum-wage coverage are also exempt under overtime provisions. Employers may, if they wish, pay overtime to these exempt employees, but are not required to do so by the FLSA. Additional employees exempt under overtime provisions include farm workers, motion picture theater employees, some employees of some nonmetropolitan broadcasting stations, sales employees paid on a commission basis, employees of railroads and air carriers, domestic workers residing in the house of their employer, taxi drivers, and seamen on American vessels.

Equal Pay   The Equal Pay Act of 1963 was passed as an amendment to FLSA. Basically, the Equal Pay Act prohibits wage differentials based on sex between men and women employed in the same establishment when they have jobs that require equal skill, effort, and responsibility, and that are performed under similar working conditions. It is under the Equal Pay Act that some of the comparable worth lawsuits have been pursued; these suits have not generally been successful. The most successful case for advocates of the notion of comparable worth, *AFSCME v. State of Washington*, was brought under Title VII of the Civil Rights Act discussed in Chapter 1 and later in this chapter.

There are several reasons why the Equal Pay Act is not conducive to comparable worth ideas. The requirement of equal skill, effort, and responsibility means that all three factors must be equal. Equal skill refers to the experience, training, ability, and education required to perform a job. Equal effort does not occur if the more highly paid job has tasks requiring greater effort or if the more highly paid job requires a greater amount of time for such tasks. Equal effort is not the sole criterion of job value, however. If tasks of similar effort result in significantly different economic values to the employer (for example, making computer components versus making nails), the employer may be justified in paying different rates. Minor differences in responsibility do not generally justify pay differentials. Likewise, working conditions must differ significantly if pay differentials are to be justified.

Some conditions that may lead to lower pay for women than for men are specifically approved under the Equal Pay Act. Wage differentials resulting from legitimate seniority systems, merit systems, or any system that ties earnings directly to quantity or quality of production (for example, commission sales, or piecework) are permissible. Part-time workers need not be paid as much as full-time workers. Even differentials paid to heads of families are permitted, as long as female heads of families are paid the differential as well as males.

Employers who are in violation of the Equal Pay Act's prohibition on sex-related pay differentials may not lower pay to correct the violation. Instead, the pay of the affected group must be raised to meet that of the favored group. There are no exempt employees under the Equal Pay Act. Nearly all employers and labor unions negotiating for employees are subject to the provisions of the Equal Pay Act.

Record-Keeping Requirements   Under the FLSA, employers must collect, store, and report great quantities of information about their compensation system and wage and hour data on nonexempt employees to the Wage and Hour Division of the Department of Labor. The information for nonexempt employees includes:

1. Employee name, address, occupation, and sex
2. Hour and day that workweek begins
3. Total hours worked each workday and workweek
4. Total basic pay on daily or weekly basis
5. Regular hourly pay rate for any week that the employee works overtime
6. Total overtime pay for the workweek
7. Deductions from or additions to wages
8. Total wages paid during the pay period
9. Date of payment and pay period covered
10. Special information when uncommon pay arrangements exist (for example, estimated tips) or when board, lodging, or other facilities are counted as part of pay.

Acts Concerning the Prevailing Wage

There are three acts, the Davis-Bacon Act of 1931, the Walsh-Healy Public Contracts Act of 1936, and the McNamara-O'Hara Service Contract Act of 1965, that, though passed at separate times, all have one goal in common: when organizations do work for the United States government they must pay the "prevailing" wages to their employees. These laws, particularly the Davis-Bacon Act, have been under fire by business organizations in the last several years and have been just as heatedly defended by labor organizations. The primary issue is that of what constitutes a "prevailing" wage. The Department of Labor is authorized to make this decision; its determination has generally been whatever union workers in the area get. (In the case of Walsh-Healy, wages throughout the industry rather than in one area are used.) Because union workers tend to make more than nonunion workers, business managers argue that these laws help to establish unions and force nonunion contractors (1) to pay higher wages than they otherwise would to workers on government jobs (thereby causing internal or individual inequity in the organization), (2) to avoid government contracts, or (3) to pay artificially high wages. Labor leaders argue that repeal of the laws, or changes in the interpretation of prevailing wage, would weaken or destroy unions and union contractors. This issue is likely to remain with compensation administrators for some time.

The Davis-Bacon Act of 1931   Davis-Bacon applies to all contractors holding federal or federally assisted contracts in excess of $2,000 for construction, alteration, repair, painting, or decorating of public buildings or public works. All laborers and mechanics employed under such contracts are covered. The act requires that wage rates and fringe benefits found by the Department of Labor to prevail in the area be paid. In addition, contractors must submit certified payroll records each week to the contracting agency. An associated law, the Copeland Act of 1934, was passed to prevent abuse of Davis-Bacon wage floors. Under the Copeland Act, it is illegal for a Davis-Bacon contractor to demand kickbacks from employees or to make certain prohibited deductions from wages.

The Walsh-Healy Public Contracts Act of 1936   Walsh-Healy is similar to Davis-Bacon, but it applies to employers holding federal contracts in excess of $10,000 for the manufacture or provision of materials, supplies, and equipment. Among other provisions, Walsh-Healy requires covered employers to pay the wage rate that prevails in the industry, as determined by the Department of Labor, and to pay overtime at not less than one and a half times the basic rate for all hours worked in excess of eight in one day or forty in a workweek, whichever results in greater pay.

The McNamara-O'Hara Service Contract Act of 1965   This act extends Davis-Bacon concepts to the services sector of government contracting. For employers holding service contracts or subcontracts of $2,500 or less, service employees must be paid not less than minimum wage. For employers holding service contracts or subcontracts in excess of $2,500, employees must be paid not less than the wage rates and fringe benefits found by the Department of Labor to prevail in the area, or the wage rates and fringe benefits contained in the previous contractor's collective bargaining agreement.

Wage and Price Controls

There have been several attempts to regulate wage increases on the national level in order to control inflation. During World War II, the National War Labor Board was authorized to administer wages and wage changes. During the period of the Korean War, the Wage Stabilization Board performed similar functions. Peacetime controls have been fewer and less effective. Under the Economic Stabilization Act of 1970, President Nixon was authorized to issue orders and regulations thought necessary to stabilize prices, rents, wages, and salaries at levels not less than those prevailing on May 25, 1970. Running through several phases, the Nixon controls were unpopular and largely unworkable. Even less effective at controlling inflation was the program created under the Carter administration. A Council on Wage and Price Stability was formed, but with no real enforcement powers. The program died when President Reagan took office in 1981. Currently there are no wage or price controls in effect, but compensation analysts should be aware that such programs could be legislated in the future. People who feel that government can effectively control wages and prices are likely, under conditions of high inflation, to lobby for such legislation. Even some businessmen, who note that in the past wages always seemed to be more effectively frozen than prices, push for regulation in this area.

The Consumer Credit Protection Act of 1968

Title III of the Consumer Credit Protection Act of 1968 deals with wage *garnishment*. Wage garnishment occurs when a creditor goes to court and gets a garnishment order. The order, which has the force of law, requires the employer of the debtor to deduct some portion of the debtor's pay and to deliver it to the creditor. Prior to passage of the law, some employers simply fired any employees against whom a garnishment order had been obtained.

Under the law, a court cannot order a garnishment on the aggregate disposable earnings of a debtor for any workweek in excess of the lesser of either (1) 25 percent of the debtor's disposable earnings for the workweek, or (2) the amount by which the debtor's disposable earnings for the week exceed thirty times the minimum wage authorized under FLSA. *Disposable earnings* are defined as compensation less legally required withholdings (that is, FICA, income tax, and so on).

Garnishment restrictions do not apply to all debts. Federal and state tax debts, alimony and child support, and orders under Chapter XIII bankruptcy filings are exempt from Title III. The law also allows for the preemption of state law. If state laws allow larger garnishments than the federal law, then federal law preempts state law. But on the other hand, if the state law restricts the court to even smaller garnishments, then it preempts the federal law. The law also forbids employers to fire debtors because of a single garnishment order. If the debtor has a second garnishment order, then the employer is free to fire him.

Old Age, Survivors, Disability, and Health Insurance Program (OASDHI)

The OASDHI is perhaps the most pervasive of all compensation-related legislation in the United States. More than nine out of ten workers are covered by its provisions, which form the base of most benefit programs. The only workers not covered are federal civilian employees covered by other United States retirement systems, employees of state and local governments when those government units have chosen not to participate, some agricultural and domestic workers, and employees of some nonprofit organizations that have chosen not to arrange coverage.

The programs legislated under OASDHI are the base of most benefit packages and form the backbone of the social programs in the United States. Included are retirement, survivors, and disability insurance, known collectively as Social Security; hospital and medical insurance for the aged and disabled, known as Medicare/Medicaid; black lung benefits for coal miners; Supplemental Security Income; unemployment insurance; and public assistance and welfare services, including aid to families with dependent children (AFDC). The principal programs of interest to employers, because they are directly taxed to support them, are Social Security, Medicare/Medicaid, and unemployment insurance.

Social Security, Medicare, and Medicaid   Social Security — retirement, survivors, and disability insurance — and hospital and medical insurance for the aged and disabled are paid for by a tax on employers and employees. These taxes, authorized by the Federal Insurance Contributions Act, constitute the FICA deductions noted on every paycheck. FICA taxes are not levied on total salary: in 1950, for example, the wage limit for deductions was only $3,000. As demands for benefits have risen and as the costs for those benefits have risen on a per unit basis, both the salary subject to FICA tax and the tax rate itself have increased. In 1975, for example, the levy was 4.95 percent for Social Security plus 0.90 percent for Medicare/Medicaid, or a total levy of 5.85 percent. This levy was applied against the first $14,100 earned by the employee. In 1987, the combined FICA levy was 7.15 percent, and it was applied against the first $43,800 earned.

The employee is not the only one who pays FICA taxes, though: the employer pays in an equal amount. Thus, in 1987, the real tax rate for FICA needed to support these programs was 14.30 percent of the first $43,800 earned by each employee or as much as $6,263.40 per employee. The rate and levy base were raised again in 1988 to 7.51 percent on the first $45,000 earned, as benefit costs and the number of individuals qualifying for benefits continue to grow.

OASDHI places other constraints on employers besides direct taxes. Employees who receive tips are required to pay FICA on those tips. Employers are required to collect data on tips and deduct the tax due on those tips from regular wages. Record-keeping requirements also exist. The employer must keep track of, and report, the amounts and dates of wage payments (including tips), the name, address, occupation, and social security number of each employee receiving wages, and employees' periods of employment.

In addition, the employer must provide each employee a W-2 form by January 31 for the previous calendar year. It must show the name, address, and social security identification number of the employer, the name, address, and Social Security number of the employee, the total amount of wages subject to FICA taxes paid to the employee during the year (including tips), and the amount of FICA taxes deducted from wages. If taxes are still owed on tip income, this information must be reported as well.

Unemployment Insurance   The unemployment insurance program is a state-administered program that operates with federal participation under general requirements set out in OASDHI. The function of unemployment insurance is to provide partial income replacement for a limited period when a worker loses his job through no fault of his own.

Funding for unemployment claims comes from a tax levied by states on employing organizations. The amount of tax depends on the benefit levels granted by the state and on the employer's record. That is, the more people who file for and are granted employment benefits after being discharged by an employer, the higher the tax the employer must pay. In a few states, employees must also contribute to unemployment funds.

Federal law requires employers to pay a tax of 6.2 percent on the first $7,000 of each employee's nonexempt annual wages (as of January 1, 1985). Some states have imposed a higher taxable wage base and a higher tax rate; Alaska, for example, (as of 1986) takes up to 6.2 percent of the first $21,600 and Michigan takes up to 10.8 percent of the first $9,500. When the standard rate is charged to the standard base, 5.4 percent goes to the state and .8 percent goes to the federal government. When a higher rate is paid or is charged against a higher base, the excess over .8 percent goes to the state. This tax base does not include mandatory deductions for OASDHI, which are exempt. The standard rate is the rate that would be assigned to an employer just starting business. Generally, after three years, a good rating of the employer's record, or "experience rating," will lower this percentage.

There are several ways for states to determine the experience rating. The most common method, used by over thirty states, is an actuarial method that attempts to ensure enough money in the unemployment fund reserve to cover benefit outflow. This reserve ratio formula is based on the difference between the employer's contribution over a period of time and the total benefits received by former workers of that employer. Tax rates are assigned according to a schedule of rates for specified sets of reserve ratios. The higher the ratio, the lower the rate. The ratio itself is calculated by dividing the reserve attributable to the employer by the employer's current payroll.

A second method used in some states is the benefit ratio formula, under which the ratio used is benefits paid out over the last three years divided by current payroll. Again, a schedule of rates is used to assign tax rates. A third method makes use of a benefit wage ratio. In this system, the number of dismissals per benefit year, weighted by salaries, is divided by total taxable wages. Schedules similar to those used in other plans provide a means of calculating the tax. The simplest method is to calculate the percentage decline in payroll and use a schedule of rates for different percentages of decline.

Regardless of the method by which the tax is computed, it is crucial for compensation analysts to make sure that line managers and other personnel specialists understand how the system works because the greater the number of successful filers, the greater the tax to the organization. A former worker must register at a public employment office and file an unemployment claim. The worker's previous job must be a covered job, and there must be some set amount of earnings or employment in some specified base period, usually one year, prior to filing. The worker may not be sick or disabled, but must be able to work. The worker must be available for work and willing to take a suitable job if one is offered. In addition to being available, workers must actively seek work and must not refuse an offer of suitable work.

Workers covered by unemployment insurance must have lost their jobs through circumstances beyond their control; that is, they cannot have quit, without good cause, or have been discharged for a just cause. In most states, workers may not be unemployed because of a labor dispute in which they are participating. We note here that many workers violate one or more of these conditions for receiving unemployment benefits. Both workers and employers have the right to appeal unemployment insurance benefit eligibility decisions, and it is important for the company to challenge claims when appropriate to prevent tax rate increases. It is also important for employers to discharge only those workers who truly warrant it, and to be able to document the misconduct that resulted in discharge.

Workers' Compensation

Workers' compensation programs are operated by the states, and laws vary from state to state. Because of widely varying costs to employers and benefits to workers there have been, from time to time, national commissions that have suggested mandating standards on the federal level. In 1972, a National Commission on State Workmen's Compensation Laws set forth nineteen recommendations aimed at standardizing state laws and reducing the insurance premiums paid by employers.

The goal of workers' compensation laws is to provide immediate money for medical care and support to workers who are injured on the job, and to provide support to dependents if the worker is killed. Thus, workers' compensation is essentially an insurance program to cover work-related injury and health problems. Some state laws require all employers to pay for such insurance. Other states allow employers to be self-insured. Many states leave workers' compensation coverage to private insurance carriers. In others (Ohio, Nevada, North Dakota, Washington, West Virginia, and Wyoming), the state is the carrier.[2] In some states, employers have a choice between state and private carriers.[3]

Benefit payments are usually based on a worker's wages at the time of the injury and on the number of dependents he or she has. There are maximum and minimum payments for specified injuries and for total claims. Time limits for benefit payments are also common.

Costs to employers are, like any other insurance costs, a function of base rates, influenced by discounts for quantity purchases and the employer's past record. In 1978, average costs to employers noted in one survey ranged from a weekly cost of $0.68 per $100 of payroll in North Carolina to $4.18 per $100 of payroll in the District of Columbia.[4] These costs are likely to have gone up considerably in the last several years.

The Employee Retirement Income Security Act of 1974

The Employee Retirement Income Security Act of 1974 (ERISA) was passed to regulate the pension programs of employers. Although ERISA does not require employers to offer pension programs, it does require employers who do offer pension programs to follow certain rules if they want favorable tax treatment for both their contributions and their employees' deferral of income.

Briefly, ERISA applies to all employees twenty-five years or older who have completed one year or more of service. Some workers can be excluded, primarily those employees under a collective bargaining agreement wherein pension benefits are the subject of negotiation. Tax benefits for pension plans apply only to ERISA-qualified plans; the plans must cover 70 percent of all employees of the organization, or 80 percent of eligible employees where at least 70 percent of all employees are eligible, or some fair share of employees in a plan that does not favor officers, stockholders, or highly compensated employees. Basically, then, ERISA prohibits pension programs set up to benefit management only. A look at the law's provisions would help to explain the range of its application.

Vesting　Under ERISA, an employee gains ownership of accrued pension rights over a period of employment time, even if he or she then leaves the organization. This process is called *vesting*. Vesting requirements under ERISA vary, but basically there are three methods an organization can use. The simplest is the ten-year service rule; an employee is fully vested after ten years of service. A second method is the graded five- to fifteen-year service rule, under which the employee first gains 25-percent vesting in accrued pension rights after five years, then gains 5-percent additional vesting for each year of service for years six through ten, and finally 10-percent additional for each year of service in years eleven through fifteen. The third method, the rule of forty-five, requires 50-percent vesting when the sum of the employee's age and years of service equals forty-five (providing at least five years of service have been completed), then 10-percent vesting for each year of service thereafter. An additional limit on this method is that the employee must be 50-percent vested after ten years of service and 100-percent vested after fifteen years of service.

The Tax Reform Act of 1986 has revised the vesting rules, with the revision to take effect January 1, 1989. At that time, employers who choose the original vesting plan (discussed earlier) will be required to vest employees 100 percent after five years of service. Employers who choose a graded vesting approach will be required to vest employees 20 percent after three years of service and have 100 percent vesting after seven years of service.

Accrual of Benefits   Computation of accrued benefits is subject to three constraints. Under the 3 percent rule, the employee must accrue for each year of service (up to 33⅓ years) at least 3 percent of the benefit payable under the plan if the employee began participation at the earliest age and retired at normal retirement age. Under the 133⅓ percent rule, the annual rate of accrual cannot exceed the accrual rate for a prior year by more than one-third (133⅓ percent of the prior year's rate). This prevents employers from backloading pension benefits. Finally, under the fractional rule, the benefits accrued for any year of service should equal an employee's projected benefit at normal retirement age prorated on the basis of the actual years of participation to normal retirement. Thus, if an employee has participated in a retirement program for twenty-five years, and by normal retirement age is expected to have participated a total of fifty years, then he or she should have 50 percent of expected benefits accrued.

Survivor Benefits   Plans qualifying for ERISA tax treatment must provide an option for employees to receive benefits in the form of a 50-percent joint and survivor annuity. A spouse must give written permission for this option not to be taken.

Funding   ERISA-qualified plans must be funded. That is, employers must actually fund plans, and not simply carry obligations on the books, with a minimum annual contribution equal to a normal cost plus amortization over thirty years of unfunded accrued liabilities for all plan benefits.

Termination Insurance Under ERISA, the Pension Benefit Guarantee Corporation (PBGC) was set up under the direction of the Labor Department. The function of the PBGC is to insure vested benefits in case organizations default on their obligations. As of 1986, a covered employer paid $8.50 per plan participant per year into the PBGC; vested benefits of up to $1,789.77 per month were guaranteed.[5]

Benefit Limitations ERISA restricts the amount of benefits paid to employees. Under a defined benefits plan, benefits may not exceed $90,000 per year or 100 percent of the employee's average compensation for the highest three consecutive earnings years, whichever is lower. Defined contribution plans are limited to contributions equal to 25 percent of compensation or $30,000, whichever is less. Cost-of-living adjustments are allowed.[6]

The Multiemployer Pension Plan Amendments Act (MPPAA) of 1980

The MPPAA amended the portions of ERISA dealing with the obligations of employers who participate in multiemployer pension plans. These plans are largely the result of collective bargaining agreements: employers are required to bargain with a union over pension benefits, and a recent court case, *NLRB v. AMAX Coal Co.*, 101 S. Ct. 2789, June 29, 1981, determined that a union may legally bring pressure on an employer to join a specific multiemployer plan. The MPPAA requires an employer, once in such a plan, to assume the liabilities for the fund, even upon withdrawal. These liabilities may not necessarily be based on rights accrued to the employees of the employer, and they may in fact be completely out of the employer's control.

Equal Employment Opportunity

The equal employment opportunity programs consist of several laws and executive orders. The principal laws are the Civil Rights Act of 1964, Title VII as amended by the Equal Employment Opportunity Act of 1972, the Age Discrimination in Employment Act of 1967 as amended in 1978, the Vocational Rehabilitation Act of 1973, Section 503, the Vietnam Era Veterans Readjustment Assistance Act of 1974, and Executive Orders 11246 of 1965 and 11375 of 1967. While these laws have an effect on all human resource management functions, their major influence to date has been on the selection and placement functions.

Basically, the laws prohibit discrimination based on race, color, sex, religion, age, or national origin in any of the terms, conditions, or privileges of employment by employers, employment agencies, and labor unions. For government contractors, laws and executive orders require that, in addition to the above-protected groups, employers must not discriminate against Vietnam era veterans or the handicapped, and also must take positive steps (or affirmative action) to correct the results of past discrimination. Because compensation decisions are covered by the law, employers must be prepared to justify any differentials between the sexes (the issue of comparable worth), races, or the majority and any protected group, with the same rigor (that is, by means of reliability and validity studies) that would be applied to any other human resource management decisions needing justification.

Summary of Compensation Laws

Although our discussion of legal constraints touched only on the major points of laws, it should be clear that, in some areas, the compensation specialist has little leeway. FLSA, Davis-Bacon, Walsh-Healy, and McNamara-O'Hara all place lower limits on wage structures. In addition, FLSA defines the legitimate wage–effort bargain in terms of time, and specifies extra payment for work performed beyond that time. At various times, wage and price controls have set ceilings on the wage structure and have limited or prevented wage increases.

Benefit packages are constrained in two ways. OASDHI and worker compensation laws specify that certain benefits will be offered and also specify how much the employer must pay to offer them. ERISA places restrictions on how pension programs must be run, gives employees certain rights that they did not previously enjoy, and requires insurance coverage of benefit obligations.

The various equal employment opportunity laws, including the Equal Pay Act of the FLSA, speak to the establishment and administration of pay and benefit systems and set the guidelines for their proper application. Although their effects on pay and benefit systems have so far been limited to comparable worth issues, there is pressure to validate pay systems in the same way human resource management departments have been validating recruiting and selection systems. Legal constraints on employers with respect to wages and benefits are likely to become more complex and more stringent. The compensation analyst should be aided by legal specialists, then, to help ensure the legality of decisions made.

The Internal Revenue Code

The Internal Revenue Code (IRC) affects compensation programs in several ways, some of them fairly obvious. Most people know that the code requires employers to withhold income tax from checks paid to employees, to send that withholding to the IRS, and to report to employees and the IRS the total amounts withheld.

Less familiar are the constraints the Internal Revenue Code places on benefits. Because the compensation package consists of both wages and benefits, and because there is some tradeoff between the two, it might seem reasonable that all benefits be taxed on the same basis as straight salary. In fact, this is not so. First, the IRC does consider some benefits taxable, but not all of them. Second, some benefits providing deferred income are taxed, not when the employer enters into an obligation to provide the benefit, but when the employee actually receives the benefit. This is true of pensions, profit-sharing plans, and ESOPs (Employee Stock Ownership Plans), which are discussed further in Chapter 10. The IRC's third influence on benefits is the treatment of the employer's costs in providing benefits. Thus, for example, under ERISA, a company for tax purposes may deduct pension payments from income only if that money is being invested to fund future pension benefits; current pension benefit payments may not be deducted.

Under the IRC, the Revenue Act of 1978, the Economic Recovery Tax Act of 1981, the Tax Reform Act of 1986, and other tax laws, certain benefits are nontaxable. Health, accident, and disability benefits are nontaxable; so is group term life insurance with a value up to $50,000. Services or perquisites may or may not be taxable. Whether they are taxed appears to depend upon the answers to the following questions that the IRS asks when looking at services and perquisites:

1. Is the expense really an expense of doing business and being reimbursed by the employer rather than an expense being borne by the employee?

2. Are the beneficiaries the obvious ones? A country club membership for the director of public relations makes sense; one for the head of research and development may not. In general, services or perquisites provided only to executives will be considered taxable.

3. What costs are involved? Are they significant in comparison with the recipient's income? What would be the cost of keeping track of these expenses and charging them to the individual recipients?

4. What do other, similarly situated organizations do?[7]

One recent law deserves mentioning here: the Tax Reform Act of 1986. This act involved a substantial and fundamental change in the tax treatment of compensation and benefits. Repeal of capital gains provisions have made many deferred income and investment programs less attractive to highly compensated employees. Lowering of the general tax rate to a maximum marginal rate of 27 percent also decreases the need for deferred income programs. The act sharply limits the amount that can go into tax deferred accounts. Benefits become more likely to be subject to taxation. Discrimination rules (dealing with the proportion of less highly paid employees covered by and utilizing a benefit program if the program is to receive favorable tax treatment) have been greatly tightened.

Although the details of the Tax Reform Act of 1986 are beyond the scope of this book, we hope our brief overview of the subjects touched upon indicate the pervasiveness of IRS constraints on compensation and benefit programs. The important matter for our purposes is to indicate that an understanding of tax laws is crucial to the construction of a comprehensive compensation program. Benefits that do not receive favorable tax treatment may benefit no one. Deferred income programs not meeting IRS requirements may be so reduced in value both to employer and employee that their power to attract, retain, and motivate may be negative.

Labor Unions

Labor unions place constraints on compensation programs in several ways that create a supportive interaction between several federal laws and labor unions. Davis-Bacon and similar laws, for example, require that government contractors pay prevailing wages. The Department of Labor determines what the prevailing wage in an area is; the cases in which this prevailing wage is not the union rate are rare. Thus, unions help determine the wages even for nonunionized employees.

Another constraint placed on compensation managers occurs only when a union is running an organization drive against an employer. The Labor Management Relations Act of 1947, also known as the Taft-Hartley Act, makes it an unfair labor practice to change the wage rates or benefits for employees during the organization drive. Thus, under such circumstances the compensation program of the organization is effectively frozen. A second unfair labor practice prohibited by the Taft-Hartley Act is any refusal to bargain over wages or benefits. It is the outcome of and the necessity for such bargaining that place the greatest constraint on compensation programs. It is not so much the actual settlement figure in a contract that constrains the compensation administrator. The constraint lies in the resulting inability of the compensation administrator to manage the compensation program, to make those changes that he or she believes the employer and the employee need, and to adjust the program to maximize its effectiveness in attracting, retaining, and motivating employees.

A look at the typical provisions in a union contract, abstracted from *Basic Patterns in Union Contracts,*[8] indicates the areas of constraint common in unionized organizations. With respect to wages, aside from the actual wage rate to be paid initially and increases to be made over the life of the agreement, there are frequently clauses for cost-of-living adjustments, and wage-opening provisions allowing for the renegotiation of: (1) wages during the life of the contract; (2) the status of negotiated increases under federal wage controls; (3) shift differentials; (4) reporting pay; (5) callback pay; (6) pay for temporary transfer; (7) hazardous work premiums; (8) travel expenses, work clothes and tools; and (9) nonperformance bonuses. In some cases, there are clauses dictating the form of piecework or incentive rates, time study procedures (determining what a legitimate output for an employee is and thus the base of costing piecerate jobs), job evaluation methods, and job classification procedures. Hiring rates and wage progressions are also frequently specified. Thus, nearly every aspect of the basic wage and wage-setting process is removed from the administrative discretion of the compensation manager.

Employee benefit discretion is equally constrained. Contract clauses frequently specify formulas for determining retirement benefits, with special provisions for disability retirement, early retirement, the financing and funding of pensions, vesting procedures, and the administration and termination of plans. As we noted earlier, under the legal requirements of ERISA, the union may legitimately force bargaining (though it still must negotiate any concessions) concerning which multiemployer pension plan a company will join.

Contracts usually include provisions for life insurance, accidental death or dismemberment coverage, sickness and accident insurance, long-term disability, occupational accident insurance, hospitalization, surgical insurance, doctor's visits and major medical, maternity benefits, dental and optical care, prescription drugs, and the administration of insurance benefits. Severance pay, guarantees of work or pay, supplemental unemployment benefits, and other income-maintenance clauses also exist in many contracts. Various premiums for overtime work and weekend work are covered by many contracts along with provisions for paid lunch, rest, cleanup, and other nonproductive times. Holidays and holiday pay (pay for employees who must work on holidays) are specified, as are vacation entitlements and vacation pay.

In summary, when an organization is unionized, it may expect to deal with union demands on every aspect of the wage and benefit package. Because of this, and especially because unions insist that seniority, rather than performance, should be the deciding factor in many matters such as raises and promotions, compensation practices often do not achieve external, internal, or individual equity.

Summary

We have explored the major groups of factors that cannot be ignored by managers in compensation practice: (1) federal laws and regulations, (2) tax regulations, and (3) unions.

The Fair Labor Standards Act establishes rules for minimum wages and overtime payments among its provisions. The Equal Pay Act of 1963 prohibits wage differences between men and women employed on the same job by the same employer. The Davis-Bacon Act, Walsh-Healy Act, and McNamara-O'Hara Act all require that organizations contracting with the U.S. government pay "prevailing" wages to their employees. At various times, the United States has tried to stem inflation through the imposition of wage and price controls. Old Age, Survivors, Disability, and Health Insurance (OASDHI) is a far-reaching social insurance program funded through contributions by employers and employees. We also examined similar laws providing protection in the event of job loss (unemployment insurance), job-related illness and disability (worker compensation), and pension loss (Employee Retirement Income Security Act). We then examined a series of equal employment opportunity laws (for example, Title VII of the 1964 Civil Rights Act, and the Age Discrimination Act of 1967) that prohibit discrimination against protected groups through pay practices.

Finally, this chapter has explored the impact of tax laws and the influence of labor unions on the practice of compensation.

Notes

[1] Wage and Hour Division, U.S. Department of Labor, *Handy Reference Guide to the Fair Labor Standards Act*, W. H. Publication 1282 (Washington, D.C.: U.S. Government Printing Office, 1978).

[2]*Compensation*, BNA Policy and Practice Series (Washington, D.C.: The Bureau of National Affairs, 1986), p. 365:3.

[3]Ibid., pp. 365:17–365:20.

[4]M. W. Elson and J. F. Burton, Jr., "Workers' Compensation Insurance: Recent Trends in Employee Costs," *Monthly Labor Review* (March 1981), 45–50.

[5]*Compensation*, pp. 343:92–343:94.

[6]Ibid.

[7]D. A. Weeks, *Compensating Employees: Lessons of the 1970s* (New York: Conference Board, 1979), p. 63.

[8]*Collective Bargaining — Negotiations and Contracts*, vol. 2, and *Basic Patterns in Union Contracts* (Washington, D.C.: Bureau of National Affairs, 1979–   ).

7

Job Pricing

After you have studied this chapter, you should be able to address the following key issues and questions:

1. Where does one obtain good information about competitive wages and salaries?

2. Is it better to do one's own wage and salary survey or to use available surveys?

3. What are benchmark jobs and how are they used in compensation practice?

4. How should the labor market for a job be defined?

5. What kind of information should be sought in a wage and salary survey?

6. What is the best method for conducting a wage and salary survey?

Introduction

A major goal of any compensation program is to maintain external equity, that is, to pay employees salaries and benefits equivalent to those paid to similar employees in other organizations. In fact, if there were an ideally efficient labor market, there would be a single wage for any given job, and compensation systems would be based on such rates. The market, however, is not all that efficient, and for any given job we find a wide variety of wage/benefits packages, tempered by geographic, industrial, performance, and seniority differentials. A wage and salary survey, then, is designed to help the compensation analyst make informed decisions about wage rates that will more or less maintain external equity in the compensation system, allowing for labor market imperfections.

Wage and salary surveys can be used as a diagnostic tool, as well. Behaviorally, compensation systems are designed to attract, retain, and motivate employees. High turnover or job offer rejection rates may be due to compensation levels, or to other similar factors. Wage and salary survey data can help the staffing manager judge the role that compensation levels play in staffing problems. Such survey data are also very important to labor relations experts preparing to negotiate a new contract.

Regardless of the uses to which the wage and salary survey data are put, the compensation analyst in need of such data faces a "make-or-buy" decision. An organization can run its own survey (or take part in a joint effort), or it can use data collected by others. The tradeoff is generally between up-to-date comparisons with jobs of interest (running one's own survey) and lower cost data (data collected by others), which are easier to obtain, but may not be directly relevant to the internal job mix. In the following sections, we will look first at the development of a custom survey and then at the use of data collected by others.

Wage and Salary Surveys: The In-House Project

Several standard steps are followed in conducting a wage and salary survey:

1. selecting the jobs to be surveyed
2. defining relevant labor markets
3. selecting the firms to be surveyed

4. determining the information to ask
5. determining the data collection technique
6. administering the survey.

Selecting the Jobs to Be Surveyed

The first step in conducting a wage survey is the selection of *benchmark* jobs. This is the set of jobs the organization will take to the market to price. No wage and salary survey is likely to include data on all jobs in the organization. First of all, many jobs are unique to specific organizations; that is, there is no market. To attempt to get survey information on such jobs would be futile, since no other organization would have equivalent jobs. In addition, if the survey attempts to get information on too many jobs, the time it will take to complete the survey form will become so great that many respondents will refuse to cooperate. Finally, the compensation specialist may not need information on every job: as we shall see in the next chapter, job evaluation processes can make such information unnecessary. (If an organization is adopting a market pricing strategy, the analyst will attempt to get survey data on as many jobs as possible. Even in this case, the analyst is more likely to use multiple survey sources rather than try to collect all needed data from a single survey.)

The jobs that are chosen for the survey are known as benchmark, or *key* jobs. They make up a sample that reflects the organization as a whole. Most surveys include at least 25 to 30 percent of the total number of jobs as key jobs. In selecting key jobs, the compensation analyst uses a number of guidelines.

1. Key jobs should be readily definable. All aspects of the job should be describable in common English.

2. A key job should be common in the marketplace. Many organizations should employ people in a key job. There is no point in surveying for salary data on a job if you are the only organization possessing such a job.

3. Key jobs should vary in terms of job requirements such as education and experience, and in terms of other compensable factors. This diversity is of primary importance when survey data are combined with job evaluation data to build a salary structure.

4. Likewise, key jobs should represent all salary levels within the organization.

5. Key jobs should not be in the process of changing. If duties, skills, and responsibilities associated with a job are changing, then different organizations are likely to be reporting data on noncomparable jobs. In addition, salary data for changing jobs will become obsolete in a short time.

6. The group of key jobs should account for a sizable part of the employee population. Given two jobs similar in all other key job criteria, the compensation analyst will ordinarily choose for the survey the job that employs the most workers.

7. Entry-level jobs and other jobs with which the employer faces market competition will ordinarily be treated as key jobs.

8. Key jobs for an organization will probably include any jobs with which the organization is having problems such as an inability to hire or excessive turnover.

9. Finally, though less important, key jobs should probably include some jobs traditionally used on wage and salary surveys. Inclusion of such jobs increases the probability that respondents will provide the data requested.

Defining Relevant Labor Markets

Having selected a set of benchmark, or key jobs, the compensation analyst must then determine the *relevant labor markets* for those jobs. For wage and salary surveys, the relevant labor market for a job is (1) the geographic area(s) within which one would ordinarily expect to recruit all potential employees for that job, and (2) the geographic area(s) to which one would ordinarily expect to lose employees in that job. Most of the time these markets are identical, but they need not be. Thus, one might hire mechanical engineers from a national mark — this would be the case if recruiting was done primarily at schools of engineering — but lose engineers largely to local and regional competitors.

The relevant labor market is determined by the source of supply. The labor markets usually differentiated by compensation analysts are local, regional, national, and international.

Local Labor Markets A *local labor market* is usually defined as being within easy commuting distance of an organization. A secretary, for example, is usually hired from a local labor market; an employer would not normally recruit in another city for secretarial employees. Likewise, a secretary is not likely to commute for two hours to a job, since an equivalent job is likely to be available at a lesser distance. The secretarial salaries of interest to the compensation analyst, then, are those offered by other organizations within that commuting area. Most blue-collar and white-collar jobs compete in the local labor market, too; external equity may be preserved by paying salaries that are in line with local market data.

Regional Markets   Some jobs have more regional markets. Schoolteachers, for example, tend to think of salary equity in terms of a state, or perhaps several states. Other technical, administrative, and professional jobs also tend to have labor markets that are not national but are broader than local markets. Accountants, MBAs, some engineers, and many technicians will be recruited only from a multistate area; most job movement within such professions will also be confined to regional markets. Thus, the compensation analyst interested in these kinds of jobs will have to determine the relevant region to survey. Recruiting experience and interviews with departing employees will help to place the boundaries on regional markets.

National Markets   There are a few jobs for which truly national job markets exist. These jobs tend to be highly skilled managerial and professional jobs. Doctors, college professors, executives, and some scientists and engineers will tend to operate in national job markets. When dealing with national markets, the individual compensation analyst is much less likely to prepare a formal wage survey; he or she will tend to rely more heavily on data collected by others.

International Markets   Fortunately for the compensation analyst, there are few jobs for which there is truly an international market. Some transportation jobs, such as airline piloting, could be considered as such. Generally, analysts rely on national market data for such jobs.

Selecting the Firms to Be Surveyed

Having determined the geographic area to which the survey will be restricted, the compensation analyst must then decide which firms within the area will be surveyed. There are several issues the compensation analyst must take into account when selecting firms to survey.

Labor Supply Competitors   The firms chosen should include those hiring the same kinds of employees as the surveying firm. These firms should be hiring substantial numbers of employees to fill the jobs being surveyed. Interviews with employees who are leaving may supply leads for potential survey firms.

Compensation Systems Similarities The firms chosen should include some that use the same job evaluation system as the surveying firm. Salary similarities will provide some indication of the kind of job evaluation judgments being made. Conversely, comparability of job evaluation practices among employers will help to make surer salary comparisons.

Industry If possible, some of the firms chosen should be in the same industry as the surveying firm. This is because wages are influenced by the type of industry; a firm in the same industry is likely to have similar wages, all other things being equal. In addition, a firm in the same industry is likely to have all the jobs being surveyed, and those jobs are more likely to be similar to jobs in the surveying firm than jobs with the same title in a different industry.

Size Wages and benefits tend to vary according to the size of an organization. Thus, the compensation analyst should select firms of varying sizes, making sure to get some larger firms that account for substantial numbers of incumbents. In addition, firms with larger numbers of incumbents in surveyed jobs are more likely to have recruited and hired employees for those positions more recently than firms that have only one or two incumbents. These larger firms are thus more likely to have salaries that reflect current market pressures.

Number of Firms to Survey The compensation analyst must decide how many firms as well as which firms to survey. There is no magic number. In a small market with a few large employers, two or three firms may provide all the data needed. In larger local markets, as many as 200 or 300 positions may be surveyed within dozens of firms. National labor market surveys and some regional surveys will use sophisticated sampling strategies to ensure representative, "good" data. Such a strategy may require a survey of 1,000 to 1,500 firms.

Determining the Information to Ask

When deciding what information to request of surveyed organizations, the compensation analyst is faced with a choice of incomplete information versus no information at all. A complete but long survey may inadvertently discourage the cooperation of the surveyed organizations because of its length. Thus, what follows below is the information the compensation analyst would usually like to know. How much information the analyst will actually acquire depends upon the influence he or she has, the number and kinds of jobs being surveyed, the method of data collection, whether other survey requests have been received by the surveyed organization, and random factors beyond the control of the compensation analyst.

The information wanted by the compensation analyst will be one of four kinds. The first is general information about the surveyed organization, which helps the compensation analyst judge whether that organization is similar to his or her own. This category also includes information that helps the compensation analyst to identify the organization for further contact if necessary. The information requested in this section of the survey would include:

1. Identification data. The organization's name and address, and the contact person's name, title, and telephone number would be included.

2. Location of organization. If there were several locations, each would be noted and the total number of locations given. If the survey was local, a map might be provided for the respondent to pinpoint his location. This information would help the compensation analyst to determine the effect of commuting ease on salary differentials.

3. Industry. The surveyed organization's principal line(s) of business should be requested. If possible, Standard Industrial Classification (SIC) codes should be used. SIC codes, developed by the Department of Commerce, are used for industry breakouts in almost all statistical reporting of the U.S. government and by most private firms, as well. Their use would allow the compensation analyst to cross-check survey results with most other wage data available. In addition, the use of SIC codes would facilitate use of wage survey data in a variety of other labor market research projects (such as productivity comparisons) that the analyst may wish to undertake at a later date.

4. Size indicators. This would include sales volume, total number of employees, and number of employees at each location (if it is a multilocation organization).

5. Organization chart. The organization chart should include all jobs being surveyed.

6. Workweek length, hours worked per day.

7. Unions. All union representation should be noted, along with a description of the bargaining units.

Wage and Salary Policies   Wage and salary policy information is needed by the compensation analyst to understand the context in which specific wage rates operate. All policies affecting work-related pay should be surveyed. Included in such policies would be:

1. The job evaluation system in use. A short description would be sufficient here. Chapter 8 describes the four major types of job evaluation systems; in addition, there are several commercial packages used by many organizations.

2. The overall salary structure. An example of a structure is given in Chapter 8. Confidentiality is a major limitation on obtaining this information.

3. Merit adjustments to wages and salaries. The compensation analyst would want to know the basis for merit adjustments (such as supervisory ratings or other performance appraisal methods) to base pay, and the frequency and size of increases. This information would help the analyst judge the stability of the salary data received.

4. Across-the-board increases. Of particular interest to the compensation analyst would be any increase that is tied to cost-of-living adjustments (COLAs), again, to help judge the stability of salary levels. The frequency of such increases also would be needed.

5. Miscellaneous performance-related payments. These are payments that, unlike merit adjustments, do not affect base pay. Profit-sharing programs, cost-reduction programs such as the Scanlon Plan, or other bonus systems related to performance and resulting in nonrecurring payments would be of interest.

6. Miscellaneous pay differentials. Policies that affect the pay of individual employees, such as overtime, shift differentials, or holiday pay, would be included here. Two individuals in the same job could get different take-home pay because of such differentials. In addition, the pay of the individuals would be likely to change differently over time.

Benefits Policies   The compensation package today includes much more than direct pay. Benefits may, in fact, amount to as much as one-third of the total compensation package. (Benefit packages are described in Chapter 10.) The compensation analyst needs to know benefit levels, because many organizations trade off benefits for direct salary levels; thus, comparison must be made between total compensation packages and not just wage levels. Major benefits that need to be surveyed include:

1. The pension policy. Company contributions (as a percentage of salary), vesting timetables, and retirement policies should be surveyed. If the organization pays the employee's contribution to social security (FICA tax) as well as its own, this should be noted.

2. Insurance. The level of contribution to life, health, dental, optical, and other insurance programs would be of obvious interest to the compensation analyst.

3. Pay for time not worked. The organization's policies regarding vacations, holidays, and sick leave should be known. It also would be important for the compensation analyst to know about conversion policies, carryover policies, and other organizational treatments of such pay for time not worked. Other leaves (such as jury duty, paternity/maternity leave, marriage leave, and so on) for which employees receive partial or full payment should be described. Information regarding paid lunches and rest breaks should also be sought.

4. Major miscellaneous benefits. The compensation analyst may wish to survey organizations for their miscellaneous benefits, such as credit unions, reimbursements for education, stock ownership programs, subsidized cafeterias or other services, thrift plans, or any other benefit that has substantial economic worth to the average employee and may have been substituted for direct wage payment.

Individual Job Data   The compensation analyst will want to collect a variety of information on each job in the survey. In some cases, the analyst will provide the information and ask for agreement. Thus, a job title and job description will be provided, and in many cases, the *Dictionary of Occupational Titles (DOT)* job code will be given, too.[1] This information is given to ensure that the organization being surveyed knows exactly what job the analyst is interested in. Space should be provided for the surveyed organization to note major departures from the job description. Frequently, a "job match" checkoff is provided, which allows the respondent to specify whether the job in his or her organization matches, is a more valuable, or is a less valuable job than that in the survey job description.

In addition, the analyst is likely to provide questions about on-the-job relationships, the amount of supervision received, the skills and training required of entry-level employees, and the number of employees supervised (if applicable). With this basic descriptive data ensuring job comparability covered, the analyst also will ask for other information including:

1. Job incumbent data. This information should include the number of employees in a job, turnover rates, average seniority levels, average performance ratings, and the age of employees.

2. Wage and salary data. Six figures are frequently asked for. The first three are related to the salary structure ideal: the minimum wage for the job, the maximum for the job, and the midpoint of the range. The other three figures are related to the actual salaries paid: the current starting salary, the average pay given for the job, and the highest pay.

While the analyst would prefer both actual *and* structure data, the analyst would prefer actual wages to structure data if forced to choose. This is because companies compete against the actual salaries paid by others in the labor market, not their structures. As one consultant we know is fond of reminding his clients: "It would be foolish to base your compensation decisions on the structures and policies of others, since those structures and policies might be as poorly designed as yours!"

3. Miscellaneous data. This information would include anything that might account for the wage levels attached to the job, such as special perquisites (for example, a company car) or other benefits not given to all the employees of the organization.

Determining the Data-Collection Technique

There are basically three methods of collecting wage and salary data: the telephone interview, the mailed questionnaire, and the group meeting. (The Bureau of Labor Statistics uses trained interviewers, who meet with each respondent face-to-face; this method is not economically feasible for any other organization. Even the major survey firms use telephone or mailed survey techniques.) The method chosen by the compensation analyst will depend on the amount of information wanted, the number of organizations to be surveyed, the scope of the relevant labor market, and the time and budget available.

Telephone Interviews   Telephone interviews are usually limited to collection of small sets of data from continuing contacts. Any compensation analyst would be unlikely to give out extensive information to an unknown caller. However, the telephone interview is quite useful when conducted within the informal network that exists in a profession. It is also useful for following up on mail surveys to clarify responses or to get missing data.

The Mailed Questionnaire   Mailed questionnaires are the most common data-collection technique for wage and salary surveys. They allow for the use of a structured format that ensures getting the same information from all participants. Because respondents can fill out the questionnaire at their own pace, more information can be requested. However, it is also much easier for respondents to ignore or put aside the questionnaire.

The Group Meeting   Some wage and salary surveys, usually in local labor markets, have been done in group meetings. A list of the jobs to be surveyed is distributed beforehand, and compensation analysts taking part can bring relevant information with them to the meeting. The advantages of such a meeting are that group discussion and feedback can ensure that all information received is truly comparable, that differences can be ironed out, and that further information can be sought as it is requested.

The use of this form of data collection poses some risk to the participants and to their organizations, since the practice could be construed as wage fixing, and thus in violation of antitrust law. If participants confine themselves to the exchange of current wage rates and do not discuss future plans, the risk of antitrust violation is considerably reduced. (The same warning applies to mailed questionnaires and telephone interviews, but these are less likely to be seen as a conspiracy to fix wages.)

Administering the Survey

The actual structure of the survey used will be determined by the data-collection technique decided on and the precise information being sought. However, the administrative techniques used for a mail survey are generally applicable to other types. Before sending out a questionnaire (or calling an unknown respondent), one should contact the organization to be surveyed, explain the purpose of the survey, briefly outline the kinds of information that will be requested, and try to get a commitment for cooperation. Confidentiality of individual survey responses is guaranteed; that is, only aggregated or anonymous information will be published.

A copy of the results of the survey is promised to those who participate in the survey by supplying data. Usually the survey will be provided with the respondent organization's data removed and the surveying organization's added. Respondents thus will have information for the external market that is not contaminated with internal information. This is the inducement that usually leads many of those contacted to cooperate, for the wage and salary information gained from the survey may be of as much use to them as to the initiating organization. Plus, such information is, of course, obtained by the respondent organization at a much lower cost than if they were to conduct the survey themselves.

The compensation analyst will have to decide how much information he or she can safely ask for and still have other organizations cooperate. The amount of information really needed to solve the problems that inspired the survey in the first place must also be considered.

A budget for the survey should be drawn up before starting the project. Aside from printing, postage, and telephone costs, the major expense will be the labor of the compensation analyst and the clerical staff in developing and mailing questionnaires, and in tabulating and analyzing the collected information.

If questionnaires are constructed, the compensation analyst should consider both the ease with which respondents can answer questions asked and the ease with which completed questionnaires can be coded for analysis. It is better to give respondents questions that can be answered by yes or no, or with a checkmark in a multiple-choice response ("supervises __ no __ 1–2 __ 3–5 __ 6–10 __ 11 or more employees"), than to use an open-ended question. Although organization charts, the overall salary structure, and some other items will not fit such a format, most information can be gathered in this way.

The construction and conduct of surveys is a complex art, and great care must be taken if the data collected are to be usable. A full discussion of this topic is beyond the scope of this book. For those proposing to undertake survey research (or any other business-related research, for that matter) we recommend a book that we have written devoted entirely to that topic (C. H. Fay and M. J. Wallace, Jr., *Research-Based Decisions*, New York: Random House, 1987).

Outside Wage and Salary Surveys

Many organizations do not have the time or the money to devote to the ongoing collection of wage and salary data. In many cases, they get some or all of the data they need by participating in surveys conducted by other firms. They may also cooperate with other surveying organizations such as the Bureau of Labor Statistics of the U.S. Department of Labor, industry groups, private companies, and local groups such as chambers of commerce. In this section, we will look at some of the major outside sources of wage and salary data available to the compensation manager. There are four primary sources: the aforementioned Bureau of Labor Statistics, other federal government groups, professional groups, and private firms. We will also look briefly at maturity curves.

The Bureau of Labor Statistics

The Bureau of Labor Statistics (BLS) is the major publisher of wage and salary survey data. The BLS puts out three major series of survey data: area wage surveys, industry wage surveys, and the *National Survey of Professional, Administrative, Technical, and Clerical Pay.*

Area Wage Surveys   The BLS makes surveys of approximately ninety-six areas across the United States for a limited number of jobs. These areas are surveyed to provide wage and salary data used in administering the Service Contract Act of 1965, which requires government contractors to pay prevailing wages (see Chapter 6). A sample of the Service Contract Act survey for Albuquerque, New Mexico, is shown in Exhibit 7.1. Also, more extensive area wage surveys are made for seventy Standard Metropolitan Statistical Areas (SMSAs). The more extensive area surveys differ from the Service Contract Act surveys in two ways.

First a larger number of jobs are surveyed. For example, Exhibit 7.2 shows the jobs for which wage and salary data were collected for an area wage survey of San Francisco–Oakland, California, in 1985. Second, the kinds of data provided are somewhat different. In addition to the kinds of data shown in Exhibit 7.1 (similar data are provided for all jobs in Exhibit 7.2), indexes of earnings and percentage increases for selected occupational groups are given for selected periods. Average pay relationships within establishments for selected occupations are also provided. Thus, the compensation analyst can discover, for example, that in the Albuquerque area, in September 1986, a Secretary V earned almost twice that of a Secretary I in the same firm, on the average. Likewise, the shipping packers and material handling laborers earned only 81 percent, on average, of a forklift operator's salary in the same firm.

Industry Wage Surveys   The Bureau of Labor Statistics publishes surveys on approximately seventy industries, both manufacturing and nonmanufacturing. An example is the *Industry Wage Survey: Machinery Manufacturing, No-*

vember 1983 (published in April 1985). This survey includes wage and salary data based on a sample of 830 organizations in twenty-three geographic areas (e.g., Boston and Houston), giving the number of workers and mean salary data. Wage distributions for thirty-one jobs in each area are provided. Other information also published in the survey includes whether wages are based on time (so much per hour) or incentive (such as piecework or group bonus). Additional data reported include scheduled weekly hours, shift differentials (both flat cents per hour and uniform percentage differentials are reported), and paid holidays and vacation practices and amounts.

Other benefits are reported, but instead of reporting costs/values of the benefits, the percentage of workers who possess specified benefits are given. These benefits include health insurance and retirement plans, funeral and jury duty leave, technological severance pay, and cost-of-living adjustment (COLA) provisions.

The precise information reported in the industry surveys varies, depending on the industry. Generally, the data most relevant to a compensation analyst in the industry for which a given survey applies are provided. These surveys are among the best available because they are based on rigorous sampling and survey technology. Unfortunately, this care incurs reporting delays. However, any compensation analyst in a covered industry will look at the industry survey as the starting point in dealing with external wage data.

The National Survey of Professional, Administrative, Technical, and Clerical Pay (PATC)   The PATC covers twenty-six professional, administrative, technical, and clerical occupations, differentiating these into one hundred and twelve occupational levels. A sample table from the PATC, showing the occupations and levels surveyed, is presented in Exhibit 7.3. Examination of this exhibit should emphasize the wide variety of jobs included in this survey. The PATC also provides complete information on salary distributions. Like the industry surveys, the PATC is the starting point for external market data for the jobs covered.

Other Government Surveys

Other branches of the federal government conduct, or contract out, wage and salary surveys. One such survey is the *National Survey of Compensation Paid Scientists and Engineers Engaged in Research and Development Activities*, prepared for the U.S. Department of Energy by Battelle Columbus Laboratories. This

Exhibit 7.1 Area Wage Survey: Hourly Earnings[1] of Selected Occupations in Albuquerque, NM, September 1986

Occupation[2]	Number of workers	Hourly earnings (in dollars)[1]								
		Mean	Median	Middle range	3.35 and under 3.50	3.50 – 4.00	4.00 – 4.50	4.50 – 5.00	5.00 – 5.50	5.50 – 6.00
Secretaries	950	9.16	9.69	7.93– 9.94	–	–	–	1	26	25
Secretaries I	121	6.74	6.75	5.71– 7.56	–	–	–	1	26	10
Secretaries III	330	9.30	9.27	8.08–10.39	–	–	–	–	–	–
Secretaries IV	86	11.15	11.30	9.62–12.09	–	–	–	–	–	–
Secretaries V	16	12.73	13.14	10.86–14.89	–	–	–	–	–	–
Typists	25	6.97	6.78	5.10– 8.68	–	–	–	4	3	1
Typists I	15	5.75	5.77	4.93– 6.60	–	–	–	4	3	1
Word processors	90	7.01	6.68	6.00– 7.63	–	–	–	–	4	18
Word processors I	48	6.26	6.00	5.75– 6.72	–	–	–	–	4	18
Word processors II	42	7.86	7.62	6.68– 8.53	–	–	–	–	–	5
File clerks	82	5.22	5.27	4.86– 5.52	6	2	11	10	26	15
File clerks I	61	4.84	5.15	4.00– 5.50	6	2	11	10	16	14
Messengers	8	5.89	5.71	– –	–	–	–	–	–	5
Receptionists	20	5.56	5.36	4.92– 6.00	–	–	2	4	7	1
Switchboard operators	39	5.39	5.16	4.85– 5.95	–	4	3	6	10	7
Key entry operators	243	6.17	6.21	5.10– 6.62	–	–	–	43	31	24
Key entry operators I	203	5.90	6.06	5.00– 6.62	–	–	–	43	29	23
Key entry operators II	40	7.50	7.06	6.49– 8.49	–	–	–	–	2	1
Computer operators	207	9.60	9.09	7.87–11.16	–	–	–	–	–	6
Computer operators I	51	7.34	7.42	6.08– 8.74	–	–	–	–	–	6
Computer operators II	108	9.74	9.77	8.23–10.58	–	–	–	–	–	–
Computer operators III	48	11.70	11.68	9.99–12.35	–	–	–	–	–	–
Drafters	335	11.13	11.22	9.14–13.25	–	–	–	–	7	9
Drafters II	23	6.76	6.65	6.25– 7.50	–	–	–	–	3	1
Drafters III	78	9.33	9.25	8.40–10.34	–	–	–	–	–	–
Electronics technicians	1,178	11.35	11.17	9.70–12.69	–	–	–	–	–	–
Electronics technicians I	195	8.54	8.43	7.90– 8.99	–	–	–	–	–	–
Electronics technicians II	462	11.60	10.79	9.89–13.44	–	–	–	–	–	–
Electronics technicians III	521	12.17	12.03	11.09–12.98	–	–	–	–	–	–
Maintenance electricians	133	11.82	12.00	9.50–13.32	–	–	–	–	–	–
Maintenance painters	23	12.65	13.26	11.64–13.52	–	–	–	–	–	–
Maintenance machinists	52	12.53	13.10	12.00–13.26	–	–	–	–	–	–
Maintenance mechanics (machinery)	175	10.83	11.00	9.50–12.00	–	–	–	–	–	–
Motor vehicle mechanics	176	13.01	14.69	9.98–14.87	–	–	–	–	–	–
General maintenance workers	101	6.36	6.01	5.00– 7.66	–	–	6	–	31	13
Stationary engineers	34	13.03	13.84	11.45–14.09	–	–	–	–	–	–
Truckdrivers	1,034	9.33	9.11	7.60–10.60	18	12	66	62	13	23
Truckdrivers, light truck	179	6.02	4.88	4.00– 8.19	18	12	34	26	9	11
Truckdrivers, medium truck	455	9.72	9.11	7.00–14.20	–	–	32	36	4	12
Truckdrivers, tractor-trailer	308	10.60	10.60	8.50–11.22	–	–	–	–	–	–
Shipping packers	37	6.88	7.15	6.81– 7.15	–	–	–	–	–	2
Material handling laborers	61	6.84	6.11	5.00– 8.96	–	–	6	1	18	1
Forklift operators	197	8.51	8.37	7.59– 9.13	–	–	–	–	2	–
Guards	534	5.46	3.86	3.50– 6.60	126	158	32	2	28	42
Guards I	447	4.32	3.50	3.45– 5.21	126	158	32	2	28	42
Janitors, porters, and cleaners	853	4.54	3.55	3.35– 5.05	298	194	90	53	31	25

[1] Excludes premium pay for overtime and for work on weekends, holidays, and late shifts. Also excluded are performance bonuses and lump-sum payments of the type negotiated in the auto and aerospace industries, as well as profit-sharing payments, attendance bonuses, Christmas or year-end bonuses, and other nonproduction bonuses. Pay increases - but not bonuses - under cost of living allowance clauses and incentive payments, however, are included. Hourly earnings reported for salaried workers are derived from regular salaries divided by the corresponding standard hours of work. The wages of learners, apprentices, and handicapped workers are excluded. The mean is computed for each job by totaling the earnings of

Source: Area Wage Survey: Albuquerque, N.M., September 1986 (Washington, D.C.: U.S. Bureau of Labor Statistics, 1986), p. 2

Number of workers receiving straight-time hourly earnings (in dollars) of —

6.00 – 6.50	6.50 – 7.00	7.00 – 7.50	7.50 – 8.00	8.00 – 8.50	8.50 – 9.00	9.00 – 9.50	9.50 – 10.00	10.00 – 10.50	10.50 – 11.00	11.00 – 11.50	11.50 – 12.00	12.00 – 13.00	13.00 – 14.00	14.00 – 15.00	15.00 – 16.00	16.00 and over
26	48	42	78	62	67	38	308	95	43	25	19	26	12	3	3	3
5	24	16	28	4	5	2	–	–	–	–	–	–	–	–	–	–
–	11	20	45	36	45	19	11	83	38	7	8	2	3	2	–	–
–	–	–	–	2	6	7	11	6	4	10	11	22	5	–	–	2
–	–	–	–	–	1	–	2	–	1	1	–	2	4	1	3	1
1	6	–	–	–	10	–	–	–	–	–	–	–	–	–	–	–
1	6	–	–	–	–	–	–	–	–	–	–	–	–	–	–	–
15	18	8	9	7	4	1	–	–	6	–	–	–	–	–	–	–
8	11	5	–	2	–	–	–	–	–	–	–	–	–	–	–	–
7	7	3	9	5	4	1	–	–	6	–	–	–	–	–	–	–
1	5	2	3	–	–	–	–	1	–	–	–	–	–	–	–	–
–	2	–	–	–	–	–	–	–	–	–	–	–	–	–	–	–
2	1	–	–	–	–	–	–	–	–	–	–	–	–	–	–	–
3	1	–	2	–	–	–	–	–	–	–	–	–	–	–	–	–
3	3	2	–	1	–	–	–	–	–	–	–	–	–	–	–	–
55	51	10	9	5	10	–	2	1	–	–	–	–	2	–	–	–
48	44	2	4	5	2	–	2	1	–	–	–	–	–	–	–	–
7	7	8	5	–	8	–	–	–	–	–	–	–	2	–	–	–
10	8	18	19	14	25	9	10	16	20	9	3	32	–	–	8	–
9	7	8	5	2	14	–	–	–	–	–	–	–	–	–	–	–
1	1	10	13	12	10	3	6	13	17	3	2	17	–	–	8	–
–	–	–	1	–	1	6	4	3	3	6	1	15	–	–	8	–
8	11	5	19	7	10	21	19	27	18	8	23	56	18	39	21	9
2	7	2	8	–	–	–	–	–	–	–	–	–	–	–	–	–
2	–	3	11	5	7	14	10	9	8	7	–	2	–	–	–	–
–	–	6	47	49	56	85	125	106	83	102	87	179	82	112	23	36
–	–	6	6	47	49	45	37	2	4	3	–	–	–	–	–	–
–	–	–	–	–	11	30	89	73	40	49	19	27	14	89	4	17
–	–	–	–	–	–	18	34	31	39	50	68	152	68	23	19	19
–	–	–	–	–	–	1	41	6	–	5	–	20	50	7	–	3
–	–	–	–	–	–	–	–	–	–	–	10	–	13	–	–	–
–	–	–	–	–	–	8	–	–	–	–	–	8	34	2	–	–
–	–	–	1	–	10	15	48	–	–	20	–	76	1	–	–	4
–	–	–	–	–	4	16	25	4	–	9	6	14	4	63	23	8
9	5	9	10	8	8	2	–	–	–	–	–	–	–	–	–	–
–	–	–	–	–	1	–	–	1	4	3	2	1	11	10	1	–
14	36	14	62	34	145	124	16	30	118	15	–	5	–	227	–	–
3	–	1	15	21	1	4	6	16	1	–	–	1	–	–	–	–
9	20	9	30	12	–	120	6	–	20	–	–	4	–	141	–	–
2	16	4	16	–	77	–	3	2	97	15	–	–	–	76	–	–
4	10	21	–	–	–	–	–	–	–	–	–	–	–	–	–	–
9	6	1	–	–	4	–	1	14	–	–	–	–	–	–	–	–
5	12	9	35	84	–	5	–	36	–	4	4	–	–	1	–	–
12	22	8	11	4	2	–	–	–	–	59	28	–	–	–	–	–
12	22	8	11	4	2	–	–	–	–	–	–	–	–	–	–	–
56	6	2	19	59	–	–	14	2	1	1	–	1	1	–	–	–

all workers and dividing by the number of workers. The median designates position—one-half of the workers receive the same as or more and one-half receive the same as or less than the rate shown. The middle range is defined by two rates of pay; one-fourth of the workers earn the same as or less than the lower of these rates and one-fourth earn the same as or more than the higher rate.

² For occupations with more than one level, data are included in the overall classification when a subclassification is not shown or information to subclassify is not available.

Exhibit 7.2 Sampling of Job Titles Covered in Extensive Area Wage Surveys

Occupation and industry division

Secretaries
  Manufacturing
  Nonmanufacturing
    Transportation and utilities

Secretaries I
  Nonmanufacturing

Secretaries II
  Manufacturing
  Nonmanufacturing

Secretaries III
  Manufacturing
  Nonmanufacturing
    Transportation and utilities

Secretaries IV
  Manufacturing
  Nonmanufacturing
    Transportation and utilities

Secretaries V
  Manufacturing
  Nonmanufacturing
    Transportation and utilities

Stenographers

Stenographers I
  Nonmanufacturing

Typists
  Nonmanufacturing

Typists I
  Nonmanufacturing

Typists II
  Nonmanufacturing

Word processors
  Manufacturing
  Nonmanufacturing
    Transportation and utilities

Word processors I
  Manufacturing
  Nonmanufacturing
    Transportation and utilities

Word processors II
  Manufacturing
  Nonmanufacturing

File clerks
  Manufacturing
  Nonmanufacturing

File clerks I
  Nonmanufacturing

File clerks II
  Nonmanufacturing

File clerks III
  Nonmanufacturing

Messengers
  Nonmanufacturing
    Transportation and utilities

Receptionists
  Nonmanufacturing

Switchboard operators
  Nonmanufacturing

Switchboard operator-
  receptionists
    Manufacturing
    Nonmanufacturing
      Transportation and utilities

Order clerks
  Manufacturing
  Nonmanufacturing

Order clerks I
  Manufacturing
  Nonmanufacturing

Order clerks II
  Manufacturing
  Nonmanufacturing

Accounting clerks
  Manufacturing
  Nonmanufacturing
    Transportation and utilities

Accounting clerks I
  Manufacturing
  Nonmanufacturing
    Transportation and utilities

Accounting clerks II
  Manufacturing
  Nonmanufacturing
    Transportation and utilities

Accounting clerks III
  Manufacturing
  Nonmanufacturing

Accounting clerks IV
  Manufacturing
  Nonmanufacturing
    Transportation and utilities

Payroll clerks
  Manufacturing
  Nonmanufacturing
    Transportation and utilities

Key entry operators
  Manufacturing
  Nonmanufacturing
    Transportation and utilities

Key entry operators I
  Manufacturing
  Nonmanufacturing
    Transportation and utilities

Key entry operators II
  Manufacturing
  Nonmanufacturing

Source: Area Wage Survey: San Francisco–Oakland, California, Metropolitan Area, March 1985 (Washington, D.C.: U.S. Bureau of Labor Statistics, 1985), pp. 3–5.

particular survey is of interest because it utilizes the *maturity curve* approach to salary structure. Sample data from this survey are presented in Exhibit 7.4. Notice that salary data are presented in terms of years from a terminal degree. This approach is frequently used for professional workers, whose increases come about largely through longevity. Maturity curves as wage-setting devices are further discussed both on pp. 185–189 and in Chapter 8.

Professional Groups

Many professional groups provide wage and salary survey data for specialized occupations, industries, or locales. An example of one professional survey is the ACA *Salary Budget Survey*, sponsored by the American Compensation Association. This survey, based on actual and planned salary data from nearly 3,000 U.S. and Canadian organizations, provides a wide range of data not available in the BLS area wage survey. A sample page, showing (a) highlights of the 1986–1987 survey, and (b) more detailed information on range spreads, grade increments, increase intervals, and other salary budget information for U.S. firms in 1986, is shown in Exhibit 7.5.

Another survey conducted jointly by the American Society for Personnel Administration and A. S. Hansen, Inc., is the *ASPA/Hansen Salary Survey on Personnel and Industrial Relations Positions*. The 1986 data for the position of senior compensation analyst are shown in Exhibit 7.6.

Regional and local groups also conduct salary surveys for selected jobs in limited areas. These surveys vary widely in quality depending on the expertise of the sponsoring group. Correctly done, they may well be the most useful surveys available to the compensation analyst because the market is defined exactly as the analyst needs it, and the jobs covered are likely to be those that are of most interest to the analyst (i.e., those local labor market jobs that characterize the market).

An example of a good local survey is the *Salary Survey Report* published by the Washington Personnel Association. Any local group thinking of conducting a survey could readily use the Washington Personnel Association survey as a model. Data are provided on survey participants and a statistical profile of organization types is given. A very important section details the survey methodology used and provides specific definitions of all terms (e.g., average new hire rate reported and change in weighted average of survey data). Salary administration practices also are reported (for example, 57 percent of the respondents increased salary ranges in the last six months, 51 percent pay shift differentials, 50 percent internally publicize their salary structure).

Exhibit 7.3   PATC Survey Summary

Occupation and level[2]	Number of employees[3]	Monthly salaries[4]	
		Mean[5]	Median[5]
Accountants			
I	13,846	$1,752	$1,741
II	29,311	2,129	2,083
III	46,228	2,595	2,541
IV	23,733	3,274	3,249
V	8,227	4,103	4,025
VI	1,397	5,129	5,050
Auditors			
I	1,756	1,795	1,791
II	2,928	2,176	2,124
III	4,709	2,677	2,657
IV	2,022	3,309	3,249
Public accountants			
I	11,606	1,706	1,707
II	11,595	1,893	1,873
III	8,897	2,219	2,166
IV	4,275	2,676	2,624
Chief accountants			
II	1,454	3,997	4,000
III	475	5,240	5,151
IV	230	6,701	6,568
Attorneys			
I	1,377	2,584	2,525
II	3,199	3,303	3,250
III	4,347	4,177	4,082
IV	3,500	5,328	5,248
V	1,847	6,533	6,497
VI	587	8,431	8,488
Buyers			
I	6,914	1,770	1,749
II	22,990	2,197	2,167
III	18,323	2,798	2,735
IV	4,798	3,442	3,406
Computer programmers			
I	15,974	1,736	1,749
II	38,540	2,046	2,041
III	46,996	2,444	2,426
IV	21,524	2,910	2,905
V	9,492	3,578	3,612
Systems analysts			
I	21,402	2,428	2,400
II	47,518	2,907	2,907
III	38,943	3,500	3,450
IV	15,506	4,126	4,032
V	2,666	4,867	4,816
VI	233	5,981	5,958
Job analysts			
I	103	1,853	1,841
II	350	2,107	2,001

Occupation and level[2]

Job analysts
III
IV

Directors of personnel
I
II
III
IV

Chemists
I
II
III
IV
V
VI
VII

Engineers
I
II
III
IV
V
VI
VII
VIII

Engineering technicians
I
II
III
IV
V

Drafters
I
II
III
IV
V

Computer operators
I
II
III
IV
V

Photographers
I
II
III
IV
V

Accounting clerks
I
II
III
IV

Source: National Survey of Professional, Administrative, Technical, and Clerical Pay, March 1986 (Washington, D.C.: U.S. Bureau of Labor Statistics, 1986), pp. 11–13.

Number of employees [3]	Monthly salaries [4]	
	Mean [5]	Median [5]
624	$2,550	$2,432
520	3,184	3,090
1,849	3,318	3,200
2,082	3,861	3,880
1,179	5,321	5,165
395	6,264	6,023
3,580	1,878	1,866
6,673	2,267	2,249
10,244	2,845	2,791
9,257	3,462	3,435
7,266	4,223	4,198
3,632	5,066	5,075
848	6,217	6,033
40,469	2,322	2,365
71,336	2,599	2,595
145,165	2,976	2,956
157,033	3,556	3,532
111,913	4,231	4,203
52,105	4,907	4,881
13,395	5,717	5,650
3,097	6,585	6,545
5,797	1,407	1,380
17,342	1,693	1,666
32,193	1,991	1,972
35,397	2,368	2,346
19,399	2,726	2,700
2,982	1,088	1,083
12,102	1,321	1,300
25,970	1,683	1,665
24,371	2,054	2,038
14,362	2,584	2,541
10,704	1,144	1,125
37,530	1,435	1,408
25,698	1,794	1,749
8,059	2,046	2,012
1,260	2,416	2,426
401	1,386	1,331
873	1,908	1,916
791	2,251	2,189
331	2,632	2,601
104	2,924	2,842
36,023	$1,043	$1,000
133,183	1,224	1,187
79,215	1,496	1,456
22,354	1,823	1,766

Occupation and level [2]	Number of employees [3]	Monthly salaries [4]	
		Mean [5]	Median [5]
File clerks			
I	20,916	861	842
II	10,110	1,013	958
III	2,100	1,302	1,255
Key entry operators			
I	68,827	1,096	1,049
II	30,770	1,408	1,343
Messengers	9,842	1,023	945
Personnel clerks/assistants			
I	2,521	1,183	1,174
II	4,414	1,409	1,350
III	3,255	1,641	1,621
IV	1,298	1,975	1,915
Purchasing clerks/assistants			
I	4,014	1,166	1,127
II	5,585	1,440	1,387
III	4,197	1,865	1,837
IV	1,037	2,449	2,350
Secretaries			
I	59,859	1,361	1,300
II	69,450	1,526	1,485
III	110,604	1,763	1,708
IV	49,403	1,987	1,956
V	16,038	2,338	2,282
Stenographers			
I	6,811	1,531	1,512
II	5,648	1,812	1,846
Typists			
I	25,125	1,049	1,021
II	12,842	1,404	1,334
General clerks			
I	11,811	873	850
II	59,359	1,061	1,014
III	65,101	1,292	1,250
IV	33,472	1,610	1,552

[1] For the scope of the survey, see table A-1 in appendix A.

[2] Occupational definitions appear in appendix C.

[3] Occupational employment estimates relate to the total in all establishments within the scope of the survey and not to the number actually surveyed. For further explanation, see appendix A.

[4] Excludes premium pay for overtime and for work on weekends, holidays, and late shifts. Also excluded are performance bonuses and lump-sum payments of the type negotiated in the auto and aerospace industries, as well as profit-sharing payments, attendance bonuses, Christmas or year-end bonuses, and other nonproduction bonuses. Pay increases – but not bonuses – under cost-of-living allowance clauses, and incentive payments, however, are included.

[5] The mean is computed for each job by totaling the earnings of all workers and dividing by the number of workers. The median designates position; one-half of the workers receive the same as or more and one-half receive the same as or less than the rate shown. The middle range is defined by two rates of pay; one-fourth of the workers earn the same as or less than the lower of these rates and one-fourth earn the same as or more than the higher rate.

Exhibit 7.4   Maturity/Salary Data for Scientists and Engineers: Doctorate Degree—Nonsupervisory Employees—Total Survey: Working as Occupation—Electrical and Electronic Engineering

SALARY	0	1	2	3	4	5	6	7	8	9	10	11	12	13	14
6751-7950															
6251-6750															
5751-6250															
5251-5750										1					
4751-5250												1	2	2	3
4651-4750											1		1		2
4551-4650										1		1	2	1	1
4451-4550														3	1
4351-4450							1					2	1	1	2
4251-4350									1	1		3	1	3	1
4151-4250								1	1		2	4	1	1	2
4051-4150											1	2	2	1	1
3951-4050							4	2	3	2	2	4	5	3	2
3851-3950							2	1	1	1	1	4	2	7	5
3751-3850					1		1		2	5	1	2	3	1	2
3651-3750							2	2	2	4	1	4	3	6	2
3551-3650						2	4	3	3	2	5	2	4	4	2
3451-3550						2	2	1	5	6	2	3	1		1
3351-3450								2	1	1	2	4	4	2	2
3251-3350						3			1	3	3	2	2	2	1
3151-3250		1		1		1	1	2		2	4	4	1	1	2
3051-3150			1	1		1			2	2	2	2			3
2951-3050					1			2	1	1	3			1	1
2851-2950								2		2	2	1	1	2	1
2751-2850								1	1	1	1			1	
2651-2750						2		1	1	3	1	1	1		
2551-2650						1						1			
2451-2550															
2351-2450															
2251-2350															
2151-2250															
2051-2150															
1951-2050															
1851-1950						1									
1751-1850															
1651-1750															
1551-1650															
1451-1550															
1351-1450															
1251-1350															
1151-1250															
1051-1150															
951-1050															
851- 950															
751- 850															
SUM		1	1	2	2	9	21	21	25	38	31	51	37	43	38
%							3	5	7	10	13	17	20	24	27
MEAN		3200	3100	3150	3400	3167	3595	3462	3564	3532	3503	3724	3846	3879	3918
0.90						3605	4022	4045	4033	4010	4140	4346	4615	4540	4760
0.75						3537	3937	3737	3837	3780	3775	4112	4087	4258	4375
0.50		3200	3100	3150	3400	3200	3637	3500	3566	3516	3475	3712	3800	3871	3890
0.25						2712	3462	3012	3375	3175	3193	3287	3475	3593	3425
0.10						2640	3253	2855	3000	2830	2905	3020	3285	3180	3110
	0	1	2	3	4	5	6	7	8	9	10	11	12	13	14

YEARS SINCE

Source: Battelle Columbus Laboratories, *Report on 1985 National Survey of Compensation Paid Scientists and Engineers Engaged in Research and Development Activities.* Prepared for the U.S. Department of Energy, Office of Industrial Relations, 1985. Page H44.

15	16	17	18/19	20/21	22/23	24/25	26/27	28/29	30/31	32/33	34/35	36/40	41/50	SUM	%
										1		1		2	100
			2	2	1		1	2		1		1	1	11	99
		1	1	5	5	3	3	1	5	4	5	4	3	34	96
1	1		5	9	15	4	8	7	4	4	2	7	3	73	
11	6	6	13	16	27	18	13	8	7	5	3	12	7	160	90
1	1	3	5	7	5	5	3	2	4	3	2		1	46	76
1	3	4	5	5	2	4	5	2		4	2			48	72
1		3	4	10	8	5	4	2	1	7	3		1	53	68
3	2	3	4	6	4	7	4	3	1	2	3		2	54	64
4	1	3	11	7	6	6	4	5	1	2	1	3		64	59
4	6	5	8	10	5	3	5	5	6	1	3	3	1	77	54
3	3	2	7	10	4	3	2			2	4	5		53	47
7	3	3	8	4	7	6	3		2		3		1	80	43
1	6	2	2	4	3	4	2	3	1	1			1	58	36
3	2	1	9	4	6	3	1	1	1		2		1	52	31
1	4	3	3	2	4		1			1	1	1	1	48	27
5	1		2	5			1					2		47	23
4	3	4	3	3	2	2		1	1	1		1	1	48	19
3	2	2	4	4	1	2		3		1	1	1		42	15
1		1	4	2	1		1		1			1		30	11
1		1	2	2	2							1	1	30	9
	1		2					1						18	6
				2				1						13	5
			1	1		1								14	3
						1								6	2
	1	1	2		1							1	1	15	
				1										3	1
					1									1	
	1													2	
55	47	48	107	120	111	75	65	54	35	30	35	52	29	1183	
32	36	40	49	59	68	75	80	85	88	90	93	98	100		
4169	4072	4213	4231	4413	4585	4535	4628	4554	4580	4890	4640	4712	4707	4250	
5012	4980	4980	5015	5450	5572	5241	5687	5430	5500	6100	5900	5745	5960	5265	
4575	4412	4600	4635	4800	5032	5012	5087	5100	4981	5725	4962	5200	5141	4717	
4100	4033	4230	4206	4350	4543	4480	4560	4450	4575	4775	4514	4550	4500	4190	
3645	3718	3750	3791	3975	4032	4108	4175	4125	4195	4200	4208	4125	4075	3705	
3462	3435	3440	3342	3483	3727	3833	3887	3590	3866	3600	3825	3610	3740	3304	

15	16	17	18	20	22	24	26	28	30	32	34	36	41	SUM	%
			19	21	23	25	27	29	31	33	35	40	50		

FIRST DEGREE

Exhibit 7.5 American Compensation Association Salary Survey

American Compensation Association

1987-1988 Salary Budget Survey Report

The 1987-1988 Salary Budget Survey is the fourteenth such survey conducted by the American Compensation Association. Over 2,750 U.S. firms with over eight million employees and 111 Canadian firms with approximately 425,000 employees supplied data representing a broad cross section of industrial, insurance, service, utility, finance, government, education, and health-care organizations.

Highlights of the Survey

United States Firms

- 1987 salary budget increases for nonexempt, exempt and officers/executives declined for the sixth consecutive year.
- The actual salary budget increases for 1987 are slightly lower than the projections for 1987.
- The salary budget increase projections for 1988 closely reflect of the 1987 actual data.
- Summary data follows.

Exhibit 7.5 (*continued*)

	1986	Actual Salary Budget Increases				
		1987				
United States	National	National	Eastern Region	Central Region	Southern Region	Western Region
Nonexempt salaried employees	5.7%	5.0%	5.3%	4.7%	4.8%	5.0%
Exempt salaried employees	5.9%	5.2%	5.5%	5.0%	5.0%	5.2%
Officers/Executives	6.3%	5.5%	5.7%	5.3%	5.2%	5.4%

	1987	Projected Salary Budget Increases				
		1988				
United States	National	National	Eastern Region	Central Region	Southern Region	Western Region
Nonexempt salaried employees	5.4%	5.0%	5.3%	4.8%	4.9%	5.0%
Exempt salaried employees	5.5%	5.2%	5.4%	5.0%	5.1%	5.2%
Officers/Executives	5.7%	5.4%	5.7%	5.3%	5.2%	5.4%

Exhibit 7.5 (*continued*)

Actual Salary Budget Trends

United States	1976	1977	1978	1979	1980	1981	1982	1983	1984	1985	1986	1987	Proj. 1988
Nonexempt	8.4%	8.4%	8.5%	8.2%	10.1%	10.6%	9.1%	6.8%	6.4%	6.2%	5.7%	5.0%	5.0%
Exempt	8.2%	8.2%	8.4%	8.0%	9.9%	10.5%	9.1%	6.9%	6.5%	6.4%	5.9%	5.2%	5.2%
Officers/Executives	8.2%	8.4%	8.5%	7.8%	9.7%	10.6%	8.9%	6.9%	6.8%	6.7%	6.3%	5.5%	5.4%

- Salary structure increases for 1987 dropped to 3.5 percent from the 4.5 percent level projected for 1987 and are significantly lower than the 5.0 percent experienced in 1986.

- The projections for 1988 salary structure increases at 3.8 percent show a slight increase over 1987 actual data.

- Summary data follows.

Actual Salary Structure Increases

United States	1986 National	1987 National	Eastern Region	Central Region	Southern Region	Western Region
Nonexempt salaried employees	4.7%	3.3%	3.8%	3.1%	3.0%	3.0%
Exempt salaried employees	4.9%	3.5%	3.9%	3.4%	3.2%	3.2%
Officers/Executives	5.3%	3.6%	4.0%	3.5%	3.3%	3.2%

Exhibit 7.5 *(continued)*

United States	Projected Salary Structure Increases					
	1987	1988				
	National	National	Eastern Region	Central Region	Southern Region	Western Region
Nonexempt salaried employees	4.3%	3.7%	4.0%	3.6%	3.4%	3.6%
Exempt salaried employees	4.5%	3.9%	4.2%	3.9%	3.7%	3.7%
Officers/Executives	4.7%	3.9%	4.2%	3.9%	3.7%	3.7%

United States	Actual Salary Structure Trends											
	1977	1978	1979	1980	1981	1982	1983	1984	1985	1986	1987	Proj. 1988
Nonexempt	7.3%	7.6%	7.5%	8.6%	9.3%	7.5%	4.9%	5.4%	5.2%	4.7%	3.3%	3.7%
Exempt	7.3%	7.4%	7.5%	8.7%	9.4%	7.8%	5.1%	5.7%	5.5%	4.9%	3.5%	3.9%
Officers/Executives	7.2%	7.4%	7.5%	8.6%	9.6%	7.3%	4.7%	5.9%	5.7%	5.3%	3.6%	3.9%

Exhibit 7.5 *(continued)*

AMERICAN COMPENSATION ASSOCIATION
1987/1988 Salary Budget Survey

National
1987 Actual Increases

Nonexempt Salary Employees

INDUSTRY	GENERAL INCREASE		COLA		MERIT INCREASE		TOTAL INCREASE	
	No. Cos.	%	No. Cos.	%	No. Cos.	%	No. Cos.	%
Aerospace	9	3.5	7	2.2	70	4.2	75	4.5
Airlines	1	6.0	—	—	7	3.4	8	3.7
Apparel Manufacturing	2	5.0	—	—	9	5.0	11	5.0
Automotive & Farm Equipment	1	5.0	—	—	24	4.8	25	4.8
Building Materials	—	—	—	—	14	4.5	14	4.5
Chemical	6	4.4	—	—	54	4.7	58	4.8
Communications	10	3.3	—	—	57	4.8	63	4.9
Computer Service & Software	1	2.5	1	2.0	80	5.5	80	5.6
Construction/Engineering	4	3.9	1	1.5	27	4.6	31	4.6
Consultants	7	5.4	3	3.3	84	6.0	90	6.1
Cosmetics	—	—	1	6.0	10	5.3	11	5.4
Diversified	7	3.9	1	1.8	68	4.6	69	5.0
Education	22	3.2	1	1.8	36	4.1	46	4.8
Electrical & Electronic	7	3.6	3	1.5	158	4.7	160	4.8
Finance/Banks	12	4.0	2	2.5	324	5.3	330	5.4
Food & Beverage	5	4.3	—	—	77	5.0	79	5.0
Forest & Paper Products	—	—	—	—	23	4.3	23	4.4
Gas Transmission Lines	1	4.0	—	—	14	4.2	15	4.2
Government	31	3.5	5	3.8	34	3.3	52	4.6
Hospital & Health Care	58	3.2	7	3.1	177	4.4	202	4.9

Hotel/Motel	2	5.0	—	—	12	5.2	13	5.2
Instrument Manufacturing	2	4.0	—	—	17	4.9	19	4.8
Insurance	11	4.6	2	4.2	152	5.7	155	6.0
Manufacturing	17	4.3	1	8.3	247	4.5	260	4.5
Mining	1	2.2	1	2.0	22	3.2	22	3.4
Nonprofit, Miscellaneous	5	3.9	3	3.2	45	5.0	48	5.3
Ofc./Computer/Bus. Equip.	1	6.0	—	—	28	5.7	28	6.0
Petroleum	1	4.0	1	4.0	35	3.7	35	3.8
Petroleum Services	—	—	—	—	12	2.4	12	2.4
Pharmaceutical	2	2.2	2	1.3	55	5.4	55	5.6
Printing & Publishing	7	3.6	—	—	55	4.8	57	5.1
Research & Development	2	4.7	—	—	32	5.1	33	5.3
Restaurant	—	—	—	—	21	5.4	21	5.4
Retail	9	3.7	1	5.7	74	5.0	80	5.1
Rubber	—	—	1	3.2	8	2.9	8	3.3
Steel, Alum., Copper, Ni.	1	4.4	—	—	21	2.8	22	2.9
Textiles	3	4.0	—	—	12	4.7	15	4.6
Tobacco	—	—	—	—	5	5.9	5	5.9
Transportation	2	4.3	—	—	26	4.7	27	4.8
Utilities	26	3.5	3	2.6	90	4.0	105	4.3
Other	10	3.9	1	1.3	176	4.9	180	5.0
TOTAL U.S. FIRMS	286	3.7	48	2.9	2492	4.8	2642	5.0
					Nonmanagement Employees			
TOTAL CANADIAN FIRMS	41	4.1	4	4.4	77	4.2	104	4.9

Source: *Report on the 1987–1988 Salary Budget Survey* (Scottsdale, Ariz.: American Compensation Association, 1987), pp. 2–4. Used by permission.

Exhibit 7.6   ASPA/Hansen Survey

JOB CODE: 045	JOB TITLE: SENIOR COMPENSATION ANALYST

JOB DESCRIPTION

ASSISTS IN THE DEVELOPMENT, INSTALLATION AND ADMINISTRATION OF COMPENSATION PROGRAMS. EVALUATES SALARIED, MIDDLE AND TOP MANAGEMENT POSITIONS. ASSISTS IN ADMINISTRATION OF MERIT RATING PROGRAM, REVIEWING CHANGES IN WAGES AND SALARIES FOR CONFORMANCE TO POLICY. AUDITS EVALUATION OF POSITIONS AND APPLICATION OF EXISTING CLASSIFICATIONS TO INDIVIDUALS. CONDUCTS COMPENSATION SURVEYS AND PARTICIPATES IN COMPENSATION SURVEYS CONDUCTED BY OTHER COMPANIES. ASSISTS IN UPDATING THE SALARY STRUCTURE. TYPICALLY REPORTS DIRECTLY TO COMPENSATION MANAGER OR COMPENSATION AND BENEFITS MANAGER.

SUMMARY OF ALL REPORTED SALARIES AND BONUSES

Data Reported in $000's	Firm Count	Incumbent Count	10th Percentile	25th Percentile	50th Percentile	Average	75th Percentile	90th Percentile
Salary (All Incumbents)	382	532	23.0	27.0	31.4	31.8	35.8	41.1
Salary (Bonus Non-Eligible)	332	470	23.4	27.0	31.4	31.7	35.6	40.3
Salary (Bonus Eligible)	50	62	20.0	25.4	31.3	32.3	37.0	47.8
Bonus (Bonus Reported)	35	39	0.7	1.2	2.0	2.7	3.4	6.7
Total (Bonus Reported)	35	39	21.6	27.0	31.3	33.5	37.8	45.2
Total (All Incumbents)	382	532	23.1	27.0	31.4	32.0	35.9	41.1

DEGREE OF MATCH:	LESS THAN DESCRIPTION 8.1 %	VERY CLOSE MATCH 76.5 %	MORE THAN DESCRIPTION 15.3 %

	Minimum	Midpoint	Maximum	%	
				Percent Eligible for Bonus: 12.7	Avg Bonus as % of Salary: 8.9
Average Salary Range	26.2	33.0	39.8	No. of Firms Reporting Range: 375	Compa-ratio (Based on Average): 95.0
Median Salary Range	26.1	32.9	39.5	No. of Firms in Compa-ratio: 362	Compa-ratio (Based on Median): 95.2

Exhibit 7.6 *(continued)*

| JOB CODE: | 045 | JOB TITLE: | | SR. COMPENSATION ANALYST | | | | | | | | | | |

SUMMARY ANALYSIS BY TOTAL ASSETS

Range	Average Scope (Millions)	Firm Count	Incumbent Count	Base Salary				Average Bonus	Average Total Compensation	Average No. of Ees. Supervised	Percent Eligible for Bonus	Average Bonus as Percent of Salary	Number of Firms Reporting Range	Average Salary Range Midpoint
				25th Percentile	50th Percentile	Average	75th Percentile							
UNDER $1 Bil	171.4	13	15	22.6	27.0	27.2	31.1	1.5	27.3	1	13.3	5.9	11	28.3
$1–5 Bil	3,011.2	23	27	22.0	24.0	26.2	31.6	1.6	26.5	0	18.5	6.3	22	29.4
OVER $5 Bil	19,240.1	34	52	25.9	31.2	33.0	38.0	5.3	33.6	1	13.5	14.5	33	32.5

SUMMARY ANALYSIS BY PREMIUMS

Range	Average Scope (Millions)	Firm Count	Incumbent Count	Base Salary				Average Bonus	Average Total Compensation	Average No. of Ees. Supervised	Percent Eligible for Bonus	Average Bonus as Percent of Salary	Number of Firms Reporting Range	Average Salary Range Midpoint
				25th Percentile	50th Percentile	Average	75th Percentile							
UNDER $80 Mil		3	5										3	
$80 < 400 Mil		7	8										7	26.7
$400 – 1 Bil	668.2	13	17	28.5	31.0	31.0	33.5	3.0	31.2	1	5.9	12.2	13	31.6
OVER $1 Bil	3,695.7	14	28	27.0	34.2	35.4	41.1		35.4	0			13	35.3

SUMMARY ANALYSIS BY OPERATING BUDGET

Range	Average Scope (Millions)	Firm Count	Incumbent Count	Base Salary				Average Bonus	Average Total Compensation	Average No. of Ees. Supervised	Percent Eligible for Bonus	Average Bonus as Percent of Salary	Number of Firms Reporting Range	Average Salary Range Midpoint
				25th Percentile	50th Percentile	Average	75th Percentile							
UNDER $40 Mil		5	6										5	
$40 < 90 Mil	67.5	11	11	24.1	26.6	28.3	32.0		28.3	2			9	29.8
$90 – 200 Mil	128.5	20	25	23.4	26.9	27.7	30.2	0.6	27.7	0	8.0	2.1	19	29.2
OVER $200 Mil	2,615.9	24	50	26.8	30.9	31.8	37.8		31.8	1			23	31.4

Exhibit 7.6 (*continued*)

JOB CODE: 045   JOB TITLE: SR. COMPENSATION ANALYST

SUMMARY ANALYSIS BY GROSS SALES / GROSS REVENUE

Range	Average Scope (Millions)	Firm Count	Incumbent Count	Base Salary 25th Percentile	Base Salary 50th Percentile	Base Salary Average	75th Percentile	Average Bonus	Average Total Compensation	Average No. of Ees. Supervised	Percent Eligible for Bonus	Average Bonus as Percent of Salary	Number of Firms Reporting Range	Average Salary Range Midpoint
UNDER $40 Million		3	3										3	
$40 < 100 Mil		5	7										4	
$100 < 200 Mil	136.4	21	21	26.0	29.7	29.1	32.6	1.5	29.4	0	23.8	6.4	19	31.3
$200 < 350 Mil	252.9	24	28	25.0	30.3	30.2	34.7	1.3	30.4	1	21.4	4.7	24	32.5
$350 < 650 Mil	476.1	31	37	26.5	30.8	30.8	35.6	1.7	30.8	0	5.4	5.9	28	33.0
$650 < 1.5 Bil	978.1	57	83	29.4	33.7	33.9	37.3	2.7	34.1	0	16.9	8.4	55	35.6
OVER 1.5 Bil	3,407.4	59	87	29.0	33.0	33.6	36.5	4.0	33.9	0	13.8	10.8	57	36.5

SUMMARY ANALYSIS BY TOTAL EMPLOYMENT

Range	Average Scope	Firm Count	Incumbent Count	Base Salary 25th Percentile	Base Salary 50th Percentile	Base Salary Average	75th Percentile	Average Bonus	Average Total Compensation	Average No. of Ees. Supervised	Percent Eligible for Bonus	Average Bonus as Percent of Salary	Number of Firms Reporting Range	Average Salary Range Midpoint
UNDER 250	102	22	30	26.9	31.4	30.7	33.6	2.6	31.2	1	16.7	8.1	21	31.9
250 - 650	436	19	22	25.0	29.1	30.8	36.4		30.8	1			18	30.7
850 - 1,300	972	43	48	24.6	29.1	28.8	31.9	2.2	29.1	1	14.6	8.1	42	31.5
1,300 - 3,500	2,316	109	129	24.8	29.1	29.4	32.8	1.5	29.5	1	14.7	5.9	103	31.3
3,500 - 10,000	5,608	120	182	27.0	32.7	32.6	37.0	3.1	32.7	0	9.3	9.2	111	34.1
OVER 10,000	37,863	70	121	30.2	34.0	34.8	38.0	4.5	35.2	1	11.6	12.0	68	35.6

Exhibit 7.6 (continued)

JOB CODE: 045   JOB TITLE: SR. COMPENSATION ANALYST

SUMMARY OF ANALYSIS BY LOCATION

Location	Firm Count	Incumbent Count	Base Salary				Average Bonus	Average Total Compensation	Average No. of Ees. Supervised	Percent Eligible for Bonus	Average Bonus as Percent of Salary	Number of Firms Reporting Range	Average Salary Range Midpoint
			25th Percentile	50th Percentile	Average	75th Percentile							
PHOENIX AZ	8	10	24.9	29.9	29.4	33.8	7.1	30.8	0	20.0	21.9	8	34.4
LOS ANGELES CA	14	28	31.4	34.1	34.8	36.9		34.8	1	3.6		14	35.7
SAN FRAN. CA	10	16	29.7	35.7	34.5	41.3	3.0	34.6	0	12.5	12.2	10	35.0
HARTFORD CT	6	10	27.7	29.9	31.0	36.5		31.0	0				
STAMFORD CT	7	10	29.6	33.3	33.7	36.5		33.7	0			7	35.8
WASHINGTON DC	12	14	21.8	28.8	29.8	35.8	1.9	29.9	0	7.1	6.7	11	30.1
ATLANTA GA	12	14	22.6	26.7	28.3	32.8	2.3	28.7	0	35.7	12.0	11	29.5
CHICAGO IL	28	40	25.0	32.3	31.7	35.5	1.9	31.8	1	5.0	6.1	26	34.2
BALTIMORE MD	8	11	25.0	27.5	28.5	32.0		28.5	1	9.1		7	31.2
BOSTON MA	15	16	27.5	28.3	30.2	30.8	1.4	30.6	0	25.0	4.7	13	32.0
MINNEAPOLIS MN	11	17	28.5	33.3	34.3	40.6	1.2	34.4	1	23.5	4.4	11	33.3
NEWARK NJ	12	15	23.0	29.2	30.7	37.3		30.7	0	13.3		12	34.3
NEW YORK NY	31	37	29.0	31.9	34.7	37.5	4.7	35.6	1	24.3	11.6	29	35.5
PHILADELPHIA PA	14	21	25.5	28.3	28.9	32.2	1.7	29.0	1	9.5	7.4	14	31.3
DALLAS TX	12	14	27.5	31.0	32.5	36.6	2.8	32.7	0	21.4	10.0	12	34.9
HOUSTON TX	10	15	28.1	32.1	33.3	38.4		33.3	0	13.3		10	35.3

Exhibit 7.6 (continued)

JOB CODE:	045	JOB TITLE:	SR. COMPENSATION ANALYST

SUMMARY OF ANALYSIS BY TYPE OF INDUSTRY

Type of Industry	Firm Count	Incumbent Count	Base Salary				Average Bonus	Average Total Compensation	Average No. of Ees. Supervised	Percent Eligible for Bonus	Average Bonus as Percent of Salary	Number of Firms Reporting Range	Average Salary Range Midpoint
			25th Percentile	50th Percentile	Average	75th Percentile							
Manufacturing/non-durable	45	59	29.8	32.7	33.9	37.3	1.3	34.0	0	13.6	4.1	45	36.2
Manufacturing/durable	51	70	29.2	32.7	32.8	36.0	2.0	32.9	0	18.6	7.2	48	33.8
Transportation	11	16	29.1	31.3	31.5	34.8		31.5	0			11	33.3
Utilities	28	44	29.8	34.0	33.8	38.1	1.4	33.8	1	9.1	3.8	28	36.6
Wholesale/Retail Trade	19	23	26.8	32.2	32.1	36.8	4.9	33.6	1	34.8	13.5	18	34.7
Finance	69	96	23.7	29.0	30.4	35.6	3.6	30.8	1	13.5	11.4	65	30.8
Insurance	40	65	27.1	31.9	32.7	35.8	2.0	32.8	1	1.5	7.7	39	32.7
Service/Profit	37	44	24.6	28.5	29.1	34.6	2.2	29.4	0	20.5	7.9	32	30.8
Service/Non-profit	25	37	26.1	29.0	30.7	33.8	1.4	30.8	1	8.1	5.1	24	31.6
Educational Services	14	22	23.4	25.1	25.7	28.1		25.7	1			14	26.8
Government	14	23	26.9	37.4	34.3	40.8		34.3	1			11	31.7
Construction/Mining	2	2										2	
Oil & Gas Exploration/Drilling	3	4										3	
Real Estate	2	2										1	

Source: ASPA/Hansen Human Resource Management Compensation Survey, 1986. Used by permission of Mercer Meidinger Hansen, Inc.

A sample page from this survey covering a compensation analyst's job is shown in Exhibit 7.7. The same information is provided for 127 other job titles. Because salary levels may vary by location in the Washington area, separate data are given for suburban Virginia, suburban Maryland, and the District of Columbia, as well as for the total area. Breakouts are provided by organization type, as well. Because a major competitor in the Washington area labor market is the federal government, the GS (General Schedule) rating of the job is provided. A table of the GS pay schedule also is provided; at the time of the survey, a compensation analyst's (GS 11) pay range was between $26,381 and $34,292.

Private Firms

A large number of private firms also provide salary data. A comprehensive listing of these firms and other sources of wage and salary data can be found in the *Prentice-Hall Personnel Policies* series volume *Compensation.* Compensation analysts should have access to the Prentice-Hall series, and to similar publications from the Bureau of National Affairs (*Policy and Practice Series: Compensation*) and Commerce Clearinghouse (*Personnel Guide*).

Maturity Curves

A variant to pricing a specific job in terms of the external market is the *maturity curve.* Maturity curves represent wage data for professions, for example, engineers, accountants, or physicians, rather than for specific jobs. A typical maturity curve presents wage or income data for the profession as a function of time since professional degree. An example of a maturity curve is seen in Exhibit 7.8.

In effect, maturity curves are substitutes for wage information about specific jobs. They simply report wage or income trends for professionals as a function of time in the profession. An external equity criterion is served in setting wage rates for employed professionals according to maturity curves to the extent that a firm wants to keep an employed professional on an income par with the rest of his or her profession.

Maturity curves, however, do not address issues of internal and individual equity very well. Income trends in a profession have little or nothing to do with the real value of an employed professional to his or her organization. Similarly, should a company make pay distinctions among those employed in a given profession according to their time at work since they acquired

Exhibit 7.7 Washington Personnel Association Survey

WASHINGTON PERSONNEL ASSOCIATION

1986 SALARY SURVEY REPORT

COMPENSATION ANALYST, 36

1. <u>POSITION DESCRIPTOR</u>

ADMINISTERS WAGE AND SALARY PLANS FOR EXEMPT AND NON-EXEMPT PERSONNEL. ASSISTS IN ESTABLISHING PAY PROCEDURES AND APPROVING SALARY ADJUSTMENTS. CONDUCTS WAGE AND SALARY SURVEYS TO OBTAIN DATA TO SUPPORT CHANGES IN POLICY, PRACTICE AND RATES OF PAY. ASSISTS MANAGERS IN INTERPRETING WAGE AND SALARY POLICIES AND PROCEDURES. PREPARES WAGE AND SALARY REPORTS. WORKS UNDER GENERAL DIRECTION. THIS IS USUALLY AN EXEMPT POSITION.

	SURVEY TOTAL	LOCATION SUB. VA.	LOCATION SUB. MD.	LOCATION DIST. OF COL.	RET	NP	FIN	PS	ORGANIZATION TYPE LG	HC	EI	RD/M	TELC	PUB	INS	OTH
2. BASE SALARIES REPORTED																
NO. OF SURVEY RESPONDENTS	48	17	11	20	3	11	10	2	2	0	4	1	5	1	1	8
NO. OF INCUMBENTS REPORTED	64	21	15	28	4	12	11	3	3	0	9	2	8	1	1	10
10TH %ILE ($000 OMITTED)	22.1	26.0	17.8	20.8	0.0	30.0	17.1	0.0	0.0	0.0	0.0	0.0	0.0	0.0	0.0	22.0
25TH %ILE ($000 OMITTED)	28.9	30.1	21.8	22.5	0.0	30.2	18.8	0.0	0.0	0.0	21.6	0.0	31.0	0.0	0.0	24.5
50TH %ILE ($000 OMITTED)	30.4	30.4	25.5	28.5	20.0	30.5	22.5	20.5	26.5	0.0	23.5	0.0	34.0	0.0	0.0	27.0
75TH %ILE ($000 OMITTED)	30.8	30.7	29.3	33.0	0.0	30.8	25.6	0.0	0.0	0.0	27.9	0.0	38.0	0.0	0.0	31.8
90TH %ILE ($000 OMITTED)	31.6	30.9	39.5	38.2	0.0	30.9	28.9	0.0	0.0	0.0	0.0	0.0	0.0	0.0	0.0	51.0
WTED AVG. ($000 OMITTED)	29.4	30.0	26.4	28.6	21.8	30.3	22.8	20.5	29.8	0.0	26.5	25.5	33.6	34.5	32.5	32.1

3. SALARY RANGES REPORTED

NO. OF SURVEY RESPONDENTS	43	16	10	17	2	9	9	2	2	0	4	1	5	0	1	8
MINIMUM ($000 OMITTED)	24.1	25.1	21.3	24.7	20.2	24.6	19.3	16.8	25.6	0.0	21.9	20.6	28.0	0.0	22.6	30.4
MIDPOINT ($000 OMITTED)	30.3	31.6	27.0	30.8	23.4	30.6	24.9	21.7	31.6	0.0	27.5	25.8	35.0	0.0	29.2	38.6
MAXIMUM ($000 OMITTED)	36.9	39.1	32.8	37.4	31.2	37.3	30.5	26.7	37.6	0.0	33.0	31.0	41.9	0.0	35.8	46.5

4. NEW HIRE RATES REPORTED

NO. OF SURVEY RESPONDENTS	16	6	4	6	1	1	4	1	2	0	0	0	2	0	1	4
LOWEST ($000 OMITTED)	15.0	15.0	16.7	19.4	0.0	0.0	15.0	0.0	0.0	0.0	0.0	0.0	0.0	0.0	0.0	20.8
AVERAGE ($000 OMITTED)	23.9	21.6	21.6	27.6	20.8	29.7	17.8	20.0	25.6	0.0	0.0	0.0	36.2	0.0	22.6	23.5
HIGHEST ($000 OMITTED)	39.4	29.7	27.1	39.4	0.0	0.0	20.2	0.0	0.0	0.0	0.0	0.0	0.0	0.0	0.0	26.9

5. COMPARISON TO PRIOR YEAR

% CHANGE IN WTED AVG.   5.3

6. FEDERAL GOVERNMENT

SERIES: 223   GS: 11

Source: *1986 Salary Survey Report* (Washington, D.C.: Washington Personnel Association, 1986), p. 79. Used by permission.

Exhibit 7.8   Maturity Curve—Scientists and Engineers

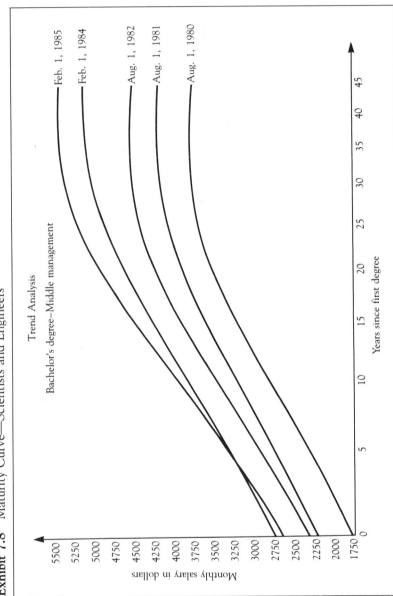

Trend Analysis

Bachelor's degree—Middle management

Source: Battelle Columbus Laboratories, *Report on 1985 National Survey of Compensation Paid Scientists and Engineers Engaged in Research and Development Activities.* Prepared for the U.S. Department of Energy, Office of Industrial Relations, 1985. Page J7.

their professional degrees, factors such as individual performance and company loyalty (seniority, or time with the employer) are not recognized.

Utilizing Survey Data

Regardless of whether wage and salary data are generated through an in-house survey or purchased from external sources, the compensation analyst needs to compare survey data with the figures from his or her own organization. A number of comparisons are needed; the following exhibits developed for the Heavyweight Manufacturing Company show how both in-house and purchased data can be used.

Heavyweight has a salary structure consisting of nine salary ranges. Adjustments to the midpoints in these salary ranges have been proposed by the compensation analyst; the comparisons to be made are between survey data and the proposed structure. It should be noted that survey data always lag behind current salary levels; the analyst would expect his or her own organization's current salaries to be greater than survey data, and would expect a proposed system to exceed survey levels by a considerable amount (depending on the actual and forecasted levels of inflation). Exhibit 7.9 shows the first comparison, that of Heavyweight's midpoints to average salaries in the survey. Note that average salaries rather than structure midpoints are used: Heavyweight is competing against the salaries paid by other employers in the labor market, not their structures.

To help account for the lack of currency of the data, the compensation analyst has obtained the range adjustments contemplated by organizations in the survey; these data are shown in Exhibit 7.10. The analyst has also acquired data from two trade association surveys, also shown in Exhibit 7.10, indicating annual percentage range adjustments for several previous years. Finally, the compensation analyst has graphed comparison data; this comparison is seen in Exhibit 7.11. In this case, the comparisons are between the proposed Heavyweight wage curve (constructed by connecting the midpoints of each pay grade) and (1) current industry wage data from Exhibit 7.9 and (2) industry wage data adjusted for expected increases, based on data in Exhibit 7.10. This comparison indicates that Heavyweight's proposed structure will continue to exceed industry wage levels.

Of course, the kinds of comparisons the compensation analyst will make depend on the kinds of problems leading the organization to conduct a wage and salary survey in the first place. However, both tabular and graphic pre-

Exhibit 7.9 Heavyweight Manufacturing Company Midpoint Comparison

Grade	Survey Population	Heavyweight Midpoint[a]	Sample Wage Survey Metalworking Personnel Group—December, 1999 Survey Average Wage	Salary Proposal July 1, 2000 Plus or Minus Survey Dollars	Percent
3	33	$4.85	$4.46	$+.39	+8.7%
4	91	5.37	4.93	+.44	+8.9
5	10	5.91	5.44	+.47	+8.6
6	4	6.40	5.87	+.53	+9.0
7	27	7.04	6.46	+.58	+9.0
8	20	7.70	7.08	+.62	+8.8
Overall (Weighted)	185	$5.82	$5.35	$+.47	+8.8% above average of midpoints

Heavyweight
Current Population   384

(Results of 1998 survey =   11.1%
above average of midpoints)

[a]Midpoints represent midpoint of salary structure ranges.

Source: R. Beatty, N. F. Crandall, C. H. Fay, R. Mathis, G. T. Milkovich, and M. J. Wallace, Jr., *How to Administer Wage–Salary Programs and Perform Job Evaluations*. © 1979 by the authors. Used by permission.

Exhibit 7.10   1999 Wage Trend

	Metalworking Sample Survey		Salary Proposal July 1, 2000
Date	Company	Surveyed Employee Population	Actual or Anticipated Wage Adjustment
6–1–1999[a]	Zankowski's Metalworks	52	6.0%
9–1–1999	Gama Products	78	5.2
9–1–1999	Mannix, Inc.	57	5.0
2–1–2000	Alpha Manufacturing	145	5.7
1–1–2000	Lumman's Laminations, Inc.	198	5.4
2–1–2000	Tip & Tater Company	86	5.5
3–1–2000	Alco Electronics	123	4.8
7–1–2000[a]	Exco Heavy Construction	—	Unknown
7–1–2000[a]	Machined Tools	—	Unknown
—	Tool & Die Designers	—	Unknown
Overall		739	5.4%

[a]Unionized Firms—Zankowski's a deferred wage increase and contracts to be negotiated for other two firms.

	Other Trend Data				
Survey	1995	1996	1997	1998	1999
AMA Sample Survey Trend	3.7	4.0	4.7	5.6	6.5
Metalworking Trades Survey	2.0	1.6	4.4	7.1	4.7

Source: R. Beatty, N. F. Crandall, C. H. Fay, R. Mathis, G. T. Milkovich, and M. J. Wallace, Jr., *How to Administer Wage–Salary Programs and Perform Job Evaluations.* © 1979 by the authors. Used by permission.

Exhibit 7.11   Comparison of Proposed Heavyweight Midpoints to Metal-working Survey Average Wage

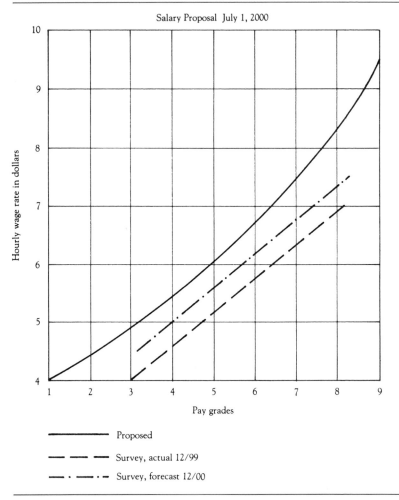

Source: R. Beatty, N. F. Crandall, C. H. Fay, R. Mathis, G. T. Milkovich, and M. J. Wallace, Jr., *How to Administer Wage–Salary Programs and Perform Job Evaluations.* © by the authors. Used by permission.

sentations of the information received will increase the value of that information and the ease of proposing changes to management.

Summary

In this chapter, we have examined the procedures most organizations follow in pricing their job structures, and have identified several key points to remember about this process. First, the manager must select the jobs to be priced (benchmark jobs); these are key jobs because they provide the links between the organization's own internal wage structure and the structure of wages prevailing in external labor markets. Next, the manager must decide on the source of the data to be acquired; we have examined two major ways of obtaining market information. First, the manager can design his or her own survey. Such a practice results in gaining highly specific information, but it is extremely expensive and demands high levels of research skills. Second, the manager can obtain information from existing surveys. We have summarized the major steps one should follow if one decides to conduct his or her own survey and have also reviewed the major surveys already in existence. Finally, we have examined the procedures one should follow in using and analyzing survey data.

It is crucial for the compensation analyst to get wage and salary survey data if external equity is to be maintained. Whether the analyst chooses to do his or her own survey or to acquire survey data from other sources depends on the specific problem(s) facing the organization. Most larger organizations will probably acquire data from both sources.

Naturally, even the most comprehensive survey will not "tell" the analyst what a specific job should be paid. A wide range of salaries exists for most jobs. The base salary for senior compensation analysts, for example, is as low as $23,000 and as high as $47,800, depending upon the industry and other circumstances (see Exhibit 7.6). Wage and salary surveys only provide benchmarks for the compensation analyst. Before setting up a wage structure, the analyst must consider internal equity issues, that is, the relative value of jobs within the organization.

Postscript

We began our discussion of wage-setting practices and techniques as we began our discussion of the theory of wage determination, with processes related to external rather than internal equity. Although this reverses the order found in most books, we feel it is important to underline the sovereignty of external equity influences on wages over internal equity influences. Certainly the power of a wage or salary to attract employees is based solely on external equity considerations. The retention power of a wage or salary is also influenced heavily by external equity considerations. When external and internal equity considerations are in conflict, we suspect, though lacking scientific evidence, that external equity takes precedence. Comparable worth advocates have certainly found this to be the case. Any organization constructing a wage and salary structure *de novo* is likely to start with market data. In the ongoing organization, of course, internal and external equity processes are likely to be carried out simultaneously, with strong effects upon each other. Such a simultaneous presentation is, unfortunately, not possible in the format of a book.

Notes

[1] U.S. Department of Labor, *Dictionary of Occupational Titles*, 4th ed. (Washington, D.C.: U.S. Government Printing Office, 1977).

Job Evaluation and the Wage–Salary Structure

Key Issues and Questions for This Chapter

After you have studied this chapter, you should be able to address the following key issues and questions:

1. What is job evaluation?
2. What is the relationship between job evaluation and internal equity?
3. What are the major types of job evaluation available to managers?
4. What are compensable factors?
5. How is job analysis a part of job evaluation?
6. What are the steps in administering job evaluation?
7. What major job evaluation programs are available to managers?
8. What are the steps in building an internal wage structure?

Introduction

As we noted in Chapter 7, most organizations do not rely solely on market data to establish a wage structure. First of all, it is difficult for any organization to collect wage and salary data for all jobs in the organization. Most jobs in any organization have some characteristics unique to that organization. Secretaries in one organization, for example, may be expected to operate automated data retrieval equipment requiring special training; in another organization, secretaries may have to deal with no higher technology than the electric typewriter. There are also jobs in many organizations for which there is no market; that is, the job is truly unique to that organization. The so-called administrative assistant is a job for which this is frequently the case. The variety of abilities, skills, company-related experiences, and specific training often required belies the generality of the title. Secondly, even when market data are available for a job, those data do not consist of a single wage but are made up of a broad range of wages reflecting location, size, industry, employee demographics (such as seniority and performance level), and other factors.

Third, even if single rates (with adjustments for location, and so on) were available for all jobs in the company through surveys, such rates might not satisfy internal equity demands. The value of an engineer to company A and company B relative to the value of a lawyer to those two companies could vary significantly, depending on environmental pressures. If company A had a history of discrimination cases but its products were very successful, and company B had few legal problems but had significant quality control problems, the relative worth of lawyers and engineers could vary considerably. Finally, many organizations prefer to maintain the ability to use wages as an administrative tool; while heeding the market, they also wish to administer their own wages within the sometimes broad limits imposed by the market.

Thus, for many organizations, lack of information and the existence of internal equity considerations suggest that market data alone are not adequate to build the wage and salary structure. In these organizations, the structure is usually built on internal equity considerations and then adjusted to meet market forces. These internal equity decisions, when formalized, become the process known as *job evaluation*, that is, what jobs are worth to the organization: which jobs are of similar value, which are worth more, and which are worth less. After describing current approaches to job evaluation, we will show how the results of job evaluation are merged with market data to achieve the final wage–salary structure by organizations with this point of view.

In other organizations, a decision has been made to pay primarily on the basis of external equity considerations. This market pricing strategy has been made feasible largely because the advent of high-speed electronic computers allows ready access to current market data. In fact, few organizations have either a purely internal pricing strategy or a purely external pricing strategy. Most organizations end up in a compromise between the two extremes. Market pricing strategies and several varieties of implementation will be discussed at the end of this chapter.

Job Evaluation

The immediate purpose of job evaluation is to create a hierarchy of jobs based on their value, or worth, to the organization doing the evaluating. Job evaluation is the process by which one tries to ensure internal equity — that jobs of comparable worth receive comparable wages. It is not, in theory, concerned with the value of the job in the external market. (However, as Schwab[1] and other compensation theorists have noted, job evaluation as practiced by most organizations is primarily an administrative procedure designed to develop market rates for non-key jobs and otherwise to justify pay levels. Most compensation analysts are all too familiar with the forced reevaluation of jobs to bring evaluation scores more into line with known market rates.)

Job evaluation usually consists of six steps:

1. determining the sources of value
2. conducting the job analysis
3. establishing job families
4. choosing an evaluation method
5. conducting the evaluation
6. establishing a wage structure.

After the initial establishment of a structure, the structure also must be adjusted on some periodic basis. We will consider each of these steps in turn.

Compensable Factors — Sources of Value

The first major decision to be made by the management of the organization is the source of value in jobs. Some job evaluation techniques require that these sources of value be made explicit, but all job evaluations require that the organization think about what aspects of a job have value to the organization. These sources of value are known as *compensable factors*. In the discussion of internal equity in Chapter 3, we examined the demand-side and supply-side aspects of job value. In practice, compensable factors may be classified into *job inputs* (what employees bring to the job) and *job outputs*. Inputs include experience; education; effort; responsibility for people, assets, or workflow; and ability to function under various working conditions. Job outputs include work outcomes such as production, profit, or results.

Job Analysis

Having decided on the sources of job value, the compensation analyst must develop job descriptions that will allow him or her to estimate the degree to which jobs possess the factors that create value. This is generally done through *job analysis*. It is important to differentiate job analysis and job evaluation. Job analysis is a systematic study of the tasks making up a job, the employee skills required to do the job, time factors, situation-specific factors (such as the technology used), certain physical aspects (for example, lighting and temperature), information flows, interpersonal and group interactions, and historical traditions. From good job analysis procedures, job descriptions can be written. One reason it is important for the compensation analyst to make decisions about sources of value before selecting a job analysis technique or developing job descriptions is to ensure that the job analysis procedure addresses those dimensions of a job that give it value to the organization.

Ordinarily, the compensation analyst will not be the individual doing the job analysis. Because job analysis is the basis for many human resource management processes — such as performance appraisal, selection, and training — each of which requires knowledge of different aspects of a job to different degrees, most organizations have specially trained job analysts who can coordinate the analysis with the needs of other personnel specialists. Thus, the compensation analyst receives a series of job descriptions to work with from the job analyst.

A typical job description the compensation analyst might get is shown in Exhibit 8.1. This description, after a general summary of the job, lists the key tasks performed by the employee and the amount of time devoted to each task. A task-statement data sheet at the end of the description notes the equipment used, the knowledge, skills, and abilities required for each task, and the level of difficulty or consequence of error associated with each task.

Exhibit 8.1   Job Description

Date Issued: _____

Job Title: Secretary II

Summary of Job:

Under general supervision independently performs assigned administrative and secretarial duties. Maintains log of executive staffs' activities and whereabouts. Executes special assignments as requested by various staff personnel.

Job Tasks:

Task 1:   10% — Keeps records of special activities for various staff representatives.

Task 2:   60% — Performs general secretarial duties for all four members of executive staff (correspondence, reports, and telephone duties).

Task 3:   10% — Communicates and answers telephone. Supplies appropriate information when possible and directs caller to appropriate other if not.

Task 4:   10% — Executes special assignments as requested.

Task 5:   10% — Maintains staff appointment calendars and itineraries. Coordinates trip details and schedules with travel department.

Supervisory Responsibilities: None

Supervision Received: Direct 25% — General 25%

External Contacts: Customers, operating managers, travel department

Equipment Used: Telephone, IBM Selectric, Electronic Calculator, Copier, Dictaphone.

Employee: _____
Supervisor: _____

Exhibit 8.1   (*continued*)

Working Conditions

    Hazards: None

    Work Environment: Comfortable

    Noise Level: Below normal office exposure

    Lighting: Excellent

    Temperature: Controlled 70–72 degrees

    Miscellaneous: —

Job Training

    A.   Required Experience: (Include other jobs) 2–3 years secretarial exposure

    B.   Formal Educational Experience: Time in semesters/quarters

        Vocational Courses: —

        High School Courses: Shorthand, typing

        College Courses: —

        Continuing Education: —

    C.   Internal Training Programs: Telephone etiquette/message-taking

Task Statement: 1–5

    1.   Equipment Utilized: Typewriter, telephone, Dictaphone®, calculator, copier

    2.   Knowledge Required: Filing, business forms, telephone etiquette, general business experience

    3.   Skills Required: Typing, shorthand, and mathematical

    4.   Abilities Required: As indicated, and good at thinking on his/her feet.

    5.   Time Spent and Frequency of Performance: —

    6.   Level of Difficulty/Consequence of Error: Varies by particular task/basically error-free

---

Source: Adapted from R. Beatty, N. F. Crandall, C. H. Fay, R. Mathis, G. T. Milkovich, and M. J. Wallace, Jr., *How to Administer Wage–Salary Programs and Perform Job Evaluations.* © 1979 by the authors. Used by permission.

Further information is provided on supervisory responsibilities, supervision received, external contacts, and equipment used on the job. Finally, different aspects of working conditions are noted and the variety of training (both formal and on-the-job) is listed. Similar data sheets would be provided to the compensation analyst for all jobs in the job family under evaluation.

Most compensation analysts treat the job descriptions received with a good deal of skepticism unless they are developed by experienced job analysts. Most employees understand fully the impact of the job description on final pay levels, and the compensation analyst can expect to find in the description (even in the absence of deliberate falsehood) a self-serving bias that tends to exaggerate the job characteristics an incumbent believes are related to salary level if the employee writes his or her own description. One of the authors, for example, received an offer from a social worker in state government who, representing a number of individuals with the same job title, wished to hire someone to help rewrite the job description of the social worker series, making sure that the words used in the description would support a higher salary level than it currently received. No suggestion of falsehood was raised; rather it was a question of the appropriate semantics. The proper words, the author was assured, would trigger grade level associations in the minds of the state compensation analysts who would review the reclassification request.

The compensation analyst greets with even more skepticism the assurance that there are good up-to-date job descriptions for all the jobs in an organization. Again, this is not so much the case when a professional level job analyst working in the organization makes the claim. Typically, many of the job descriptions are old (and the jobs they "describe" have changed radically), many are up-to-date but exaggerated, many are just plain wrong, all have at least one significant piece of information missing, and there are descriptions for jobs that no longer exist and jobs for which there are no descriptions.

This pessimistic view of the situation is important to note because any salary structure based on job evaluation will be only as good or bad as the job descriptions on which the job evaluations are based. If the job descriptions are inaccurate, the job evaluation results will be at least as inaccurate and there will be little hope that any form of equity will be served.

Job Families

Job families are groups of jobs that have some set of characteristics in common. We can speak of clerical, sales, managerial, and production jobs; each of these constitutes a job family. Job families may also be defined more broadly, as for example, nonexempt and exempt job categories. In undertaking a job evaluation, the compensation analyst first must decide the range of jobs to which the job evaluation process will be applied (and thus, the number of job-worth structures that will be constructed). Thus, all jobs could be evaluated under one system, and a single job-worth structure set up as a result. Or, alternatively, a job-worth structure could be set up for each job family. There are several arguments for having a single job-worth structure, but most of them are based on one of two factors. First, an organization ends up with a simple wage and salary structure, in that one job is paid in one range, and a second job in a second range. In the end, jobs are paid in common units (dollars), and the job-worth structure is common to all jobs, too. If different structures are developed, say for managers and supervisors, points of overlap, between lower managers and upper-level supervisors, for example, can create problems.

Second, aside from difficulties from the organization's point of view, employees may not feel internal equity goals are being met if they compare their pay to the pay of others whose jobs are valued under a different system, or to the pay they receive when they are moved to a different job which is valued under a different system. This is a litigious age, and an employer may find it difficult to justify valuing one set of jobs on one basis while valuing another on a second basis, particularly if the two systems result in an adverse effect on any legally protected group.

Countering these arguments, proponents of multiple job-worth structures point out that most organizations do have separate pay systems, for example, exempt versus nonexempt, or union versus nonunion, and for a variety of practical reasons often wish to recognize those differences in the job-worth structure. If the compensation analyst does decide on separate job-worth structures, he or she will use a variety of criteria to help determine which jobs should be clustered into which job families. The job-worth structures will then be constructed for each of those job families.

The criteria used for clustering jobs into families should be related to characteristics addressing the value of a job in the market and to the organization. Such factors make the process of job evaluation easier and include:

1. common skills
2. common occupational qualifications
3. common technology

4. common licensing

5. common working conditions.

These five criteria can be used to identify job families within which jobs can be readily evaluated using a common set of compensable factors. Likewise, they separate groups of jobs that need very different kinds of compensable factors for evaluation.

Criteria related to administering the final wage and salary system include:

1. common union jurisdictions

2. common work place

3. common status with respect to the law (for example, exempt versus nonexempt)

4. common career paths

5. organizational tradition

6. special compensation arrangements (for example, sales personnel and executives).

Administrative criteria used to cluster jobs have no impact on the evaluation itself, but they do affect the process of implementing and administering the final structure. Thus, ordinarily, all jobs in a bargaining unit are evaluated and placed in a single structure: the organization does not wish to be constrained by a union contract specifying evaluation method, wage level, or other issues if the job is not part of the bargaining unit. Similarly, it is desirable to have as many jobs as possible in a single work place in a single system because employees are most likely to make equity comparisons within a work site. Having the possibility of different evaluation systems in different sites allows greater administrative discretion without risking unfavorable internal equity judgments.

It is desirable to keep jobs in the same career paths evaluated under the same system to facilitate compensation decisions as employees move through the path. Tradition and organization culture are most important when organizations merge. Maintenance of separate evaluation systems and salary structures, at least initially, may reasssure the employees of a takeover target of some stability in pay and relative job status. A later folding in of the takeover target system into that of the parent underlines the subordinate status of the takeover target.

Typical job families used in job evaluations based on these criteria include sales, managerial, supervisory, production, technical, and clerical, though other categories are sometimes used.

Job Evaluation Techniques

Once the information about jobs has been gathered and the jobs have been arranged into families, the next step is to select the appropriate job evaluation technique. Hundreds of job evaluation techniques have been developed over the years. The great majority of them, however, fall into one of four general types, which are differentiated by two major issues. The first issue concerns the directness of the evaluation: whether a job being evaluated is compared to some other job directly (that is, ranking), or whether it is measured against some standard to produce a rating, with the rating then being compared with the ratings of other jobs. The second issue concerns the specificity of the evaluation: whether the comparison is made on the basis of the whole job, or whether specific factors in jobs are compared. These characteristics suggest a classification table for the four major types of job evaluation as depicted in Exhibit 8.2. We shall look at all four types: first at the two whole-job systems, then at the two systems utilizing specific job factors.

Ranking   The ranking of jobs is the simplest evaluation system available. When there are fewer than twenty jobs to be evaluated, ranking is probably an acceptable method. It is simple, fast, and inexpensive. There are two

Exhibit 8.2   Four Approaches to Job Evaluation

	Whole Job	*Specific Job Factors*
Job vs. Job	ranking method	factor comparison method
Job vs. Standards	classification method	point method

Source: Adapted from R. Beatty, N. F. Crandall, C. H. Fay, R. Mathis, G. T. Milkovich, and M. J. Wallace, Jr., *How to Administer Wage–Salary Programs and Perform Job Evaluations.* © 1979 by the authors. Used by permission.

ways of ranking jobs. The first is a forced ranking, done either by one individual or a committee. In either case, one job is chosen as having most value to the organization, a second as having next most value, and so forth, until one job is chosen as having the least value to the organization. There are several problems inherent in this technique.

First, there are no standards for comparison. Job A may be seen as more valuable than job B because it requires much more responsibility; job B may be seen as more valuable than job C because of educational differentials, and so on. This lack of standards makes rankings particularly vulnerable to bias when most of the incumbents of some but not all jobs are women or minorities. In addition, forced rankings do not allow for jobs having equal value. Nor are changes in job value readily accommodated by the ranking method. Ranking does not indicate how much *more* value job A has than job B, and value differentials are essential if internal equity is to be preserved. Most individuals appear to have trouble ranking many jobs: people can agree on which jobs have most value and which have least, but the mid-level jobs are difficult to differentiate.

To get around this, proponents of ranking techniques have used paired comparisons, in which each job is compared to every other job and the job of more value in each pair is noted. The score for a job is the number of times it is considered the more valuable; ranks are based on these scores. There are two drawbacks to the paired-comparison technique. First, there is still no guarantee that comparisons are made on the same basis. A second equally serious drawback is that as the number of jobs to be ranked rises arithmetically, the number of paired comparisons to be made rises geometrically. The formula showing the number of comparison decisions to be made is:

$$CD = \frac{N(N\text{-}1)}{2}$$

where N is the number of jobs to be ranked. Thus, with seven jobs to be ranked, the analyst must make $(7)(6) \div 2 = 21$ comparison decisions; with twenty jobs to be ranked, the number of comparison decisions rises to $(20)(19) \div 2 = 190$! On the whole, then, ranking is simply not a very satisfactory method of evaluating jobs, except in a very small organization. Even then, better alternatives, such as market pricing, exist.

Classification The classification method of job evaluation is a job-to-standard comparison technique that solves a number of problems inherent in simple job ranking. The compensation analyst using the classification method first decides how many categories, or classification steps, the job value structure is to be broken down into. A typical number of classes is around eight; the number might vary from five to fifteen.

The second step in the classification method is writing definitions for each class. These definitions are the standards against which the jobs will be compared. Exhibit 8.3 shows a part of a classification system developed for clerical workers. Notice that although several factors are used to define class levels, a job is compared to these standards on the whole-job basis, not on a factor-by-factor basis. The compensation analyst compares the jobs to be evaluated with the class definitions, placing jobs in appropriate classifications.

Although classification does provide specific standards for comparison and does accommodate changes in the value of individual jobs, it too has some drawbacks. There still is not much detail in the standards, and a rigid relationship between job factors of value is assumed. In Exhibit 8.3, for example, it is assumed that no clerical job will exist that entails complex work and supervisory responsibility but that has no public contact. As a result of this system, many jobs in large organizations using the classification method are likely to be forced to fit into classes that they don't entirely match when it comes to job evaluation. The fact that some jobs do not exactly fit their classes may lead to some disagreement about the equity of the final value structure.

Exhibit 8.3   Clerical Worker Classification System

CLASS I	Simple work, no supervisory responsibility, no public contact
CLASS II	Simple work, no supervisory responsibility, public contact
CLASS III	Work of medium complexity, no supervisory responsibility, public contact
CLASS IV	Work of medium complexity, supervisory responsibility, public contact
CLASS V	Complex work, supervisory responsibility, public contact

A related problem is tied to the decision of how many classifications there should be. If there are too few classes for the number of jobs in an organization, it will be difficult to differentiate job value, and thus wage levels, sufficiently. If there are too many, the drafting of class definitions will be difficult, and the results of placing particular jobs in certain classes will be more open to dispute. The rigid structure of most classification systems leads administrators to work around the system "via administrative finesse" to achieve their compensation aims.[2] On the positive side, a classification system can be constructed simply, quickly, and inexpensively. It is also an easy system to understand (if not to get agreement on); organizations that have open pay plans may find that a classification system helps in its communications with its employees. While the federal government has established a point factor system for many of its jobs, the majority of federal jobs (about three-fifths) are still evaluated using a classification system.

Factor Comparison   In factor comparison, jobs are compared against other jobs on the basis of how much of some desired factor they possess. It therefore ranks certain aspects of jobs rather than whole jobs. It is also one of the most complex of job evaluation systems and requires considerable training if it is to be done well.

The first step is for the compensation analyst to acquire job descriptions from which judgments can be made about the factors the jobs possess. Traditionally, five factors are used in the factor comparison method: the mental, physical, and skill requirements of the job, the responsibility entailed by the job, and the working conditions associated with the job.

From the entire set of jobs to be evaluated, the compensation analyst then selects ten to fifteen key jobs. (The nature of key jobs was fully described in Chapter 7.) For factor comparison, the primary requirements are two: key jobs must show considerable variation on the five factors, and there must be well-defined rates—rates that the organization considers legitimate.

To start the actual evaluation process, the analyst ranks each job on each factor. This is conventionally done vertically; an abbreviated version is shown in Exhibit 8.4. The vertical ranking is identical to whole-job ranking except that jobs are ranked on each factor with respect to the amount of that factor present in, or required by, the job.

The next stage is to take the market rate for each of the key jobs and apportion that rate across factors. An example of this apportionment is shown in Exhibit 8.5. In this stage, the compensation analyst is deciding how much of the salary associated with a specific key job is being paid for mental

Exhibit 8.4   Factor Comparison Method:
Step 1—Vertical Ranking

Key Jobs	Factors				
	Mental Requirements	*Physical Requirements*	*Skill Requirements*	*Responsibility*	*Working Conditions*
Job A	1	5	2	3	3
Job B	2	4	4	1	6
Job C	3	6	1	6	4
Job D	4	1	6	2	1
Job E	5	3	5	5	2
Job F	6	2	3	4	5

NOTE: The rank of 6 is highest.

Source: Adapted from: R. Beatty, N. F. Crandall, C. H. Fay, R. Mathis, G. T. Milkovich, and M. J. Wallace, Jr. *How to Administer Wage–Salary Programs and Perform Job Evaluations.* © 1979 by the authors. Used by permission.

Exhibit 8.5 Factor Comparison Method:
Step 2—Allocation of Wage Across Factors
Step 3—Ranking of Allocations Across Jobs

	Factors					
Key Jobs	Mental Requirements	Physical Requirements	Skill Requirements	Responsibility	Working Conditions	Current Market Rate (Dollars/Hour)
Job A	.40 (1)	2.00 (5)	0.40 (1)	0.75 (3)	0.30 (4)	3.85
Job B	1.75 (2)	1.50 (4)	1.95 (3)	0.20 (1)	2.20 (6)	7.60
Job C	2.15 (3)	2.05 (6)	2.70 (5)	4.10 (6)	0.35 (3)	11.35
Job D	3.00 (4)	0.25 (1)	2.80 (6)	0.40 (2)	0.10 (1)	6.55
Job E	3.20 (5)	1.35 (3)	2.50 (4)	2.50 (5)	0.25 (2)	9.80
Job F	4.10 (6)	0.75 (2)	1.80 (2)	2.10 (4)	0.70 (5)	9.45

NOTE: The rank of 6 is highest.

Source: Adapted from: R. Beatty, N. F. Crandall, C. H. Fay, R. Mathis, G. T. Milkovich, and M. J. Wallace, Jr. *How to Administer Wage–Salary Programs and Perform Job Evaluations.* © 1979 by the authors. Used by permission.

requirements, how much for physical requirements, and so on. This allocation is made for each key job. When allocations have been made for all key jobs, the dollar figures for each factor are ranked across the jobs. These rankings are shown in Exhibit 8.5 in parentheses. For example, job F has more of its market wage allocated to mental requirements than does any other job, so it receives the highest rank of 6.

The purpose of this ranking becomes clearer in Exhibit 8.6, where a comparison of the two rankings is presented. The vertical rankings are based on the factors' importance to the jobs, or on the extent to which they form a basis for the jobs' value. The allocation rankings indicate the relative pay currently given the jobs for each factor. If the jobs are truly key jobs, there should be little or no difference between the two sets of numbers. The reconciliation shown in Exhibit 8.6, then, is basically a validity check on whether the jobs chosen are truly key jobs. It can be seen in the exhibit that generally there is no difference in the two sets of rankings, except with respect to the skill requirements for job C. The current market rate allocated to job C's skills is considerably higher than the skill requirements would indicate. It may be that these skills are currently in short supply or that union pressure has forced up wages. Regardless of the reason, job C is not a key job, and must be discarded from the evaluation for the time being. The elimination of job C brings the rest of the rankings into exact agreement.

The compensation analyst is then ready to set up a job evaluation scale to be used in evaluating the other jobs in the organization. An example of such a scale is shown in Exhibit 8.7. The data from Exhibit 8.5 have been rearranged to show ascending dollar values for each factor. The amount allocated to each factor for the key jobs is indicated by the anchoring of value levels by the key jobs. It is for this reason that the validation of key jobs in the previous stage is so important. As another check, the compensation analyst will take an additional set of key jobs and value them using the scales. That is, key job G will be compared on each factor with respect to jobs A through F and a value level determined. Total value assigned to the job will be summed, and that value will be compared with market data. There should be a close match for the additional set of key jobs. If there is, the compensation analyst can then use the scales, with the additional key jobs as further anchors of value, to evaluate the rest of the jobs in the organization.

Factor comparison does have some advantages over both ranking and classification systems. It is much more reliable than either of the other two because of the two rankings made. It also addresses internal and external

Exhibit 8.6 Reconciliation of Vertical Ranking and Allocation of Wages Ranking

Key Jobs	*Mental Requirements*	*Physical Requirements*	*Skill Requirements*	*Responsibility*	*Working Conditions*
Job A	V-1 A-1	V-5 A-5	V-2 A-1	V-3 A-3	V-3 A-4
Job B	V-2 A-2	V-4 A-4	V-4 A-3	V-1 A-1	V-6 A-6
Job C	V-3 A-3	V-6 A-6	V-1 A-5	V-6 A-6	V-4 A-3
Job D	V-4 A-4	V-1 A-1	V-6 A-6	V-2 A-2	V-1 A-1
Job E	V-5 A-5	V-3 A-3	V-5 A-4	V-5 A-5	V-2 A-2
Job F	V-6 A-6	V-2 A-2	V-3 A-2	V-4 A-4	V-5 A-5

Factors

Source: Adapted from: R. Beatty, N. F. Crandall, C. H. Fay, R. Mathis, G. T. Milkovich, and M. J. Wallace, Jr. *How to Administer Wage–Salary Programs and Perform Job Evaluations.* © 1979 by the authors. Used by permission.

Exhibit 8.7   Job Evaluation Scale for Additional Jobs

Job Value	Mental Requirements	Physical Requirements	Skill Requirements	Responsibility	Working Conditions
.00					Job D
.20				Job B	Job E/Job A
.40	Job A	Job D		Job D	
.60			Job A	Job A	Job F
.80		Job F			
1.00					
.20		Job E			
.40		Job B			
.60			Job F		
.80	Job B	Job A	Job B	Job F	
2.00					Job B
.20					
.40			Job E	Job E	
.60			Job D		
.80					
3.00	Job D				
.20	Job E				
.40					
.60					
.80					
4.00					
.20	Job F				
.40					

Factors (column group heading over Mental, Physical, Skill, Responsibility, Working Conditions)

Source: Adapted from: R. Beatty, N. F. Crandall, C. H. Fay, R. Mathis, G. T. Milkovich, and M. J. Wallace, Jr. How to Administer Wage–Salary Programs and Perform Job Evaluations. © 1979 by the authors. Used by permission.

equity issues at the same time. However, there are some major drawbacks to the use of this system. Extensive training is needed to use it effectively. As dollar values change, particularly in periods of inflation, the whole system has to be changed. More seriously, market rates tend to change differently for different jobs, thus compelling extensive reworking of the system. Some compensation analysts argue that not all jobs can be analyzed accurately in terms of the five factors traditionally used. Finally, as the example of job C indicates, the reconciliation of internal and external equity issues is incomplete.

Conceptually, the factor comparison system is a primitive form of mulitple regression, a statistical technique that fits internal job evaluation factors to external market rates. The internal value of jobs exists only in terms of external market rates, though those rates are allocated based on internal norms. Given that much more sophisticated and reliable (to say nothing of ease of use) market pricing techniques are available that allow for broader choice of compensable factors, it seems strange that anyone would persist in a factor comparison approach, or even some of its variants. In the balance, the factor comparison system of job evaluation is cumbersome and not appropriate when labor markets have any instability. As a final note, picture yourself in the position of a compensation analyst trying to explain to a worker why a job is valued as it is under this system.

Point Factor Method   The point factor method, or one of its variations, is the most commonly used job evaluation method, and the one that seems most sensible for use by many organizations. The first step in the point factor method is to choose the factors to be used to rate each job. Some typical compensable factors are education, experience required, need to work independently, physical demands, visual/mental demand, responsibility for equipment, responsibility for material, responsibility for the safety of others, supervisory responsibility, working conditions, accident and health hazards, contact with the public, and manual dexterity. In fact, any aspect of a job for which a company is willing to pay can be a compensable factor.

Having chosen the compensable factors, the compensation analyst must define each factor in some detail and then develop a scale for each factor. A sample factor scale, for education, is shown in Exhibit 8.8. Notice that besides the definition of the factor itself, there is a definition for each level of the scale. There is no optimal number of scale levels, nor do all factor scales have to have the same number of levels.

The compensation analyst then decides how many points will be used

Exhibit 8.8   Point Factor Method Compensable Factor Scale

Education — 300 points

    This factor measures the amount of formal education required to satisfactorily perform the job. Experience or knowledge received through experience is not to be considered in evaluating jobs on this scale.

Points

20	Level 1	Eighth-grade education
90	Level 2	High school diploma or eighth-grade education and four years of formal apprenticeship
160	Level 3	Two-year college degree or high school diploma and three years of formal apprenticeship
230	Level 4	Four-year college degree
300	Level 5	Graduate degree

---

in the system as a whole. Although this is an arbitrary number, we have recommended the use of 1,000 since it is easy to work with and provides enough points to make meaningful differentiations. The total number of points must be allocated across factors. Given the factors education, experience, physical demands, responsibility, and working conditions, the analyst might decide to have education worth 300 points, experience worth 300 points, responsibility worth 200 points, and physical demands and working conditions each worth 100 points. This weighting of factor value cannot be done in an entirely arbitrary fashion. Rather, the analyst must look at key jobs in the organization and decide how much each of the factors contributes to the value (note, not the wage) of the job to the organization.

    Overall organizational strategy serves as a guide to these decisions. In a high-tech professional organization, for example, education might be rated most heavily. In contrast, a retail services organization might weight education much less heavily. Some generalities are probably safe to make. Although only rough estimates can be made, it is clear that in most organizations education is of much more value than the ability to tolerate poor working conditions.

When points have been assigned to each factor, the points assigned to each level of a factor must be determined. Our education scale, for example, has been weighted fairly heavily: 300 points out of 1,000. The analyst must now decide how many points to assign each level. The highest level of a scale is always assigned the full number of points allocated to the factor; thus, a graduate degree would be assigned 300 points. The lowest level on a factor scale is usually assigned some points, since an eighth-grade education is not equivalent to no education at all. For the job family we are considering, it seems equitable to value an eighth-grade educational level at 20 points. Scale levels between the base level and the top level can be assigned such that the differences between levels are (in terms of points assigned) equal. We have assigned equal intervals to this scale; thus the intermediate levels are assigned 90, 160, and 230 points. To calculate equal intervals, use the formula:

$$I = \frac{(\text{Max} - \text{Min})}{(N - 1)}$$

where I equals the width of the interval, Max equals the highest value of the scale, Min equals the lowest scale value, and N is the total number of scale levels desired. In our example, $I = (300 - 20) \div (5 - 1) = 280 \div 4 = 70$.

A similar process is carried out for each factor scale. Jobs are then compared to scales and points assigned to the job for each factor. Factor points are totaled, and the resulting scores may be compared to show the relative value of each job.

The advantages of the point factor system lie in its greater reliability and its immunity to the fluctuations in market rates. Changes in jobs may be accommodated. Once created, the scales are relatively easy to use. The points assigned to jobs not only give differences in value, but also indicate the size of those differences. The disadvantages are (1) the point method is expensive and time-consuming to develop, and (2) the accuracy of the scales may be questioned, for although they are based on the judgment of the compensation analyst, there is no way to prove that they accurately reflect value. However, some statistical checks (for example, against employee perceptions) can be used to support factor scales.

Even though the point factor system is the most commonly used system, some compensation theorists are currently questioning its value. Lawler, for example, notes a number of shortcomings of the point factor system for the modern organization:[3]

1. Being duty based, it tells people what not to do.
2. It reinforces bureaucratic hierarchy.
3. It reinforces the idea that people are worth what they do.
4. It focusses too heavily on internal pay relationships.
5. It hinders strategic compensation management.
6. It generates a high investment in the status quo.
7. It rewards dishonest job descriptions and encourages point-grabbing behavior.
8. It is expensive to develop and administer.
9. It does not support horizontal career moves or specialist career roles.
10. It creates pay increases tied to promotion and thus spends money reinforcing promotion rather than performance or skill acquisition.
11. The system is frequently used for assignment of perquisites and other noncompensation purposes.

While many compensation professionals would not agree with all of Lawler's criticisms, there is a renewed interest in alternate ways of thinking about bases for pay in organizations today. Many of these alternatives are discussed in Chapter 12.

Finally, we should note that after completing the point factor job evaluation process, the analyst has only a set of points reflecting the internal equity value of a set of jobs, and not a wage and salary structure. These values remain to be translated into such a structure.

Administering the Job Evaluation Process

The discussion of job evaluation so far has been written as if it were a one-person job; that is, as if the compensation analyst handled all aspects of the process. In fact, nothing could be further from reality, especially in larger organizations.

Even in using the simple whole-job ranking method, a committee usually does the ranking. Compensable factors are usually developed by a committee consisting of management, compensation specialists, and representatives of at least some of the jobs in the job family being evaluated. When a job family is represented by a union, there is usually an official of the union on the committee.

The same kind of participation takes place when jobs are actually being evaluated. The inclusion on the committee of some people who know the jobs is useful because written job descriptions may be misleading to individuals not familiar with the way the jobs are actually done. Finally, it is important that all decisions of the job evaluation committee (or of the compensation analyst) be written down in a job evaluation manual. In this way, consistency among committee members and consistency over time can be ensured. The manual also provides important documentation in the event of a comparable worth lawsuit.

Miscellaneous Job Evaluation Systems

A variety of commercial job evaluation systems are used in many types of organizations. The leading systems, in terms of popularity, are the Hay system and the NMTA Associates' National Position Evaluation Plan. There are many other job evaluation systems available and most compensation consulting firms have their own versions. A number of software packages are currently being marketed that facilitate job evaluation projects.

The Hay System The Hay system is a system that evaluates jobs with respect to "know-how," "problem-solving," and "accountability." Treiman views it as a "modification and simplification of factor comparison methods."[4] The Hay system combines external market rates with the job evaluation process, rather than creating a job value hierarchy and then pricing it. It is aimed at evaluation of upper-level jobs in organizations, both professional and managerial. Hay utilizes standardized "guide charts," but customizes them to fit the needs of individual clients. The guide chart scales are geometric, thus allowing for greater salary differentiation for arithmetic differences in job factors.

National Position Evaluation Plan The National Position Evaluation Plan has evolved from the old National Electrical Manufacturers Association (NEMA) job evaluation system. Sponsored by eleven management/manufacturers associations, the plan is offered under the umbrella group known as NMTA Associates. The plan is a point-factor system with four units, each utilizing common criteria, that can be used to evaluate all jobs in an organization. Unit I is used to evaluate manufacturing, warehousing, service, distribution, and maintenance jobs. Unit II evaluates nonexempt clerical, technical, and administrative jobs. Unit III is used in evaluating exempt professional, technical, administrative, sales, and supervisory jobs. Executive jobs are evaluated using unit IV. The commonality of criteria used in the units is a strength of the NMTA Associates plan, since it allows for a single hierarchy of job evaluation points for all jobs in an organization.

Building the Wage and Salary Structure

At this point, if the compensation analyst used the point factor method, he or she would have the number of points assigned to the jobs in the organization and, on the basis of wage and salary surveys discussed in Chapter 7, also would have reliable market data for a variety of key jobs. What is needed now is to construct a wage structure from these two data sets. Although a wage structure could be constructed that provided a specific range of wages for each job in the organization (including a starting, midpoint, and maximum wage figure), organizations have largely avoided such structures. Several reasons for not using separate ranges for each job have been advanced:

1. In a company with many jobs the structure would be unwieldy and possibly unworkable.

2. Neither job evaluation nor wage survey data are sufficiently precise, reliable (having agreement between sources), or stable (over time) to justify such a structure.

3. Internal equity issues are unlikely to be served by such a structure, because of the problems noted in reason 2. Aggregation is likely to smooth over small inconsistencies in survey and evaluation rankings.

In brief, neither survey data nor job evaluation data are thought to be good enough to create one salary range per job. (It should be noted that some organizations do not agree with this view: we shall explore their approach when we discuss market pricing.) Therefore, organizations create wage structures with a number of ranges, or grades, into which are aggregated all the jobs in the organization. This structure has several characteristics controlling its construction; these are the questions the compensation analyst must keep in mind when building the structure:

1. How many classes (or ranges) is the structure to have?
2. How far apart should midpoints of those ranges be?
3. How wide should each range be?
4. How much should the ranges overlap?

To answer these questions, the compensation analyst also has to know the answer to some additional questions:

5. How is the organization going to relate to the market with respect to pay levels? Will it exceed, fall short of, or match the market?

6. On what basis is the organization going to make individual pay decisions? Will all incumbents receive the same salary, or will there be differentials for seniority, performance, or some other factor?

Number of Ranges

The number of ranges to be used depends on several things. A major determinant is the number of jobs evaluated, their hierarchical level in the organization, and their reporting relationships. That is, a supervisor and subordinate would not ordinarily be in the same pay range. The greater the number of layers of hierarchy an organization has, the greater the number of pay ranges it will require. Career development issues also influence the number of ranges. When an individual is promoted to a new job, a raise is expected; career paths can typically be mapped by moves between ranges.

Range Parameters

The distance between midpoints is largely determined by the number of classes. When the number of ranges has been determined, the compensation analyst can look at job evaluation points assigned to various jobs and see whether there are obvious breaks. Another method is to divide the total number of job evaluation points possible (under the example used for the point factor system there were 1,000) by the number of ranges decided on. Thus, if it were decided to have ten ranges, range 1 would consist of all jobs receiving between 1 and 100 points; range 2 would consist of all jobs receiving between 101 and 200 points, and so on.

The midpoints would be based on salary survey data for the jobs in the range in this case; thus, the distance between midpoints would be derived from marketplace differentials.

Range Spread

The width of a given range, or the rate range *spread,* can be determined in different ways. One way is to look at market rate data of jobs falling within the classification and to base rate ranges on those data. A second way is to use a percentage band (usually between 5 and 30 percent) above and below the midpoint of each range. When this is done, the smaller percentages are used on lower ranges, and the larger percentages on the upper.

The midpoints and ranges chosen depend on the policies of the organization reflected in questions 5 and 6. The organization must decide if it is going to exceed or fall below the market, or just match it. This decision is called the *competitive wage* policy, or the *market stance* policy. To implement this policy, the organization chooses a survey statistic (median, upper quartile, lower quartile) and consistently uses that statistic for each key job surveyed. It may choose to adjust these figures in a consistent fashion; for example, it may say, "We will pay 15 percent above the median salary reported for this class."

Individual pay policies influence range spreads. If the organization is going to pay for performance, then a wider range is needed to reflect differentials than if no merit pay is to be given. The same is true of seniority payments. In the typical organization, employees are brought into the lower end of a range and move to the midpoint in two or three years if performance is satisfactory; movement thereafter is less rapid. Promotion policies also influence range spreads. If most people in a job are promoted to the next level within three years or fired, the range need not be broad.

Range Overlap

Many of the same issues governing range width influence ideal range overlap. As with range spread, there is no "right" overlap. The problems that occur when overlap exists include:

1. A promoted employee who was at the top of the old range must be placed above the base of the new range, or receive a cut in salary.

2. Supervisors may have employees working for them who make more money than they do, which can cause morale problems.

However, to avoid overlap completely would create an alternative problem: jobs would have artificial constraints on pay ceilings.

All other factors being equal, organizations with more classifications can expect more overlap; each organization has to judge the degree of overlap acceptable on the basis of the issues noted. An example of a typical wage structure is shown in Exhibit 8.9.

In building the wage structure, the compensation analyst must relate job evaluation points to wage survey data. Salary data for key jobs in each point range must be noted. Some analysts average out salary data to arrive at a midpoint; thus, if there are market data on four different jobs in range 8, the analyst would average those for rates (always using the same statistic,

Exhibit 8.9   Wage Chart

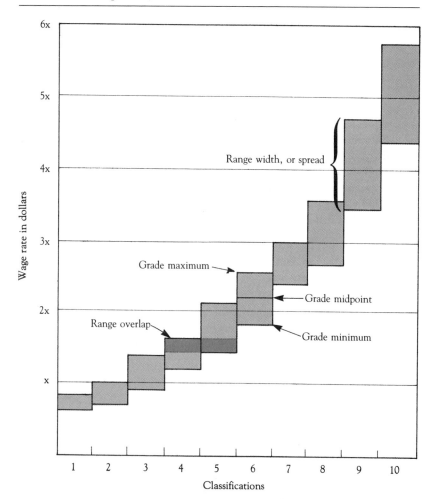

such as median or mean) and use that as the midpoint. A weighted average might be used, which would take into account both the number of incumbents in the surveyed positions, and the number of incumbents in the same positions in the analyst's own organization. Others use more complex statistical techniques to derive not only the midpoint but also the minimum and the maximum of the range. Actual range construction is an art; it is an iterative process in which the compensation analyst tries to meet the constraints of internal policy and still allow the organization to provide external equity.

A glance at Exhibit 8.9 may give the impression that the typical salary structure developed by an analyst has the regularity of that example. As any experienced compensation analyst can tell you, nothing is less likely. The midpoints of the ranges are unlikely to have the even progression noted. Typically, the analyst has to make adjustments for a pleasant, aesthetic effect to be achieved. This "smoothing" is typically done by calculating the percentage increase in the initial midpoints and then averaging these to get the mean increase, or progression, between midpoints. This calculated increase then is applied to the actual midpoint of the lowest range to get the calculated midpoint of the next highest range. The calculated percent increase is applied to this midpoint to get the calculated midpoint of the next highest range, with the process being repeated until the highest range's midpoint is calculated. Several arguments have been advanced for this smoothing:

1. Neither the survey data nor the evaluation process are so perfect as to be absolutely certain that the midpoints of the structure derived using them are "correct."

2. In communicating the structure to management the aesthetic appearance of the structure makes it seem more "scientific" and thus more acceptable. An uneven progression of midpoints is likely to raise questions for which there may be no convincing answers.

3. The even progression of midpoints makes administration of the system easier because standard increases for promotions can be given regardless of where the promoted employee falls in the salary structure. Similar administrative advantages exist with respect to merit and seniority differentials.

4. Use of even progression of midpoints underlines the importance of internal equity to the organization because the job evaluation hierarchy takes precedence over market differentials. This last argument is one for the compensation analyst to ponder. If the salary structure is smoothed, it is quite possible that external equity considerations will suffer, and that the organization may, in spite of a competitive pay policy, underpay with respect to some job categories. One audit need is for the compensation analyst to compare final salaries paid by his or her organization to salaries in the market for the same job.

Adjustments to the Structure

From time to time, adjustments will need to be made to the structure. Inflation drives labor prices upward, jobs change in their relative value to the organization, and jobs themselves change as technology changes. Employees entering jobs change, as well. The wage structure will have to be adjusted to meet these changes. In some cases, the compensable factors and their weightings will be questioned; in other cases, scale values will need to be changed. These changes will make it necessary to reevaluate all jobs. In a more normal situation, the need will be only to reevaluate selected jobs.

Adjustments that should be made are adjustments to movements in labor markets and to major changes in the organization. Adjustments that should be avoided are general cost-of-living adjustments, whether they are simple across-the-board adjustments or formal programs tied to the Consumer Price Index.

Finally, the structure should be taken seriously, but not as a straightjacket. Job evaluation is a tool, and wage survey data are estimates and averages. Building the structure is a matter of judgment, not a precise science. If done carefully, the structure should handle almost all jobs and the base salary for all but a few employees. There will always be a few employees who require special treatment. The compensation analyst, recognizing the uniqueness of these situations, should handle them outside the wage and salary structure and not distort the structure to accommodate these few cases. In short, adjustments to the wage and salary structure should not be confused with individual employee adjustments.

Market Pricing

As we noted earlier, some organizations like to emphasize external equity concerns above internal equity concerns, and, in a sense, define internal equity in terms of the market. The compensation analyst in such an organization has two tasks: (1) to get the best market data available for all jobs in the firm, and (2) for those jobs for which there are no market data, get the best estimate of what the market would pay for those jobs if there were a market. The means of acquiring the best market data was described in Chapter 7. Developing estimates of market rates for jobs for which there are no markets and the options available in developing structures for them will be described in this section.

To develop estimates of what the market would pay for a job if there were a market for it requires the development of a model relating market wages and job characteristics for key jobs, and then applying that model to jobs with unknown or nonexistent markets. The typical model used for such purposes is the *linear multiple regression* model, although other models, such as *nonlinear multiple regression* and *multiple-goal programming* can be used.

The linear multiple regression model takes the form:

$$W = a + b_1 x_1 + b_2 x_2 + \ldots + b_n x_n$$

where W represents the estimated wage of a job, a is some constant generated by the model, $x_1, x_2, \ldots, x_n$ are the amount of some characteristic (such as education required) of the job, and $b_1, b_2, \ldots, b_n$ are weights associated with respective job characteristics.

Typically, the job characteristics used in market pricing strategies as the x's, or independent variables, are standard job evaluation factors similar to those used in point factor systems. Certainly from a theoretical point of view, the use of compensable factors as independent variables makes sense, for the analyst can, with certain reservations, interpret results and make sense of them in communications both with management and employees. Thus, the compensation analyst might be able to say: "In this organization, the annual salary of a job is equal to $2,000, plus $563 for every year of education required by the job, plus $320 for every year of experience required by the job, plus $417 for every subordinate supervised, plus . . ." and so forth.

In fact, no such theoretical justification for the independent variables is necessary. As long as the independent variables are related specifically to the jobs, the market pricing model may produce usable results for prediction, though not for explanation. Generally, a middle ground is chosen, with many more independent variables than the usual compensable factors being tried in the model, and those being the best predictors retained. The best known market pricing model using this approach is that conducted using the PAQ, or Position Analysis Questionnaire.

The PAQ, developed by Ernest McCormick and his associates, is a job analysis technique that captures more than 150 aspects of a job. As it happens, when PAQ variables are used in the model, the variables that are able to predict wage variations best are fairly similar to standard compensable factor measures. Other systems akin to the PAQ are offered by most of the compensation consulting firms.

Having determined the set of independent variables that will be tested in the model, the compensation analyst regresses market wages on the set of independent variables. Typically, the regression analysis is conducted using a standard statistical software package on a mainframe or a personal computer. Many regression software packages designed specifically for compensation purposes are now available. These have the advantage of automatically providing reports couched in terms familiar to the compensation analyst. Some, however, are too simplistic in their approach, and may provide misleading results for the compensation analyst unfamiliar with the statistical principles underlying the model.

The output of the regression analysis includes the regression model with the set of independent variables that best predicts the wage data, the weight associated with each variable (the "*b's*" in the formula above) and the value of the constant. In addition, a multiple correlation coefficient (and/or a multiple coefficient of determination, which is the square of the correlation coefficient) is provided. This coefficient provides an estimate of the "fit" of the data; that is, how closely variation in the weighted linear combination of the independent variables is related to variation in wages. One would expect the coefficient of determination associated with a market pricing model to be in excess of .90 if the model is to have much use. A second measure that should be provided is the standard error of the estimate. This statistic allows the compensation analyst to calculate an error band around any specific estimate made using the regression formula. For the model to be of much value, the standard error of the estimate should probably be no more than 1.5 to 2 percent of any predicted salary.

Given a useful model, the compensation analyst has several choices. Even using the model, it is possible to divide the salary levels produced into grades and to create a standard structure similar to those discussed earlier. Jobs are placed in grades based on their wage value as estimated by the model. If there is a market rate for a job and that rate is not in the same range as that predicted by the model, the analyst must decide the grade in which the job "really" belongs. Given the trouble to which the analyst has gone to develop the model, aggregation into grades seems a pointless waste of information. Most of the arguments advanced in favor of grades described above are similarly advanced here, although the internal equity emphasis rings hollow.

If the analyst decides to use the model directly and not use grades, he or she is still faced with two possibilities. For jobs for which there are no market rates, the prediction of the model is used. However, when there is a market rate, and it is different from the model prediction, the analyst must choose between the two figures. Some organizations use the model prediction, referring to it as a policy line. Other organizations use actual market data if they are available and the policy line if they are not. The primary argument against the use of either a policy line or actual market rate/policy line combination is the administrative complexity of dealing with a salary structure in which every job has a different midpoint.

It is our view that, with the advent of high-speed electronic computers and their accessibility to compensation professionals in the form of mini- and microcomputers, this argument is no longer compelling. If (1) external equity is the primary concern of an organization, (2) adequate market and job data are available, and (3) a model with sufficient predictive power (i.e., a high coefficient of determination and low standard error of the estimate) is developed, then market pricing is the preferred strategy. Even when other strategies are followed it is advisable for the compensation analyst to develop a market pricing model as an audit technique of the salary structure.

Summary

This chapter has examined procedures involved in building an internal wage structure. We began our discussion with the recognition that the external labor market, in reality, allows managers a rather comfortable amount of discretion in setting specific rates for jobs. Thus, internal as well as external equity becomes an issue. Job evaluation was defined as a procedure that allows the manager to combine external and internal equity concerns by systematically establishing pay ranges for every job in the organization.

We then explored the six steps involved in job evaluation: (1) determining sources of job value (identifying compensable factors), (2) conducting a job analysis to develop information about each job, (3) establishing job families (common groupings of similar jobs), (4) choosing an evaluation method, (5) conducting the evaluation, and (6) establishing the wage structure.

We examined four major methods of job evaluation: (1) ranking, (2) classification, (3) factor comparison, and (4) point factor systems. We also examined the process of conducting the evaluation and building the wage structure.

Finally, we presented a specialized technique, called market pricing, that employs the use of multiple linear regression and has become quite popular among practitioners in recent years. The technique of market pricing allows the manager to combine external market and internal job evaluation judgments in a consistent fashion.

Notes

[1]D. P. Schwab, "Job Evaluation and Pay Setting: Concepts and Practices," in E. R. Livernash (ed.), *Comparable Worth: Issues and Alternatives* (Washington, D.C.: Equal Employment Advisory Council, 1980), pp. 67–78.

[2]J. M. Shafritz, *Position Classification: A Behavioral Analysis for the Public Service* (New York: Praeger Publishers, 1973), p. 23.

[3]E. E. Lawler, III, "What's Wrong With Point-Factor Job Evaluation," *Compensation and Benefits Review* 18(2) (March-April 1986): 20–28.

[4]D. J. Treiman, *Job Evaluation: An Analytic Review* (Washington, D.C.: National Academy of Sciences, 1979), p. 21.

9

Individual
Wage Determination

Key Issues and Questions
for This Chapter

After you have studied this chapter, you should be able to address the following key issues and questions:

1. Why should organizations pay people on the same job different amounts?

2. What is individual equity and why is the issue important?

3. What are the major bases for creating individual pay differences?

4. What conditions are necessary for a pay-for-performance or merit system to work?

5. What impact do performance appraisals have on pay-for-performance systems?

6. What are the major methods for providing incentive payments that are not a part of base pay and that do not automatically recur each year?

Introduction

An organization could take a wage and salary structure as described in Chapter 8 and use the single rates developed as midpoints as the sole basis for individual pay. To do so would, if the structure were correctly constructed, satisfy the external and internal equity requirements we have described earlier. However, determining individual pay solely on a job-worth basis is very rare, and for good reasons:

1. Organizations that wish to use pay strategically need to have pay differentials available within an individual job. This allows them to communicate a changed emphasis on important job roles.

2. Pay differentials provide organizations with an important tool for emphasizing organizational norms without having employees change jobs (e.g., promotion).

3. Same-job pay differentials allow the organization to recognize that different employees holding the same job may make substantially different contributions to meeting organizational goals, a matter of individual (as opposed to external or internal) equity.

4. Same-job pay differentials allow the use of pay to motivate employees.

5. Lack of same-job pay differentials violates the internal equity norms of most employees, reduces pay satisfaction, and makes it more difficult for the organization to attract and retain competent employees.

6. Organizations need some administrative discretion to keep compensation systems useful. Same-grade pay differentials allow the organization to recognize minor market differentials between jobs in the same grade, for example. Temporary labor market shortages for one job might require starting some employees in a grade at a higher salary than employees holding other jobs in that grade. Without some administrative discretion, most salary structures would require frequent, and expensive, adjustments if external equity requirements were to be met.

For these reasons, most organizations opt for a structure that allows different pay for individuals in the same job, or job grade.

The first concern when looking at individual pay, then, is determining the basis on which individuals in the same job, or job grade, will receive different salaries. This is a matter of organizational policy, and should be determined by top management. We will spend most of this chapter looking at criteria for pay differentials that can forward organizational goals. These criteria, usually lumped together as "merit" criteria, include seniority and performance. However, most compensation specialists recognize that other individual pay criteria, which do not necessarily forward organizational goals, are commonly used.

Some forms of compensation, for example, are distributed on an equal basis: health insurance and the Thanksgiving turkey are examples. Other forms of compensation are allocated on the basis of need; these are usually benefits (such as counseling), but are sometimes individual wage decisions ("We should give Jones that raise; they just had triplets"). All cost-of-living adjustments are in response to employee need.

A third type of individual pay decision not based on merit is that based on power. In some cases, the power is market-based ("The competition has just offered me a job at 20-percent more than I make now; if you can't meet that, I'm going to have to accept their offer"). In other cases, the power is based on intraorganizational relationships (if, for example, your in-laws are major stockholders in a corporation, you will probably be paid a higher salary than merit would justify). The fourth nonrational determinant of individual pay differences is luck. A few good breaks (the boss happens to be at the office the one Saturday you dropped in to catch up on some work; a client gets angry at the competitor and places a large order with you) or bad breaks (the boss has a hot domestic dispute going at review time and is in a rotten mood; cash flow problems of a client cause them to cancel the large order they placed with you) can have significant effects on individual salaries.

There is not much the compensation analyst can do about nonrational determinants of individual pay. They certainly cannot be programmed. The best approach is to control them as much as possible; those that cannot be controlled should be recognized for what they are, and the entire system not be distorted to justify a few exceptions.

The best way for the organization to manage individual pay decisions is to set out policies governing individual pay and to draw up procedures to implement those policies. In this chapter, we will look at the two major determinants of individual pay: seniority and performance. A means of adjusting for each is shown individually, and a joint adjustment is also shown.

Seniority

There are two ways in which an organization can adjust for seniority. The more common way is to reward employees for loyalty to the organization;

that is, employees receive a pay increment for every year they have served the company. Typically, these pay increments are tied to grade: an employee in job A who has worked in that job longer than a second employee will be paid more. However, when the first employee is promoted to job B, he will make less than an employee, X, who had filled job B longer, even if that employee, X, has worked for the organization for a shorter time than the first employee. Seniority in this case works *within* a grade and not across grades. A second way organizations sometimes pay for seniority is not to make adjustments to the pay structure to account for service, but to develop and use a maturity curve.

Pay Adjustments for Seniority

The first step for the compensation analyst preparing pay adjustments for seniority is to draw up a policy providing guidelines for such adjustments. Options to be considered include:

1. how long an employee has to work before receiving a seniority adjustment

2. the number of adjustments possible in a single job (shall seniority be rewarded indefinitely, or is there a limit?)

3. the size of the seniority adjustment, and differential adjustments across job levels and years of service.

Exhibit 9.1 shows a seniority pay adjustment guideline that takes these options into account. Annual increases are given to employees, but only through the tenth year of service in the same job classification. Adjustments shrink as a percentage of total salary both with years of service and with increase in salary classification. The philosophy behind this adjustment policy is that the organization believes that employees who perform well will be promoted to higher pay grades. Because the adjustment made after year 1 creates a higher base for year-2 adjustment, a lower adjustment, in terms of percentage increase, can be made in year 2. Note that these adjustments are independent of any other adjustments made to the structure. Midpoints and entire ranges may be shifted to respond to changes in the labor market, the inflation rate, or changes in the company's technology level, size, or location.

A different form of adjustment may be embodied in the salary structure itself. A good example of this is the general schedule (GS) pay system of the United States government, seen in Exhibit 9.2. The GS pay system takes the adjustment policy shown in Exhibit 9.1 and constructs a graded pay

Exhibit 9.1   Seniority Pay-Adjustment Policy (Percentage increase)

Classification	Years of Service									
	1	*2*	*3*	*4*	*5*	*6*	*7*	*8*	*9*	*10*
1	4.5	4.4	4.2	4.0	3.8	3.6	3.4	3.2	3.0	2.8
2	4.5	4.4	4.2	4.0	3.8	3.6	3.4	3.2	3.0	2.8
3	4.5	4.4	4.2	4.0	3.8	3.6	3.4	3.2	3.0	2.8
4	4.4	4.3	4.1	3.9	3.7	3.5	3.3	3.1	2.9	2.7
5	4.4	4.3	4.1	3.9	3.7	3.5	3.3	3.1	2.9	2.7
6	4.4	4.3	4.1	3.9	3.7	3.5	3.3	3.1	2.9	2.7
7	4.3	4.2	4.0	3.8	3.6	3.4	3.2	3.0	2.8	2.6
8	4.3	4.2	4.0	3.8	3.6	3.4	3.2	3.0	2.8	2.6
9	4.3	4.2	4.0	3.8	3.6	3.4	3.2	3.0	2.8	2.6
10	4.2	4.1	3.9	3.7	3.5	3.3	3.1	2.9	2.7	2.5

structure with seniority adjustments built in. Either system is satisfactory; however, the GS pay system must be revised frequently if it is to accommodate market and inflationary influences. (An additional constraint on the GS structure is political pressure to hold government costs down.) A percentage table of seniority adjustments need not be revised so frequently.

Maturity Curves

Maturity curves, discussed as a method for pricing jobs in Chapter 7, are sometimes adapted as a variant in making individual pay distinctions among professionals such as scientists and engineers. The underlying assumption of the maturity curve is that the value of a worker to an organization increases with years in the field. Maturity curves reward not organizational loyalty but professional longevity.

Exhibit 9.2 General Schedule Pay Rates, 1986

Grade	1	2	3	4	5	6	7	8	9	10
						Step				
1	$9,339	$9,650	$9,961	$10,271	$10,582	$10,764	$11,071	$11,380	$11,393	$11,686
2	$10,501	$10,750	$11,097	$11,393	$11,521	$11,860	$12,199	$12,538	$12,877	$13,216
3	$11,458	$11,840	$12,222	$12,604	$12,986	$13,368	$13,750	$14,132	$14,514	$14,890
4	$12,862	$13,291	$13,720	$14,149	$14,578	$15,007	$15,436	$15,865	$16,294	$16,723
5	$14,390	$14,870	$15,350	$15,830	$16,310	$16,790	$17,270	$17,750	$18,230	$18,710
6	$16,040	$16,575	$17,110	$17,645	$18,180	$18,715	$19,250	$19,785	$20,320	$20,855
7	$17,824	$18,418	$19,012	$19,606	$20,200	$20,794	$21,388	$21,982	$22,576	$23,170
8	$19,740	$20,398	$21,056	$21,714	$22,372	$23,030	$23,688	$24,346	$25,004	$25,662
9	$21,804	$22,531	$23,258	$23,985	$24,712	$25,439	$26,166	$26,893	$27,620	$28,347
10	$24,011	$24,811	$25,611	$26,411	$27,211	$28,011	$28,811	$29,611	$30,411	$31,211
11	$26,381	$27,260	$28,139	$29,018	$29,897	$30,776	$31,655	$32,534	$33,413	$34,292
12	$31,619	$32,673	$33,727	$34,781	$35,835	$36,889	$37,943	$38,997	$40,051	$41,105
13	$37,599	$38,852	$40,105	$41,358	$42,611	$43,864	$45,117	$46,370	$47,623	$48,876
14	$44,430	$45,911	$47,392	$48,873	$50,354	$51,835	$53,316	$54,797	$56,278	$57,758
15	$52,262	$54,004	$55,746	$57,488	$59,230	$60,972	$62,714	$64,450	$66,198	$67,940
16	$61,296	$63,339	$65,392	$67,425	$68,700	$68,700	$68,700	$68,700	$68,700	$68,700
17	$68,700	$68,700	$68,700	$68,700	$68,700	$68,700	$68,700	$68,700	$68,700	$68,700
18	$68,700	$68,700	$68,700	$68,700	$68,700	$68,700	$68,700	$68,700	$68,700	$68,700

Source: *Salary Table No. 71, General Schedule* (Washington, D.C.: Office of Personnel Management, 1986).

Maturity curves usually reflect market values more closely than other seniority adjustments. The major differences between maturity curves and regular pay adjustments for seniority are two. The first, as noted above, is that maturity curves reward seniority in the field, not the organization. The second and more important difference for the compensation analyst is that maturity curves do not address internal equity at all. External equity is served by use of wage survey data, and individual equity is served (in part, at least) through the curve itself. No provision is made for internal equity: there is no job evaluation. For this reason, maturity curves tend to be confined to professional jobs for which there is a very clear market rate. They are not suitable for most jobs in most organizations.

Two-Tier Pay Plans

A final method for establishing base pay rates is called a two-tier pay plan. Such plans represent an attempt to reduce labor costs drastically and have been popular among organizations that traditionally have been faced with either multinational or domestic price competition.

Under a two-tier plan, two classes of employees are defined for each job: a group of tenured employees who have hire dates before some defined date, and a group of nontenured employees who were hired after that date. Employees in the first tier retain their current pay rates, while the lower-tier employees are hired to do the same jobs at substantially lower rates. Some two-tier plans have provisions for allowing new employees to move to the upper tier after a specified amount of time.

A number of older organizations have attempted two-tier pay plans in order to cope with untenable labor cost situations in the automobile industry, the rubber industry, and the retail food industry. The advantage of a two-tier system is that it allows for a short-run reduction in labor cost while honoring earlier wage commitments. Some also argue that it allows the firm to avoid layoffs, or going out of business entirely.

Two-tier systems, however, have a number of disadvantages. First, they violate equity norms by setting up a "second-class" citizenship among employees. Second, research demonstrates that higher turnover among employees in the lower tier is most likely to occur, defeating the cost containment objective in the first place. Finally, to the extent that minorities and women are adversely affected, any firm using a two-tier system runs some risk of fair employment practice law violation.

Two-tier pay systems are not a pleasant chapter in the history of American management. They represent a failure of companies to control their labor costs and to remain productive and competitive. They may be the best among difficult choices in the short run, but they will not likely be a long-term solution to compensation problems.

Performance

We saw in Chapter 4 that pay can affect performance. Performance can also affect pay. The focus of this section is on adjustments to base pay rates as a result of some level of performance. A second means of paying for performance, which we will look at later in this chapter, is giving one-time payments, or lump-sum bonuses, as a reward for performance. These payments do not affect base pay, nor is any adjustment made to the pay structure. One-time payments are becoming more popular for several reasons. Because they do not add permanently to the employee's base pay, the employee must earn the merit differential each year: it is the compensation equivalent of "What have you done for me lately?" Second, because (especially after several years) less of the total compensation budget is sunk into base pay, more money is available to make dramatic differentials in pay based on performance. Finally, the levels of many benefits are a function of base pay: by keeping base pay reduced, total benefit costs can be controlled, as well.

Typically, performance adjustments to base pay rates are based on individual performance appraisal systems. Bonus systems, on the other hand, may be individual, group, or company-wide plans and are typically based not on performance appraisal systems but on dollar measures of productivity or cost savings.

In either case, several conditions must exist before a pay-for-performance system can work. Organizations in which any of these conditions are missing will find that performance-based pay systems have little effect except for the expenditure of money and employee morale.

Required Conditions for a Performance-Based Pay System

The first condition for the establishment of a performance-based pay system is that employees must have some control over their performance, and be able, either individually or as a group, to perform better or worse. It would be hard to justify a merit system for assembly-line workers based on amount of output, since the speed of the line is typically set by an engineer, and the employee cannot produce more than is sent past the work station. Likewise, about the only control a gate guard has over performance is showing up for the job. Many workers are so dependent on the actions of others that they have little control over their individual performance. In such cases, group performance may be the basis for merit pay decisions.

A second condition for merit pay is that any performance differential must be important to the organization. It may be that the organization requires only minimal levels of performance; higher levels are irrelevant or even undesirable. A cleaning service, for example, may only need to have the halls swept and the wastepaper baskets emptied in a client's office. The same degree of shine and polish that one might desire at home is not required.

The third condition is that the organization must be able to measure performance in a valid and reliable way. This is probably the most difficult condition for most organizations to meet; for that reason a section on performance appraisal systems follows.

The other conditions for a workable merit pay system center on the compensation system itself. First, the organization must be willing to budget enough money to the system so that changes in pay will be meaningful to employees. Second, the pay system must truly match performance differentials with pay differentials. High performance must be well rewarded; mediocre performance must not be well rewarded. Employees must accept the performance measurement system and the links between performance and pay as fair and equitable. This means that employees must have some realistic information regarding what the organization considers good performance, what linkages exist between performance and pay, and what pay levels exist in the organization.

Performance Appraisal

Performance appraisal is a major area of personnel administration, with an extensive literature of its own. A comprehensive treatment is obviously beyond the scope of this book.[1]

There are a number of appraisal decisions that must be made, though, so we will look at those decisions only as they affect compensation systems. The first issue to be decided is the use to which appraisal data shall be put. There are three broad categories of use: to make personnel decisions, to help develop employees, and to conduct research. For compensation purposes, the decision-making characteristics of performance appraisal system outputs are of primary interest.

The compensation analyst is not interested in development of employees; thus, the requirements placed on appraisal systems by developmental uses (that is, the output of information telling the employees' areas of excellence, areas of shortcomings, and ways to improve) will not be covered here. Research uses of appraisal data may be important to the compensation analyst who wants to see what aspects of performance respond to merit pay systems, and to experiment with the effects of pay adjustment on performance level. However, it is the effect on personnel decisions that is of primary concern to the compensation analyst. That decision aspect places one major constraint on performance appraisal systems: data output from the system must have the capability of being summarized in a single number that can be compared against standards for a specific job and across all types of employees regardless of job or level in the pay structure. For example, employee A, a forklift truck operator with a performance appraisal rating of 7, is a better employee than employee B, an administrative assistant to the vice president of sales with a rating of 5.

Who should be appraised? From the point of view of the compensation analyst, it is only necessary to appraise employees for whom merit adjustments are to be made. Therefore, salesmen on straight commission and unionized workers paid flat rate plus seniority adjustment need not be appraised.

What performance should be appraised? There is no such thing as an objective performance waiting to be appraised. The organization must define performance for each job in terms of overall organizational goals. In addition, the definition of "effective" performance on a job is likely to change as organizational goals and requirements change, and as the environmental pressures on the organization change.

For the compensation analyst, *performance* is whatever aspect of employee behavior, makeup, or job outcomes the organization wishes to increase by rewarding it. Compensation definitions of performance may not always agree with other organizational definitions. Thus, individuals caught in illegal activities on behalf of the organization frequently say that although the organization may pay lip service to legal and ethical practices, raises come to the employee who price fixes, bribes government officials, or makes payoffs to corrupt union officials. The compensation analyst will have to reconcile these differences, making sure that the organization rewards only what it really wishes to motivate, and that the performance appraisal system captures those aspects of performance on which rewards should be based.

Four criteria the compensation analyst will use to judge the performance appraisal system are its relevance, reliability, freedom from bias, and practicality. Evidence of relevance, or validity, would indicate that appraisal measures are in fact tapping those aspects of performance the organization wishes to reward. Thus, the compensation analyst might compare appraisal systems with management statements of what it wishes to reward to look for similarities and differences. For the compensation analyst, the reliability that is of interest is interobserver reliability. An employee should receive the same score on the appraisal system regardless of the appraiser. The appraisal system is most likely to fail in reliability because of rater bias. Rater bias refers to the information processing errors that all managers are subject to make rather than to blatant prejudice. Major rater errors include:

1. *Restriction of range errors.* Some managers, especially with salary increases at stake, give all their subordinates high ratings. This is known as *leniency error.* Other managers like to make their employees "reach." "After all," they say, "no one is really that good." Other managers, to avoid offending anyone, rate everyone about the same.

2. *Contrast error.* Some managers will not rate their subordinates against standards, but contrast them to other employees. The major problem with this practice is that most of us are so imbued with the idea of the normal distribution that we force small sets of employees into such distributions. Thus, one outstanding employee may be compared to several good ones, and the good employees marked down to average as a result.

3. *Weighting errors.* Several errors result from improper weighting of appraisal data. Managers tend to rate individuals similar to themselves in background or attitude higher than other individuals with comparable performance. Irrelevant data, which should be weighted zero, enter into the appraisal. Many managers are apt to take into account more recent performance, which accounts for the tendency of some workers to go all out just prior to a performance review. "Halo" error occurs when a manager is so impressed with one aspect of a subordinate's performance that he rates the subordinate highly overall. Thus, a faculty member with a high research output is likely to be rated as a good teacher. Poor student evaluations may be excused, or even taken as evidence that the faculty member is really making the students learn, rather than just amusing them. Regardless of its source, rater bias gets in the way of linking performance and merit correctly, and appraisal systems must be as impervious to it as possible.

Practicality of the performance appraisal system, as far as the compensation analyst is concerned, has two components. The first is the acceptance of the system by raters and ratees. Rater acceptance is necessary if the system is to be taken seriously. Raters must see that use of the appraisal system allows them to reward employees they view as high performers and withhold rewards from employees they view as mediocre. Ratee acceptance of the system is necessary if employees are to make performance-reward linkages. The other area of practicality is the degree to which the system will stand up under legal scrutiny. Merit pay decisions, like all other personnel decisions, are subject to the requirements laid down by Title VII of the Civil Rights Act and the administrative interpretation of that Title by the Equal Employment Opportunity Commission.

There are five systems used to measure performance for pay adjustment purposes: global ratings, comparative procedures, trait systems, behavioral systems, and objective work outcomes. Each of these will be discussed in terms of its value for merit pay uses.

Global Ratings   A manager making a global rating simply assigns to each employee a number that represents overall performance level. Such systems are only as good as the manager doing the ratings. Global ratings are likely to show the effects of bias, and this bias will detract from both the reliability and the relevance of the ratings. Resulting data will be as much a measure of the manager who is making the rating as the employees on whom it is made. From a compensation point of view, global appraisal measures are more likely to be used after raise decisions are made than before them ("Joe deserves a 10-percent raise; that means I'll have to give him a 7 on the appraisal"). Preserving individual equity, especially across departments, using global ratings is not likely. It is equally unlikely that one could successfully defend the organization in a pay discrimination suit in which global appraisals are a contested issue.

Comparative Ratings   Although methods differ, all comparative rating procedures end up with a ranking of some set of employees. Comparative ratings are not much of an improvement over global measures from a compensation point of view. First of all, these procedures use global measures and thus are subject to all of their problems. However, there are additional problems. Rankings are not comparable from one rating unit to another: being the third best employee in one unit is not the same as being third in another unit. Rankings also have no absolute meaning. All employees in a unit may be superb, but ranking will force some employees to the bottom raise classification. In another unit, all employees may be wretched beyond belief, yet the best of these misfits will receive the same raise as the best worker in the first unit described. Any attempt to preserve internal equity through a comparative system such as this is hopeless.

Trait Systems   Trait systems have undoubtedly been the most widely used performance appraisal system. Usually, they appear as graphic rating scales. Such scales typically begin with ratings of quality and quantity of work (not traits, but rather quasi-global measures) and continue with ratings of initiative, cooperation, judgment, leadership, creativity, responsibility, commitment, tact, mental alertness, and decisiveness. Trait scales, though widely used, are inadequate in terms of the four criteria mentioned on p. 237 (relevance, reliability, freedom from bias, and practicality). They are particularly subject to rater bias and thus to lack of reliability. Most psychologists now question the ability of managers to make clinical decisions about traits. The relationship of traits to a job is difficult to demonstrate, anyway. An employee might demonstrate excellent leadership qualities in organizing fellow workers for a union, but management is unlikely to consider this good performance.

Trait ratings have little practicality, too. Although easy to construct and use (badly), they are not likely to stand up to court challenges. For the compensation analyst, trait ratings have another, equally serious flaw. Most traits are, by definition, stable behavioral patterns not likely to change. A good leader, for example, is likely to remain so; an individual with no initiative is unlikely to change suddenly. If the function of merit adjustments to base salary is to motivate specific behaviors, those systems should operate at those levels. Adjustments to base pay should not be made for an unchangeable characteristic of an employee; doing so would be equivalent to making continuous adjustments because the employee has red hair. If the trait can be said to exist, and is measurable, then employees should be selected on the basis of the trait.

Behavioral Systems   Behavioral systems are based on employee behaviors rather than global comparisons with other employees or traits. They can avoid the problems of these other systems because they are less subject to rater error than are traits or comparative systems. Unlike objective or dollar outcomes, behaviors can be associated with the individual performance of any job. Properly constructed, a behavior-based appraisal system can be relevant, reliable, and relatively free from error. Such a system is likely to be upheld if challenged in court.

A behavior-based system is also of greater benefit to a compensation analyst than previously mentioned systems. Because behaviors can be associated with an individual employee, the appraisal system can be used as a basis for individual pay adjustments. In addition, an employee has more control over individual behaviors than over traits or outcomes. Performance standards stated in behavior terms can be readily communicated to employees; thus it is possible for employees to see linkages among what they do, the performance ratings they are given, and the salary adjustments they receive.

There are two major forms of behavioral systems commonly used today. The first is the behavioral expectation scale, or BES (also known as behaviorally anchored rating scales, or BARS). The second is the behavioral observation scale, or BOS.

Behavioral Expectation Scales (BES). BES development is based on the *critical incident technique,* a job analysis procedure. A first sample of job-knowledgeable people provides examples of effective, ineffective, and neutral behaviors. These incidents are clustered by content area, and the clustered dimensions are named and defined.

The incidents defined by this first group of job-knowledgeable people are placed in random order. A second sample of job-knowledgeable people takes the dimensions defined by the first group and assigns each incident to one of them. This process is called *retranslation,* and serves as a validity check on the relationship of incidents and dimensions. Only those incidents matched with the same dimension they were connected with by the first group are retained.

These incidents are not important in themselves but, as examples of behavior, they indicate some level of effectiveness on a dimension. A group of employees rates each incident for effectiveness in terms of the dimension. Only those incidents whose effectiveness is agreed upon are retained. Of the incidents left, between five and seven are chosen that illustrate different levels of effectiveness with respect to the dimension. Because the behaviors used are illustrative, raters need not have seen the actual behavior performed; anchor behaviors serve as examples of many behaviors of equal effectiveness or ineffectiveness. The usual practice is to state the anchor behaviors in terms of expectations. A sample BES is shown in Exhibit 9.3.

Raters using BES typically are required to write down one or more behaviors observed by the rater during the rating period to justify the BES score given to the employee. There are usually eight to twelve different BES scores used in this system. For compensation purposes, scores on each dimension are averaged. The BES will be different for each job, but the average score will be comparable across all jobs as a measure of performance.

Behavioral Observation Scales (BOS). The other major appraisal system based on behaviors is the behavioral observation scale. Also known as a *summated*

Exhibit 9.3   A Behavioral Expectation Scale for a Retail Clerk

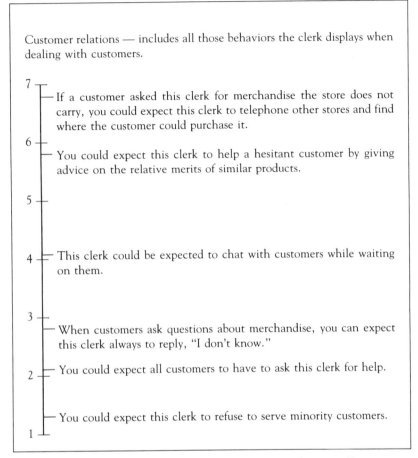

Customer relations — includes all those behaviors the clerk displays when dealing with customers.

7
— If a customer asked this clerk for merchandise the store does not carry, you could expect this clerk to telephone other stores and find where the customer could purchase it.

6
— You could expect this clerk to help a hesitant customer by giving advice on the relative merits of similar products.

5

4 — This clerk could be expected to chat with customers while waiting on them.

3
— When customers ask questions about merchandise, you can expect this clerk always to reply, "I don't know."

2 — You could expect all customers to have to ask this clerk for help.

— You could expect this clerk to refuse to serve minority customers.

1

Source: M. J. Wallace, Jr., N. F. Crandall, and C. H. Fay, *Administering Human Resources: An Introduction to the Profession* (New York: Random House, 1982), p. 483. Used with permission.

rating scale or *behavioral checklist,* the BOS differs from the BES both in method of development and appearance of the final scale. A BOS is similar to a BES in that they are based on the same job analysis technique, critical incidents.

A sample of job-knowledgeable people provides critical incidents related to job performance. For the generation of a BOS, only effective and ineffective incidents are sought, not neutral ones. A job analyst takes all the critical incidents generated and clusters similar incidents into behavioral items. Thus, four specific incidents relating to lateness would be generalized to "Arrives at work on time." The behavioral items are then categorized into job dimensions. Thus, "Arrives at work on time" would be placed in a category with other similar aspects of "work habits."

A second analyst, taking the behavioral items and performance dimensions, tries to duplicate the first analyst's judgments about the relations of incidents to items and items to dimensions. This step, similar to retranslation, provides a check on the reasonableness of the items and dimensions. In addition, two checks are made on content validity of the items and dimensions. A preliminary appraisal instrument is a five-point *Likert scale* in which each item indicates the frequency of a behavior for the person being appraised. A sample of one dimension and its associated items is shown in Exhibit 9.4.

The preliminary appraisal instrument is then used to rate employees. Item analysis or factor analysis is used to refine the instrument, eliminating behaviors that do not differentiate effective from ineffective performance. When a manager uses the BOS to rate an employee, the employee's scores are averaged to give an overall rating of performance.

Objective Work Outcomes   Objective work outcomes are all of the kinds of hard data that management uses to judge the effectiveness of the organization. Examples are profit, scrap rates, net sales, cost of goods sold, maintenance costs, and age of accounts receivable. There is no doubt that these bottom-line data are crucial for measuring organizational performance. As more organizations try to support the achievement of strategic goals through the compensation program, objective work outcomes have assumed more importance as essential elements of performance appraisal systems.

Because individual and group results are closer than other forms of performance measures to organizational outcomes, they are the preferred form of appraisal measure. Rewards policies built around cost-related outcomes allow the compensation program to further organizational strategies by:

1. rewarding results most supportive of organizational strategy
2. directing employee attention to business plans supporting organization strategy
3. reinforcing attention to individual and group performance planning
4. supporting performance management programs.

Exhibit 9.4   A Behavioral Observation Scale

A Behavioral Observation Scale

Work Habits

1.   Argues with a foreman in front of others.
     Almost always   1   2   3   4   5   Almost never
2.   When unsure about a problem, discusses it with supervisor.
     Almost never   1   2   3   4   5   Almost always
3.   Knows the information provided in technical bulletins and manuals on the equipment in his area.
     Almost never   1   2   3   4   5   Almost always
4.   Knows where to get special equipment or supplies to get the job done.
     Almost never   1   2   3   4   5   Almost always
5.   Is ignorant of the capabilities and limitations of equipment.
     Almost always   1   2   3   4   5   Almost never
6.   Arrives to work on time (e.g., no later than 6 A.M.).
     Almost never   1   2   3   4   5   Almost always
7.   Stays on the job.
     Almost never   1   2   3   4   5   Almost always
8.   Meets deadlines with minimum overtime (if possible).
     Almost never   1   2   3   4   5   Almost always
9.   Keeps a sense of humor (smiles) even in difficult situations.
     Almost never   1   2   3   4   5   Almost always
10. Has the smell of liquor on his breath.
     Almost always   1   2   3   4   5   Almost never
11. Spends more time behind the desk than in the work area.
     Almost always   1   2   3   4   5   Almost never
12. Resists change, complains, and/or is slow to implement it.
     Almost always   1   2   3   4   5   Almost never
13. Does not delegate work (must do everything himself).
     Almost never   1   2   3   4   5   Almost always
14. Does not check to see that a job area is clean after completion of the job.
     Almost always   1   2   3   4   5   Almost never
15. Does not get written reports in on time.
     Almost always   1   2   3   4   5   Almost never

Source: M. J. Wallace, Jr., N. F. Crandall, and C. H. Fay, *Administering Human Resources: An Introduction to the Profession* (New York: Random House, 1982), p. 485.

During the 1970s, management developed interest in a technique of managing that centered on objective or "hard" performance measures, and that was known as *management by objectives* (MBO).[2] Managers who follow MBO set goals for their subordinates in terms of "hard" or objective measures of outcomes and results. Many organizations have experimented with performance appraisals and rewards based on MBO. Thus, a manager might be measured against the budget performance of his department and receive a bonus or even merit adjustment according to such measures.

Kane and Freeman, though, have recently noted some severe problems that a strict adherence to MBO can create and note that many organizations that once used MBO solely as a reward device are moving towards more behavior-oriented measures of job performance.[3] The major problem of using objective or MBO-style results as measures or indicators of individual merit lies in the nature of work in our society. There are simply too few jobs for which objective results can truly capture an individual's actual performance. Kane and Freeman note additional problems associated with only measuring merit according to results:[4]

1. *Rate-setting problems.* Traditional MBO systems create incentives for setting goals as low as possible in order to maximize the incentive bonus received.

2. *Comparability problems.* Traditional MBO systems can lead to inconsistent standards of merit being applied throughout an organization. One boss may set very easy objectives while another may set very tough ones. Merit determination would result in unfair rewards distribution under such circumstances.

3. *Procrustean definition of objectives. Procrustean* definitions are those that force a common mold or shape on all things. In this case, MBO tends to force any definition of performance merit to fit a very narrow mold consisting of tangible results measures, even though they do not adequately capture all important dimensions of an individual's performance.

4. *Excessive emphasis on the short run.* Perhaps the most difficult problem with MBO is the tendency to focus on very short-run results, like quarterly performance, while ignoring more difficult to measure but even more important long-term aspects of performance. Quarterly or even annual reward cycles tend to force managers to think only of short-term results when determining merit.

5. *Inflexibility.* Many MBO systems tend to set goals in concrete, allowing no way to change standards and goal levels as conditions and events

change. As organizations change or when environments become turbulent, it may be impossible to set meaningful goals in terms of hard objectives. Basing merit on an MBO system under such circumstances would be inequitable.

Some sales jobs are compensated solely on the basis of cost-related outcomes. This is the commission system. Piecerate systems are also rewarded on the basis of cost-related outcomes. However, most jobs in this society are not independent; rather they are tied in closely with many other jobs. Isolating the effect of one worker would be impossible. Consider a planning group drawing up long-range plans for a hospital system. Such a group might consist of managers, health care economists, a human resource planning specialist, union representatives, and even representatives of city government or patient groups. How would you isolate the contribution of the human resource planner on some basis that would allow equitable annual salary adjustments?

When objective work outcomes are available for a job and the effects of one individual on those outcomes can be isolated, they are an excellent basis for individual merit adjustments. But because this cannot always be done, they have limited use as the sole basis for individual merit adjustments. However, as we shall see, they do form the basis of most pay-for-performance schemes that do not involve adjustments to individual base rates.

Compensable Performance Dimensions

Organizations wishing to use the compensation system as a performance management tool need to think very carefully about the performances they have in mind for each job and to translate those into standards. A useful way of linking the performance system and the compensation system is to think in terms of compensable performance dimensions.

When we think about the factors we want to reward in a job, we speak of *compensable factors; compensable performance dimensions* are the individual employee parallel. Thus, in looking at a specific position/employee, we need to identify the function of that individual with respect to organizational goals and to what four, five, six, or more things we want to reward. These things are the compensable performance dimensions. We then need to specify how we know that performance on those dimensions has earned a reward, and how much.

In most cases, a performance dimension will be characterized by both objective work outcomes and job-related behaviors. This sequencing of performance dimension determination before outcome and behavior specification is crucial. We must make sure that we measure what is important to reward rather than reward what is easy to measure.

How to Make Adjustments for Performance   Adjusting pay for performance is similar to adjusting for seniority. Such adjustments can be made either in terms of percentage increases to base pay or in terms of relationship to midpoint. Typically, no differentiation in grade is made; if a 4 on a five-point performance scale gets an 8-percent raise, that will hold true whether the employee is in class 1 or class 6 of the salary structure. An example of a range placement policy is shown in Exhibit 9.5. In fact, this adjustment is not determined strictly by merit, for a distinction is made based on experience in the job. In a sense, this matrix simply has different definitions of performance depending on experience: performance that is considered "acceptable" for someone who is just learning the job differs from that considered "acceptable" for someone fully experienced in all functions of the job. The fully experienced "acceptable" performer is thought to contribute more to the organization and is therefore worth more.

Combined Adjustments for Performance and Seniority   Many organizations make adjustments for both seniority and performance. This can be done through a *placement-in-range matrix,* an example of which is shown in Exhibit 9.6. In this system, even unsatisfactory employees can reach the range midpoint through seniority, though it takes five years. The excellent employee can get to the midpoint of the range in two years, but it takes ten years to reach the top of the range.

Three problems arise from using a matrix such as this. The most serious problem is the need to adjust the entire structure in response to market fluctuations. If employees are brought in at 80 percent of the midpoint, then the midpoint must rise when market rates do, and everyone in that classification must be raised. It is very difficult to get managers to accept the idea of holding employee salaries constant to a range midpoint, especially when market rates are increasing rapidly. On the other hand, not to adjust to the market in this fashion results in a fairly common situation: the new worker with no experience makes more than an excellent worker with one year of experience, who makes more than the excellent worker with two years of experience, and so on. This was the experience of MBAs during much of the 1960s and 1970s. While entry-level salaries moved by, say, 15 to 20 percent each year, employers were reluctant to give raises of this magnitude

Exhibit 9.5 Guide to Salary Placement in Range

		Performance				
	Unsatisfactory	*Acceptable*	*Fully Satisfactory*	*Excellent*	*Highly Exceptional*
4. Fully experienced and trained in several functions of higher-level position(s)	Employee on Probation or Terminated	100% of midpoint	105% of midpoint	110% of midpoint	115% of midpoint to maximum
3. Fully experienced in all functions of job		95% of midpoint	100% of midpoint	105–110% of midpoint	110–115% of midpoint
2. Experienced in most functions of job		90% of midpoint	95% of midpoint	100% of midpoint	105% of midpoint
1. Still learning basic functions of job		Minimum	80–85% of midpoint	85–90% of midpoint	90–95% of midpoint

Source: R. Beatty, N. F. Crandall, C. H. Fay, R. Mathis, G. T. Milkovich, and M. J. Wallace, Jr., *How to Administer Wage–Salary Programs and Perform Job Evaluations.* © 1979 by the authors. Used by permission.

Exhibit 9.6   Guide to Placement in Range Based on Seniority and Performance (Percentage of midpoint)

Years in position	Performance level				
	1	*2*	*3*	*4*	*5*
1	80%	82%	84%	86%	88%
2		86	88	90	100
3	Probation	90	94	100	104
4		95	100	104	108
5	T	100	102	108	110
6	E R	100	103	110	112
7	M I	100	104	112	114
8	N A	100	105	114	116
9	T E	100	105	116	118
10		100	105	118	120

to current employees. The result, of course, was considerable turnover in the affected jobs.

A second problem arises from fluctuations in performance level. A third-year employee who earned a level 5 the previous year but who performed at a level 3 in the third year should be placed at 94 percent of the midpoint. This obviously will not occur.

The final problem is the reaction of many managements to a lack of freedom in setting individual salary levels. One response has been to state the percent of midpoint as a range, so that, for example, an employee might be brought in at between 80 and 82 percent of midpoint. Although use of

a matrix tends to ensure internal equity, it also removes management discretion with respect to salary levels. If the appraisal system is reliable and
valid, this problem is not serious.

Many organizations do not use placement-in-range approaches to distribute merit increases. Instead, employees get merit increase percentages to
current salary based on performance level. In its simplest form, this approach
might dictate that all employees scoring a 5 on a five-point performance scale
would receive an 8-percent increase, those scoring a 4 would receive a 6-
percent increase, and so forth. A problem with this simplest approach is that
no allowance is made for seniority (should the organization wish to reward
loyalty) and no allowance is made for an employee's current place in the
salary range. An employee at 120 percent of midpoint would receive a raise,
even if it put her out of range.

One way to solve these problems is to develop a matrix that adjusts the
percentage increase an employee receives both by his or her place in the
range and by performance level. An example of such a matrix is shown in
Exhibit 9.7. In this matrix, the columns relate to the individual employee
compa ratio (defined in Chapter 11, see page 309); rows are based on performance rating. Although percentage increases could be given as a range,
here they are single increase options. Other approaches include giving merit
increases as a percentage of range midpoint rather than actual salary (thus
assuring that while similar performers in the same range get identical cash
increases, the increase in terms of percentage of actual salary is smaller for
the employee higher in the range) and staggering the time between increases
for performers of different levels (so that higher performers not only get more,
but are eligible for further increases sooner and more often than lower
performers).

Exhibit 9.7   Merit Increase Matrix

Performance Rating	Compa Ratio				
	less than 85	85–94	95–104	105–114	115 and over
5	14%	12%	10%	8%	6%
4	11%	9%	7%	5%	3%
3	9%	7%	5%	3%	—
2	4%	2%	—	—	—
1	—	—	—	—	—

Economic Restrictions on Merit Adjustments   One of the major requirements for effective merit pay programs noted above is that merit differentials between high and low performers be sufficiently great to emphasize to employees that high performance is well rewarded and that low performance is not rewarded at all. In many organizations, an attempt to maintain these differences and at the same time minimize the compensation budget is embodied in a policy of forced merit distributions. The underlying assumption is that the quality of performance of the employees is normally distributed amongst them (that is, in any group of ten employees, there will be one outstanding one, two good ones, four average performers, two mediocre ones, and one loser). The second assumption is that managers will inflate merit ratings of all subordinates to avoid making hard decisions about merit measured against standards. A final assumption is that, if all employees in a work unit receive identical raises, they will view the raises as across-the-board increases and the increases will have no motivating effect. At the same time, if everyone gets the same increase, that increase will of necessity be relatively small for everyone.

In our opinion, a forced distribution merit policy is a program for failure. The goal of human resource management programs is high performance by all employees. If normal distributions of performance occur in the organization (assuming that performance is normally distributed in the overall population), all human resource management programs have failed, for a normal distribution will occur in a sample only if that sample is randomly drawn. In most organizations, there are sophisticated recruitment and selection procedures that should bring only the most qualified employees into the organization. Training and development activities should prepare employees to operate at high levels of performance. The merit pay system and other motivational processes should be getting these high-ability employees to make greater efforts to perform. The performance appraisal system should be documenting performance problems and the performance management system should be helping to solve performance problems. When necessary, discipline and separation policies should be weeding out the truly poor performers. If all these programs are working as planned, everyone should be performing at high levels. A truly normal distribution of performance is a sign that the human resource management system is in trouble, for we might expect similar distributions of performance by simply hiring people off the streets, putting them in jobs, and pretty much ignoring them.

A second characteristic of normal distributions is that such distributions will occur in randomly drawn samples only as those samples approach some large size. Even with 100 units, such a distribution might not appear. To expect such a distribution to appear in a group of ten or fewer indicates a complete lack of understanding of the underlying statistical principles.

Behaviorally, a forced distribution merit increase policy can have devastating effects. For managers forced to make such artificial divisions, the merit pay program forces unjustifiable decisions. Two or more employees who believe their performance levels are equivalent but who see very different pay increases being offered may find it difficult to accept the internal equity of the compensation program. Organizations supporting such programs may wonder why turnover is high and why overall performance does not improve.

When discussing this topic with compensation analysts and line managers, we usually hear that not everyone will operate at peak performance. We could not agree more. The point that we try to make is that organizations must develop good measures of performance and high performance standards, and be prepared to reward employees who meet those standards. Having all employees operate at the highest levels of performance is success rather than failure. If in fact all employees in an organization are operating at these levels, sufficient income should be generated to reward all employees. Equity theory suggests that if all employees are operating at equal performance levels, they will see equal merit increases as appropriate.

Skill-Based Pay

In addition to making adjustments in pay to recognize seniority and performance, some organizations also adjust pay according to the level of skill or knowledge one has achieved on his or her job.[5] Under a *pay-for-knowledge* or *skill-based* pay plan, rates are set for people, not jobs. A typical plan will establish four to six successive levels of job knowledge to be attained. The Topeka plant of General Foods provides a good example of skill-based pay at work.[6] Every employee enters the plant at a base starting salary rate. Upon qualifying for each successive skill level, the employee's salary rate is increased. In most cases, a new employee achieves the top level (qualifies at all skill levels) within two years. In effect, the structure of skill-based pay rates replaces a more traditional job evaluation system that would establish successive rates for increasing job levels.

Although skill-based pay originated among the professions (physicians, teachers, scientists, and accountants, for example), it has become increasingly popular among hourly paid employees, where skill acquisition and flexibility in task assignment are important. Proponents of skill-based pay point to the following advantages of such systems:[7]

1. Skill acquisition is motivated. The plan encourages employees to become adept at a variety of tasks, not just one.

2. Labor is used more efficiently. Skill-based pay systems encourage employees to learn a wide variety of tasks, creating more flexibility in allocation and use of the workforce.

3. Employees adapt well to startups. Skill-based pay encourages the development of human assets. Companies in startup modes, opening new plants, have found skill-based pay to be an effective way to develop job skills among new employees.

Skill-based pay systems are not without problems, however. Research on pay for knowledge demonstrates the following difficulties:[8]

1. Employees top out when all tasks have been learned. Most skill-based pay programs allow employees to top out within two years. The obvious questions employees ask when this happens is, "What's next?" Will my salary be adjusted further? Most skill-based pay installations combine skill-based pay with some other system, like merit pay, to overcome this problem.

2. Mature plants cannot provide mobility. Skill-based pay works best in high growth operations that provide upward mobility for all employees. If the business is declining, there may not be room at the top for all employees who aspire to learn new skills.

3. There are measurement problems. Some skill-based pay plans have failed because of inadequate definition and measurement of various qualification levels. Such plans have degenerated into "credentialling" schemes for employees to qualify for higher wage rates.

4. It requires investment in training. Skill-based pay only makes sense when critical skills must be developed. It seems logical that if skill-based pay is called for, the firm is also willing to make substantial investments in the training and development activities such skills will require.

5. It conflicts with traditional job evaluation plans. Traditionally, management has navigated with job evaluation plans that measure a job's value and has set hierarchical pay rates for jobs accordingly. People are paid rates for the job they hold — not the skills they have. Skill-based pay upsets that apple cart by blurring job distinctions and focusing, instead, on the various tasks each employee can learn and perform. It is not uncommon for a skill-

based pay plant to have only one or two job designations, where traditionally they might have had fifteen or twenty.

6. Skill-based pay plans conflict with market rates. Traditionally, management groups have identified many different jobs in their organizations and priced each one according to well-defined market rates (see Chapter 7). Under skill-based pay plans, only one or two positions are, very generally, defined. Pricing them competitively is difficult, because well-defined market rates may not exist. Skill-based pay plans, then, tend to set competitive external rates at the entry level, and are less concerned with external comparisons above such levels.

It should be apparent that skill-based pay systems are not for every organization and only make sense in a rather highly defined situation. Research shows that they work best in process-production plants in a startup mode, where skill acquisition is extremely important.[9] Many of the new automobile and other manufacturing startups in the southeastern United States (for example, Nissan's Smyrna, Tennessee, plant, Toyota's Georgetown, Kentucky, plant, and James River's paper packaging products plant in Gordonsville, Tennessee) have made effective use of skill-based pay to develop new workforces and introduce team-based, autonomous work groups.

One-Time Direct Performance Payments

The individual adjustment techniques we have reviewed so far in this chapter result in a permanent adjustment in an employee's base pay as well as in an adjustment to the relation of that employee's pay rate to the internal wage structure. An alternative to such procedures is the direct performance payment, which makes no permanent adjustment in a person's base pay but, rather, allows a person's earnings to vary directly and continuously with some measure of work output. Some of these direct performance payment systems are based on individual performance; others are based on group, or even organization-wide effort.

Individual Direct Performance Payments

Individual direct performance payments take on three basic forms: (1) piecerate incentives, (2) sales commissions, and (3) bonuses. All three result in direct income to the employee based on individual achievement and vary directly with performance.

Piecerates   Under most circumstances, piecerates are designed to take external market rates for a job into account in determining a piecerate formula under which a worker will be paid. Usually, management establishes the external market rate as the "fair" rate a person of average skill, working at a normal level of effort, should make on the job. A job analysis is then carried out to determine how many units of acceptable quality a person should be able to turn out per hour. This work rate is then defined as a standard.

Suppose, for example, that an employer is attempting to set a piecerate for machinists turning out a part on a lathe. A market survey indicates that machinists on such a job earn $10 per hour. A job analysis is carried out that determines that a machinist of average skill working at a normal rate should be able to turn out 10 units per hour. The piecerate for the job is then calculated by dividing the market rate ($10 per hour) by the output standard (10 units per hour) to get a piecerate of $1 per unit. The machinist who produces 10 units per hour earns $10 for that hour. The machinist who produces 20 units per hour earns $20 that hour.

In practice, piecerates are most often set up in a way that guarantees some minimum hourly wage rate. Thus, for example, a typical piecerate will guarantee a machinist $10 per hour, but will pay earnings based on the piecerate when such earnings exceed $10 per hour.

Piecerates are not without problems. First, the nature of the job must be such that a single output measure (quantity alone, for example) is sufficient to measure performance. Where jobs involve complex dimensions of performance, piecerates will be impossible. Second, employees (and unions) often come to mistrust management's intentions in setting the work output standard. Suppose that, in our earlier example, management sets the output standard at 10 units per hour and finds that 90 percent of the machinists within two weeks are producing 40 units per hour and earning $40 per hour. Management will very likely reanalyze the job and determine that 20 or 30 units per hour is a more reasonable standard. Thus, they reduce the piecerate from $1.00 per unit to $0.50 or $0.33 per unit. The machinists thus end up working harder to earn the base wage of $10 per hour. In many cases, employees and management have come to distrust each other, destroying the incentive effects of a piecerate system. Indeed, many labor unions are on record against piecerate systems because they claim such policies do not protect the economic interests of the worker.

A third problem with a piecerate system is that employees can sometimes work themselves out of a job and into a layoff. In this case, employees respond to the piecerate and perhaps double their hourly earnings until management finds itself with an inventory of output that will last for the next four months. Their reaction is to lay the employees off for this period, having no more work for them. Many employees in this situation will gladly trade off maximum hourly earnings in the short run for long-run employment stability.

Finally, piecerates have the potential of disrupting informal status systems within a work group. Social scientists for many years have recognized the informal group problems that develop when traditional relationships between earnings of traditional work groupings are disrupted when a particularly eager worker maximizes his or her earnings.[10] A great deal of formal research and informal managerial experience suggests that informal groups develop extremely effective sanctions to discourage such "rate busters."

Commissions   Commissions are almost exclusively used as a form of payment for sales representatives. A simple sales commission formula would set a representative's commission as some percentage of the gross or net sales for which he or she is responsible. Thus, a person on a 5-percent commission who generates $500,000 in sales would earn $25,000.

Other commission formulas can be more complex. Suppose, for example, that a company wanted to (1) ensure a sales representative of some base amount of annual earnings and (2) create an incentive to expand sales in a representative's territory. Say the company is in the chemical business, and a sales representative's performance is measured by the number of gallons of various chemicals he or she is responsible for selling. The commission formula may look like this:

> Base: $18,000 per year
>
> Commission: 1¢ per gallon on the first 2 million gallons
>
>   2¢ per gallon on additional gallons

If the sales representative sold three million gallons, her earnings would be:

> $18,000   (base)
>
> 20,000   (1¢ commission × the first 2 million gallons)
>
> + 20,000   (2¢ commission × the third million gallons)
>
> $58,000   (total earnings)

The problems (in setting fair rates and readjusting them) inherent in piecerates apply to commissions, as well. Compensation planners must be very careful to set commission rates in line with the specific kinds of behaviors they wish to influence.

Bonuses   The third form of individual direct performance payment is a bonus. A bonus is simply a lump-sum payment made on top of a base salary. Bonuses can be tied to any aspect of performance, and specific bonus formulas take on a wide variety of forms.

A sales bonus, for example, may take the following form: a sales representative's base annual salary is set at $25,000 per year; a bonus formula is set up that provides an additional payment of $10,000 if a particular sales objective is met. If the objective is met, the sales representative earns a total of $35,000. Very often, bonuses are set up on a sliding scale with increasingly difficult targets. The greater the performance, the higher the bonus.

Some Considerations for Implementing Individual Direct Performance Payments   The most frequent form of individual one-time performance payment is some form of piecerate or commission. Such payments are possible only in situations where performance can be well defined in terms of output (sales dollars generated, number of items completed) and where individual employees work independently of each other. In some cases, there is a basic wage paid, with set production rates or net sales expected as a minimum, and then a bonus paid for production or sales in excess of the base. If the organization is going to make individual performance payments of this kind, it should have those employees affected in a separate wage and salary structure, because the flexibility required for such systems is not possible in the standard wage and salary structure. Job evaluation in traditional terms is not applicable to these jobs; the output possible is the only factor of interest. A commission or piecerate system must be explained in detail to employees because income will fluctuate from pay period to pay period.

Determining the size of commissions or piecerates is a different process from making other pay decisions. Wage survey information is still necessary in terms of external equity considerations. The primary set of data used for both internal and individual equity is economic: value added by the employee, based on accounting information. It is necessary to find out, for example, what an additional unit of sales is worth to the organization. The commission paid to the sales personnel will be some portion of that average marginal net revenue to provide an income for the salesperson that is competitive with income provided by similar jobs.

Direct Performance Payments to Groups

Direct performance payments to groups are similar to those to individuals. For example, with a group, such as a small sales team or an assembly team, that performs with well-defined outputs and with relative independence from other workers or groups of workers, group piecerates or bonuses are paid on a basis similar to that of individual payments.

Payments to groups, however, must take into consideration the group that is not homogeneous: for example, a sales team for a computer company may be made up of a hardware specialist, an accountant, and a management analyst. The organization must find a way to factor out the contributions of each member of the team in a way that is satisfactory to all group members. One-time performance payments are, for this reason, not much used unless all members of the group do obviously comparable work or there exists some commonly accepted way of allocating bonus payments to individual members of the group. The computer company sales team members, for example, all have jobs for which there are well-defined external markets, and base salaries can be set with respect to those markets. Bonus payments to such a group would likely be allocated on the basis of base salary; that is, if the management analyst has a base one-third higher than the accountant, she would receive one-third more bonus.

Organization-Wide Direct Performance Payments

Much more widespread are payments shared by all members of the organization. Generally, these payments are based on one of two performance concepts: a sharing of profits generated by the efforts of all employees altogether or a sharing of money saved as a result of employees' cost-reduction efforts.

Profit-Sharing Programs   Some compensation specialists argue that profit-sharing programs are membership benefits like insurance or pensions. This is largely because the linkage between performance and reward for the individual is so weak. Like almost all group or organization-wide plans, an individual's share of the total profit-sharing pool is based on salary as a percentage of total payroll; that is, if the total annual profit-sharing pool were equal to the total annual payroll, each employee would receive a bonus equal to his or her annual salary. Even though profit-sharing programs may not be effective motivators of performance, most companies using them as immediate salary supplements act as if they are, and the rhetoric accompanying payouts refers to rewards for performance, not to membership. Of course, many organizations use profit sharing as a source of deferred income for employees in connection with, or as a substitute for, other pension programs: these "profit-sharing" programs are an employee benefit and will be discussed in Chapter 10. However, the profit-sharing programs designed for annual payouts are part of pay for performance.

Profit-sharing programs are probably most effective in a small organization, where organizational performance is largely dependent on close cooperation between members of the organization. Advertising agencies, brokerage houses, accounting firms, and similar service organizations where professional and managerial efforts are the bulk of expense for the organization are more likely to use profit sharing than are manufacturing organizations, although many organizations of all types are shifting towards profit-sharing concepts and practices, as noted in Chapter 12.

The key issue for management in a profit-sharing program of this nature is what proportion of net is to be taken to form the pool for distribution to employees. There is no set answer for this, obviously; labor market pressures, other organizational needs, and tradition provide the guidelines.

Gainsharing–Productivity Programs   A major shortcoming of profit-sharing plans is that the measure employed (for example, net return on investment, ROI) is not directly influenced by the activities of any group of employees. Gainsharing plans were developed to overcome this problem and are very similar in form to profit sharing, except that the measure of productivity is defined in terms of factors that work groups can affect.

All gainsharing plans have two features in common: (1) a structured approach toward measuring productivity and (2) a formal employee involvement process.[11] Gainsharing programs develop highly structured measures of productivity (measuring the volume of output per units of input). Usually, outputs and inputs are defined in terms of dollars (for example, value of product sold divided by actual controllable costs) or in terms of standard hours (budgeted hours for production divided by actual hours). The idea behind gainsharing is the same as that behind profit sharing: a pool of money is created when productivity gains exceed some target or baseline. Under most gainsharing plans the pool is evenly split between the company and workers. The workers' half of the pool is generally paid out each quarter in the form of lump-sum gainsharing payments that are separate from wage payments.

Gainsharing plans are becoming increasingly popular as a way of designing an incentive system that is affordable and that highlights the need for productivity improvement as a way to compete. One study, for example, estimates that more gainsharing plans have been developed and installed in the last five years than in all of the previous twenty years combined.[12] The most commonly known gainsharing plans are the Scanlon plan, the Rucker plan, and Improshare. But a recent survey has found that very few firms use any of these plans in their original form. The majority of gainsharing installations have been tailored to the specific needs and situation of the organization.[13] The Scanlon plan is the earliest of the three, and defines productivity in terms of standard costs. Under the plan, a base ratio of payroll costs/net sales is created. The ratio is tracked throughout the year. Periodically (usually each quarter), performance is assessed with the ratio. If the ratio drops below the base line, 50 percent of the additional dollars saved goes into a gainsharing pool and is paid back to all members of the group in the form of bonus payments. Some plans hold a small amount of the bonus back in a reserve fund to smooth out variations in productivity that may occur during the year.

Improshare operates in a very similar fashion to Scanlon, except that the productivity measure involves standard hours rather than dollar labor costs.[14] Under Improshare, standard hours are established for production during a productivity survey. Up to two years of productivity data are established as a baseline against which to measure future performance under the plan. The Rucker plan is a third variation of productivity measurement that uses value-added-minus-production costs.

The following have been cited as advantages gained by firms that employ gainsharing as a productivity technique:[15]

1. Teamwork is enhanced and coordinated within work groups.

2. Employees focus their attention on business operations and goals.

3. Employees become knowledgeable about the entire business, not just their immediate job activities.

4. Employees work harder and smarter.

5. Individuals and groups generate ideas for doing things more effectively.

6. Work assignments are more flexible.

In spite of the advantages gainsharing promises, Lawler notes that gain-sharing requires some very unique conditions in order to succeed. He cites the following as conditions that favor gainsharing:[16]

1. Small organization, usually fewer than 500 employees

2. Organization old enough that the learning curve has flattened — standards can be set on historical data

3. Market good for the output — the company can readily sell all its production

4. Product costs largely under the control of employees — they can readily influence costs of production

5. Little or no capital investment planned

6. Technology stable with no plans for changes in methods or equipment

7. Little or no use of overtime

8. Financial measures sound and creditable

9. Organizational climate open and characterized by high levels of trust

10. No union or a union willing to negotiate a gainsharing plan

11. Management style highly participative, involving employees in decision through use of task forces and work teams

12. Product lines stable with no plans for new product introductions or changes.

The absence of any of the above features can pose a threat to gainsharing. Product market conditions and technology are particularly difficult problems to overcome in designing and installing a gainsharing plan. Swings in the demand for a company's product, for example, will often swamp a gainsharing formula. Thus, if a company cannot sell all the units produced, the gainsharing formula will show no gains, even though the groups are working more efficiently.

Similarly, changes in technology and capital investment will threaten gainsharing plans by making current measures and formulas obsolete. The introduction of new machinery may cut the time to produce a unit by 20 percent. Is this saving to be credited to the workers or to the capital investment?

Finally, gainsharing or cost-saving plans require a substantial investment in participative management. Plans such as gainsharing line up very well with a broad management style that is characterized by high degrees of employee involvement. In gainsharing, this usually takes the form of employee involvement teams who not only participate in the design of the gainsharing plan but also continue to function as teams finding more efficient ways to operate.

The other feature of most cost-reduction plans is the set of suggestion committees designed to have employees give input on means of reducing costs. This participative feature, with screening of ideas by management and employee representatives, is what makes it probable that costs can, in fact, be reduced. The advantages of cost-reduction plans are the employees' lack of resistance to change and their active involvement in keeping costs down.

Thus, the Eddy-Rucker-Nickels Company, a major consultant for installation of gainsharing programs, notes that the reward aspect of a gainsharing program is only one-third of the program: the other two, equally important, are feedback of results to employees (and further information sharing) and involvement/participation of employees in productivity-increasing activities.[17] Examples of such activities include self-directed work teams, quality circles, or a network of departmental productivity representatives combined with a structured suggestion program.

Miscellaneous Payments

Several other miscellaneous payments made to employees are not permanent adjustments to the wage and salary structure but are more stable add-ons to individual pay. The three most common add-ons are shift differentials, differentials for temporarily unpleasant or hazardous working conditions, and geographic differentials.

Shift differentials are based on the feelings of many employees that they deserve an extra bonus for working during periods other than Monday through Friday from nine to five. In most cases, unorthodox work hours are rewarded by extra pay per hour; in some cases additional benefits, such as a paid "lunch" hour, are given.

Some jobs have occasional temporary duty (usually at a different location) that is unpleasant, hazardous, or both. An example would be a maintenance operator, one of several who worked in a main plant, who on occasion would be required to visit remote sites. Because the amount of time spent at such sites would vary, and because assignments would vary with whomever was present when maintenance was required, how many remote visits were required at one time, and so forth, the organization might provide an add-on hourly pay for those times. These differentials should not be used when the hazard or unpleasant working condition is a standard, daily feature on the job; in these cases, job evaluation builds rewards into the wage and salary structure.

The third common differential is used by organizations with a single salary structure that is applied to employees in different geographic locations, especially when there are frequent transfers of employees between locations. Rather than account for local labor market differences for specific jobs by developing specific salary structures for each location, these organizations have general geographic differentials that apply to all jobs in the structure. Typically, these differentials are based on some combination of general market levels in the different locations and cost-of-living differentials.

Finally, some organizations set up pay bonuses for special situations. A company with recruiting problems might offer a "bounty" to employees who refer qualified applicants who are subsequently hired. Rewards might be offered to employees with records of no, or low, absenteeism. Specific suggestions are rewarded by many organizations with one-time bonuses. Certainly all of these bonuses are "pay for performance," yet they are rarely the work of the compensation specialist. The compensation administrator will have to coordinate these payments with the compensation program in general.

Summary

We have examined the procedures involved in paying individual employees within the wage structure. We noted that organizations often choose to make pay distinctions among individuals (even those employed on the same job) to reflect a number of factors including seniority and performance effectiveness. Thus, individual pay determination often reflects management's desire to recognize merit and promote incentives for people to remain with the organization and perform at high levels.

We examined the most common form of incentive system today, called merit or pay for performance. Such plans call for adjustments to base pay according to an employee's performance level. We showed that such plans are critically dependent on the effectiveness and credibility of the performance appraisal system in use.

Finally, we examined the use of incentive payments for performance that are not rolled into base pay and must be re-earned each period. We looked at individual incentive systems that include piecerates and commissions. We also examined group incentive plans including gainsharing and profit sharing.

Notes

[1]Three recent books that do treat the area comprehensively are: R. W. Beatty and H. J. Bernardin, *Appraising Human Performance* (Boston: Kent, 1982); G. P. Latham and K. N. Wexley, *Increasing Productivity Through Performance Appraisal* (Reading, Mass.: Addison-Wesley, 1981); and L. S. Baird, R. W. Beatty, and C. E. Schneier, *Performance Appraisal Sourcebook* (Boston: Human Resource Development Press, 1982).

[2]R. G. Greenwood, "Management by Objectives," *Academy of Management Review* 6 (1981); Jeffrey S. Kane and Kimberly A. Freeman, "MBO and Performance Appraisal: A Mixture That's Not a Solution, Part I," *Personnel* (December 1986): 26–36; Kane and Freeman, "MBO and Performance Appraisal: A Mixture That's Not a Solution, Part II," *Personnel* (February 1987): 26–31.

[3]Kane and Freeman, ibid.

[4]Kane and Freeman, "MBO and Performance Appraisal, Part I."

[5]Edward E. Lawler, III, *Pay and Organizational Development* (Reading, Ma.: Addison-Wesley, 1981); G. D. Jenkins and N. Gupta, "The Payoffs of Paying for Knowledge," *National Productivity Review* 4 (2) (1985): 121–30; Jenkins and Gupta, *Exploratory Investigations of Pay for Knowledge Systems* (Washington, D.C.: U.S. Department of Labor, 1986), BMLR #108, 1986; Edward E. Lawler, III, and G. E. Ledford, Jr., "Skill-Based Pay — A Concept That's Catching On," *Personnel* (September 1985): 30–37; H. Tosi and L. Tosi, "What Managers Need to Know About Knowledge-Based Pay," *Organizational Dynamics* 14 (3) (1986): 52–64.

[6]R. E. Walton, "Work Innovations at Topeka: After Six Years," *Journal of Applied Behavioral Science* 13 (1977): 422–33; Walton, "The Topeka Story: Teaching an Old Dog Food New Tricks," *The Wharton Magazine* 2 (2) (1978): 38–48.

[7]Jenkins and Gupta, "The Payoffs of Paying for Knowledge"; Lawler, *Pay and Organizational Development;* Lawler and Ledford, "Skill-Based Pay"; Jenkins and Gupta, *Exploratory Investigations;* Tosi and Tosi, "What Managers Need to Know."

[8]Ibid.

[9]Lawler, *Pay and Organizational Development.*

[10]W. F. Whyte, *Money and Motivation* (New York: Harper & Row, 1955).

[11]Lawler, *Pay and Organizational Development.*

[12]Carla O'Dell (with Jerry McAdams), *People, Performance, and Pay: America Responds to the Competitiveness Challenge* (Scottsdale, Ariz.: American Compensation Association, 1986).

[13]Ibid.

[14]Improshare is a registered service mark of Mitchell Fein, Inc., and is offered to organizations through Arthur Young.

[15]Lawler, *Pay and Organizational Development.*

[16]Ibid.

[17]R. C. Scott, "Gainsharing to Improve and Protect Profit," opening remarks at the Productivity, Inc., Conference, Dearborn, Michigan, April 30, 1985.

10

Benefits Programs

Key Issues and Questions
for This Chapter

After you have studied this chapter, you should be able to address the following key issues and questions:

1. What is a total compensation plan?
2. What are benefits?
3. How can a manager obtain information about benefits?
4. What are the major components of a benefit program?
5. Can benefits be used to attract, retain, or motivate employees? If so, how can this be accomplished?

Introduction

The compensation analyst who has developed a salary structure with policies for individual placement in the structure based on merit, seniority, or some combination of the two has only half the compensation job done. The other half is creating a benefit structure that will complete the compensation package. Many "comp" people sometimes forget that total compensation is the sum of direct pay *plus* benefits. The goals of the benefit structure are similar to those for the wage and salary structure, in that they should also attract, retain, and motivate employees, and should do this in the least costly fashion for the employer. The benefit structure should also be complementary to the wage and salary structure and planned with the wage and salary structure in mind; many benefit levels (for example, life insurance and pensions) are a function of salary level.

A full discussion of benefits is beyond the scope of this book. (For those with an interest in a more comprehensive view of benefits, PWS-KENT Publishing Co. has published a new revised edition of Robert McCaffery's *Managing the Employee Benefits Program* as a companion volume to this book in the Human Resource Management Series, entitled *Employee Benefit Programs: A Total Compensation Perspective.*)

Salaries and Benefits

Why not just pay people salaries and let it go at that? There are a variety of reasons why benefits are popular, and popular they are. (One survey of 186 companies, for example, traced a growth in benefits from 1959 to 1980 from 24.7 percent of payroll to 41.4 percent of payroll.)[1] The reasons for their popularity are as follows:

1. During World War II, wage controls made it difficult to use salaries as a means of attracting, motivating, or retaining employees. Changes in benefits were easier to make, and employers started to compete in terms of benefits.

2. For many benefits, it is more cost efficient for the company to provide them than for the individual. Group coverage for insurance, for example, is cheaper per dollar protection bought than individual coverage.

3. Internal Revenue Code treatment of benefits (at least through 1986) makes them preferable to wages. Many benefits are nontaxable to the employee and are deductible by the employer. With other benefits, taxes are deferred. In addition, inflation has caused "bracket creep" for most employees. That is, salaries themselves have grown artificially high because the dollar

has become worth less; employees must pay taxes at a higher rate for the same purchasing power. Inflation, then, tends to make benefits preferable to wages, too.

4. Unions have found it profitable to bargain over benefits. If a union gains certain benefits, say total dental care, and the benefit is granted in terms of services given, any price increases are likely to be absorbed by the employer with no further bargaining necessary. This is also the case in nonunion situations. A benefit (such as a company car or cafeteria service) once granted is unlikely to be withdrawn.

5. Management finds it convenient to bargain over benefits, or to grant benefits in nonunion organizations. In a sense, the granting of benefits confers an aura of social responsibility on employers; they are "taking care of" their employees.

6. Many benefits, such as social security, are mandated by the federal government. Others may be required under state law. There are other benefits, such as pensions, that are controlled under both federal and state law, as noted in Chapter 6.

Benefits Surveys

Before starting to set up a benefit structure, the compensation analyst will want to obtain the same type of survey data for benefits as he or she obtained for salaries. In Chapter 7, we indicated the necessity of asking surveyed organizations for levels of various benefits granted. The information is needed both for interpreting wage-level data and for determining benefit levels needed to be competitive. Factors such as labor market or industry type that are used in determining the scope of the survey were also noted in Chapter 7. If the purpose of the survey is to gather information only on benefits, key jobs will not be used. This is because benefits tend to be distributed fairly equally across the organizations; if one worker gets dental insurance, all do. The exceptions to this general rule are executive perquisites and certain deferred income programs. Thus, surveys such as the *U.S. Chamber of Commerce Employee Benefits Survey* concentrate on nonexecutive employees; others, such as Executive Compensation Service (a subsidiary of The Wyatt Company) report on executive perquisites, stock plans, and other salary and benefit data for supervisory and managerial employees.

Because benefits tend to be given by organization rather than by job (as are salaries), and because organizations tend not to compete over benefit packages as much as they do over salary levels, much more published information seems to be available to compensation analysts on benefits than on wages. An additional cause of this greater availability of information is that many benefits are supplied to organizations by outside companies; these vendors are willing to supply whatever information they have as part of the sales effort.

The standard survey of employee benefits is published annually by the U.S. Chamber of Commerce. Exhibits 10.1 and 10.2 show the basic kinds of information contained in the survey. The benefit data in the Chamber of Commerce survey are conservative with respect to benefits actually paid by organizations. Except for the data on banks, financial institutions, and some hospitals, these data do not include benefits paid to managerial or professional employees, but only those paid to hourly employees and salaried employees whose pay varies with the number of hours worked. Managerial and professional employees tend to get higher benefits, both absolutely and as a percentage of base pay. A second point to note is the Chamber's use of "percent of payroll." When it is stated that total benefits for all industries are 40 percent of payroll, that means that for every dollar spent for direct wages or salaries, an additional $0.40 is spent on benefits. Thus, benefits in this case amount to about 28.5 percent of the total compensation package. The third point is that not all benefits are included in the Chamber of Commerce survey. These benefits, which are primarily services, may or may not be mentioned by survey respondents in miscellaneous categories. Nevertheless, this survey is the standard; any compensation specialist should obtain it as a matter of course.

There are also many other sources of benefit survey data. The three loose-leaf services (Bureau of National Affairs, Commerce Clearinghouse, Prentice-Hall) all have one or more volumes including coverage of current benefit practices; survey data are reported by these services on a timely basis. *Compensation & Benefits Review* frequently publishes articles relating current practices data; in addition, there is a front section called "Compensation Currents" that provides summary information from many commercial benefit surveys. *Employee Benefit Plan Review* and *Employee Benefits Journal* have articles and issues devoted to benefit levels. Finally, many of the wage and salary surveys discussed in Chapter 7 provide information on benefits, as well. Regardless of the source of information, it is important for the compensation specialist to obtain survey data on benefits just as on wage levels, and for the same reason: if external equity in the compensation package is to be preserved, the benefit portion of that package must be planned in relation to the market.

Benefits Policy

If it is important for the compensation specialist to know what the average organization in the market is offering in the way of benefits and benefit levels, it is crucial that he or she not follow such averages slavishly but, rather, build a benefits program based on organizational policy. There are many decisions to be made on benefits policy; some are similar to policy decisions for wages and salaries. In the most general form, a benefits policy must address the following questions:

1. What benefit goals does the organization have? Benefit programs may be used to ensure employee security and health, provide deferred income, reward employee loyalty, fulfill the social obligations of the organization, underline status differences between different groups of employees, or provide an incentive to join the organization.

2. What benefit levels will the organization provide? It may choose to meet, exceed, or follow the market, just as it may with wages. There may be a tradeoff between wage and benefit levels.

3. To what extent will the organization require employees to support benefit levels? Such support may come in the form of coinsurance, where employees pay some part of premiums, or copayment, where employees pay some part of the bill for actual services received, or both. One survey, for example, found that only 47 percent of the nearly 5,000 companies responding paid the full cost for employees' hospitalization, surgical, and major medical benefits; and only 69 percent paid the full cost of group life insurance.[2]

4. What specific benefits will the organization provide? Will employee wishes help formulate the program, and if so, to what extent?

As we noted in Chapter 6, federal law, state law, and union bargaining contracts constrain the organization with respect to all four aspects of benefit policy. Competition for employees places further constraints on the organization; although benefits are not well publicized or much used as recruiting tools, many employees know enough about some specific benefits (day care,

Exhibit 10.1 Employee Benefits as Dollars per Year per Employee, by Type of Benefit and Industry Groups, 1985

Type of benefit	Total, all industries	Manufacturing industries															Nonmanufacturing industries							
		Total, all manufacturing	Food, beverages, and tobacco	Textile products and apparel	Pulp, paper, lumber, and furniture	Printing and publishing	Chemicals and allied products	Petroleum industry	Rubber, leather, and plastic products	Stone, clay, and glass products	Primary metal industries	Fabricated metal products (excluding mach. and trans. equipment)	Machinery (excluding electrical)	Electrical machinery, equipment, and supplies	Transportation equipment	Instruments and miscellaneous manufacturing industries	Total, all nonmanufacturing	Public utilities (electric, gas, water, telephone, etc.)	Department stores	Trade (wholesale and other retail)	Banks, finance companies, and trust companies	Insurance companies	Hospitals	Miscellaneous nonmanufacturing industries*
Total employee benefits as dollars per year per employee	8,166	8,653	8,425	4,599	7,786	7,292	10,086	12,303	8,095	7,511	11,344	8,659	9,408	8,573	9,649	6,948	7,819	10,622	4,292	5,697	6,552	7,608	6,745	7,731
1. Legally required payments (employer's share only)	2,058	2,348	2,453	1,456	2,588	1,801	2,138	3,000	2,537	2,336	3,178	2,492	2,679	2,116	2,314	2,011	1,852	2,075	1,423	1,807	1,661	1,688	1,712	2,011
a. Old-Age, Survivors, Disability, and Health Insurance (FICA taxes)	1,428	1,471	1,461	969	1,461	1,397	1,598	2,104	1,396	1,472	1,578	1,401	1,574	1,493	1,522	1,361	1,397	1,689	940	1,171	1,243	1,338	1,332	1,390
b. Unemployment Compensation	344	452	400	328	372	240	314	284	470	499	687	587	637	384	416	398	267	179	298	408	355	282	214	298
c. Workers' compensation (including estimated cost of self-insured)	261	413	503	158	752	158	224	606	671	362	912	501	451	232	371	236	154	195	179	217	60	65	144	213
d. Railroad Retirement Tax, Railroad Unemployment and Cash Sickness Insurance, state sickness benefits insurance, etc.**	25	12	89	0	3	6	3	6	0	4	1	3	17	8	5	15	34	11	7	10	3	4	22	110
2. Pension, insurance, and other agreed-upon payments (employer's share only)	2,762	2,850	2,671	1,358	2,489	1,901	3,292	4,298	2,450	2,432	4,727	2,923	3,247	2,575	3,449	1,901	2,700	4,082	1,234	1,724	2,077	2,753	2,056	2,618
a. Pension plan premiums and pension payments not covered by insurance-type plan (net)	905	731	678	296	422	427	972	1,876	392	553	1,470	669	807	610	1,070	321	1,029	1,905	212	273	563	998	703	1,014
b. Life insurance premiums; death benefits; hospital, surgical, medical, and major medical insurance premiums, etc. (net)	1,561	1,842	1,713	1,002	1,880	1,269	1,894	1,981	1,731	1,794	2,817	2,070	2,159	1,654	2,028	1,353	1,362	1,789	690	1,237	1,252	1,327	1,070	1,374
c. Short-term disability	61	91	84	30	104	46	122	118	81	14	133	78	100	109	99	67	41	59	20	34	32	62	36	23

d. Salary continuation or long-term disability	44 / 87	25 / 91	26 / 92	7 / 8	6 / 59	29 / 52	63 / 137	83 / 146	39 / 38	18 / 34	24 / 107	11 / 64	20 / 117	19 / 99	26 / 164	34 / 70	58 / 84	73 / 117	13 / 26	28 / 95	53 / 80	75 / 86	44 / 70	58 / 68
e. Dental insurance premiums	17	6	18	9	3	18	1	7	14	0	0	6	1	1	10	15	24	32	270	29	13	11	33	5
f. Discounts on goods and services purchased from company by employees	29	8	17	0	11	0	29	42	0	0	3	4	1	17	2	2	43	33	0	3	44	88	42	39
g. Employee meals furnished by company	58	56	43	5	4	59	75	46	155	19	173	21	42	67	50	39	59	75	3	25	41	105	58	37
h. Miscellaneous payments (vision care, prescription drugs, separation or termination pay, moving expenses, etc.)	752	772	739	537	685	756	1,068	698	752	822	755	851	768	793	771	684	739	926	515	602	643	648	822	651
3. Paid rest periods, lunch periods, wash-up time, travel time, clothes-change time, get-ready time, etc.	2,044	2,053	1,879	964	1,861	1,875	2,565	3,317	1,917	1,638	2,256	1,792	2,192	2,269	2,529	1,605	2,038	3,040	950	900	1,293	2,039	1,968	1,929
4. Payments for time not worked	1,049	1,101	1,036	528	1,100	1,055	1,277	1,854	1,086	885	1,393	1,020	1,205	1,137	1,141	842	1,012	1,479	471	466	622	961	1,082	935
a. Paid vacations and payments in-lieu of vacation	611 / 286	681 / 186	583 / 233	380 / 25	617 / 106	534 / 240	823 / 367	946 / 421	629 / 121	513 / 196	635 / 56	658 / 70	765 / 140	750 / 229	939 / 347	526 / 197	561 / 356	885 / 503	344 / 114	257 / 145	391 / 219	676 / 311	391 / 370	517 / 381
b. Payments for holidays not worked																								
c. Paid sick leave																								
d. Payments for State or National Guard duty; jury, witness, and voting pay allowances; payments for time lost due to death in family or other personal reasons, etc.	99 / 549	84 / 630	27 / 683	32 / 284	38 / 163	45 / 958	99 / 1,023	96 / 990	80 / 438	44 / 282	171 / 429	44 / 601	82 / 521	153 / 819	102 / 585	40 / 747	109 / 491	173 / 499	21 / 170	32 / 664	60 / 878	92 / 480	126 / 187	97 / 522
5. Other items	234	331	377	181	45	594	463	202	240	151	185	309	270	536	151	124	140	241	115	330	480	90	48	207
a. Profit-sharing payments	131	119	107	26	31	97	280	747	39	99	169	98	45	83	164	124	140	241	22	86	208	179	20	110
b. Contributions to employee thrift plans	69	91	86	49	60	222	204	8	53	4	38	101	116	84	52	76	54	33	15	172	61	63	22	66
c. Christmas or other special bonuses, service awards, suggestion awards, etc.	63	36	14	21	11	39	32	24	48	29	13	30	30	74	40	40	82	67	6	75	92	85	77	101
d. Employee education expenditures (tuition refunds, etc.)	51	53	99	7	15	7	44	8	59	0	22	62	60	42	178	51	49	104	12	1	36	64	19	38
e. Special wage payments ordered by courts, payments to union stewards, etc.																								

*Includes research, engineering, education, government agencies, construction, etc.
**Figure is considerably less than legal rate, because most reporting companies had only a small proportion of employees covered by tax.
***Less than 50c.

Reprinted with the permission of the Chamber of Commerce of the United States of America from *Employee Benefits 1985*, ©1986 Chamber of Commerce of the United States of America.

Exhibit 10.2   Employee Benefits as Percent of Payroll, by Type of Benefit and Industry Groups, 1985

Type of benefit	Total, all industries	Total, all manufacturing	Food, beverages, and tobacco	Textile products and apparel	Pulp, paper, lumber, and furniture	Printing and publishing	Chemicals and allied products	Petroleum industry	Rubber, leather, and plastic products	Stone, clay, and glass products	Primary metal industries	Fabricated metal products (excluding mach. and trans. equipment)	Machinery (excluding electrical)	Electrical machinery, equipment, and supplies	Transportation equipment	Instruments and miscellaneous manufacturing industries	Total, all nonmanufacturing	Public utilities (electric, gas, water, telephone, etc.)	Department stores	Trade (wholesale and other retail)	Banks, finance companies, and trust companies	Insurance companies	Hospitals	Miscellaneous nonmanufacturing industries
Total employee benefits as percent of payroll	37.7	39.7	39.7	32.3	35.3	34.3	43.0	39.1	40.0	34.0	49.6	42.1	40.1	39.1	41.5	34.4	36.3	41.2	30.7	31.5	34.5	37.6	34.4	33.9
1. Legally required payments (employer's share only)	9.5	10.8	11.6	10.2	11.7	8.5	9.1	9.5	12.5	10.6	13.9	12.1	11.4	9.7	10.0	9.9	8.6	8.0	10.2	10.0	8.8	8.3	8.7	8.8
a. Old-Age, Survivors, Disability, and Health Insurance (FICA taxes)	6.6	6.8	6.9	6.8	6.6	6.6	6.8	6.7	6.9	6.7	6.9	6.8	6.7	6.8	6.6	6.7	6.5	6.5	6.7	6.5	6.6	6.6	6.8	6.1
b. Unemployment Compensation	1.6	2.1	1.9	2.3	1.7	1.1	1.3	0.9	2.3	2.3	3.0	2.9	2.7	1.8	1.8	2.0	1.2	0.7	2.1	2.3	1.9	1.4	1.1	1.3
c. Workers' compensation (including estimated cost of self-insured)	1.2	1.9	2.4	1.1	3.4	0.7	1.0	1.9	3.3	1.6	4.0	2.4	1.9	1.1	1.6	1.2	0.7	0.8	1.3	1.2	0.3	0.3	0.7	0.9
d. Railroad Retirement Tax, Railroad Unemployment and Cash Sickness Insurance, state sickness benefits insurance, etc.**	0.1	0.1	0.4	...	...	...	...	...	...	...	...	...	0.1	...	...	0.1	0.2	...	0.1	0.1	...	...	0.1	0.5
2. Pension, insurance, and other agreed-upon payments (employer's share only)	12.8	13.1	12.6	9.5	11.3	8.9	14.0	13.6	12.1	11.0	20.7	14.2	13.9	11.7	14.8	9.4	12.5	15.8	8.8	9.5	11.0	13.6	10.5	11.5
a. Pension plan premiums and pension payments not covered by insurance-type plan (net)	4.2	3.4	3.2	2.1	1.9	2.0	4.1	6.0	1.9	2.5	6.4	3.3	3.4	2.8	4.6	1.6	4.8	7.4	1.5	1.5	3.0	4.9	3.6	4.4
b. Life insurance premiums; death benefits; hospital, surgical, medical, and major medical insurance premiums, etc. (net)	7.2	8.5	8.1	7.0	8.5	6.0	8.1	6.3	8.6	8.1	12.3	10.1	9.2	7.5	8.7	6.7	6.3	6.9	4.9	6.8	6.6	6.6	5.5	6.0
c. Short-term disability	0.3	0.4	0.4	0.2	0.5	0.2	0.5	0.4	0.4	0.1	0.6	0.4	0.4	0.5	0.4	0.3	0.2	0.2	0.1	0.2	0.2	0.3	0.2	0.1

Item																											
d. Salary continuation or long-term disability	0.2 0.4	0.1 0.4	0.1 0.4	0.1 0.1	••• 0.3	0.1 0.2	0.1 0.1	0.1 0.4	0.1 0.3	0.2 0.2	0.3 0.6	0.3 0.5	0.2 0.2	0.1 0.2	0.1 0.5	0.1 0.3	0.1 0.5	0.1 0.4	0.1 0.7	0.2 0.3	0.3 0.4	0.3 0.5	0.1 0.2	0.2 0.5	0.3 0.4	0.4 0.4	0.2 0.4	0.3 0.3
e. Dental insurance premiums	•••	•••	0.1	•••	•••	•••	•••	•••	•••	0.1	•••	•••	0.1	•••	•••	•••	•••	•••	•••	•••	0.1	•••	1.9	0.2	0.1	0.1	0.2	•••
f. Discounts on goods and services purchased from company by employees	0.1	•••	0.1	0.1	•••	0.1	0.1	0.1	0.1	•••	•••	•••	0.1	0.1	•••	•••	0.1	0.1	•••	0.1	0.2	0.1	•••	0.2	0.1	0.1	0.2	•••
g. Employee meals furnished by company	0.1	•••	0.1	•••	•••	0.1	0.1	•••	0.1	0.8	0.3	0.1	0.8	0.4	0.8	0.2	0.3	0.1	0.2	0.2	0.1	0.2	•••	•••	0.2	0.4	0.2	0.2
h. Miscellaneous payments (vision care, prescription drugs, separation or termination pay, moving expenses, etc.)	0.3	0.3	0.2	•••	•••	0.3	0.1	0.1	0.3	0.8	0.1	0.1	0.8	0.1	0.1	0.2	0.3	0.3	0.2	0.2	0.3	0.3	•••	0.1	0.2	0.5	0.3	0.2
3. Paid rest periods, lunch periods, wash-up time, travel time, clothes-change time, get-ready time, etc.	3.5	3.5	3.8	3.1	3.6	4.6	2.2	3.7	3.7	3.3	4.1	3.6	3.3	3.3	3.4	3.6	3.4	3.7	3.6	3.4	3.3	3.3	3.4	3.2	0.5	3.4	4.2	2.9
4. Payments for time not worked	9.4	9.4	8.9	8.4	8.8	10.9	10.5	9.5	7.4	9.9	8.7	10.3	9.4	10.9	9.5	11.8	6.8	6.8	5.0	6.8	10.1	10.0	8.5
a. Paid vacations and payments in lieu of vacation	4.8	5.1	4.9	5.0	5.0	5.4	5.9	5.4	4.0	6.1	5.0	5.2	5.1	4.9	4.2	4.7	5.7	3.4	2.6	3.3	4.7	5.5	4.1
b. Payments for holidays not worked	2.8	3.1	2.7	2.8	2.5	3.5	3.0	3.1	2.3	2.8	3.2	3.4	3.3	4.0	2.6	2.6	3.4	2.5	1.4	2.1	3.3	2.0	2.3
c. Paid sick leave	1.3	0.9	1.1	0.5	1.1	1.6	1.3	0.6	0.9	0.2	0.3	1.0	0.6	1.5	1.0	1.7	2.0	0.8	0.8	1.2	1.5	1.9	1.7
d. Payments for State or National Guard duty; jury, witness, and voting pay allowances; payments for time lost due to death in family or other personal reasons, etc.	0.5 2.5	0.4 2.9	0.2 2.0	0.2 0.7	0.2 4.5	0.4 4.4	0.3 3.1	0.4 2.2	0.2 1.3	0.7 1.9	0.2 2.9	0.7 3.7	0.3 2.2	0.4 2.5	0.2 3.7	0.5 2.3	0.7 1.9	0.1 1.2	0.2 3.7	0.3 4.6	0.5 2.4	0.6 1.0	0.4 2.3
i. Other items	1.1	1.5	1.3	0.7	2.8	2.0	0.6	1.2	0.7	0.8	1.5	2.4	1.2	0.6	2.3	0.8	0.2	0.8	1.8	2.5	0.4	0.2	0.9
a. Profit-sharing payments	0.6	0.5	0.2	0.1	0.5	1.2	2.4	0.2	0.4	0.7	0.5	0.4	0.2	0.7	0.6	0.7	0.9	0.2	0.5	1.1	0.9	0.1	0.5
b. Contributions to employee thrift plans	0.3	0.4	0.3	0.3	1.0	0.9	•••	0.3	•••	0.2	0.5	0.4	0.5	0.2	0.4	0.3	0.1	0.1	1.0	0.3	0.3	0.1	0.3
c. Christmas or other special bonuses, service awards, suggestion awards, etc.	0.3	0.2	0.1	0.1	0.2	0.1	0.1	0.2	0.1	0.1	0.1	0.3	0.1	0.2	0.2	0.4	0.3	•••	0.4	0.5	0.4	0.4	0.4
d. Employee education expenditures (tuition refunds, etc.)																							
e. Special wage payments ordered by courts, payments to union stewards, etc.	0.2	0.2	0.5	0.1	•••	0.2	•••	0.3	•••	0.1	0.3	0.2	0.3	0.8	0.3	0.2	0.4	0.1	•••	0.2	0.3	0.1	0.2

*Includes research, engineering, education, government agencies, construction, etc.

†Figure is considerably less than legal rate, because most reporting companies had only a small proportion of employees covered by tax.

**Less than 0.05%.

Reprinted with the permission of the Chamber of Commerce of the United States of America from *Employee Benefits 1985*, ©1986 Chamber of Commerce of the United States of America.

dental coverage) that these can make a difference in attraction and retention rates.

Although developing a benefits policy is a complex task, there appear to be general patterns that emerge for different kinds of organizations. One consulting firm, for example, notes the level and characteristics of noncash components for different types of organizations.[3] Exhibit 10.3 shows the interaction of noncash and cash components of typical compensation programs for several kinds of organizations.

Components of the Benefits Package

There are three major components of the benefit package: security and health benefits, pay for time not worked, and services provided by the organization at reduced cost or no cost. In this section of the chapter, we will look at the major benefits that make up each of these components and provide some information on levels of benefits commonly provided and policy questions to be faced by the compensation specialist.

Security and Health Benefits

The component of employee benefits devoted to ensuring security and health is the most regulated. Some of the constraints placed on these benefits were noted in Chapter 6. The major benefits classified as security and health include OASDHI segments (especially social security, unemployment, and workers' compensation), insurance, severance pay, pensions, and other capital formation devices.

Old Age, Survivors, Disability, and Health Insurance (OASDHI)   The program that most employees know as *social security* includes more than just that. It includes retirement insurance, survivors' insurance, disability insurance, hospital and medical insurance for the disabled and aged (Medicare), black-lung benefits, and supplemental security income. OASDHI also includes provision for unemployment insurance (discussed separately) and public assistance/welfare, such as aid to families with dependent children.

OASDHI benefits are financed equally by employer and employee through Federal Insurance Contributions Act (FICA) payments. FICA taxes are based on two factors: the tax rate and the size of the taxable base. Both of these factors have been increasing in recent years and are likely to continue doing

Exhibit 10.3 Organizational Style and Compensation Mix

Type of Organization	Working Climate	Reward Management Components				
		Cash		Noncash		
		Base Salary	Short-Term Incentives	Level	Characteristics
Mature industrial	Balanced	Medium	Medium	Medium	Balanced
Developing industrial	Growth, creativity	Medium	High	Low	Short-term-oriented
Conservative financial	Security	Low	Low	High	Long-term, security-oriented
Nonprofit	Societal impact, personal fulfillment	Low	None	Low-medium	Long-term, security-oriented
Sales	Growth, freedom to act	Low	High	Low	Short-term-oriented

Source: Reprinted by permission of the publisher, from "Compensation Currents," *Compensation Review*, Second Quarter 1981, p. 12. ©1981 by AMACOM, a division of the American Management Associations. All rights reserved.

so. In 1987, the tax rate was 7.15 percent, including both social security and Medicare funding, and the base rate rose to $43,800. Thus, an employee could have payed as much as $3,131.70 in FICA taxes in 1987 (as compared to a maximum of $1,975.05 in 1981). The employer must match these payments, as well.

The social security system is in a state of disarray, but to herald its demise may be premature. If the system is to remain solvent, either FICA taxes must be raised or benefits must be lowered. In any case, individuals cannot expect to maintain a preretirement life-style on social security benefit payments alone. Social security was never intended to provide more than a "minimum floor of protection" against risks.[4] It will never be more than that, even if it does survive. Although it is a major expense for employers (equivalent to 6.6 percent of payroll in 1985)[5] and employees, it is not seen by most productive workers as a major "benefit."

Unemployment Insurance   Mandated under OASDHI, the unemployment insurance programs are administered at the state level, and are supported through employer contributions. In 1985, employer taxes required to support unemployment payments amounted to about 1.6 percent of payroll.[6] State laws vary, but basically the tax rate on employers is based on an "experience rate." Those employers who lay off more employees pay more; those with lower contributions to unemployment rates pay less.

Workers' Compensation   Workers' compensation is a program administered by the states under varying state laws and paid for by the employer. Rules and regulations vary from state to state, as do employer contributions. In 1985, however, the costs of workers' compensation to employers were estimated to be about 1.2 percent of payroll.[7] The function of workers' compensation programs is to provide support to those workers who are injured on the job or who sustain job-related medical problems (such as asbestosis, black lung, or cancer associated with prolonged exposure to some chemicals). Payouts made under workers' compensation programs include payment of medical bills, support if the medical problem makes further work impossible (disability payments), burial expenses, and aid to widows and dependent children.

As with unemployment insurance, workers' compensation taxes are frequently experienced-based: companies whose workers sustain most work-related injury/illness problems pay the most. Except in a few states (such as Ohio), most workers' compensation insurance is underwritten by private companies. Large organizations can also insure themselves. Thus, organizations can fit workers' compensation programs into the total benefit package with more flexibility than is allowed the treatment of other legally mandated programs.

Insurance   Insurance is a large benefit expenditure for most organizations, equivalent to 8.1 percent of direct payroll costs in 1985.[8] Many different types of insurance are offered to employees, including life insurance, accidental death and dismemberment, health, dental and optical insurance, prescription drugs, psychiatric care, and auto insurance. All these types of insurance share some characteristics that make them good benefits from both the employer's and employee's point of view.

An employer may feel a responsibility for the health of an employee and his or her family. But in any case, the employee beset by health problems and the worry about how to pay for them is not likely to be productive. In addition, the availability of paid care may induce employees to take care of problems they would otherwise live with; again, productivity may be improved. Employers may deduct expenditures on insurance premiums from taxable income; employees receive these benefits (within legislated limits) as nontaxable income. The insuring of a large group allows coverage at a rate lower than would be available to individuals. Also, employees are not required (generally) to submit to physical examinations or other qualifying tests, which makes insurance available to more employees at lower costs. Finally, group programs tend to have lessened administrative costs and record-keeping requirements because these can be added into other personnel functions.

Health insurance is the most frequently provided type of insurance. Many programs are available: some hospitalization programs guarantee certain services; others provide dollar amounts for specific services according to a schedule. Surgical insurance is sometimes separated out from general medical/hospital care. Basic plans, such as Blue Cross, provide coverage for most health needs. Additional coverage can be provided through major medical insurance. If an organization is located near a health maintenance organization, or HMO (these provide comprehensive prepaid medical coverage), the Health Maintenance Organization Act requires that HMO membership be a health insurance option for employees.

Other forms of health-related insurance are now becoming more common, too. Dental insurance now accounts for benefit payments equivalent to 0.4 percent of the payroll.[9] Nearly three-fifths of the plans in one survey provided dental care.[10] Usually, bridgework and orthodontia are excluded from coverage, especially if the employer pays the full premium. Prescription drugs are increasingly paid for by the employers' plans. In those organizations in which some behavioral problems (abuse of controlled substances or stress-related antisocial behavior, for example) are recognized as symptoms of illness rather than as sins, treatment rather than punishment is the preferred solution. In these organizations, insurance is provided for outpatient psychiatric counseling. Insurance for routine eye care is now provided by many organizations (two-fifths of plans covered in one survey did so);[11] fewer provide coverage for frames and lenses. A rarer form of insurance, hospice care for the terminally ill, is now offered by such companies as RCA and Westinghouse, and through insurers such as Blue Cross.[12] Although 500 hospice programs are available, geographic coverage is spotty and employee reaction is mixed so far.

Accidental death and dismemberment insurance is provided by many organizations. It can be a useful supplement to workers' compensation, and is particularly useful for employees who travel for the organization. Regular life insurance is also provided by most organizations. The type of insurance provided is usually group term life insurance (coverage is for the period of a specified term, and premiums do not build up assets) provided in some multiple of base annual salary. Most companies pay the premium for coverage between 1.5 and 2.5 times an employee's annual salary; many plans allow the employee to buy additional coverage at the group rates.

A final form of insurance that is beginning to be offered as a benefit is auto insurance. A few companies now offer such insurance, paying about 40 percent of the premium. Two problems preventing more widespread adoption are the federal tax code (which treats employer premium payments for auto insurance as taxable income to the employee) and the Taft-Hartley Act (which does not include group auto insurance as a legitimate benefit under collectively bargained trust funds jointly administered by labor and management).[13]

Severance Pay   Because of unemployment compensation, many organizations give no severance pay; others still provide payment to employees when they leave, usually in lieu of notice.[14] One survey of 131 major corporations reported that 90 percent provided severance pay to salaried employees; 48 percent provided such protection to involuntarily terminated hourly workers. Amounts ranged from two weeks to one year's pay; 79 percent of the respondents continued benefits during the severance-pay period. Some executives were reported to receive as much as three years' pay.[15] Other benefits provided for terminated employees include placement services such as resume banks, job-finding seminars, and the use of office space to operate from while in the process of job hunting.

Pensions

Pensions and their variants (such as profit-sharing plans and stock option programs) have two distinct purposes. The first is to ensure that employees will continue to have some income after they retire. The second is to defer income realization, and therefore defer income taxation, until after retirement and thus have the income taxed at a lower rate. For executives, a related purpose is capital formation by providing opportunities to realize capital gains and thus avoid high rates of taxation on standard income. With the passage of the Tax Reform Act of 1986, capital gains tax provisions were abolished, and such income, starting in 1987, became taxable at regular income tax rates. Thus a major incentive for some forms of benefit provision has, for the time being, disappeared.

Under many pension programs, both employer and employee make contributions. The employee contribution is usually some percentage of base pay. Employer contributions depend on whether a defined contribution or defined pension is provided.

If the plan is a *defined contribution plan,* the employer provides a specific amount, usually based on some percentage of the employee's salary. Employer (and employee, if applicable) contributions are invested and the employee, upon retiring, receives whatever income the total investment has generated. Thus, the employee bears all the risk in such a system. If investments are wise, a high retirement income will be generated.

However, *defined benefit plans* are far more common; one survey of more than 800 employers found over 90 percent of them had this type of pension plan.[16] In a defined benefit plan, the employer contribution is usually based on the amount required to provide expected payouts at retirement. Thus, these contributions depend on the employee's current age, years of service, current and projected compensation, expected retirement date, expected life span, spouse's expected life span, and interest rate assumptions. Benefits under most pension plans may be paid out only when the employee terminates, whether through normal retirement, early retirement, death, discharge, or quitting. The amount paid out in benefits varies with the type of termination, and may be either a lump sum (in the cases of discharge or quitting), installment (in the case of retirement or early retirement; these are the most frequent in all cases), or both (in the case of death, where a survivor may receive both a capital amount and installment payments).

As we have noted, defined benefit contributions by employers are based on actuarial requirements or expected pension payouts. Defined contribution plans, on the other hand, are usually based on a percentage of employee salary; employer obligations are unrelated to organizational success. For this reason, many employers use a variant of the pension: the profit-sharing plan.[17] The major features of a profit-sharing plan are implied by the title. Usually, employees make no contribution to the plan. The employer's contribution is a function of before-tax profit, and thus will vary from year to year. The contribution is usually allocated among employees on the basis of annual salary, ignoring age and seniority. At termination of employment, whether through retirement, death, discharge, or quitting, the benefit in the employee's account is distributable, usually in a lump sum. In some cases, an employee can draw on the profit-sharing account before termination.

Another means of tax deferral or tax avoidance for employers and employees is the *employee stock ownership plan* (ESOP). Actually, there are three primary types of ESOPs.[18] The stock bonus plan is the first form of ESOP. A trust is established to benefit employees, and the company contributes its own stock (or money to be used to buy its own stock). A limit of 15 percent of salary is imposed. Vesting rules apply, and the employee gets stock only on retirement or other termination of employment. The organization can deduct the contribution; the employee is not liable for taxes until he or she actually receives stock from the trust.

A *leveraged* ESOP is similar to the stock bonus format, except that the trust can go into debt to purchase stock of the organization. The corporation guarantees the loan and contributes cash to service the loan. Created under the Tax Reduction Act of 1975, *TRASOPs* comprise the third form of ESOP. A TRASOP is an investment credit ESOP in which both employer and employee contribute to the trust fund on a matching basis. Vesting is 100 percent and immediate, but stock in an employee's account may not be distributed for seven years, except on termination of employment, death, or disability. Employers receive investment tax credit for TRASOP contributions.

There are a number of advantages to an employer in using an ESOP rather than regular pension or profit-sharing plans.[19] The advantages are that:

1. There is no reduction in working capital, because payments are made in corporate stock.

2. Retention and motivation goals may be served when employees have an "ownership stake" in the organization.

3. The ESOP trust may help the organization avoid takeover; however, the courts may not allow ESOP trust shares to be voted.[20]

4. ESOP contributions are not based on profit, so operating losses (and resultant tax benefits) can be credited; at the same time, contribution levels are not a function of payroll, so contributions can be lessened in adverse economic times.

5. Service of employees prior to ESOP establishment does not create employer liability, as could service prior to establishment of a pension program.

ESOP disadvantages include increased costs of administration and dilution of ownership. Employees are not always enthusiastic about ESOPs, and unions generally oppose them.[21] When companies are closely held, the value of stock contributed to the ESOP may be questioned.

Many employers are looking at stock options again as a tax-deferred income opportunity for executive employees. Under the Economic Recovery Tax Act of 1981, individuals may be granted *incentive stock options* (ISOs) of up to $100,000 each year. Gain on stock from option price to exercise price is not paid until the stock is sold; under the Tax Reform Act of 1986, any gains are taxed as income. ESOPs are still accorded favorable tax treatment under the Tax Reform Act of 1986, and in fact some new advantages have been added.[22] Incentive stock option provisions have been somewhat liberalized under the new law, and thus may be more attractive.[23]

Regardless of the kind of pension program an organization decides to set up, the employer has several decisions to make:

1. What mix of pension, profit-sharing, ESOP, and option benefits will be offered?

2. How much will employees get?

3. How will differences in benefits be determined? Some possibilities are seniority, profits, salary level, age, or a mix.

4. How much will employees contribute to the plan?

5. Will benefits be subject to cost-of-living adjustments?

6. Will other employee income (such as social security) affect benefit levels?

7. When will benefits start? Can employees retire early for reduced benefit levels?

8. What happens to benefits if employment terminates for reasons other than retirement?

9. How are payouts to be made (lump sum, income flow, or combination)?

10. How is vesting to be handled?

11. Can the employee draw on benefit funds (e.g., borrow against them) while still working for the organization?

12. How is the fund to be administered?

13. To what extent will employees participate in fund administration?

14. How is the fund to be insured against economic adversity?

The answers to many of these questions are constrained by the IRS, ERISA (Employment Retirement Income Security Act), ADEA (Age Discrimination in Employment Act), and other federal laws. Still, employers have some choice with respect to all of them, and they should be prepared to make policy decisions.

Pay for Time Not Worked

Most employees do not work eight hours a day, five days a week, fifty-two weeks a year; yet almost all salaried employees are paid as if they did. In essence, most organizations pay employees for time they do not work as well as for time they do. The most widely recognized forms of pay for time not worked are vacation, holidays, and sick leave, but other types exist, as well. Pay for time not worked is important to the compensation analyst because an increase in paid time off is equivalent to an increase in wage rate. Total payment for time not worked amounted to nearly 10 percent of direct wages in 1985.[24]

Vacation Pay   The cost of vacations (or pay in lieu of vacations) was about 5 percent of direct payroll costs in 1985.[25] The vacation policies of interest to compensation specialists are summed up by answers to the following questions:

1. Who should get vacation time and how much? Usually vacation is a

reward for service; employees who have worked a longer time for an organization receive more vacation time. The loose-leaf services provide information on current vacation practices. Typically, white-collar workers get more than blue-collar, executives get more than hourly workers, and part-time workers may get none at all. Current practices are shown in Exhibit 10.4.

2. What if a holiday, sickness, or other "time off with pay" event occurs during the vacation?

3. To what degree can vacation time not taken be saved and carried over to another pay period? Can vacation time be combined with authorized nonpaid absences?

4. Under what circumstances will employees get extra pay rather than paid time off? Some organizations use accrued vacation time as a form of severance pay. If the organization wants the employee to forego vacation, will it pay double for that time period?

5. When is vacation pay to be given? When long-term employees have a month or more of vacation, their paid time off might cover two or three paydays. Most organizations give all vacation pay in advance; others observe regular paydays.

Holidays Holidays cost employers the equivalent of 2.8 percent of total payroll costs in 1985.[26] In 1986, about half of the companies in one survey offered ten or more holidays; 21 percent offered eleven or more.[27] These holidays included:

New Year's Day	Martin Luther King's Birthday
Thanksgiving Day	Easter Sunday
Labor Day	Columbus Day
Independence Day	Presidents' Day
Memorial Day	Easter Monday
Christmas Day	Day after Christmas
Good Friday	Veterans' Day
Day after Thanksgiving	Employee's Birthday
New Year's Eve	Floating Holiday
Washington's Birthday	Christmas Eve
Election Day	

Exhibit 10.4 Vacation Time in Companies Having Plant and Office Employees

Length of Service	1 Week		6–9 Days		2 Weeks		11–14 Days		3 Weeks		4 Weeks		5 Weeks		Other	
	Office	Plant	Office	Plant	Office	Plant	Office	Plant	Office	Plant	Office	Plant	Office	Plant	Office	Plant
6 months	34.1%	20.0%	7.1%	5.9%	1.2%	—	—	—	—	—	—	—	—	—	3.5%*	5.9%*
1 year	27.1	47.1	—	—	68.2	45.9%	3.5%	3.5%	1.2%	1.2%	—	—	—	—	—	2.3*
2 years	5.9	20.0	3.5	4.7	82.4	65.9	4.7	5.9	3.5	2.3	—	—	—	—	—	1.2*
3 years	—	4.7	1.2	1.2	89.4	84.7	3.5	4.7	5.9	4.7	—	—	—	—	—	—
5 years	—	—	1.2	1.2	49.4	60.0	10.6	5.9	38.8	32.9	—	—	—	—	—	—
10 years	—	—	—	—	4.7	4.7	2.4	1.2	72.9	76.4	18.8%	16.5%	—	—	1.2**	1.2**
15 years	—	—	—	—	3.5	3.5	1.2	1.2	44.7	43.5	48.2	49.4	1.2%	1.2%	1.2**	1.2**
20 years	—	—	—	—	3.5	3.5	—	—	18.8	20.0	63.5	62.4	13.0	12.9	1.2***	1.2***
25 years	—	—	—	—	3.5	3.5	—	—	18.8	17.6	40.1	42.4	35.3	34.1	2.3***	2.4***
30 years	—	—	—	—	3.5	3.5	—	—	17.6	16.5	38.8	38.8	34.2	35.3	5.9***	5.9***

*Varies from 1 to 5.5 days.
**18 days.
***Varies from 22 days to 6 weeks.

Source: "Prentice-Hall Survey: 1986 Vacation Policies," *Prentice-Hall Personnel Management: Policies and Practices* (Englewood Cliffs, N.J.: Prentice-Hall, 1986), p. 224.

Holiday policies affecting compensation include:

1. The holidays to be observed. For those holidays that fall on different weekdays each year, what happens when the paid holiday falls on a Saturday or Sunday? On a Tuesday or Thursday? Will Friday or Monday be granted in these cases?

2. Is everyone eligible for holiday pay? Eligibility questions involve hourly workers who miss the day before or after the paid holiday, as well as part-time workers, and workers who are laid off, on sick leave, or on vacation.

3. Pay rates. There are two issues here. The first involves the rate of pay for pieceworkers, commission workers, and workers getting a shift premium. The second involves the rate of pay for employees who are required to work on holidays.

4. Extra religious holidays. If all employees get Christmas off, should members of other religions get holy days off with pay, too? (Many organizations solve this problem by granting one to three "individual" holidays with pay to all employees.)

Sick Leave   Sick leave pay equaled about 1.3 percent of total payroll costs in 1985.[28] As with other forms of pay for time not worked, the organization must develop policies that speak to compensation issues:

1. Who gets sick leave, and how much? Does this vary by type of employee?

2. Does sick leave build up or does it disappear at the end of the year? Can unused sick leave be traded for extra pay? What happens to accrued sick leave when an employee terminates?

3. What level of pay will be given for sick leave? This applies mainly to workers who get shift premiums or who are on some piecerate system.

Some employers have found sick leave to be one of the more abused benefits. Instead of differentiating vacation and sick leave, employees are simply given a set amount of time when they are not required to work but will still be paid. Such a policy encourages workers not to report in sick unless they are in fact sick; more important, it saves the employer the expense of an audit system for sick leave.

Miscellaneous Pay for Time Not Worked   There are also a number of miscellaneous paid times borne by organizations. Reservists generally are paid for the time they spend in summer camp, and some reservists get full or partial pay if they are called back to military service. Voting time is paid for by many employers; thirty states require workers to have time off to vote.[29] Presidential election days are more likely to result in full paid days off; for local elections, an hour may be all that is granted. Jury duty, marriage leaves, bereavement leaves, and leaves associated with childbirth are all recognized policy issues in most organizations. Some companies give time off with pay to male employees to care for a newborn or adopted child. Other organizations grant "social services leaves" with full salaries and fringe benefits to employees who do such things as help small companies fight employees' drug and alcohol problems or help disabled persons make their homes barrier-free for wheelchairs. Still other employers provide paid sabbaticals for employees or pay for time devoted to public service activities.

Employers also pay employees for internal nonwork time. Coffee breaks, rest breaks, and lunch breaks are commonly paid for. Employers frequently give workers time to clean up and time to prepare for work. Travel time is sometimes paid for, as well. The issue for the compensation analyst is how much of the money spent on nonwork time has some return to the organization. Does it help in attracting, retaining, or motivating employees? How does that paid time interact with wage levels?

Services

Compensation analysts have not traditionally been as concerned with services to employees as with the other three categories of benefits. Yet, these services are frequently more visible to employees than health or security benefits, or pay for time not worked. This visibility makes the inclusion of paid services into the equity equation a high probability; thus compensation analysts should look at employee service benefits as an integral part of the compensation package. There are many kinds of services. Many of the services fill other human resource function needs, and so must be considered on broader ground than compensation program requirements alone. A full study of services is beyond the scope of this book, but we will look at a few services that exemplify the total range.

Services differ from other benefits in that they are provided to all employees as a matter of course. Some services, such as executive perquisites, are limited to a class of employees. Others, such as relocation benefits, are provided on the basis of need. Finally, some services, although theoretically available to all employees, are in fact limited to those who are interested in the service (gymnasium facilities), or who can afford to pay for it (charitable matching, credit unions). More than 2,500 companies, for example, sponsor or pay for day care for their employees. Proctor and Gamble has created two community child care centers in Cincinnati and set up a child care resource and referral service. Campbell Soup subsidizes half the fees for children in its center in Camden, New Jersey.[30]

Perquisites   A perquisite is a benefit tied to a specific job. These benefits may be sizable: perquisites for chief executive officers were found by one researcher to average more than $24,000 a year.[31] The most widespread executive "perk" is a company car for private use. Other perks include country club membership, payment for spouses to accompany executives on trips, entertainment expenses, and physical examinations. Financial counseling, including tax preparation, legal advice, and investment advice for top executives, is frequently offered; one survey found more than one-third of all executives responding had such counseling.[32]

Many perquisites are considered by the IRS to be attempts to provide extra untaxed income to favored employees; therefore such perks often are declared taxable income. The necessity of the service for the employee to carry out his or her job is frequently the deciding factor. In spite of their taxable nature, perquisites are prized by many employees who receive them beyond their dollar value. In some cases, the prestige of receiving the perquisite may be as important as the monetary or convenience value of the perquisite itself.

Charitable Matching   Many organizations give money to charitable groups as a public relations gesture. Frequently, employee input is sought. One means of doing this is to match gifts employees make to institutions. The National Center for Higher Education puts out a list of nearly four hundred corporations that will match employees' gifts to universities, secondary schools, and in some cases elementary schools. Nearly 50 percent of these organizations match on a greater than dollar-for-dollar basis.

Special Facilities   Meal and coffee-break facilities are the most common special facilities. Subsidized meals are not infrequent, especially when commercial restaurants are not readily available to employees. In addition to meal facilities, many organizations provide health facilities or employee "country clubs."

Special Occasion Bonuses   Bonuses include service awards, Christmas checks, and turkeys at Thanksgiving. Generally, these bonuses are small in terms of individual costs, but collectively they can be quite expensive.

Savings Plans, Credit Unions, and IRAs   In an attempt to help employees build up capital, many organizations sponsor savings plans. Some employers match part of employees' savings as a motivation to save. Credit unions are similar programs, usually without employer matching of deposits. However, employers usually provide space and employees to run the credit union.

Under the Economic Recovery Tax Act of 1981, individuals covered by corporate pension programs can, in addition, invest up to $2,000 per year in tax-deferred Individual Retirement Accounts (IRAs). Few organizations are managing IRAs for their employees, but many are making it easier for employees to set up IRAs by allowing insurance companies, brokers, and mutual funds to sell IRAs to employees on company time.[33] (Under the Tax Reform Act of 1986, many workers have become ineligible for the tax advantages of IRAs. Only employees with adjusted gross income of less than $25,000 [$40,000 for a joint return] are eligible for full IRA deductions; employees with adjusted gross incomes in excess of $35,000 [$50,000 for a joint return] cannot take any IRA deductions.[34]) In addition, many organizations set up payroll deduction plans to make it easy for employees to participate in savings plans, credit unions, and IRAs.

Miscellaneous Services   Organizations provide hundreds of other miscellaneous services to employees such as partial payment of adoption fees,[35] arrangement for discount buying services, or even company housing. Approximately 9 million Americans even receive prepaid legal plans as an employee benefit.[36]

Why should a compensation specialist be concerned with such benefits? Many employees think of these fringe benefits as essential parts of the compensation package. Consider the case of Pepper Rogers, former head football coach at the Georgia Institute of Technology. When fired in 1979, his $42,300 contract had two years to go; and the school continued to pay that amount. However, Mr. Rogers's fringe benefits (including perquisites) ended, and by his estimation they were worth $496,980 for 1980 and 1981 combined.[37] This is an extreme case, but many employees see their fringes as an integral part of the job, and thus these benefits become important to the compensation package in attracting, retaining, and motivating employees.

Cafeteria Benefits Plans

Traditional benefits plans have not been flexible enough to reflect differences in employee life situations. A single plan with the same retirement, insurance, and other packages has been offered to all employees with no regard to marital status, working status of spouse, number of children, or life stage. In recent years, a number of firms have introduced *cafeteria benefits plans* or *flex benefits systems* that allow each employee some degree of freedom in choosing and tailoring benefit elements to his or her situation.[38]

Under a typical flexible or cafeteria benefits plan, an employee is provided with a base plan. Everyone, for example, must carry minimal levels of life, health, and income protection insurance. Everyone also has minimal contributions to pension plans. Beyond these minimums, however, the employee has the freedom of allocating benefit dollars among a variety of options. A middle-aged husband and father of three college-age children, for example, may wish to go very heavily into life insurance, while an older employee with few obligations may wish to shelter as much current income as possible into a retirement plan. Some extreme plans even allow an employee to move cash in and out of the direct pay program into the benefits program.

Experts have cited three major drawbacks to cafeteria plans. First is the problem of irresponsible choices by employees. What (if any) is the responsibility of the company for an employee who makes no preparation for retirement, or who carries no life insurance? Most plans address this problem by requiring everyone to carry a base plan providing minimal levels of such protection. A second problem concerns a phenomenon known as *adverse selection*. According to this problem, those who are least likely to develop an insured problem, (for example, heart disease) ignore the insurance, while those who are in the highest risk categories (for example, smokers or overweight people with family histories of heart disease) load up on coverage. The result is that the cost of insuring for a given benefit level increases. Requiring all employees to carry base plans can also mitigate the impact of adverse selection. The third problem concerns costing a cafeteria plan. To the extent that such situations as adverse selection occur, estimating the premiums necessary to provide economically reasonable coverage challenges the actuary and the financial planner.

Experts cite a number of offsetting advantages to cafeteria benefits plans, though. Perhaps the clearest is that of heightening the incentive value of the benefits plan to the employee by allowing him or her to tailor provisions to his or her own needs. Many have hypothesized that higher levels of pay satisfaction will result and that the total pay program will have a stronger effect on employees. Finally, proponents of flexible benefits programs argue that involving the employee in benefit choices will more effectively communicate a total compensation vision. The employee will have a better understanding and appreciation of the total compensation program.

Summary

We have explored an increasingly significant part of the total compensation package called benefits. Benefits refer to a wide range of rewards beyond direct cash payments to individuals. They can take many forms: health insurance, life insurance, employment security insurance, disability insurance, severance pay, pensions, paid vacation and other paid time off, and a wide variety of other services and perks. We also examined a policy, called cafeteria benefits, that allows each employee to make individual choices among benefit elements.

It is important for organizations to establish benefits policies by asking what objectives they seek to accomplish with benefits. Only after this question has been answered can intelligent choices be made. Benefits have become a significant part of the compensation package since World War II and now can represent up to an additional 40 percent of the base pay program. In addition, the relative size of the benefits package has been growing rapidly, forcing managers to take a "total compensation" view of their programs.

Notes

[1]U.S. Chamber of Commerce, *Employee Benefits 1980* (Washington: D.C., 1981).

[2]"Currents in Compensation and Benefits," *Compensation and Benefits Review* 18(1) (January-February 1986): 13.

[3]Compensation Currents, *Compensation Review* 2nd Quarter (1981): 12.

[4]R. J. Meyers, *Social Security* (Homewood, Ill.: Richard D. Irwin, 1975), p. 22.

[5]U.S. Chamber of Commerce, *Employee Benefits 1985* (Washington, D.C., 1986).

[6]Ibid.

[7]Ibid.

[8]Ibid.

[9]Ibid.

[10]D. R. Bell, "Dental and Vision Care Benefits in Health Insurance Plans," *Monthly Labor Review* 103 (June 1980): 22–26.

[11]Ibid.

[12]*Wall Street Journal,* Tuesday, November 3, 1981, p. 1.

[13]*Wall Street Journal,* Wednesday, January 7, 1981, p. 15.

[14]C. S. Ives, "Benefits and Services — Private," in D. Yoder and H. G. Heneman, Jr. (eds.), *ASPA Handbook of Personnel and Industrial Relations* (Washington, D.C.: Bureau of National Affairs, 1975), pp. 6-185–6-233.

[15]"Currents in Compensation and Benefits," *Compensation and Benefits Review* 18 (4) (July–August 1986): 12.

[16]"Currents in Compensation and Benefits," *Compensation and Benefits Review* 18 (6) (November–December 1986): 6.

[17]Prentice-Hall Editorial Staff, *Employee Benefits* (Englewood Cliffs, N.J.: Prentice-Hall, 1979), p. 25,054.

[18]R. G. Swad, "Stock Ownership Plans: A New Employee Benefit," *Personnel Journal* 60 (June 1981): 453–55.

[19]Ibid.

[20]G. C. Hill, "Retirement Issue: Employee Stock Plans: An Economic Cureall or a Dubious Benefit?" *Wall Street Journal,* Monday, December 8, 1980, p. 1.

[21]Ibid.

[22]*Tax Reform '86* (New York: Towers, Perrin, Forster & Crosby, 1986), p. 16.

[23]*The Tax Reform Act of 1986* (New York: The Wyatt Company, 1986), p. 33.

[24]U.S. Chamber of Commerce, *Employee Benefits 1985.*

[25]Ibid.

[26]Ibid.

[27]Prentice-Hall Editorial Staff, "P-H Holiday Time Off Survey, 1986," *Prentice-Hall Personnel Policies* (Englewood Cliffs, N.J.: Prentice-Hall, 1986), p. 329.

[28]U.S. Chamber of Commerce, *Employee Benefits 1985.*

[29]Prentice-Hall Editorial Staff, "P-H Survey: 1986 Election Day Policies," *Prentice-Hall Personnel Policies,* p. 198.

[30]"More Employers Offering Child Care Benefits," *New York Times,* Sunday, December 7, 1986.

[30]"Currents in Compensation and Benefits," *Compensation and Benefits Review* 18 (6) (November–December 1986): 2.

[32]"Currents in Compensation and Benefits," *Compensation and Benefits Review* 18 (3) (May–June 1986): 2–3.

[33]"What the New IRA Rules Do for You," *Business Week* (September 14, 1981): 122–26.

[34]*Tax Reform '86,* pp. 28–29.

[35]*Adoption Benefit Plans: Corporate Response to a Changing Society* (Philadelphia: National Adoption Exchange, 1985).

[36]"Currents in Compensation and Benefits," *Compensation and Benefits Review* 18 (2) (March–April 1986): 9.

[37]"Sacked Football Coach Sues School for Cash in Lieu of Lost Perks," *Wall Street Journal,* Thursday, October 16, 1980, p. 16.

[38]See, for example, Robert J. McCaffery, *Employee Benefit Programs: A Total Compensation Perspective* (Boston: PWS-KENT, 1988).

11

The Compensation Program

Key Issues and Questions for This Chapter

After you have studied this chapter, you should be able to address the following key issues and questions:

1. What are the major policy issues to be addressed in administering and auditing compensation programs?
2. Who has responsibility for the compensation program?
3. Who should participate in the design and administration of the compensation program?
4. What questions should be asked and what techniques used to audit a compensation program for effectiveness?
5. What steps must be taken to implement a wage structure policy?
6. What steps must be taken to implement a pay policy?
7. How should budgets be used in controlling compensation programs?

8. What details must be taken into account in order to establish individual merit adjustment?

9. How can managers estimate the cash flow impact of their compensation programs?

10. What steps must managers take to communicate compensation programs effectively?

Introduction

So far, we primarily have focused on designing compensation programs. We have examined, for example, how to build an internal wage structure through the process of job evaluation. We have shown how one prices the structure using survey data as a measure of external market wages. We have looked at the design of policies for placing individual employees within the structure based on policies reflecting individual merit. Finally, we have considered the role of benefits as part of the compensation program and examined the means for merging direct pay and benefits into a total compensation package.

In this chapter, our focus turns to implementation and administration. Once a total compensation program is designed and ready to launch, what must managers do to assure that the plan, in fact, will be administered day-to-day in a fashion that will accomplish its original objectives? Specifically, we will look at three areas that are crucial to the successful implementation and administration of compensation designs:

1. Process issues to be resolved during implementation and administration

2. Controlling, auditing, and budgeting the program

3. Communicating the program.

The best designed compensation programs will flounder if managers do not successfully resolve these three issues.

Implementation and Administration

The key to success in implementing a compensation program is to integrate the system with the broader organization. This means making sure that the compensation design dovetails with the objectives contained within strategic plans, management style and philosophy, and the culture that already exists within the organization. Nothing will fail more quickly than a compensation design that runs counter to these realities. Although we will discuss the fit between organizational strategy and compensation more thoroughly in Chapter 12, it is important to note here that compensation has the potential of being a powerful tool for implementing strategy.[1] Experts agree that compensation can be linked to strategy only if several key process issues are resolved in a way that fits in with an organization's culture.[2] Process issues are of two types: (1) the design of the compensation program, and (2) the administration of the compensation program. Managers must consider each of these areas carefully during the implementation of a compensation program in order to make sure that the design and administration of the pay program fit in with the organization and support strategy rather than conflict with it.

Compensation Design Issues

Three compensation design issues face managers: (1) the balance among external, internal, and individual equity interests; (2) the basis for making adjustments to pay; and (3) the degree to which individual earnings are placed "at risk."

Equity Emphasis   Very rarely can an organization meet external, internal, and individual equity goals completely. Thus, most managers are faced with tradeoffs among these three objectives. When there is conflict among them (for example, the market values jobs differently than an internal job evaluation system does), the organization must address the conflict in an explicit fashion and determine the order of precedence among the three. Inflationary times, for example, place compression pressures on the salary program because market wages for new hires increase at a higher rate than adjustments for those already on board. Such compression sacrifices an individual equity criterion for an external equity goal.

The major external equity issue for management to consider is the relationship between pay rates set for jobs and the rates prevailing for them in external markets. There are really three subordinate issues involved. First, does the firm want to set its rates competitive to the market? Or does it want to set them above or somewhat below the market?

Where a firm decides to set itself with respect to the market depends on a number of related human resource objectives. Staffing objectives, for example, often come up in designing compensation policy. If a firm is in a high growth phase and competing for scarce labor, it will probably want to pay above the market. It will also be pricing a greater number of its jobs directly to that market and relying less on job evaluation procedures to set wages internally. Firms that are in a mature stage of their corporate growth cycle, on the other hand, may prefer to set their wages right at the market or a little below and put more emphasis on job evaluation practices for setting wages. The latter type of firm, indeed, probably will place more emphasis on internal equity and less on external equity as a matter of policy.

A second external equity question is that of *when* the firm wants to meet the market. This is the *lead/lag problem* and concerns timing with respect to the market. Suppose, for example, that the manager knows where the market for a job stands as of some decision date. Her problem is to set internal rates to that market. These rates will constitute a structure that will be in place for some time (usually a year) before they are adjusted again. The problem is that the market is *not* stationary. It will move throughout that year, usually in an upward direction. If she sets her structure to the market as it exists on the decision date, her structure will *lag* the market the entire year and fall farther and farther behind. To avoid this situation she may choose to ratchet her structure above the market on the decision date *by an amount equal to the total amount she expects the market to move this next year*. Her structure will *lead* the market the entire year. The market will finally catch up with her structure at the end of the plan year, just as she makes a new adjustment. What do you see as the tradeoffs between a pure lag and a pure lead strategy? These tradeoffs will be discussed later in this chapter in more detail. Suffice it to say here that most companies reach a compromise by adopting a *lead/lag* policy, that is, ratcheting a structure somewhat ahead so that the market will catch it somewhere near the middle of the plan year.

The third external equity issue that organizations face has to do not with the external labor market but with the value of the dollar — inflation. Cost-of-living adjustments (COLAs) became very popular during the 1960s and 1970s; base pay was adjusted across the board for all employees according to some index of inflation (for example, the consumer price index, or CPI, of the U.S. Department of Labor). The cost pressures created by such policies during inflationary times have led most employers to abandon COLAs in the 1980s.

Once managers have achieved a balance between external and internal equity emphases, two additional internal equity questions remain: (1) the balance between direct compensation and benefits, and (2) the type of job evaluation system to use in administering internal wages.

The balance to be struck between direct compensation and benefits is primarily an internal equity issue because benefits tend to have a "leveling" effect, that is, everyone receives pretty much the same levels of benefits regardless of the position of the job in the hierarchy. Benefits are primarily a matter of entitlement — that is, people merit them through membership in the organization and not through individual qualifications. Benefits tend to dampen internal compensation differentials. Thus, the larger the proportion of total compensation that is devoted to benefits, the smaller the differences between individuals and jobs reflected in the total compensation package.

In addition to direct pay/benefit proportions, managers must also address the question of which job evaluation system to use. When managers choose a job evaluation system (including the compensable factors upon which to base job value judgments), they are making value judgments that will be reflected in final salary differentials. Many of the determinants of these policy decisions and their consequences were discussed in Chapter 8.

Award Basis   *Award basis* is an individual equity issue concerning the question of how to make individual adjustments in compensation. At one extreme, the policy could simply adjust a person's salary according to his or her time with the company. The longer one worked in the company or on a given job, the higher her pay would be. At the opposite extreme could be a policy that adjustments to pay could be earned only through performance. The higher an employee's performance level, the larger the adjustment that would be made to his pay. Both policies are common elements in most compensation designs, but they often conflict with each other. The former policy is one of entitlement. You are entitled to adjustments simply as a matter of longevity and, presumably, commitment to the employer. The latter policy is one of performance. Pay adjustments must be "earned" through performance. The balance a company strikes between these two extremes sends a clear message to employees. Adjustments based on time send a message that fits in with an entitlements culture: play by the rules, avoid obvious violations, and the system will take care of you. Adjustments based on performance send a message that fits in with a performance culture: there are no entitlements, the strong performers will prosper, the weak will not, no matter how long they have worked here.

Earnings at Risk   The third compensation design issue concerns the question of how much of a person's total earnings (direct compensation) should be rolled into base pay and how much should be at risk. As illustrated in Exhibit 11.1, direct compensation has two components: (1) base pay and (2) earnings at risk. Base pay is the basic compensation rate that is guaranteed

Exhibit 11.1   Pay at Risk

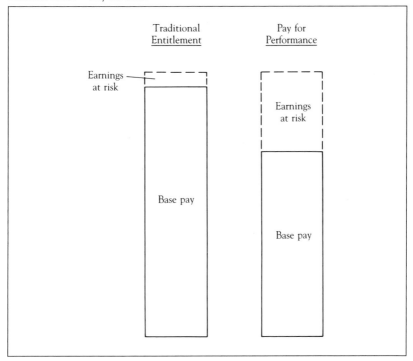

to a person. Earnings that are a part of base pay are "protected" in that once they are earned they will continue as part of one's compensation from one year to the next. Earnings that are not part of base pay are at risk, that is, they do not recur year after year and must be re-earned. Traditionally, employers have placed the majority of a person's earnings into base pay, as illustrated in Exhibit 11.1, and put very little at risk. Traditional compensation designs may place as little as 1 percent of an employee's total earnings at risk. Thus, most adjustments to an individual's pay (for merit, performance, and longevity) have been in the form of permanent adjustments to base pay.

This traditional approach to individual awards has two major drawbacks. First, the policy creates very expensive entitlements that grow over time and commit the employer to very high labor costs. Once a person has earned an adjustment, she keeps reaping the benefit over and over again in base pay increments that continue into the future. Second, the policy detracts from management's ability to make meaningful pay distinctions between individuals on the basis of performance in any given year. Combined with budget and cost-containment pressures, the effect of the traditional approach is to curtail management's ability truly to reward performance with pay.

Faced with this realization, many employers in the 1980s are attempting to move away from entitlements to a more potent pay-for-performance policy by putting more and more of an employee's earnings at risk, as illustrated in Exhibit 11.1. Some employers have recently adopted pay-for-performance designs that place as much as 25 to 30 percent of an employee's earnings at risk each year. Such a design requires people to re-earn a significant piece of their total earnings, based on individual or group performance. Pay-for-performance designs have at least three advantages. First, they free management's hands to make meaningful pay distinctions between individuals and groups based on performance, not entitlement. Second, they allow managers to relate labor costs more closely to revenues, enhancing productivity. Third, such plans should have the effect of making it more attractive to the best performers to remain and for the worst performers to seek employment (and higher earnings) elsewhere.

Putting significant amounts of pay at risk is not without problems, however. First, a true pay-for-performance system fits best in a performance culture, that is, an organization that places a high value on individual and group performance excellence. Such an organization places relatively less value on long-term commitment and does not protect long-termers. If the culture of a company does value commitment and longevity, a pay-for-performance system may very well violate cultural norms and create a great deal of disaffection. Second, a pay-for-performance system presumes management can adequately measure performance and validly determine individual and group performance merit. If the bases for determining merit are not trusted by management and employees, the pay-for-performance system will lead to suspicions of inequity and unfairness, destroying any strategic benefits the system might have.

Compensation Administration Issues

Equally important to design issues are four compensation administration issues facing managers: (1) responsibility for the plan, (2) level of participation in the plan, (3) communication openness, and (4) standardization and centralization in the administration of the plan.

Responsibility   Typically, responsibility for the design and administration of compensation programs is shared by line managers and staff compensation specialists. Broad compensation policies in larger organizations are usually set by compensation committees. Traditionally, such committees have consisted of executives who are also members of the highest operating committees of the organization. As pressure for more employee involvement has increased in recent years, however, some companies have included a broader mix of all levels of employees in such committees.

Technical issues are usually assigned to compensation specialists for action recommendations. Approval of such recommendations, however, still rests with the compensation committee. Administrative questions are often assigned to a salary administration committee, which operates at lower levels within the organization. Finally, job evaluation committees composed of a broad cross-section of employees and compensation specialists typically make specific job evaluation recommendations.

Participation   Traditionally, participation in the design and administration of compensation has been quite limited. The committees we have just described have been staffed primarily by upper-level executives and managers. Paralleling an increase in employee involvement in management, however, has been an increase in the involvement of employees at all levels and in all areas in compensation decisions.[3] Lawler notes that participation in compensation decisions should enhance the following:

1. Employee understanding of the compensation plan
2. Employee acceptance of the compensation plan
3. Employee commitment to the compensation plan
4. Employee judgments that the plan is fair.[4]

Goal setting theory, reviewed in Chapter 4, supports Lawler's contention. The research demonstrates that participation in the establishment of goals (including design elements in a compensation plan) leads to higher levels of commitment, effort, and employee performance. In fact, one study indicates that employee participation in the design of a base pay plan results in increases in job satisfaction, pay satisfaction, understanding of the pay plan, and trust in management.[5] Given these advantages, employee involvement in the design and administration of compensation plans should increase the likelihood of their success in achieving objectives. There even have been reports of some extreme practices in employee involvement in pay decisions. At

Romac Industries, for example, an employee who wants a raise must post his request on a bulletin board and submit to a secret ballot of his coworkers.[6] In fact, employee participation in compensation for most employers tends to be limited to design and does not often extend to administration; that is, employers tend to involve employees only in the initial design of the compensation program. Authority for subsequent administrative decisions under the plan is retained by management and not shared.[7]

One exception to this rule is in the area of benefits, where some employers are beginning to offer considerable latitude to employees in choosing among benefit options. Not all employees find all benefits equally attractive. A single employee with no dependents may have little use for term life insurance, while such coverage is crucial for a single parent. Many employers are responding to such differences among employees with *cafeteria* benefits plans that offer a wide variety of benefits from which to choose. Under such a plan, an employee receives a fixed dollar limit within which he can allocate his choices. Such participation should maximize the utility of the benefit plan for each employee and better enable the organization to attract and retain people.

As in the case of all other compensation policy issues, however, managers must be careful to match up the degree of employee involvement in compensation decisions with broader management philosophy and culture in the organization. An attempt to establish a high level of employee involvement in the design of a compensation system is likely to fail in an organization that otherwise practices very limited styles of management because it very well may lack credibility and be received in a very cynical fashion by employees.

Communication   Our model of employee behavior and performance, presented in Chapter 4, as well as our process equity model, presented in Chapter 5, indicate that open communication is essential for any compensation plan to have its intended impact on employees. Logic would dictate that unless compensation plan essentials are fully communicated, employees cannot understand the system and therefore cannot have predictable reactions to it.

In fact, compensation plans traditionally have been subject to secrecy policies, and communications about pay have been quite limited in many organizations. There are two reasons for secrecy policies. First, many employers take the position that disclosing compensation specifics would violate employees' rights to privacy. They take the position that an employee's earnings are his own business and no one else's. Second, many employers seek to avoid the pressure to justify compensation differentials that are questioned.

It is much easier to refuse to discuss compensation specifics than to open the system up to criticism and justification. In fact, openly communicating the specifics of a compensation plan might be risky business if the system is already inherently inequitable. Perceptions of inequity and feelings of unfairness will only be intensified under such a circumstance.

The simple fact remains, however, that a compensation plan cannot have the intended impact on behavior and performance unless it is openly communicated.[8] At the very least, the mechanics of the compensation plan must be communicated so that an employee knows how all the elements of his pay contribute to his total earnings. In addition, where individual and internal equity are concerned, he must be able to compare his level of pay and adjustments to the pay of comparable people and jobs. Many organizations protect individual privacy while openly communicating compensation plans by establishing and publishing pay ranges and rules for placement in range (as well as for any other bonuses or adjustments). Such a policy reinforces employee efforts under the plan while protecting individual information. An example of such a system is that of the U.S. government, which operates completely in the open. Knowledge of a person's position, years in service, and performance levels allows one to specify exactly what should be paid and any bonuses.

Standardization and Centralization   A final administrative policy issue concerns the degree to which the design and administration of compensation plans can or should vary within an organization. Traditionally, pay planning and administration have been highly centralized and controlled by a corporate compensation or human resource staff.[9] Under such a system, a single job evaluation plan or a single merit plan is established and used by all units within the organization. A highly centralized and standardized system assures uniformity of practice and defensibility across the organization.

Whether a centralized and standardized plan makes sense depends upon the nature of the organization to be served. If the employer is in a single business, has few locations, and is organized according to basic functions (sales, marketing, production, finance, and accounting), a highly centralized pay plan is probably appropriate. Today, many firms are experimenting with radical departures from this model, however. They have reorganized along strategic lines with each *strategic business unit* (SBU) focused on a different product and market. The influence of the corporation staff on line operations is greatly reduced and each SBU has far more latitude over operating business decisions. A decentralized compensation system probably makes more sense, in these cases, so that each SBU can tailor compensation to its own specific business situation. Indeed, there is some evidence that decentralized organizations are taking steps to move compensation design and administration out of corporate headquarters and into line operations.[10]

Controlling, Auditing, and Budgeting

Once a compensation plan has been implemented, it must be controlled so that it leads to the intended results. The basic tools for controlling include *audits* and *budgets.* An audit is simply a measurement that compares actual results to standards. A budget is a device that controls cash outlays under the plan. Although a full consideration of compensation control techniques is beyond the scope of this book, we will give an overview of the basic techniques employed by compensation specialists in:[11]

1. Adjusting or creating salary structures to achieve external market equity, internal job equity, and individual employee equity

2. Auditing the current salary structure for external, internal, and individual equity

3. Forecasting the monthly salary budget necessary to finance a given salary structure

4. Combining information about the new structure with information about the placement of employees within the structure to develop a forecast of the cash flow, that is, the actual amount of money management will spend to pay people under the compensation plan.

Importance of Distinguishing Between Structure Policy and Pay Policy

In translating the objectives of external, internal, and individual equity into reality, it is helpful for managers to distinguish between the concepts of *structure policy* and *pay policy.* Note that a salary structure is a policy device, that is, a guide to follow in establishing salary rates for jobs and people. Most of the time, for example, a salary structure specifies the minimum, midpoint, and maximum rates to be set for a job and also is used as a guide for placing individual salary rates for employees on those jobs. In this regard, it is important to understand that the salary structure is merely a guide and is not a report of the actual salaries being paid to employees.

Structure policy is the policy management follows in setting its salary structure in relation to external markets. Pay policy, in contrast, is the policy management follows in establishing actual salary rates for employees within the structure. Structure policy, then, is the rule managers follow in setting up a structure as a guide. Pay policy is the rule managers follow in actually paying people within the structure.

In order to allow you to see how the four steps in controlling compensation plans operate, we have designed a simulation for you that makes the following assumptions:

1. You are the chief compensation planner for the Fay/Wallace Corporation, a major manufacturing concern.

2. Fay/Wallace has adopted a lead/lag structure pricing policy with respect to the external market; that is, the company chooses to lead the market at the beginning of a plan year, meet the market in the middle of the plan year, and lag behind the market by the end of the plan year.

3. You are at the end of a current plan year; it is now December 31.

4. You have salary survey data from the external market that are six months old, gathered last June.

5. The best estimate you have of salary increases in the external market for this past year is 5 percent.

6. Your best estimate is that salary increases in the external market next year will be 6 percent.

7. You are concerned with five salary grades (see Exhibit 11.2 p. 306).

Many of the adjustment, audit, and budgeting techniques to be presented here were developed by Dr. John Davis, president of the consulting firm of Davis Management Consultants, Dallas, Texas. He has been instrumental in developing the quantitative courses as part of the professional certification program of the American Compensation Association (ACA) and trains compensation planners in the use of these methods under ACA auspices.

Forming a New Salary Structure

One of the first problems faced by managers and compensation planners is that of adjusting an out-of-date structure to the market or creating a new one. In either case, a new salary structure must be formed that will relate to the market for some period of time, usually a plan year. Thus, for example, the planner in December of one year is concerned with setting a new structure in place that will continue from January 1 to December 31 of the new plan year. Although we examined the problem of pricing salary structures in Chapter 7, it is useful to summarize this information here. We recommend that managers follow twelve steps in forming a new salary structure:

Step 1 — Know the Market   It is important for managers to define accurately the external markets for *each* benchmark job. As indicated in Chapter 7, factors defining the market for a given job include geography, occupational qualifications, experience, skills, licenses, competitors, and industry. Those purchasing survey data should not hesitate to require customized reports according to such parameters.

Step 2 — Check Your Job Matches   The accuracy of pricing decisions depends crucially on the accuracy of the match between benchmark jobs and the job that was surveyed in the market. One cannot rely on job titles to establish a match. Rather, the job descriptions of the benchmark jobs must be compared in detail to the job that was surveyed.

Some surveys contend that you can use job evaluation points to match your benchmarks with survey jobs. This is a very hazardous thing to do, and is not recommended because the points you have assigned to your benchmark job may not correspond at all to the way the surveyor assigned job evaluation points to the jobs in the survey. Only if the job evaluation systems employed by the manager and the surveyor are *completely identical* in design and administration would we recommend matching on points.

Step 3 — Recheck Your Internal Salary Structure   Make sure you are comfortable with the structure you are bringing to the market. Are jobs assigned to pay grades within families satisfactorily? Is there general agreement on the evaluations that have been assigned to jobs?

Step 4 — Become Familiar With Your Survey Data   If you have purchased survey data, make sure that you have a clear understanding of the methodology employed. What companies were included? What communities? What industries? How were the data obtained? When were the data obtained? How many respondents and how many incumbent positions were reported for each job? What definitions were used?

Definitions present an especially difficult problem in salary surveys. A frequent mistake, for example, is for surveys to request information about the minimum, midpoint, and maximum rates for a structure, rather than about the actual lowest and highest, and all other wages *actually paid.* This is a fundamental error because firms compete not on structures but on the wages they actually pay, and the two often are not the same.

Finally, you should become familiar with the statistics the survey has employed to summarize the data. Have means or averages and medians been reported? Is the full range of the data from highest to lowest reported? Are quartiles and percentiles reported?

Step 5 — Choose Your Comparison Statistic Once you are familiar with the survey data, you will need to choose the statistics you will use to match your structure to the market. Statistics are the crucial tools you will use to map from the market to your structure and to articulate one to the other. We recommend the following uses:

Statistic	*Use*
1. *Median* — defined as the wage above and below which 50% of the survey data falls.	Measures the middle of the market.
2. *Mean* — or average, defined as sum of the wages divided by the number of wages reported.	Measures the middle of the market. Is sensitive to extreme values and may be dragged up by a few extremely high reported wages.
3. *Q3* — Third quartile, defined as the value above which only 25% of the surveyed wages fall.	Measures the upper end of the market. Good for setting upper limits on ranges or potential earnings.
4. *P90* — 90th percentile, defined as the value above which only 10% of the surveyed wages fall.	Same as above.
5. *Q1* — First quartile, defined as the value above which 75% of the surveyed wages fall.	Measures the lower end of the market. Good for setting minimums for ranges and hiring rates.
6. *P10* — 10th percentile, defined as the value above which 90% of the surveyed wages fall.	Same as above.

Step 6 — Arrange the Survey Data Exhibit 11.2 illustrates the initial arrangement of survey data for five grades (20–24) of a proposed structure.

Exhibit 11.2   Step 6: Arrangement of Survey Data

			Survey		
Grade	No. Companies	No. Incumbents	1st Quartile	Median	3rd Quartile
24	25	225	$18,600.00	$22,962.00	$28,490.00
23	36	230	$16,134.00	$20,685.00	$24,620.00
22	36	182	$14,640.00	$18,300.00	$22,690.00
21	32	228	$11,664.00	$16,200.00	$19,764.00
20	34	235	$10,980.00	$14,450.00	$18,350.00

Note that all matches between benchmarks and surveyed jobs have been made. For each grade, the number of companies and the total number of surveyed incumbents have been listed. In addition, the first quartile, median (or second quartile), and third quartile of the data have been reported for each grade.

Step 7 — Adjust for Aged Data   There will be a time problem at this stage. Any survey is out of date the day it arrives. It typically may take three to six months from the time respondents report to the time the survey results are ready for distribution. Thus, the data are three to six months old the day they arrive. Let us assume that the data in this case are six months old. We need to know where the market is *today*. In order to adjust the data for age, it is necessary to estimate how much the market has moved since the data were collected and adjust the data forward by such an estimate.

Many surveyors and research offices keep track of wage movements through the year and can supply such estimates. In our case, with our six-month-old data, we estimate that the market will have moved up by 5 percent this year. Multiplying the fraction, 6/12 (for the half year age of the data), by the annual movement estimate of 5 percent yields an estimate of 2.5 percent that the market has moved since the data were collected. Exhibit 11.3 shows the survey data aged by the factor of 2.5 percent.

Step 8 — Form a Trial Structure   Step 8 is illustrated in Exhibit 11.4 and can be accomplished simply by setting midpoints for the new structure equal to the aged market medians. Thus, we would recommend $23,536 as the new midpoint for grade 24 and $14,811 as the new midpoint for grade 20.

Exhibit 11.3   Step 7: Survey Data Aged by 2.5%

Grade	No. Companies	No. Incumbents	*Survey*		
			1st Quartile	*Median*	*3rd Quartile*
24	25	225	$19,065.00	$23,536.05	$29,202.25
23	36	230	$16,537.35	$21,202.13	$25,235.50
22	36	182	$15,006.00	$18,757.50	$23,257.25
21	32	228	$11,955.60	$16,605.00	$20,258.10
20	34	235	$11,254.50	$14,811.25	$18,808.75

We could stop here and have achieved perfect external equity. But what about internal equity? Do the midpoint separations, that is, the rate increases as one moves up the structure, achieve internal equity? Do they reflect the value differences we want to make between jobs in different pay grades? If the answer is no, we may want to try a set of midpoint separations that come closer to internal equity.

Step 9 — Adjust for Internal Equity   Exhibit 11.5 illustrates how a compromise between external and internal equity might be achieved by trying out alternative midpoint separations to those dictated by the market. In this case, the planner believes that a 12-percent separation is the best compromise and has set each midpoint 12-percent higher than the one immediately below it beginning with grade 20.

Step 10 — Audit for Equity   The next step in forming the new structure is to audit it for external, internal, and individual equity. Exhibit 11.6 con-

Exhibit 11.4   Step 8: Form a Trial Structure

Grade	Midpoint	Midpoint Separation
24	$23,536.05	11.0%
23	$21,202.13	13.0%
22	$18,757.50	13.0%
21	$16,605.00	12.1%
20	$14,811.25	

Exhibit 11.5   Step 9: Adjust for Internal Equity

Grade	Midpoint	Midpoint Separation
24	$23,305.79	12.0%
23	$20,808.74	12.0%
22	$18,579.23	12.0%
21	$16,588.60	12.0%
20	$14,811.25	

tains a schedule for accomplishing such an audit. The schedule contains the following information for each grade: (1) the proposed structure's minimum, midpoint, and maximum; (2) the survey median (for making external equity comparisons); (3) the competitive compa ratio (defined below); (4) the midpoint separation between adjacent grades; (5) the percent overlap between adjacent grades; and (6) the range width from minimum to maximum for each grade.

Exhibit 11.6   Step 10: Audit for Equity

Minimums and Maximums from Trial Structure +/− : 18%

Grade	Minimum	Midpoint	Maximum
24	$19,110.75	$23,305.79	$27,500.83
23	$17,063.17	$20,808.74	$24,554.31
22	$15,234.97	$18,579.23	$21,923.49
21	$13,602.65	$16,588.60	$19,574.55
20	$12,145.23	$14,811.25	$17,477.28

External Equity		Internal Equity		Individual Equity
Market Median	Competitive Compa Ratio	Midpoint Separation	Percent Overlap	Range Width
$23,536.05	101.0%			43.9%
$21,202.13	101.9%	12.0%	64.9%	43.9%
$18,757.50	101.0%	12.0%	64.9%	43.9%
$16,605.00	100.1%	12.0%	64.9%	43.9%
$14,811.25	100.0%	12.0%	64.9%	43.9%

External equity. The first audit question to ask concerns how competitive the new structure is to the market. We have used a *compa ratio* to measure competitiveness. A compa ratio in this use is defined as the ratio of the market rate (numerator) to the company's midpoint (denominator). Davis has labeled a compa ratio used this way as the *competitive compa ratio* (or CCR). The CCRs for the new structure are close to 100 percent (which is not surprising, given that we've just set midpoints to the market). Note, however, that our 12-percent separation policy pulls us a little out of line, especially in grade 23 where the CCR is 101.9 percent. In this case, the market is almost 2 percent above us.

Internal equity. In Chapter 8, we discussed the development of an internal wage structure and indicated two operational criteria that must be examined to assess the degree to which a salary structure achieves the criterion of internal equity: (1) *midpoint separations* (sometimes called the *midpoint progression*), defined as the distance in percentage terms between the midpoints of adjacent grades; and (2) *percent overlap* between adjacent pay grades. The midpoint separations in this structure are 12 percent (see Exhibit 11.6). Managers would compare these separations to those they would want on the basis of job evaluation results.

The second internal equity criterion, percent overlap, is defined as the degree to which one pay grade overlaps the next one up in the structure. The formula for percent overlap is as follows:

$$\text{overlap} = \frac{(Max_i - Min_{i+1})}{(Max_{i+1} - Min_{i+1})}$$

where Max_1 = the maximum rate for pay grade i, Max_{i+1} = the maximum rate for the next pay grade up, and Min_{i+1} = the minimum rate for the next pay grade up. The data in Exhibit 11.6 suggest that there is a substantial overlap between adjacent pay grades in our structure (64.9 percent). The manager would have to ask if such overlap is warranted or if it is causing undue inequities when wage comparisons are made across pay grades. An examination of Exhibit 11.6 suggests that adjusting midpoint separations or range widths might achieve a narrowing of the overlap that currently exists.

Individual equity. The operational criterion for assessing individual equity is pay grade width or spread ("Do we have sufficient range from the minimum to the maximum rate to leave room for all the individual pay distinctions we want to make for seniority and performance merit?"). In Exhibit 11.6 we have measured range width as the difference between the minimum and the maximum rate as a percentage of the minimum rate. The range widths for our structure are 43.9 percent. The planner would have to examine the company's criteria for making individual pay adjustments and ask if these ranges are too wide or too narrow.

Interrelations among equity criteria. Note that the four equity criteria (competitive compa ratio, midpoint separation, percent overlap, and range width) are all closely interrelated. Adjusting one creates changes in the other three. Adjusting midpoints more closely to the market, for example, changes midpoint separations and range overlaps. Narrowing range widths, on the other hand, will change overlap. As a practical matter, these indices represent tradeoffs for the planner in establishing an acceptable salary structure. The challenge is to find a suitable compromise among these four criteria. Most planners may take four or five passes at a trial structure before a good fit among external, internal, and individual equity criteria is found.

Exhibit 11.7 illustrates graphically the steps we have just followed in creating a salary structure. The rectangles in the graph show the market on January 1 of the new plan year. The aged market medians, first quartiles, and third quartiles are indicated for each pay grade. The "I" bars in the graph display salary structure minimums, midpoints, and maximums for each grade.

Step 11 — Adjust for Lead/Lag Policy   The final step in forming a new salary structure is to establish the company's pricing policy for the new plan year. It is important for the manager to note that she is *setting a single structure that will remain constant for one year* (or whatever planning horizon the company has set). The marketplace is not going to remain constant during that same period. Rather, an upward movement in the market throughout the plan year can be expected (even though such increases have dropped off substantially in recent years). Thus, the planner is confronted with the problem of setting a structure as of January 1 of the new plan year that will have to ride a moving market through the following December 31. The problem is very much like aiming a gun at a moving target. Compensation planners have developed three different strategies for dealing with this problem: (1) a lead policy, (2) a lag policy, and (3) a lead/lag policy. These are illustrated in Exhibits 11.8 through 11.10.

The first strategy is a lead policy. In this case, a wage structure (the solid bars in Exhibit 11.8) is set that begins the year leading the market enough so that it will take the entire plan year for external market rates to catch up (the open bars in Exhibit 11.8). The plan ends the year in exact line with the market and competitive compa ratios (CCRs) of 1.00.

Exhibit 11.7 Fay/Wallace Market Comparison

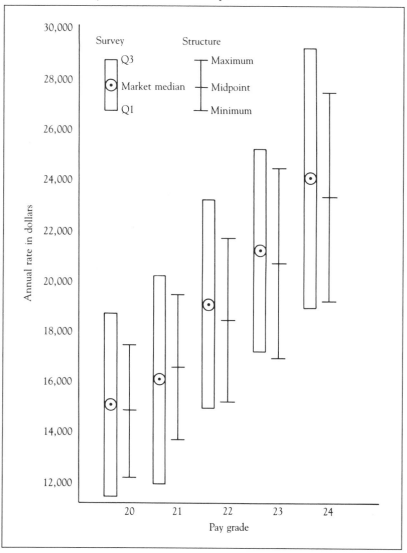

Exhibit 11.8   Target Compa Ratio: Lead Structure

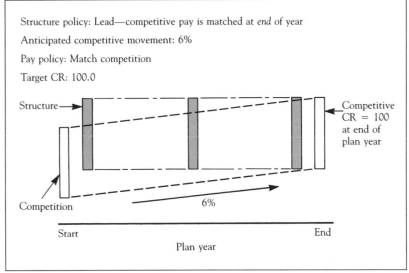

Structure policy: Lead—competitive pay is matched at *end* of year

Anticipated competitive movement: 6%

Pay policy: Match competition

Target CR: 100.0

Adapted from John H. Davis, *Quantitative Analysis for Compensation Decision Making* (Scottsdale, Ariz.: American Compensation Association, 1980), pp. 4-8 to 4-9. Used by permission.

The second strategy is a lag policy. In this case (illustrated in Exhibit 11.9), the company sets its internal salary structure exactly to the market at the beginning of the plan year and allows itself gradually to fall behind the market throughout the year.

The third strategy (illustrated in Exhibit 11.10) is a mixed lead/lag policy. According to this policy, the planner sets the salary structure sufficiently ahead of the market at the beginning of the plan year to allow market rates to catch up to the structure midway through the plan year. The company starts the year out by leading the market and finishes the year behind the market.

Actually, any degree between the extremes of a lead and lag policy is possible. The choice of strategy depends entirely on the company's concerns with the extra expense of leading the market and problems encountered in recruiting while lagging the market. In this case, we assume that the Fay/Wallace Corporation has opted for a lead/lag policy.

In order to make the final adjustment in the structure, several substeps are necessary. The first is to adopt the company's policy with regard to the

Exhibit 11.9   Target Compa Ratio: Lag Structure

Structure policy: Lag—competitive pay is matched at *start* of year

Anticipated competitive movement: 6%

Pay policy: Match competition

Target CR: 106.0

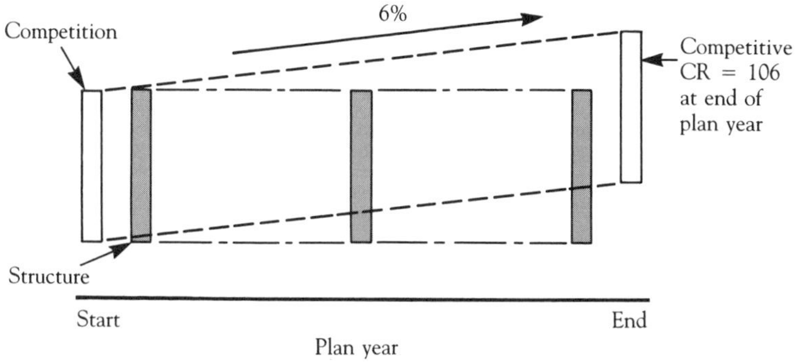

Adapted from John H. Davis, *Quantitative Analysis for Compensation Decision Making* (Scottsdale, Ariz.: American Compensation Association 1980), pp. 4–8 to 4–9. Used by permission.

market for the next plan year (we have adopted a lead/lag policy). The second is to forecast anticipated wage movements in the external market for the next plan year. In our example, we will assume that inflation has picked up and market analysts forecast an annual increase of 6 percent in wages during the next plan year. We want to be meeting the market halfway through the new plan year, in June, and, therefore, we halve this estimate (3 percent) for adjustment purposes. The third step is to adjust the structure upwards by multiplying it by 1.03. This adjustment ratchets the structure 3-percent ahead of the market and sets us up to meet the market forecast for next June. (See Exhibit 11.11.)

Forecasting Required Budgets

So far, we have established a salary structure as a policy to follow in setting salary rates and ranges for jobs. We have been dealing primarily with structure policy. Now our attention must turn to the problem of paying people within

Exhibit 11.10   Target Compa Ratio: Lead/Lag Structure

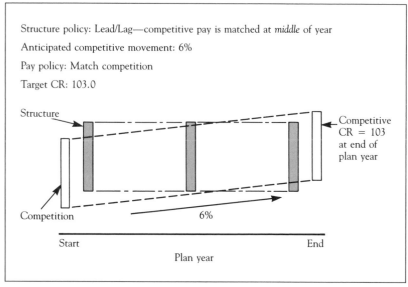

Structure policy: Lead/Lag—competitive pay is matched at *middle* of year

Anticipated competitive movement: 6%

Pay policy: Match competition

Target CR: 103.0

Adapted from John H. Davis, *Quantitative Analysis for Compensation Decision Making* (Scottsdale, Ariz.: American Compensation Association, 1980), pp. 4-8 to 4-9. Used by permission.

the new structure. There are actually two related questions for managers at this stage: (1) Where should each employee's pay be in the new ranges? and (2) How much will it cost to accomplish this? The first is a pay policy issue and the second is a budget and cash flow issue. This section and the next will describe the steps you need to take to answer these questions. This

Exhibit 11.11   Step 11: Adjust for Lead/Lag 3.0%

	New Structure		
Grade	Minimum	Midpoint	Maximum
24	$19,684.07	$24,004.96	$28,325.86
23	$17,575.06	$21,433.00	$25,290.94
22	$15,692.02	$19,136.61	$22,581.20
21	$14,010.73	$17,086.26	$20,161.78
20	$12,509.58	$15,255.59	$18,001.59

section will show you how to forecast the budget needed to finance a given pay policy and the next will show you how to forecast the cash flow that will be necessary to pay compensation under that pay policy.

Top-Down Versus Bottom-Up   Organizations vary in the way they approach the budgeting process. The approach used to develop a compensation budget should dovetail with broader management philosophies regarding involvement and participation in decision making. Traditionally, management practice in this regard has been *top-down;* that is, executives determined the budget that they could afford, established the rules for all pay decisions, and required all lower-level managers to follow them. Such an approach calls for a "macro" budget model, which we will present below.

Increasingly, however, many organizations are moving toward a more participative style that involves managers to a greater degree in decision making regarding their units.[12] Experts argue that participative decision strategies are well adapted to highly diversified organizations, characterized by varied business units, each facing different situations. A single pay policy may not be feasible for such concerns, and a *bottom-up* or "micro" budgeting model will be more appropriate. The bottom-up approach requires each manager to consider his unit's business plans, detail the compensation program necessary to achieve his plans, and recommend the budget his unit will require. We will also consider this approach below.

The Top-Down Budget   The first step in forecasting a budget is to gather information about the employees who will be part of it, that is, information about individual employee salaries to be folded into the new structure. Exhibit 11.12 contains such a report, drawn from employee records. The report shows that there are twenty-two employees at the beginning of the plan year, that their combined monthly salaries total $32,709, and that the total midpoints equal $35,215. The total salary in Exhibit 11.12 has been calculated by summing the salaries for each of the twenty-two employees; the total midpoints in the exhibit have been calculated by summing the midpoints attached to each employee's pay grade. The first thing to do is to ask where the employees' salaries as a group are in relation to the new structure. We can answer this question by calculating an overall compa ratio. We do this by dividing total salary by total midpoints. The compa ratio for this group is 92.9 percent. For technical reasons that are outside the scope of this book, dividing total salary by total midpoints is preferred over calculating the average of the individual employee compa ratios as a method for calculating the overall compa ratio.

Exhibit 11.12   The Top-Down, or Macro, Budget

	This Year			
	Number Employees	Total Salary	Total Midpoints	Compa Ratio
Plan Year Start	22	$32,709.17	$35,215.17	92.9%
Plan Year End	22	$36,271.63	$35,215.17	103.0%
Change	0.0%	10.9%	0.0%	10.9%

The overall compa ratio is an extremely important measure of pay policy and the manager's objectives in establishing individual equity. Indeed, at this point in the budgeting process, the company's structure policy and pay policy (as defined above) come together. The overall compa ratio can now be used to translate structure policy (where the company wants its pay structure to be with respect to the market) into a pay policy (that is, where the company wants its employees to be with respect to the structure).

In order to employ the compa ratio as an objective that drives the budgeting process, we will employ a tool displayed in Exhibit 11.12. The model is organized so that we can begin with current information at the top left-hand corner (Plan Year Start), move across to the right-hand side, drop down, and move back across to the lower left corner (Plan Year End) to see how much of a salary budget increase we will recommend.

Remember that Exhibit 11.12 shows us that we are beginning the new plan year with twenty-two employees; their current monthly total salary is $32,709; the total of their current midpoints (remember, the new structure) is $35,215; and their overall compa ratio is 92.9 percent. This index now becomes the focus of the planning process. Specifically, the planner and management must ask, "Where do we want our employees to be with respect to the structure by the end of the plan year?" The answer to this question depends on pay policy, which reflects where we want our people to be with respect to the structure and the market.

Recall that our structure policy, in this case, is lead/lag. In addition, we anticipate that the market will move upward by 6 percent during the new plan year. Thus, we adjusted the final structure upward by 3 percent, so that the market will meet us halfway through the next year. We now want to establish our pay policy. Suppose management decides that the employees' pay is to be competitive with the market by the end of the plan year. The midpoints of our structure will be lagging behind the market by 3 percent at that time. If we want our employees' pay to be competitive with the market at that point, we will have to aim for an overall compa ratio of 1.03 or 103 percent by the end of the plan year. That is, if the market is going to be 3 percent above our midpoints, then our employees' pay will have to be 3 percent above the midpoints to be competitive with the market.

Thus, as shown in the lower right corner of Exhibit 11.12, the planner sets a planned overall compa ratio of 1.03, or 103 percent. This is often called a *targeted compa ratio*. The targeted compa ratio defines a compensation objective to be achieved in making individual salary adjustments throughout the upcoming plan year.

Now, to answer the question of how much it is going to cost to achieve such an objective, the planner multiplies the targeted compa ratio by the total midpoints (representing the structure that will stay constant from plan year start to end) to calculate the total monthly salary budget that will be necessary by December 31 of the new plan year, if employee salaries are to be competitive with the market. The end-of-year budget necessary in Exhibit 11.12 is $36,271. This will require a 10.9 percent increase in the monthly salary budget by the end of the year.

We have used the budgeting model assuming that the 10.9 percent is the yield (that is, what we are trying to determine) and that the targeted compa ratio of 103 percent is the objective that is driving the model. Many compensation planners, however, find themselves in the position of being told what their budget increases are going to be. The model in Exhibit 11.12 is equally valuable in this situation. The manager can enter the budget increase as a constraint and then work backwards to see what kind of targeted compa ratio is going to be feasible. In effect, the manager is seeing what kinds of limits the budget places on pay policy.

Do Things Go as Planned?   So far the analysis presented in Exhibit 11.12 assumes that everything will go as planned. Every practicing manager knows from hard-won experience, though, that this is a bad assumption. During the next year, a lot of things can happen: (1) current employees (perhaps some relatively high in their ranges) will leave the company, (2) new employees will enter the company (often at relatively low rates in the ranges), (3) some employees will be promoted into higher grades, with new midpoints, (4) the company may expand or contract employment, and a whole host of other possibilities may lead to slippage in our plan.

One approach to dealing with this problem is to look back at recent history to see how things have slipped in the past, and, on the basis of that experience, adjust future plans accordingly. In our example, we can look back at the most recent budget plan (this past year) and compare what we planned last year at this time with what *actually* happened. The analysis in Exhibit 11.13 shows that at the beginning of the last plan year (one year ago) we began with twenty employees. We planned a structure with midpoints of $32,000 to carry us through the year. We targeted a compa ratio of 104 percent and recommended a new salary budget of $33,280, constituting an increase of 7.4 percent.

The lower part of Exhibit 11.13 shows what actually happened. We ended the year with twenty-two employees: an expansion of 10 percent. In addition, our midpoints dropped somewhat to $31,750 (how could this have happened?). These events led to an actual (as opposed to a targeted) compa ratio of 103 percent, somewhat below the 104 percent we had targeted.

One way to capture the results of actual experience is to calculate a statistic known as F, the *experience factor*. F is defined as the ratio of the compa ratio planned for year end to the actual compa ratio achieved. To calculate F, divide the compa ratio planned for the year by the compa ratio actually achieved. In Exhibit 11.13, $F = 1.04 \div 1.03 = 1.01$ or 101%. This means that in our case, the plan undershot by 1 percent. We can use the experience factor to adjust next year's plan in an attempt to avoid under-estimating again. In this case, as illustrated in Exhibit 11.14, we multiply our targeted compa ratio or 103 percent (see Exhibit 11.12) by the experience factor, F, of 101 percent, yielding an adjusted compa ratio of 104 percent or 1.04. Multiplying the midpoints by 104 percent yields an adjusted budget

Exhibit 11.13   Calculating the Experience Factor

	Last Year			
	Number Employees	Total Salary	Total Midpoints	Compa Ratio
Plan year start	20	$31,000.00	$32,000.00	96.9%
Planned year end	20	$33,280.00	$32,000.00	104.0%
Actual year end	22	$32,709.17	$31,750.00	103.0%
Planned change	0.0%	7.4%	0.0%	7.4%
Actual change	10.0%	5.5%	−0.8%	6.3%
Experience factor				
CR Planned/CR Actual:	101.0%			

Exhibit 11.14   This Year With Experience Factor

Total Salary	Total Midpoints	Compa Ratio
$32,709.17	$35,215.17	92.9%
$36,623.78	$35,215.17	104.0%
11.9%	0.0%	11.9%

estimate of $36,623. Thus, to achieve a compa ratio of 1.03, we will need to aim for a compa ratio of 1.04 and that will require a total salary budget of $36,623, leading to a budget increase of 11.9 percent.

You should be careful to note that the use of the experience factor in this way *assumes that history will repeat itself.* In today's business world, this is a risky assumption. The micro budget models we examine next represent an alternative to experience factors that allow managers to take all kinds of specific considerations into account in building compensation plans.

Individual Salary Increases   A final step in the budgeting process is to take the budget increase recommended and translate it into individual salary increases for every employee. One approach to the problem is to recommend a straight 10.9-percent salary increase for everyone in the unit. Most organizations, however, avoid across-the-board increases and try to pay more for merit and performance. A common top-down approach to individual salary adjustments is the salary increase matrix that we introduced in Chapter 9. A salary increase matrix proposes increases for individuals according to any criteria management may want to use. The increase matrix illustrated in Exhibit 11.15 combines performance level and an employee's position in the new range as guides for recommending individual pay increases. In this case, the analyst has tried out a policy for making adjustments that relates pay to performance. The higher an employee's performance (holding place in range or compa ratio constant), the higher the percent wage adjustment. In addition, the lower the person's compa ratio (holding performance level constant), the higher the wage adjustment.

Whether the percentage increases indicated in the exhibit will stay within the 10.9-percent budget increase recommended can be tested by examining the actual distribution of employees by performance and compa ratio category. These relative frequencies are shown in the row and column marginals of the salary increase matrix. Taking the products of the row marginals, the

Exhibit 11.15 Fay/Wallace Merit Matrix

Performance Category	Percent	Compa Ratio Category by Percent				
		<.76	.76–85	.86–.95	.96–1.05	>1.05
		0	0.03	0.12	0.85	0
5	0.07	0.15	0.14	0.13	0.12	0.11
4	0.23	0.14	0.13	0.12	0.11	0.1
3	0.55	0.13	0.12	0.11	0.1	0.09
2	0.15	0.11	0.1	0.09	0.03	0
1	0	0	0	0	0	0
Matrix	Payout					

column marginals, and the cell percentages and summing across all cells in the matrix yields a *matrix payout* that corresponds to the overall percentage increase in the budget that will be necessary to finance the matrix policy. The matrix payout, then, tells us whether the increases indicated in the matrix will keep us in budget. The matrix payout of 9.6 percent in Exhibit 11.15, for example, indicates that we can adopt the matrix and still stay within our budget of 10.9 percent.

The Bottom-Up Budget   An alternative to dictation of budgets by top management (top-down) is to provide individual managers with the responsibility and leeway to build their own business plans and recommend budgets accordingly. A bottom-up budget process is a micro approach that begins with each manager's business plan; an example is illustrated in Exhibit 11.16. The exhibit contains specific employee data for twenty-two members of a given department. Several pieces of information are displayed for each employee: (1) current grade, (2) midpoint at the beginning of the year, (3) midpoint planned for the end of the year, (4) current annual salary rate, (5) planned percentage merit adjustment, (6) planned percentage promotion adjustment, and (7) market adjustments.

The format in Exhibit 11.16 requires that the department manager consider each employee separately. Will the employee get a market adjustment to keep up with the new structure? What size merit adjustment does he deserve? If promoted, will the employee receive a promotion adjustment? (You may want to consider additional adjustments, as well.) Each of these adjustments is taken into account in calculating a new recommended salary for each employee (see the last column in Exhibit 11.16).

Note how flexible the micro model is. It allows the manager to plan explicitly for all kinds of employment decisions including merit adjustments, promotion or transfer adjustments, market adjustments, terminations, transfers, and new hires. In our case, the department manager is planning to terminate Mr. Farley, and at the same time, to add two new people this next plan year.

The output of the micro model is the same as that of the macro model, but in this case, the manager has developed a specific budget plan, rather than having a general one imposed from above. The manager can use the totals at the bottom of Exhibit 11.16 to construct a budget increase plan for the new plan year. He begins with twenty-two employees, paid a current monthly salary total of $32,709. He also begins with total midpoints of $35,215 for a beginning compa ratio of 92.9 percent. Now, however, rather

Exhibit 11.16   The Bottom-Up, or Micro, Budget

Employee	Current Grade	Begin Midpoint	End Midpoint	Current Salary	Merit Adjustment	Promotion Adjustment	Market Adjustment	New Salary
R. Anklar	24	$24,005.00	$26,885.60	$22,000.00	5.0%	5.0%	5.0%	$25,300.00
P. Burke	23	$21,433.00	$21,433.00	$17,890.00	2.0%	0.0%	5.0%	$19,142.30
J. Burkett	22	$19,137.00	$19,137.00	$17,000.00	2.0%	0.0%	5.0%	$18,190.00
H. Crosby	20	$15,256.00	$15,256.00	$12,200.00	2.0%	0.0%	5.0%	$13,054.00
J. Davis	20	$15,256.00	$15,256.00	$12,200.00	5.0%	0.0%	5.0%	$13,420.00
K. Denham	20	$15,256.00	$15,256.00	$12,400.00	5.0%	0.0%	5.0%	$13,640.00
M. Dunham	21	$17,086.00	$17,086.00	$17,000.00	0.0%	0.0%	5.0%	$17,850.00
P. Ephraim	23	$21,433.00	$21,433.00	$20,000.00	0.0%	0.0%	5.0%	$21,000.00
L. Euker	24	$24,005.00	$24,005.00	$24,500.00	2.0%	0.0%	5.0%	$26,215.00
A. Farley	24	$24,005.00		$26,000.00	0.0%	0.0%	0.0%	
C. Futrell	21	$17,086.00	$17,086.00	$17,000.00	2.0%	0.0%	5.0%	$18,190.00
A. Gantry	22	$19,137.00	$19,137.00	$17,800.00	5.0%	0.0%	5.0%	$19,580.00
Z. Gentry	22	$19,137.00	$19,137.00	$18,000.00	5.0%	0.0%	5.0%	$19,800.00
C. Harrell	22	$19,137.00	$19,137.00	$16,800.00	0.0%	0.0%	5.0%	$17,640.00
D. Hartwell	23	$21,433.00	$24,004.96	$21,300.00	0.0%	5.0%	5.0%	$23,430.00
M. Hurley	21	$17,086.00	$17,086.00	$16,000.00	2.0%	0.0%	5.0%	$17,120.00

K. Laswell	24	$24,005.00	$24,005.00	$19,500.00	5.0%	0.0%	5.0%	$21,450.00
M. Loretto	21	$17,086.00	$17,086.00	$17,800.00	2.0%	0.0%	5.0%	$19,046.00
P. Parker	20	$15,256.00	$15,256.00	$14,800.00	5.0%	0.0%	5.0%	$16,280.00
J. Smith	21	$17,086.00	$17,086.00	$14,890.00	2.0%	0.0%	5.0%	$15,932.30
P. Tarkenton	20	$15,256.00	$15,256.00	$15,430.00	5.0%	0.0%	5.0%	$16,973.00
M. Wallace	24	$24,005.00	$24,005.00	$22,000.00	2.0%	0.0%	5.0%	$23,540.00
Farley replacement	20		$15,256.00					$12,509.92
New hire #1	21		$17,086.00					$14,010.52
Total annual:		$422,582.00	$436,371.56	$392,510.00				$423,313.04
Total monthly:		$35,215.17	$36,364.30	$32,709.17				$35,276.09

New Plan Year

Summary:

	Number Employees	Total Salary	Total Midpoints	Compa Ratio
Plan year start	22	$32,709.17	$35,215.17	92.9%
Plan year end	23	$35,276.09	$36,364.30	97.0%
Change	4.5%	7.8%	3.3%	5.9%

than *assuming that the midpoints will be the same*, the manager uses plans for terminations, promotions, and new hires to calculate precisely what the end midpoints will be — $36,364. In addition, his planning shows that he will have a total of twenty-three on board, representing a net increase in employment of 4.5 percent and a new salary budget of $35,276.09 by the end of the plan year. The resulting budget increase is estimated to be 7.8 percent.

Forecasting Cash Flow

Suppose that we go with the micro budget model and agree that a 7.8-percent increase in monthly salary budgets will be necessary to finance our new compensation plan's targeted compa ratio of 97 percent. If we make all adjustments in salaries (including terminations and new hires) according to the plan indicated in Exhibit 11.16 on January 1, the first day of the new plan year, then we will spend $423,313. This represents the *cash flow* for the new plan year, *if we make all changes on the first day of the year*. But if we made no changes this year (including keeping Farley and making no new hires), we would spend $392,510, the sum of the current salaries. The difference in cash flow, therefore, would be $30,803 or 7.8 percent. In this special case, the difference in cash flow of 7.8 percent equals the difference in the budget, because *all changes occur on the first day of the plan year* and have an impact throughout the entire plan year.

But what if the company were to terminate Farley later in the year? Or hire the two new people at different times? Or, what if the company were following a policy of adjusting each employee's salary rate on the first of the month containing his anniversary date, that is, the month in which he was first hired (a very common compensation policy)? An employee hired in March, for example, would be paid his current rate in January and February and would not increase to his new rate until March. In an extreme case, an employee hired in December would wait until almost the end of the new plan year, December 1, to receive his increase under the plan. A little thought should lead you to the conclusion that timing is a key factor influencing cash flow.

The above consideration makes it crucial for the planner to distinguish between the concept of salary rate increase (for example, the percentage increase in a given salary) and cash flow, that is, the amount of money that will be expended on salaries during the plan year. Salary rate is the amount of money paid per period (for example, hour, day, week, month or year). In our example, we have expressed salaries in terms of monthly and annual rates. If Mr. Anklar in Exhibit 11.16, for example, has had his annual salary increased from

$22,000 to $25,300, he has received a salary increase of 15 percent. The cash flow change created by this increase depends upon the timing or when the adjustment to pay takes place. At one extreme we could adjust Mr. Anklar's salary on January 1. The cash flow would be $25,300 ÷ 12 months × 12 months = $25,300. The cash flow increase would be 15 percent corresponding to the 15-percent rate increase. Suppose, however, that Mr. Anklar's salary is adjusted on July 1, six months into the plan year. Now the cash flow picture changes. He earns $1,833 per month for the first six months for a total of $11,000 and $2,108 per month for the remaining six months, for a total of $12,650. His total cash flow is $11,000 + $12,650 = $23,650. The cash flow increase is only 7.5 percent while the rate increase was 15 percent. The reason the cash flow increase is smaller is because we waited for a half year before granting the salary increase.

Cash flow models allow the manager to take the timing of salary increases into account when forecasting the effect of salary rate increases on the cash flow the employer will have to expend. Exhibit 11.17 displays a cash flow model that organizes the data for the department in Exhibit 11.16. The model takes account of the action month for each employee and new hire. The action takes effect on the first day of the action month. An employee whose salary is to be adjusted earns the current salary up to this point and earns the new salary thereafter. People who are scheduled to leave earn their current salary up to this point and their salary disappears thereafter. New hires show no salary up to this point and show their new salary thereafter.

The model calculates cash flow before and after the action point for each employee in order to calculate total cash flow. The model then can make two more calculations across all employees: (1) total cash flow if no actions are taken and (2) total cash flow if all actions are taken. In our example, the total cash flow without actions is $392,510, compared to $411,375 if the actions are taken. The difference in cash flow, therefore, is $18,865 or 4.8 percent. This measures the cash flow effects of our compensation decisions and policies planned for the new plan year. Our increase policy, then, will result in a cash flow increase of 4.8 percent, even though our salary budget is forecast to increase by 7.8 percent.

Our view of cash flow increase is to ask how much more will we spend if we take actions than we would if we took no actions. This change of 4.8 percent is diagrammed in Exhibit 11.18. An alternative way of looking at cash flow increases would be to ask, "How much more cash flow will we expend than we did in all of last year?" This is a different question, as illustrated in Exhibit 11.18, and compares cash flow during the new plan year with cash flow during the previous year. In our example, the cash flow

Exhibit 11.17 Cash Flow Model

Employee	Current Salary	New Salary	Action Month	Cash Flow w/o Adjustment	Cash Flow w adjustment
R. Anklar	$1,833.33	$2,108.33	1	$22,000.00	$25,025.00
P. Burke	$1,490.83	$1,595.19	2	$17,890.00	$18,933.58
J. Burkett	$1,416.67	$1,515.83	2	$17,000.00	$17,991.67
H. Crosby	$1,016.67	$1,087.83	4	$12,200.00	$12,769.33
J. Davis	$1,016.67	$1,118.33	6	$12,200.00	$12,810.00
K. Denham	$1,033.33	$1,136.67	5	$12,400.00	$13,123.33
M. Dunham	$1,416.67	$1,487.50	9	$17,000.00	$17,212.50
P. Ephraim	$1,666.67	$1,750.00	2	$20,000.00	$20,833.33
L. Euker	$2,041.67	$2,184.58	6	$24,500.00	$25,357.50
A. Farley	$2,166.67		4	$26,000.00	$8,666.67
C. Futrell	$1,416.67	$1,515.83	3	$17,000.00	$17,892.50
A. Gantry	$1,483.33	$1,631.67	8	$17,800.00	$18,393.33
Z. Gentry	$1,500.00	$1,650.00	2	$18,000.00	$19,500.00

C. Harrell	$1,400.00	$16,800.00	8	$17,080.00
D. Hartwell	$1,775.00	$21,300.00	6	$22,365.00
M. Hurley	$1,333.33	$16,000.00	2	$16,933.33
K. Laswell	$1,625.00	$19,500.00	9	$19,987.50
M. Loretto	$1,483.33	$17,800.00	6	$18,423.00
P. Parker	$1,233.33	$14,800.00	6	$15,540.00
J. Smith	$1,240.83	$14,890.00	2	$15,758.58
P. Tarkenton	$1,285.83	$15,430.00	9	$15,815.75
M. Wallace	$1,833.33	$22,000.00	2	$23,283.33
Farley replacement	$1,042.49		4	$8,339.95
New hire #1	$1,167.54		4	$9,340.35

Total Cash Flow $392,510.00 $411,375.54
Absolute Change Cash Flow: $18,865.54
Percent Change Cash Flow: 4.8%

Exhibit 11.18   Cash Flow Analyses

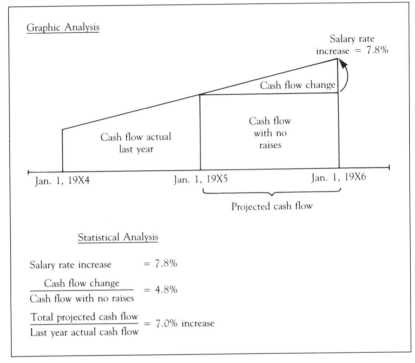

Graphic Analysis

Salary rate increase = 7.8%

Cash flow change

Cash flow actual last year

Cash flow with no raises

Jan. 1, 19X4   Jan. 1, 19X5   Jan. 1, 19X6

Projected cash flow

Statistical Analysis

Salary rate increase   = 7.8%

$$\frac{\text{Cash flow change}}{\text{Cash flow with no raises}} = 4.8\%$$

$$\frac{\text{Total projected cash flow}}{\text{Last year actual cash flow}} = 7.0\% \text{ increase}$$

increase this year over last year is 7 percent. What is the difference in these two views? The first view compares cash flow this year over what we're already committed to (current salaries). The second view compares cash flow this year over the entire previous year. The problem with the second view is that it is purely historical. There is no way to return to that year by taking actions back, so the comparison is not all that relevant to the current compensation decision. Exhibit 11.18 summarizes what we have said about cash flow and salary rate increases in this section.

Communication

Knowledge of the compensation system and the process used to construct it will not guarantee acceptance of the system. However, employees who do not know about the system and its construction are not likely to place much trust in it. How much an organization chooses to disclose to employees about the pay system will vary, but it is crucial that whatever the organization wants employees to know about the compensation system be communicated in an explicit, formal fashion.

It is important to remember that the behavioral function of the compensation system is to attract, motivate, and retain employees. As we noted in Chapter 4, compensation systems can be thought of as operating motivationally in terms of equity theory and expectancy theory. In either case, correct knowledge about outcomes for the individual is necessary.

What, then, are some specific communications needs? Employees, of course, know their gross and net salary each pay period; paychecks provide that information. A large part of the compensation package, however, is not communicated to employees in many organizations: that is the benefits package. As benefits become a larger portion of the total compensation package, many employers have begun to report to employees the value of that package. (Refer to Exhibit 5.4 on pages 113–117.)

Employers need to integrate into a formal program whatever information about the compensation process they wish employees to know. The report of the American Compensation Association/American Society for Personnel Administration joint task force dealing with pay programs suggests these six subjects for inclusion in any communication of a pay program's objectives: (1) the methods used in job analysis and job evaluation; (2) the organizational policy with respect to matching the market on pay levels; (3) the role of performance and performance appraisal in determining individual pay; (4) the pay increase policy and administration; (5) the effect of governmental and economic constraints on the amount of money available for compensation purposes; and (6) the pay policies and regulations used in compensation administration on a day-to-day basis.[13] A variety of communications techniques, both formal and informal, are suggested.

Summary

This chapter has examined three critical areas in the successful implementation and administration of compensation programs: (1) process issues to be resolved during implementation and administration; (2) controlling, auditing, and budgeting the program; and (3) communicating the program.

Process is as important as design in its influence on the success of a compensation program. In this chapter, we have looked at four processes with which the manager must be concerned: (1) who will be responsible for the design and administration of the program — typically this responsibility is shared by line managers and staff compensation experts; (2) who shall participate in designing and administering the program — we have noted that, traditionally, there has not been much employee participation in these matters, but that newer management approaches often do involve employees in the design and administration of compensation programs (which fits well with an emerging culture of high involvement management and heightens employee acceptance and "buy in" into the program); (3) how openly the compensation program, traditionally shrouded in secrecy, shall be communicated — policies of secrecy actually work against compensation programs and have shown the necessity for openly communicating pay program details; and (4) standardization and centralization — traditionally, compensation practices have been highly centralized and standardized to assure consistency of practice and results, but now many complex and large organizations are moving toward more decentralized, less standardized compensation policies.

We have also demonstrated a number of quantitative techniques for controlling, auditing, and budgeting the compensation program. Specifically, we have presented basic techniques for (1) adjusting or creating salary structures to achieve external, internal, and individual equity; (2) auditing the current salary structure for external, internal, and individual equity; (3) forecasting the monthly salary budget necessary to finance a given salary structure; and (4) combining information about the new structure with information about the placement of employees within the structure to develop cash flow forecasts.

Finally, this chapter has examined the critical process of communicating to employees about their compensation. We have discussed those aspects of the compensation program that must be communicated and understood in order for the program to have an impact on behavior.

Notes

[1] See Edward E. Lawler, III, *Pay and Organizational Development* (Reading, Mass.: Addison-Wesley, 1981).

[2] Ibid.

[3] Ibid.

[4] Ibid.

[5] G. D. Jenkins, Jr., and E. E. Lawler, III, "Impact of Employee Participation in Pay Plan Development," *Organizational Behavior and Human Performance* (1981): 11–128.

[6]D. O. Stuhaug, "Want a Raise? At Romac You Do a Little Politicking With Your Peers," *Daily Journal of Commerce and Northwest Construction Record*, Seattle, Washington, February 5, 1979, p. 1.

[7]Lawler, *Pay and Organizational Development*.

[8]Lawler, *Pay and Organizational Development*; Lawler, *Pay and Organizational Effectiveness*, (New York: McGraw-Hill, 1971).

[9]See Fred Foulkes, *Personnel and Industrial Relations in Large Organizations* (Homewood, Ill.: Richard D. Irwin, 1983).

[10]See R. Broderick, *Report to the American Compensation Association on Strategy and Compensation* (Scottsdale, Ariz.: American Compensation Association, 1985).

[11]For a complete discussion of auditing compensation programs, see R. J. Greene, "Auditing Compensation Programs for Effectiveness," *American Compensation Association Proceedings* (Scottsdale, Ariz.: American Compensation Association, 1984).

[12]Edward E. Lawler, III, *High Involvement Management* (San Francisco: Jossey-Bass, 1986).

[13]American Compensation Association and American Society for Personnel Administration, *Sound Base Pay Administration* (Scottsdale, Ariz.: American Compensation Association, 1984).

12

Strategic Uses of Compensation Practice

After you have studied this chapter, you should be able to address the following key issues and questions:

1. What events in recent years have influenced the way organizations compensate their employees?
2. What is organizational strategy and why is it important to align compensation with it?
3. How have downsizing and reorganization affected compensation practice?
4. How might compensation be used as a device for implementing business strategy?
5. How might pay be used as a lag system? As a lead system?
6. What major alternatives to time-based pay are being used by organizations?

Introduction: The Strategic Imperative

The face of the U.S. and international business environment has changed dramatically in the last decade, and conducting business will never be the same. Major industries, including automobiles, steel, transportation, communications, and banking and financial services, are operating under conditions that were entirely unknown ten years ago. Three events, in particular, have contributed to these changes: (1) increased domestic and international competition, (2) a shift from a manufacturing to a service economy, and (3) a response to these changes by many firms that includes downsizing and restructuring. Each of these changes creates a need for new business plans and new approaches toward compensation. Many companies have responded to the challenge by implementing radically different business plans and reinforcing performance under them with alternative compensation practices that depart from traditional methods. The purpose of this chapter is to examine these changes and learn how compensation can be used as a strategy for implementing and reinforcing strategic business plans.

Competition and Change

Competition

The 1980s have been an age of unprecedented increases in competition as many domestic markets have been deregulated by federal law and have become increasingly international. The transportation, communications, and banking industries, for example, were deregulated in the late 1970s. This one event brought unprecedented competition to each of these industries. Among airlines, for example, traditional carriers like Frontier, Braniff, Pan American, Continental, and Western either disappeared or were acquired by other carriers. Newly organized airlines, like Texas Air, have become the new giants, acquiring such carriers as Eastern.

In banking and finance, consumer banks find themselves in direct competition with brokerage houses, insurance companies, and retailers, like Sears, in offering financial services they once monopolized. They can no longer assume a steady volume of business and are finding that customer service is the most important factor determining business success.[1]

Communications serves as a third dramatic example of deregulation's effects. All facets of communications (long-distance service, local phone service, even the phone book) were long dominated by AT&T. Since the breakup of this giant in 1984, markets have become far more competitive, presenting a severe test for AT&T and the "Baby Bells" that were set out on their own after divestiture. AT&T now competes with MCI, Sprint, and many other long distance providers. The twenty-two "Baby Bells" compete with companies like Northern Telecom in the provision of in-home and in-office telephone equipment and switching services. Even the phone book has become a source of competition as alternative providers publish rivals to the traditional yellow pages.

Deregulation has not been the only contributor to increased competition in recent years. The 1980s have witnessed unprecedented international competition, as well. Japanese firms, for example, have established substantial shares of the American automobile, consumer electronics, machine tool, materials handling, and computer markets. Other Asian and European producers are not far behind.

The changes we have just described pose an immediate threat to old business plans. Companies that have continued to rely on old products and services have found themselves quickly losing market shares. Increased competition has forced organizations to look more carefully at three dimensions: (1) efficiency in producing goods and services, (2) product and service quality, and (3) customer service. The only way to meet this new competition is to develop and implement business plans that will improve productivity, quality, and customer service.

The Shift to Services

At the same time that competition has increased, a dramatic shift in the United States from a manufacturing-based economy to a service economy has occurred. Columnist George F. Will explains, "McDonald's has more employees than U.S. Steel. Golden Arches, not blast furnaces, symbolize the American economy."[2] Will refers to a major shift in our economy in which relatively more people are employed in the delivery of services (personal services, consumer services, industrial services, and high-technology business services) than in the manufacturing of products. The trend will continue as the service sector increases its share of gross national product and employment.[3]

The difference between selling services and selling manufactured products is substantial (as illustrated in Exhibit 12.1) and presents strategic challenges for business plans and the compensation programs designed to reinforce them.[4]

Exhibit 12.1   The Contrast Between a Traditional and a Service Economy

Traditional Economy	Service Economy
Tangible products	Intangible services
Selling stand-alone products	Selling individual performance
Focus on product characteristics	Focus on customer needs
Service is a cost and chore	Service is a strategy

The major difference is that a manufacturer (like General Motors) sells a *tangible* product (a car) that has obvious physical properties. The customer can see the car's color, for example, and product quality is primarily a problem of engineering and production.

When companies sell a service, in contrast, they are selling an *intangible*. An airline like Delta or United, for example, sells a far less tangible product than does GM. In fact, to the customer, Delta is the gate agent he meets on check-in, the flight attendant who takes his boarding pass and indicates his seat, or the service agent who handles his complaint about lost luggage. One authority on service marketing refers to the examples we have just described as "moments of truth" in customer service.[5] A moment of truth is that intensely personal experience the customer has when he deals with the service provider in a transaction. An airline might face 50,000 such moments of truth each day — so does an insurance company or any other service provider. Moments of truth add up and those companies that consistently score high in the customer's mind will prosper. Those companies that consistently score low will eventually lose market share and succumb.

The major thing a service provider sells is the *performance* of the person delivering the service. At the extreme, the sum total of an actor's or a musician's "product" is the individual performance executed before the audience. Just as a manufacturer must manage product quality (through quality control programs), so must a service provider manage service performance. In fact, variation in the quality of service performance may be far more crucial to a service business than it is to a traditional manufacturer.

Consider an assembly-line worker fitting a door panel to a car. Her work is paced by the assembly line and she has standard materials with which to work. It is important to the operation that she work at a steady pace and that the door fit within a tolerance of one-fourth of an inch. Acceptable performance in this case is to avoid any circumstance that stops the line and to mount door panels within the one-fourth-inch limit.

What is peak performance on this job? Not much different. She cannot work any faster because the line paces her. She might fit the door panel down to one-eighth of an inch tolerance, but that is not going to make that much of a difference in the overall scheme of things.

Now consider the last time you purchased a service — flew on an airliner, made a bank deposit, dined at a restaurant, attended class, or bought a shirt. Can you recall any horror stories? Any hero stories? In contrast to the case of the assembly-line worker, the difference between perfectly acceptable and peak performance can be enormous. As illustrated in Exhibit 12.2, individuals can really make a difference in service delivery, and this *margin of discretionary effort* provides an opportunity for service providers to compete.

Companies such as American Express see discretionary effort and peak service performance as key strategies for winning market shares. William Gerstner, American Express's President and CEO sees "service as our most strategic marketing weapon."[6]

Changes in Organizations

The increases in competition and the shift to a service economy that we have described create a strategic imperative for organizations. Many firms have responded to the challenge in a variety of ways, including downsizing, reorganizing operations, introducing more efficient technologies and methods, focusing more closely on product quality, and developing alternative compensation systems.

Downsizing, the removal of peripheral positions and layers of management, is one of the most frequent responses to our new business environment. Many large firms like General Electric have removed several levels of management positions in recent years. In addition, these companies have drastically cut back support staffs, like planning, and are vesting responsibility for such functions back with line managers.[7]

Reorganization is another popular response to the events we have described. Companies like Westinghouse, General Electric, and Clark Equipment Company, for example, have moved from functional design (organization centered around business functions like manufacturing, marketing, and human resources) to organization according to strategic product/service lines. The result is that divisions have only a single product or service line to produce and market, and all efforts are focused on its success. Such divisions

Exhibit 12.2   Margin of Discretionary Effort

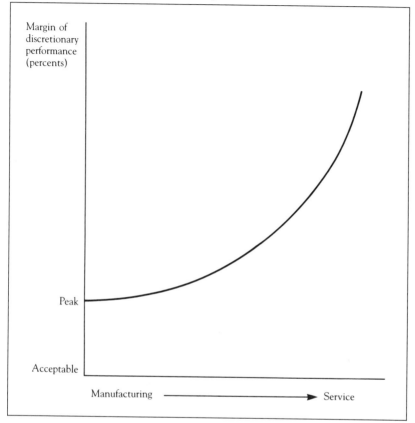

Margin of
discretionary
performance
(percents)

Peak

Acceptable

Manufacturing ⟶ Service

are treated as strategic business units (SBUs) and are measured in terms of individual contributions to the corporation's revenues and profits.

Compensation:
An Implementation Strategy

Changes in the business environment such as we have just explored present organizations with a number of strategic challenges:

1. The need to compete with discretionary effort in service performance
2. The need to relate labor costs to revenues — productivity
3. The need to stop treating compensation dollars as sunk costs
4. The need to treat compensation dollars as investments for leveraging results related to strategic plans.

Unfortunately, many experts point out that traditional compensation practices are not well suited for accomplishing anything other than managing costs. One authority notes, for example, that pay plans can have four elements, as illustrated in Exhibit 12.3, each with different consequences or roles for employees and the organization: (1) base pay, (2) benefits, (3) short-term incentives, and (4) long-term incentives.[8]

Traditional compensation plans have emphasized base pay and benefits in their pay practices. In many cases, pay plans are limited to these first two elements and do not even include short- and long-term incentives. An examination of Exhibit 12.3 shows that base pay and benefits are primarily based on *membership* in the organization, not individual or group performance achievement. Traditional compensation methods, which focus on base pay and benefits, then, enforce acceptable performance and can be used to control costs — but they do not have much effect on unleashing discretionary effort and performance, nor do they create incentives for increased productivity beyond minimum cost considerations.

Exhibit 12.3   Elements of Compensation

Element	Employee Interest	Organization Interest
Base pay	Provide standard of living	Manage external and internal equity — attract and retain employees
Employee benefits	Protect standard of living	Attract and retain employees
Short-term incentives	Prospect of more income for more effort	Motivate effort and direct behavior
Long-term incentives	Capital accumulation/ estate building	Encourage long-term view/ commitment/retention of valued employees

Source: Robert J. Greene, Reward Systems, Inc., Glenview, Ill. Used by permission.

Increasingly, experts and business leaders are asking if compensation can do more than control costs and enforce acceptable performance. Can compensation be used to support or implement an organization's strategy? One authority notes that compensation can be a powerful tool for implementing strategy both as a *lead* system, introducing change, and a *lag* system, supporting change.[9]

Pay as a lead system has four potential advantages:

1. Pay can be used to communicate business plans.
2. Pay can be used to articulate unit, group, and individual performance objectives in terms of business plans.
3. Pay establishes incentives for employees and groups to change current practices and adopt new ones.
4. Pay communicates management's intentions.

Pay as a lead system, then, is used at the beginning of business plan implementation and introduces change.

Pay as a lag system has three potential advantages:

1. Pay reinforces individual and group performance required by business plans.
2. Pay rewards discretionary effort.
3. Pay shares returns from productivity improvements and long-run goal achievement.

Pay as a lag system, then, is used continually through the plan cycle to reward, influence, and direct those behaviors required to achieve the plan.

Alternative Compensation Strategies

We noted in Exhibit 12.3 that base pay and benefit elements are good for managing external and internal equity (internal job value relationships) and that these two elements constitute traditional compensation methods that still characterize many (if not a majority) of the compensation systems in place today.

Increasingly, however, we are seeing many departures from traditional practices that include the following alternative compensation strategies:

1. *Performance-based pay.* Adjustments to pay are based on individual or group performance and are not granted simply because of organizational membership or time with the employer.

2. *Merit awards or incentives not tied to base pay.* Adjustments to pay must be earned through performance and are not rolled into base pay. Thus, they must be re-earned each year and do not constitute a payment into the future.

3. *Lump-sum bonuses.* Merit or incentive awards are granted on a one-time "lump sum" basis and are not distributed in the form of weekly or monthly pay checks.

4. *Gainsharing plans.* Compensation plans build a working model of an operation (an assembly line, for example) and measure actual performance against goals (for example, labor costs in completed units or standard employee hours in completed units). Any gain in actual dollars or hours within the standard or goal that has been set is shared with workers in the form of gainsharing cash bonuses.

5. *Skill-based pay.* Pay-for-knowledge plans create incentives for workers to learn more than one task or position in a plant. Skill-based pay systems set higher level rates for each new task or position that is mastered. The highest rate is achieved once all positions are learned.

6. *All salaried workforce.* This is a pay delivery plan that places all employees (management and hourly employees) on a single salary system. Although Fair Labor Standards Act (FLSA) overtime provisions still apply to nonexempt employees, such plans do away with the practice of punching time clocks, and provide hourly employees with the same paid time off (breaks and lunch) that are afforded salaried employees.

7. *Profit-sharing plans.* These plans establish profit goals for the organization and set aside a share of all profits exceeding the goal into a pool that is distributed back in the form of bonuses to employees.

8. *Cafeteria plans.* These are compensation plans that allow employees individual flexibility in their choices among benefit plan elements. Thus, some employees may wish to invest more in life insurance, while others may want to allocate proportionately more to retirement plan investments. Some cafeteria plans are total compensation plans, in that the employee can pool dollars going into both direct pay and benefits.

Corporate Strategy and Compensation Fit

Each of the alternative compensation strategies just outlined represents a significant departure from traditional compensation practice and should not be undertaken by employers without good reason. That is, alternative compensation designs do not make sense unless there is a larger corporate strategy to be served. If organizations are to employ compensation practices to implement business plans, there must be a logical and consistent fit between corporate strategy and compensation design. The problem, as illustrated in Exhibit 12.4, is to match up compensation plan design with an organization's strategic business plans. Business plans often contain the following elements:

1. Financial objectives
2. Market share objectives
3. Growth objectives
4. An organization design specifying units, each with performance objectives derived from the business plan.

Compensation designs have to be established that fit such objectives and conditions. Exhibit 12.4 suggests that the match between an organization's strategy and its compensation design has a bearing on individual employee, group, and organizational performance. That is, the better the fit, the better will individuals and groups perform.

Consideration of the fit between corporate strategy and compensation design raises four questions: (1) To what extent are organizations using alternative compensation designs? (2) Are there any risks associated with such designs? (3) Is there any evidence that companies currently adapt compen-

Exhibit 12.4   Strategy–Compensation Design Fit

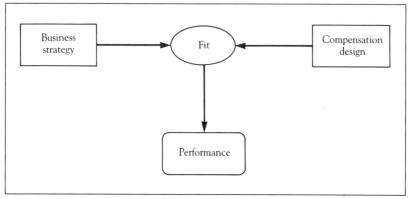

sation designs to their strategies? (4) Is there any evidence that companies that do so perform better than those that do not?

Extent of Alternative Compensation Designs

In 1986, the American Compensation Association and the American Productivity Center cooperated on a survey of some 3,000 employers regarding their use of alternative or nontraditional compensation designs.[10] The survey sought to determine the extent to which employers use (1) strategies as pay for performance, gainsharing, and profit sharing; (2) future plans with regard to such plans; and (3) the firm's positive or negative experiences with such plans.

The results of the survey suggest a strong interest on the part of many employers in alternative compensation designs. More gainsharing, skill-based pay, group-incentive, and lump-sum plans have been adopted in the last five years, for example, than in all of the previous twenty. In addition, the survey indicates that significant numbers of organizations are employing at least some elements of alternative compensation designs. The data in Exhibit 12.5, for example, show that 32 percent of employers responding to the survey use some form of gainsharing, 30 percent employ lump-sum bonus options, and 28 percent use individual incentives.

Finally, the survey indicates that many of those firms not currently using alternative compensation designs report that they have plans to design and implement such plans within the next five years. Exhibit 12.6 shows the

Exhibit 12.5   Proportion of Employers Using Alternative Pay Plans

Strategy	Percent Total	Percent Manufacturing	Percent Service
Profit sharing	32%	37%	28%
Lump-sum bonus	30%	31%	29%
Individual incentives	28%	27%	29%
Gainsharing	13%	20%	8%
Small-group incentives	14%	15%	15%
All-salaried work force	11%	13%	8%
Two-tier pay plan	11%	15%	7%
Pay for knowledge	5%	8%	2%
Earned time off	6%	5%	7%

Exhibit 12.6   Projected Percent Increase in the Use of Alternative Compensation Plans

Strategy	Projected Increase 1986–1991
All salaried	31%
Pay for knowledge	75%
Gainsharing	68%
Profit sharing	20%
Small-group incentives	70%
Individual incentives	31%
Lump-sum bonus	29%
Two-tier pay plan	33%
Earned time off	36%

projected percent increases in the adoption of alternative compensation designs over the next five years.

One of the survey's findings suggests that the move to alternative compensation designs is not random or happenstance. The evidence indicates that firms that report increases in domestic and multinational competition are far more likely to adopt such plans than those that do not. In fact, the proportion of firms adopting all salaried, pay-for-knowledge, gainsharing and profit-sharing plans is ten times greater among those facing increased competitive pressures than among those that are not.

Risks and Benefits of Alternative Compensation Designs

The ACA/APC survey suggests a strong interest among employers in alternative compensation strategy (the "new pay" as one expert calls it).[11] The rush to consider and adopt such strategies raises some uncomfortable questions about business and compensation practice. Is it just a fad? What is so new about the new pay? Are there tangible strategic benefits to be realized from such plans? Are there risks associated with adopting these designs that are not offset by any advantages?

Clearly, the new pay has potential benefits (cited earlier in our discussion of pay as a lead system and as a lag system). Such methods have the potential to communicate business plans to all employees, to articulate group and individual performance objectives in terms of business plans, to allow managers to link labor costs to productivity, and to reward those behaviors required to achieve business plan objectives.

The major effect of alternative compensation designs, though, is to put increasing proportions of an employee's earnings at risk, as illustrated in Exhibit 12.7. Pay at risk is pay that is not guaranteed each year; rather, it must be re-earned each year. There are fewer entitlements to pay as the basis for rewarding people shifts from the job one holds and seniority to specific individual and group achievements based on per-period performance. The obvious benefit of this result is that it allows managers to manage productivity closely by relating labor costs to revenues and other valued performance outcomes.

There are equally crucial costs or risks associated with the new pay, however. As illustrated in Exhibit 12.7, shifting incentive pay from base pay signals a significant change in an organization's cultural values and priorities. The message to employees is that there are no longer any entitlements. The job you hold, longevity, and commitment to the organization do not count as much any more. The organization constantly asks, "What have you done for me lately?" The person who rests on his laurels, even if performing at acceptable levels, can expect to see his pay keep up only with the middle of the market. Those who are to be paid well (in excess of the middle of the market) must maintain consistently superior performance, period after period. In addition, depending on the particular design employed, earnings might

Exhibit 12.7 Effect of Putting Increasing Proportion of Pay at Risk

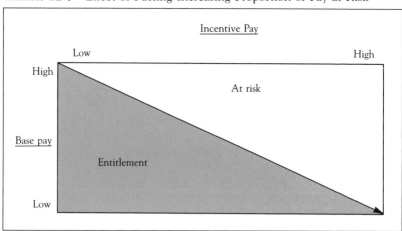

vary with factors beyond any individual's or group's control, such as market shares, stock values, and return on equity or investment.

The shift to the new pay, then, will upset traditional pay relationships and working styles. Earnings based on seniority and longevity will be replaced by the increased pressure for productivity and effort. Because people and groups may end up competing with each other, the risks associated with alternative compensation systems include alienating some long-term employees (who may be performing at perfectly acceptable levels) and creating disincentives for long-term commitment. Pay dissatisfaction and turnover may well result.

Some theorists point out, however, that these effects may be beneficial in the long run. A well-conceived pay-for-performance plan, for example, may weed out mediocre performers and attract consistently superior performers who know they can maximize total earnings through performance.

An even more subtle risk run by employers who adopt the new pay involves the definition and measurement of the performance objectives to be achieved under the plan. Under a traditional base pay system, management can afford to be vague in defining merit and performance expectations because it is not explicitly paying for performance. A traditional base pay system places a premium on longevity and very general conceptions of individual merit that enforce minimally acceptable standards of performance. So long as an employee avoids infractions and maintains generally acceptable levels of performance (as vaguely conceived by his supervisor) he can expect predictable base pay increases over time.

Under the new pay, in contrast, performance levels have a much greater influence on the earnings of individuals and groups. In addition, management commits to attaching significant dollars to differences in whatever is being defined as performance. Management, therefore, can no longer afford to be vague in defining merit and performance standards. It is under the gun to define highly explicit and measurable performance expectations that have dollar values, for three reasons.

First, there is the danger of what performance appraisal experts call *criterion deficiency* in establishing performance measures and paying for performance.[12] A deficient performance criterion is one that fails to capture all important dimensions or aspects of an employee's job. Since people tend to behave in those ways that are rewarded and avoid behaving in ways that are not, it should be no surprise that employees ignore any tasks not captured in the definition of performance that the manager uses to establish merit and reward employees.[13] Thus, if a pay-for-performance system pays for output and ignores quality on an assembly operation, management can expect high production counts as well as high rates of rejects and customer returns over time. A second problem in defining performance standards is called *criterion contamination*.[14] In this case, the system unintentionally rewards unwanted behaviors and performance. One of the authors, for example, once consulted with a large metal manufacturing firm that employed an individual incentive system that paid workers additional pay for beating a certain number of hours or minutes that had been established as standard for specific operations (for example, setting up a smelting oven, pouring ingots, sizing ingots, operating a rolling mill). The problem was that the company was attempting to shift from outdated machines and operations to state-of-the-art, computer-based methods. The standards to beat on the old jobs were dated, had slipped, and were easy to beat. It was easy to make 30 percent more than one's base pay on these jobs. Standards on the new jobs were another matter. They were less well established and harder to beat. Management's dilemma was the fact the best employees insisted on remaining on the old jobs where they knew they could fare well. They refused the new jobs and were unwilling to train for the very jobs upon which the company had staked its future. The unintended consequence of the plan was to reward behaviors that conflicted directly with the company's business plan.

Finally, managers must take care in defining performance standards under the new pay as a simple matter of economics. One of the first questions many executives ask when contemplating a pay-for-performance system or a gainsharing plan is, "How are we going to pay for this? Where is the money going to come from?" This is the wrong question to be asking and indicates that the manager has not adequately addressed the challenge of defining performance. If he has determined what performance is important for each position to be brought under the new pay plan and has determined the *value* of that performance, then he will have the answer to his question.

Managers should be careful to heed the other side of this issue. A job whose contribution to group or unit plans cannot be comfortably determined or is, at best, of marginal value, is a poor candidate for an alternative compensation system and should remain under a more traditional base-pay plan.

Matching Compensation Design with Business Strategy

The major benefit offsetting the risks associated with the new pay is the prospect of supporting business plans. Given this benefit, one would expect to find companies that adopt alternative compensation plans doing so in a way that links up with business strategy. We would expect to find, therefore, a relationship between business strategy and the types of compensation plans employed. Management experts have long proposed that management policy such as organizational structure and administrative practices flow directly from strategy.[15] Human resource experts have pointed out that we would expect to find the same to be true of human resource practices, including compensation.[16]

In order to determine whether organizations match up compensation practices with business strategy, we must define the concepts of compensation practice and strategy more carefully. Compensation practice refers to two major categories illustrated in Exhibit 12.8: (1) the design characteristics of the pay plan, and (2) its administrative aspects.[17]

Each of the eight compensation characteristics listed in Exhibit 12.8 constitutes a decision issue for anyone designing a compensation program. Each has important implications both for organizations and employees. The relative emphasis placed on entitlement based on membership versus merit based on performance, for example, will determine the degree to which a company can relate costs to revenues. At the same time, this emphasis will have a direct bearing on work climate, determining the degree to which longevity versus performance is valued and rewarded. Both compensation theory and research indicate that the eight compensation characteristics in Exhibit 12.8 are useful in comparing compensation plans across organizations.[18]

Before we can determine whether the eight compensation characteristics we have just defined vary with strategy, we first have to define the concept of strategy. *Strategy* refers to business plans that are designed to accomplish objectives. Elements of strategy include the type of product or service market within which a firm chooses to compete, the kinds of technologies or methods employed, the management style and emphasis that predominates, the way the organization is designed and administered, and the performance criteria against which the organization measures itself. Experts in the field of policy and strategy have developed numerous schemas for characterizing or sorting firms according to these dimensions of strategy. One of the most recognized of these taxonomies is that of Miles and Snow, who distinguish three basic types: (1) defenders, (2) prospectors, and (3) analyzers.[19]

As illustrated in Exhibit 12.9, defenders are firms in narrow, stable, and mature product markets. The major objective is to protect market share through customer service. Such organizations tend to have functional designs (e.g., marketing, finance, production, and information services divisions),

Exhibit 12.8   Definitions of Compensation Practice

Compensation Characteristic	Issue
Design Elements	
1. External/internal equity emphasis	Relative importance placed on external market competition versus internal job value relationships
2. Individual pay participation (individual equity)	Relative emphasis placed on entitlement based on membership versus merit based on performance in setting individual pay rates
3. Pay adjustment policy	Relative emphasis on ability to pay (productivity) versus broader business plan performance
Administrative Elements	
4. Participation in design	Degree to which employees are involved in the design of pay systems
5. Participation in administration	Degree to which employees are involved in administering pay practices
6. Centralization/ decentralization	Degree to which pay design and administration are allowed to vary across organizational units
7. Communication	Degree of openness and disclosure about pay plan design and administration
8. Formalization/standardization	Degree to which pay practices are constrained by explicit rules and guidelines

be highly formalized and centralized, and define performance in terms of cost control and financial productivity.

Prospectors present sharp contrasts to defenders. They tend to face multiple markets, many of which are in growth phases of product life cycles. They focus on innovation and a search for growth in new markets. Such firms have multiple technologies and invest more in people. Management tends to be dominated by individuals who specialize in marketing and research and development. Such organizations are structured according to product/ service lines, consisting of divisions that are often called "profit centers" or "strategic business units." There is much less formalization and centraliza-

Exhibit 12.9 Strategic Business Unit Types (Miles & Snow)

	Defender	*Prospector*	*Analyzer*
Product market definition	Narrow, stable market; concerned with protecting market share.	Changing product market emphasis; search for new markets; focus on innovation.	Characterized by mixed strategy.
Technology	Single core technology; investment in improvements.	Multiple, prototype technologies; invest more in people than in machines.	Single core technologies and investment in people.
Management	Dominated by production, finance types.	Tends to change often; dominated by marketing & R&D types.	Dominated by marketing & research; relatively stable.
Design/ administration	Functional division of labor; highly formal.	Product centered division of labor; few formal rules; market relatively open.	Divisionalized or matrix structure; combination of structured and centralized, formal work.
Performance criteria	Promotion based on past performance, cost, & budgets	Performance measured against market outcomes viz. competitors.	Performance measured on combination of cost & market outcomes.

tion — managers are freer to develop policies fitting their unique situations. Performance standards focus less on cost savings and more on market outcomes as compared to key competitors. Analyzers fall between defenders and prospectors in these dimensions. Evidence is still somewhat limited on the question of whether or not firms adapt compensation design to their business strategies. If they do, we would expect compensation designs to vary with the strategic types we have just noted. Broderick has conducted such a study, comparing defenders, prospectors, and analyzers in terms of compensation design and found systematic differences.[20] Her findings are summarized in Exhibit 12.10, which compares defenders and prospectors on compensation design elements, and in Exhibit 12.11, which compares the types of firms on compensation administration elements. In both cases, the results for analyzers fall in between, and are not tabulated.

Compensation Design   Broderick's findings (Exhibit 12.10) indicate that compensation design varies systematically with strategy. Defenders tend to emphasize internal equity (placing relative importance on internal wage relationships among jobs), base individual salary rates on entitlement (seniority,

Exhibit 12.10   Pay/Strategy Fit: Compensation Design

Issue	Defender	Prospector
Market versus internal equity	Internal	External
Award basis	Entitlement	Performance
At-risk earnings	Productivity	Business plan performance

Exhibit 12.11   Pay/Strategy Fit: Compensation Administration

Issue	Defender	Prospector
Communication/openness	Low	High
Participation/involvement	Low	High
Standardization — pay adjustments	Low	High
Standardization — administration	High	Low
Centralization	High	Low

time in grade), and provide at-risk earnings on a strict cost savings or productivity basis.

Prospectors, in contrast, place far more emphasis on external equity or market competitiveness in setting wage rates. In addition, they place relatively more importance on performance effectiveness in setting individual pay levels. Finally, they incorporate a far broader set of criteria for providing at-risk earnings — measures that examine business plan performance rather than simple cost savings. In each of these cases, analyzers fall between defenders and prospectors.

Compensation Administration   Defenders and prospectors also differ systematically with respect to compensation administration, according to Broderick's results (Exhibit 12.11). Prospectors are far more open than defenders, for example, in communicating their pay plans. In addition, they involve employees to a greater degree in the design and even administration of compensation plans. Prospectors are far more likely than defenders, for example, to establish employee task forces to explore compensation design and administration issues and make recommendations for action.

Whether defenders are more or less standardized in compensation depends on the design element. When considering rules for making individual pay adjustments, defenders have low levels of standardization while prospectors have highly standardized and explicit rules. When considering administration and centralization, however, defenders have highly standardized rules while prospectors are far less standardized.

These findings, although they are preliminary, suggest that firms do adapt compensation design and administration to their strategic plans and that as they adapt to changing business environments they adapt their compensation plans, as well.

Emerging Compensation Issues

As the trends we discussed at the opening of this chapter (multinational competition, the emergence of a service economy, and organizational restructuring) continue, we can expect increasing numbers of firms to change their strategic orientation and adapt their compensation practices accordingly. Greene, for example, suggests that firms will fold compensation planning into the overall strategic planning process at an earlier stage.[21]

Experts predict that pay strategy will change in ways that are illustrated in Exhibit 12.12. Base pay, for example, will become a smaller part of an employee's total earnings. Compensation plans of the future will focus more on total earnings than on base pay rates. Business plan accomplishments, not budgets, will trigger incentive payouts. Incentive (at-risk) earnings, will become a much larger part of total earnings. Less emphasis will be placed on the job and more on the individual in establishing pay. Thus, job evaluation practices will become relatively less important and individual merit determination (including performance appraisal) will become increasingly important as a part of compensation policy.

The changes we predict here are part of a larger reorientation in management thinking. Lawler and others have predicted that companies that will adapt well to a changing business environment will be those that practice a management style that uses high levels of employee involvement in functioning.[22] Thus, we can expect high involvement strategies in designing and administering compensation. Exhibit 12.13 suggests that communication will be far more open in future compensation plans, which will be designed with broader employee involvement rather than from the top down. In addition, compensation designs will be driven by strategy, not budgets. Finally, we will see employees given more choice in selecting compensation elements that best satisfy their needs.

Exhibit 12.12 Emerging Pay Strategy

Pay Issue	From	To
Base pay	Large %	Small %
Incentive/trigger	Budgets	Business plan performance
Incentive earnings	Small %	Large %
Pay determination	Emphasis on the job	Emphasis on the individual

Exhibit 12.13 Emerging Pay Method Issues

Issue	From	To
Communication	Secret	Open
Design	Top down	Broad involvement
Design	Traditional	Strategy-driven
Pay mix	Standard	Choice

Summary

In this chapter, we have examined the rapidly changing face of compensation as it is being practiced in the United States and Canada. A number of key events, including the onset of multinational competition, deregulation, and the emergence of a service economy, have demanded major restructuring of corporate assets. Accompanying these changes are significant alterations in the way compensation is designed and administered. We have examined a number of departures from traditional base-pay administration, including bonuses that do not fold into base pay, skill-based pay, gainsharing, profit sharing, and a variety of other nontraditional compensation methods.

Finally, we have forecasted that in the future, pay systems will concentrate less on formal job definitions and more on individual and group contributions. Base pay will become somewhat less important as a component of total earnings and variable pay (incentives not rolled into base pay) will become significantly more important.

Notes

[1]See L. Berry, J. H. Donnelly, and Thomas Thompson, *Marketing Financial Services* (Homewood, Ill.: Dow-Jones, Irwin, 1984).

[2]George F. Will, quoted in Karl Albrecht and Ron Zemke, *Service America!* (Homewood, Ill.: Dow-Jones, Irwin, 1985).

[3]See Russell Ackoff, *Revitalizing Western Economies* (San Francisco: Jossey-Bass, 1984).

[4]Albrecht and Zemke, *Service America!*

[5]Ibid.

[6]William Gerstner, cited in Albrecht and Zemke, *Service America!*

[7]"The New Breed of Strategic Planner," *Business Week* (September 17, 1984): 62–68.

[8]Robert J. Greene, "Using Reward Systems to Support Organizational Strategy." Unpublished paper, 1986.

[9]Edward E. Lawler, III, *Pay and Organizational Development* (Reading, Mass.: Addison-Wesley, 1981).

[10]Carla O'Dell, "People, Performance, and Pay: America Responds to the Competitiveness Challenge" (Scottsdale, Ariz.: American Compensation Association, 1986).

[11]Edward E. Lawler, III, "The New Pay," Center for Effective Organizations, University of Southern California, G-84-7 (55), 1986.

[12]See John Bernardin and Richard W. Beatty, *Performance Appraisal* (Boston: Kent, 1984).

[13]Lawler, *Pay and Organizational Development.*

[14]Bernardin and Beatty, *Performance Appraisal.*

[15]See Tom Burns and G. M. Stalker, *The Management of Innovation* (London: Tavistock Publications, 1961); Alfred D. Chandler, *Strategy and Structure: Chapters in the History of American*

Industrial Enterprise (Cambridge, Mass.: MIT Press, 1962); Paul R. Lawrence and Jay W. Lorsch, *Organization and Environment: Managing Differentiation and Integration* (Boston: Graduate School of Business, Harvard University, 1967); Raymond E. Miles and Charles C. Snow, *Organizational Strategy, Structure, and Process* (New York: McGraw-Hill, 1978).

[16]See Jay R. Galbraith and Daniel A. Nathanson, *Strategy Implementation: The Role of Structure and Process* (St. Paul, Minn.: West, 1978); Jay R. Galbraith, *Organization Design* (Reading, Mass.: Addison-Wesley, 1977).

[17]R. Broderick, "Report to the American Compensation Association Study of Pay Policies and Business Strategies" (Scottsdale, Ariz.: American Compensation Association, May 1985).

[18]Ibid.

[19]Miles and Snow, *Organizational Strategy.*

[20]Broderick, "Report."

[21]Robert J. Greene, "Using Reward Systems."

[22]Edward E. Lawler, III, *High Involvement Management* (San Francisco: Jossey-Bass, 1986).

Appendix: Salary Management Practices in the Private Sector[1]

I n establishing pay practices, managers frequently ask about the practices of firms similar to their own. Their interests are in staying competitive by not diverging too far from their competitors' practices and in finding ways to establish a competitive edge with respect to certain policies.

In 1987, the Advisory Committee on Federal Pay, an independent agency established under the Federal Pay Comparability Act of 1970, sought to develop comprehensive information about salary management practices in the private sector so that comparisons could be drawn for jobs in the public sector. In cooperation with the American Compensation Associaton, the group retained The Wyatt Company to conduct a survey of 10,000 compensation practitioners on their companies' practices. The information gathered covered a broad range of topics including job analysis and descriptions, job evaluation, merit pay, use of salary structures, locality pay practices, salary planning, and program administration. The results provide an excellent insight into actual salary practices. They are reproduced in this appendix to provide you with information about actual practices in compensation.

[1]*Salary Management Practices in the Private Sector,* a survey conducted for the U.S. Advisory Committee on Federal Pay, Washington, D.C., in cooperation with the American Compensation Association, by The Wyatt Company, Philadelphia, Penn., September 1987.

Salary Management Practices in the Private Sector

Introduction

The Advisory Committee on Federal Pay, in cooperation with the American Compensation Association, sponsored a survey to determine private sector salary management practices.

The Advisory Committee was created as an independent agency under the Federal Pay Comparability Act of 1970. The Committee is given responsibility to advise the president on the annual pay adjustment for the 1.4 million white-collar workers and to provide advise on compensation matters.

This research was initiated in response to the federal government's effort to more closely follow industry's compensation practices.

The Civil Service Reform Act of 1978 attempted to model the federal pay and bonus system after the private sector for the top-level executives and the next level of managers. A bonus system was introduced for the Senior Executive Service who represent the 7,000 top-level people throughout the executive branch of government responsible for managing and administering multimillion dollar programs. A similar pay-for-performance system was adopted for the next level of managers, who number about 30,000. Currently, the administration seeks to place all 1.4 million white-collar workers under a pay-for-performance merit system to replace the current within-grade step system.

Other developments are occurring within the federal system, as well. For example, the Navy Department has initiated a "manage to payroll" concept, which theoretically gives supervisors responsibility for job classification and pay levels in divisions with up to 1,000 people. A demonstration project at the National Bureau of Standards, covering 3,300 workers, will implement a total compensation comparability approach. The McClellan Air Force Base and the American Federation of Government Employees Union have agreed to a demonstration project that incorporates gainsharing of productivity savings.

Several bills have been introduced into Congress to dramatically change the current General Schedule system and give agencies extensive latitude over classification and pay, and to provide additional demonstration projects using a variety of pay approaches, including collective bargaining, locality pay, and other combinations of systems. Other bills would exclude occupations or functions from the federal pay system. As a result of these developments, the Advisory Committee believed that it was appropriate to determine prevailing industry practices.

This private sector study is valuable to the government in determining what prevailing practices exist. The next step for the government is to determine which practices are appropriate for its own work force. Government is a unique institution; it is not motivated by profit but by service; yet, in carrying out its functions, it must be mindful of efficiency and costs. Widespread changes in the current system may cause disruption and confusion among employees and may or may not be successfully transplanted from the private sector. Thus, before undertaking major revisions, the potential costs, as well as the benefits, require careful consideration. A new federal incentive system or other pay programs will not be a substitute for an adequate pay package that matches private employers, however. The federal government must also be willing to accept prevailing pay rates as well as practices in order to compete in recruiting and retaining a quality work force.

In addition to providing guidance to the federal government, the results of this survey will be useful to the private sector participants, as well. We were gratified by the number of responses received, 1,415, from a diverse group of companies of all sizes and in all industries. This study, the first of its kind, fills a void in our understanding of actual practices and the overwhelming response is testimony to the need for this information. Many respondents volunteered comments about the survey and indicated they looked forward to seeing the results.

The Advisory Committee and the ACA are deeply appreciative to all who provided thoughtful responses and welcome further comments on the survey and its findings. The Advisory Committee also wishes to thank Dr. Howard Risher, The Wyatt Company, for his contribution and assistance in developing the survey, and Dr. Charles Fay, Professor at Rutgers, for his analysis of the data. The project was conducted under the general guidance of Lucretia Dewey Tanner, Executive Director. Members of the Advisory Committee are Martin L. Duggan, Chairman; Frank G. Zarb, Partner, Lazard Freres; and W. Perry Brown, Vice President and Director of Personnel, American Cyanamid.

Advisory Committee on Federal Pay

Section I: Participating Organizations

The survey questionnaire was distributed by the American Compensation Association (ACA) to its United States members. The ACA is the primary professional association in the field of compensation management, with over 10,000 members primarily in the United States and Canada. For the purpose of this survey, the members in Canada and those who hold academic or consulting positions were excluded from the mailing. The balance of the members, 9,000 practioners, are employed by an estimated 6,000 organizations. (A number of larger organizations have two or more ACA members).

A total of 1,415 questionnaires were returned by the return date. Based on the estimated number of member organizations, this represents a 24-percent return rate. This is the largest survey of its type ever conducted.

The participating organizations represent virtually every sector of the economy. Moreover, the size and characteristics suggest that the participants are fully representative of the economy.

1. *Primary Industries:*

Durable Goods Manufacturing

10	Building Materials & Equipment	11	Heavy Machinery
22	Electrical Equipment	15	Instruments & Allied Products
126	Electronics & Computer Equipment	12	Primary Metals
17	Fabricated Metal Products	15	Transportation Equipment
		47	Other

Non-Durable Goods Manufacturing

33	Chemicals	29	Publishing & Printing
24	Drugs & Pharmaceuticals	7	Rubber & Leather Products
44	Food & Tobacco Products	9	Textile & Apparel Products
16	Paper & Allied Products	29	Other

Finance

142	Banking	4	Security & Commodity Brokers
105	Insurance	40	Other Nonbank Financial

Utilities

4	Air Transportation	7	Pipelines
60	Gas, Electric, & Water	35	Telecommunications
11	Land Transportation		

Services

66	Business Services	109	Hospitals & Healthcare
39	Education	9	Hotels & Resorts
33	Engineering & Research	12	Restaurant & Food Service

Other Industries

5	Agriculture, Forestry, & Fishing	10	Mining & Quarrying
2	Auto & Equipment Rental	6	Radio & TV Broadcasting
9	Construction	54	Retail Trade
36	Diversified	16	Wholesale Trade
29	Energy	54	Miscellaneous

2. Sales/Revenue Groups:

43	Under $5 million	197	$500.0 to 999.9 million
70	$5.0 to 24.9 million	296	$1.0 to 4.9 billion
195	$25.0 to 99.0 million	74	$5.0 to 9.9 billion
250	$100.0 to 249.9 million	63	$10.0 billion and over
173	$250.0 to 499.9 million	25	Unknown or not applicable

3. Types of Organizations:

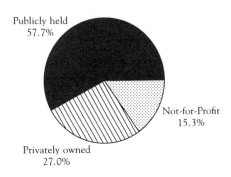

Publicly held 57.7%
Privately owned 27.0%
Not-for-Profit 15.3%

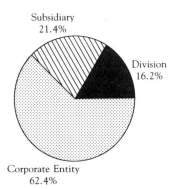

Subsidiary 21.4%
Division 16.2%
Corporate Entity 62.4%

4. Total Employment of Organizations:

Employment count	Exempt employees	Total employees
0–100	10.4%	3.1%
101–1,000	52.7	28.4
1,001–10,000	34.8	53.8
10,001–20,000	2.1	6.7
20,001–50,000	—	5.8
Over 50,000	—	2.2

5. Payroll Expenditures as Percent of Total Expenses:

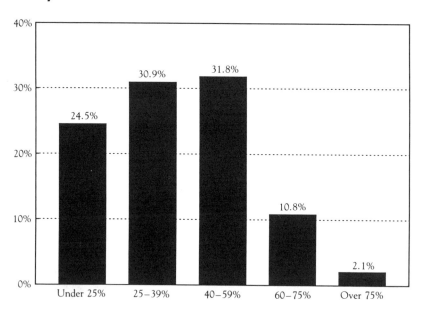

6. Percent of Work Force Represented Under Labor Agreements:

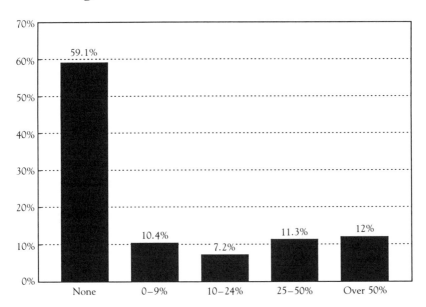

7. For Participants with Collective Bargaining, Employee Groups That Are Covered:

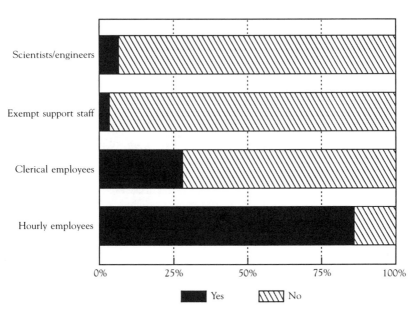

8. Headquarter's Location (10 highest reported states):

Rank/Location	Number of organizations
1 California	156
2 New York	101
3 Illinois	94
4 Pennsylvania	92
5 Texas	84
6 Ohio	71
7 Massachusetts	70
8 Michigan	59
9 New Jersey	53
10 Minnesota	49

Section II: Job Analysis and Description Practices

It is a virtually universal practice to maintain job or position descriptions. Over 90 percent of the organizations maintain descriptions for at least white-collar positions.

The nature and level of employee involvement in job analysis and the writing of position descriptions depends on the job level. At the management level, over half of the organizations involve incumbents directly in this process. Over 25 percent involve other white-collar employees throughout the process.

The most prevalent method for job analysis is the interview, with structured questionnaires as the second most widely used method.

Position descriptions are normally rewritten when jobs are restructured or upon request. Relatively few of the participants review descriptions on a scheduled basis. Less than 25 percent say that 90 percent or more of the descriptions are currently accurate or have been revised within the past two years.

In judging job analysis methods, the two most important criteria were validity and reliability. Significantly, however, the time commitment for job analysis was cited as the most serious current problem.

Although job analysis supposedly provides data for a variety of personnel purposes, respondents felt that their job analysis method best met their needs for job evaluation, performance appraisal, and recruitment/selection. These have been the traditional uses of position descriptions.

Over the next few years, respondents felt that job evaluation will continue to be the most important use of job content information. This was followed by performance appraisal and recruitment/selection.

9. Job/Position Descriptions Maintained for Employee Groups:

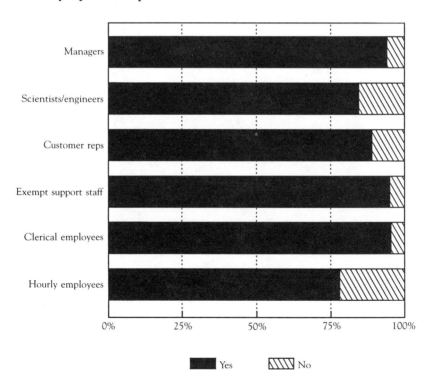

10. Involvement in Job Analysis/Writing Position Descriptions:

	Complete questionnaire	Personal interview	Write draft description	Review draft description	Approve description	None
Managers	47.8%	44.9%	52.8%	54.5%	41.2%	4.9%
Scientists/engineers	31.4	25.8	26.6	27.4	12.1	12.9
Customer representatives	36.0	27.8	25.6	28.3	13.5	14.6
Exempt support staff	47.7	37.0	38.2	39.4	17.4	9.9
Clerical employees	45.7	33.6	23.3	30.0	13.3	18.7
Hourly employees	25.5	21.0	10.8	16.5	7.7	35.9

11. Method(s) Used to Collect Job Content Information:

	Observation	Interview	Open-ended questionnaire	Structured questionnaire	Work sampling/ measurement
Managers	18.4%	62.5%	27.4%	41.6%	3.6%
Scientists/engineers	13.4	39.9	18.6	29.3	2.4
Customer representatives	18.0	43.3	20.6	33.1	3.9
Exempt support staff	22.0	56.6	27.1	41.4	4.5
Clerical employees	31.7	49.8	22.1	45.0	7.8
Hourly employees	32.9	33.5	12.5	29.4	10.0

12. *Percent of Position Descriptions That Are Current or Have Been Revised Within the Past Two Years:*

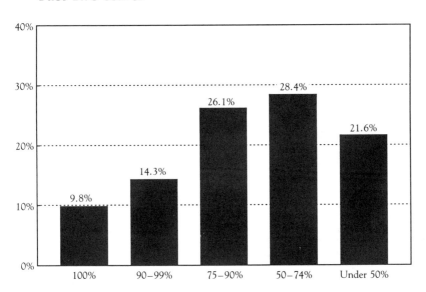

13. *Position Descriptions Normally Revised:*

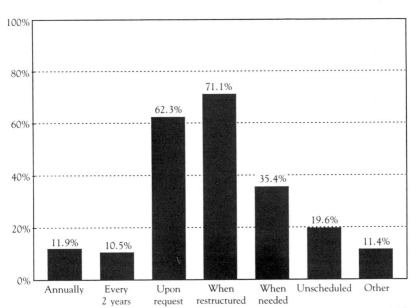

14. Criteria for Judging Job Analysis Methods:

	Rank order importance	Current problems
Employee acceptance	4.0%	31.6%
Management support	2.6	38.2
Administrative simplicity	4.4	32.9
Time commitment	4.8	54.1
Reliability	2.6	30.0
Validity	2.4	31.4

15. How Well Job Analysis Methods Meet Information Needs:

Job analysis method	Not used	Relative adequacy
Job evaluation	5.4%	3.55%
Performance appraisal	15.8	2.71
Recruitment/selection	9.5	3.12
Training needs analysis	32.4	1.49
Human resource planning	31.3	1.97
Career planning	32.1	1.92
Organization analysis	28.3	2.20
Position control	32.2	2.14
Productivity studies	55.9	1.06
Title management	31.1	2.18

16. Based on the Potential Uses of Job Content Information, Which Will Be the Most Important in the Future?

Job analysis method	Relative rank
Job evaluation	100
Performance appraisal	78
Recruitment/selection	53
Training needs analysis	39
Human resource planning	33
Career planning	23
Organization analysis	21
Position control	19
Productivity studies	15
Title management	4

Section III: Job Evaluation

Virtually every participating organization uses a formal method to evaluate or assign jobs to salary ranges or levels. Of the four basic methods, the most widely used for each of the employee groups is "market pricing." Market pricing is used by itself or in combination with one of the other methods by over 50 percent of the organizations. ("Market pricing" is the use of salary survey data to determine the prevailing wage or salary for a job in the labor market.)

The second most widely used method is the point factor approach.

Significantly, the three other methods (whole job ranking, point factor, and factor comparison) are used by most organizations in combination with market pricing. Over 95 percent of the users of whole job ranking or factor comparison methods use them in combination with market pricing. Similarly, 40 to 50 percent of the point factor users combine this with market pricing. (Since the dominant point factor system provides a basis for comparing positions across organizations, it can be used to generate estimates of market value. Some users of this method did not indicate that they use market pricing.)

Most organizations use the same job evaluation method for all exempt employees. That is to say, if they rely on market pricing, it is used to evaluate all exempt positions. Many organizations use market pricing for all positions. Among the job evaluation systems with a recognized name, the Hay guide chart method is the most widely used (28 percent of the respondents). This method is referred to by some respondents as a point factor method and by others as a factor comparison method. (This percentage does not reflect respondents that rely on only market pricing or that have an internally developed system.)

Over 50 percent of the participants have adopted their job evaluation systems since 1980. This reflects a substantial increase in interest in job evaluation over the past few years.

Although the increased interest was, to a degree, prompted by the pay equity advocates, only 35 percent of the respondents have studied their job evaluation process for its impact on women.

For firms that adopted their systems after 1980, or that are currently studying new approaches, the most important reason is inadequate confidence in their current system. Other important reasons were the changing nature of jobs and/or organizations, and the need for better job content information. Significantly, complaints from management or employees, and concern for legal liability were the least important concerns.

The most frequently cited changes to make job evaluation systems acceptable in the future are increased emphasis on improving system reliability and validity, and on communication of system objectives and administration. The least important changes would be increased employee participation in evaluation decisions and emphasis on right to appeal or file grievances.

17. *Methods Used in Job Evaluation:*

Total Responses:

	Executive/ managers	Scientists/ engineers	Customer reps	Exempt staff	Clerical employees	Hourly employees
None	2.4%	5.1%	3.4%	1.2%	1.0%	7.1%
Market pricing	65.0	45.1	49.0	59.6	56.5	46.4
Whole job ranking	22.6	14.0	15.6	20.3	20.8	16.3
Point factor	49.9	37.8	44.6	55.6	56.2	36.4
Factor comparison	11.5	9.3	10.1	12.1	11.3	7.4
Other	6.4	3.8	4.7	5.4	6.1	9.9
Combinations with Market Pricing:						
Market pricing with :						
Point factor	23.5%	17.9%	18.6%	23.4%	21.8%	14.3%
Whole job ranking	19.0	12.1	13.0	17.0	15.7	11.5
Factor comparison	7.5	5.6	6.5	7.4	6.5	4.1%

18. Employee Groups with Same Job Evaluation Process as Middle Management:

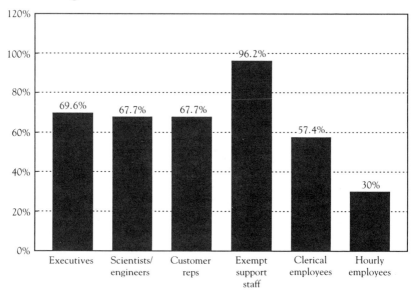

19. Job Evaluation Process for Middle Management/Supervisory Known As:

1.8%	American Association of Industrial Management	2.7%	Guideline method
		1.3	Evalucomp
27.8	Hay guide chart method	21.3	Custom designed
3.9	Position classification	18.4	Other
.6	Decision band method		

20. *The Job Evaluation Process Was Adopted:*

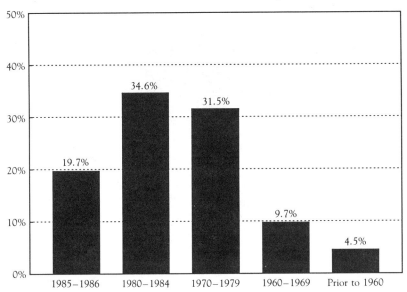

21. *Last Time Job Evaluation System Was Studied to Determine if it Was Still Valid and Effective:*

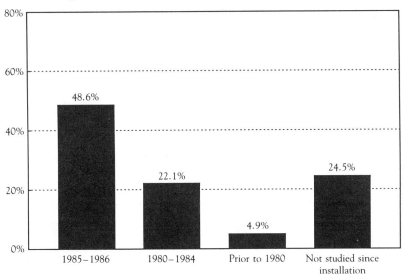

22. Job Evaluation System Studied for Impact on Women:

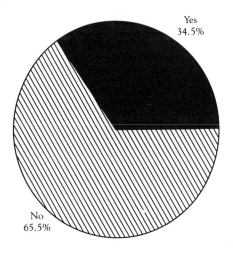

Yes
34.5%

No
65.5%

23. If Job Evaluation Was Adopted After 1980, Reasons for Considering New System:

Adopted	Studying	Reasons for
37.4%	24.0%	Inadequate confidence in current system
13.5	16.6	Inapplicability to certain types of jobs
29.2	27.2	Changing nature of jobs and/or organizations
13.8	14.6	Concern for administrative cost or efficiency
31.0	20.2	Need for better job content information
26.6	21.7	Enhanced market sensitivity
20.1	13.9	Complaints from management
19.2	10.9	Complaints from employees
18.4	15.1	Concern for legal liability
6.7	3.4	Other

24. *Most Important Changes in the Future in the Design and Administration of Job Evaluation Systems:*

41.9%   Increased employee participation in job analysis
13.5   Increased employee participation in evaluation decisions
56.7   Heavier utilization of computers to facilitate administration and to minimize possible bias
78.0   Increased emphasis on improving system validity and reliability
79.0   Increased emphasis on communication of system objectives and administration
4.7   Increased emphasis on right to appeal or file grievances
4.3   Other

Section IV: Merit Pay

Merit pay is the basis for granting salary increases to white-collar employees in over 90 percent of the survey organizations. Less than 10 percent of the participants communicate annual increases to their exempt employees as either "general" or "cost-of-living" increases.

In the majority of organizations, merit increases are granted annually. However, many organizations vary the frequency based on appraised performance level, with better performers receiving more frequent increases, and/ or position in salary range. With the latter concept, increases become less frequent as an individual's salary progresses from the minimum of the salary range toward the maximum.

The pattern of performance appraisal results was strikingly consistent. For each of the employee groups, the average survey respondent rated approximately 20 percent of the employees as "exceeded expectations" (or highest performance category). The average respondent rated less than 5 percent of its employees as "failed to meet expectations" (or lowest performance category). Despite the theoretical relevance of the normal distribution or bell-shaped curve concept, it is apparent that performance appraisal systems have an inherent bias in practice.

For employees rated as "exceeded expectations," the range of salary increases granted in the most recent fiscal year was 5.5 to 10.0 percent. The increases granted to those who "failed to meet expectations" were on average under 2 percent, with many organizations granting no increase to these employees. Over the last year or so, merit increase budgets in the private sector have averaged 4.5 to 5.5 percent (of current salaries) so outstanding performers were receiving up to twice the budgeted increase.

Virtually none of the survey organizations use a step rate or seniority-based salary increase policy for their white-collar staff.

Despite recent interest in cash incentives in the professional literature, relatively few firms are using the concept. Currently, 14 percent are using the lump-sum payment concept in lieu of salary increases. An advantage of the lump-sum increase is that it emphasizes the size of the increase, but does not lock the organization into higher fixed salaries. Group or cash incentive awards (i.e., bonuses) are prevalent only for executives and managers.

25. Formal "Merit Pay" Programs for Employee Groups:

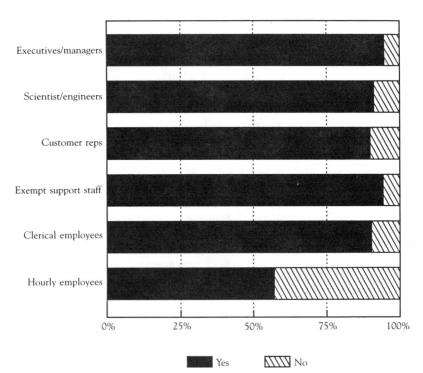

26. *Portion of Annual Salary Communicated as "General" or "Cost-of-Living":*

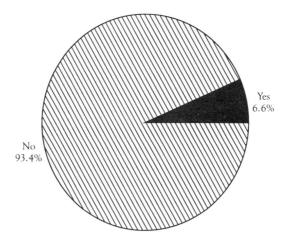

Yes
6.6%

No
93.4%

27. *Frequency or Timing of Employees Receiving Merit Pay Dependent On:*

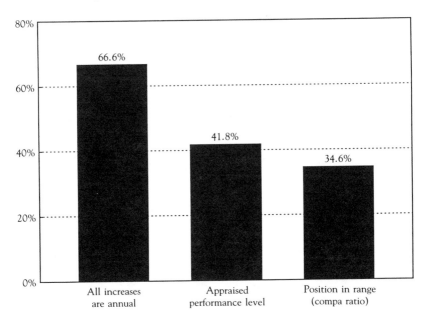

28. Approaches to Performance Appraisal:

	None	Descriptive	Rating	Other
Executives/managers	4.1%	36.1%	57.9%	30.5%
Scientists/engineers	4.3	40.5	43.4	17.6
Customer representatives	4.7	44.1	52.4	16.5
Exempt support staff	3.2	57.3	62.8	22.1
Clerical employees	4.6	49.2	69.6	12.9
Hourly employees	19.2	28.0	46.9	7.7

29. In Most Recent Fiscal Year, Percentages of Employees Rated by Performance:

	Exceeded expectations	Failed to meet expectations
Executives/managers	23.9%	3.0%
Scientists/engineers	19.7	3.2
Customer representatives	18.6	3.5
Exempt support staff	20.5	3.5
Clerical employees	19.9	4.0
Hourly employees	19.4	4.4

30. For the Same Fiscal Year, Approximate Range of Salary Increases for Employees Whose Performance Was Rated:

	Exceeded expectations		Failed to meet expectations	
	Lowest	Highest	Lowest	Highest
Executives/managers	5.8%	11.3%	.2%	1.7%
Scientists/engineers	5.3	10.2	.2	1.7
Customer representatives	5.5	9.9	.2	1.6
Exempt support staff	5.7	10.3	.2	1.7
Clerical employees	5.5	9.7	.2	1.6
Hourly employees	5.1	8.8	.3	1.4

31. *Use of a Step Rate or Seniority-Based Salary Increase Policy:*

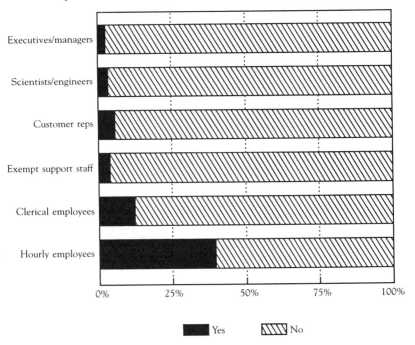

32. *Lump-Sum Payment Used in Exempt Merit Program:*

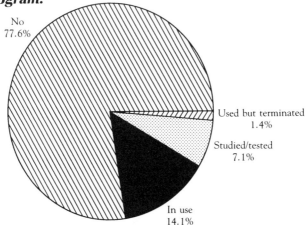

33. *Use of Group or Individual Cash Incentives for Employees:*

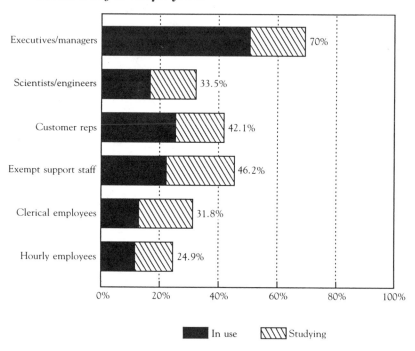

Executives/managers 70%
Scientists/engineers 33.5%
Customer reps 42.1%
Exempt support staff 46.2%
Clerical employees 31.8%
Hourly employees 24.9%

0%   20%   40%   60%   80%   100%

■ In use   ▨ Studying

Section V: Use of Salary Structure

Over 95 percent of the organizations administer salaries within a salary structure.

At least three-quarters of the respondents use the same salary structure for each of the white-collar employee groups, except clerical employees where over half use a separate salary structure. It is relatively uncommon for hourly employees to be covered under the same salary structure as managers.

In looking at the salary range width or "spread" (range maximum divided by minimum less 1.00), there is a consistent pattern across the exempt white-collar groups. The majority of survey organizations have a salary range spread of approximately 50 percent. The range spread tends to be smaller for clerical and hourly employees. This is consistent with the textbook rationale for designing salary structures.

Relatively few organizations have tested any innovative structure design concepts.

More specifically, only 10 percent of the respondents use the maturity curve concept to administer salaries for research and development professionals. This concept has been cited in personnel literature for several decades.

A related concept, "broad banding," is used by only one out of every forty respondents (several of these organizations are actually public employers.) The majority of the respondents are not familiar with the concept. This may be significant in light of the government's interest in this concept.

34. *Administers White-Collar Salaries Within Salary Structure:*

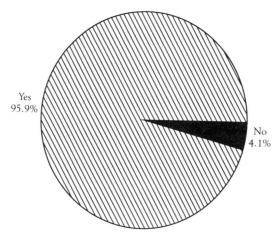

Yes
95.9%

No
4.1%

35. *Employee Groups Administered Same Salary Structure as Middle Management:*

	Yes	*No*
Executives	66.8%	33.2%
Scientists/engineers	87.0	13.0
Customer representatives	79.4	20.6
Exempt support staff	91.7	8.3
Clerical employees	43.4	56.5
Hourly employees	26.9	73.1

36. *Frequency of Reviewing and/or Adjusting Salary Structures:*

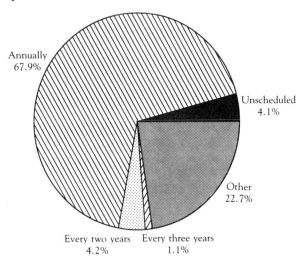

Annually
67.9%

Unscheduled
4.1%

Other
22.7%

Every two years   Every three years
4.2%   1.1%

37. *Salary Ranges for Employee Groups (Maximum ÷ Minimum less 1.00):*

	Estimated average	Less than 45%	45–55%	Over 55%
Executives/managers	57%	12%	54%	34%
Scientists/engineers	52	16	62	22
Customer representatives	49	27	57	16
Exempt support staff	50	21	61	18
Clerical employees	44	52	39	9
Hourly employees	40	64	29	7

**38. *Tried or Tested Innovative Structure
       Design Concepts:***

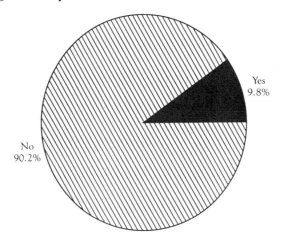

Yes
9.8%

No
90.2%

**39. *Administer Salaries with Maturity Curve
       Concept:***

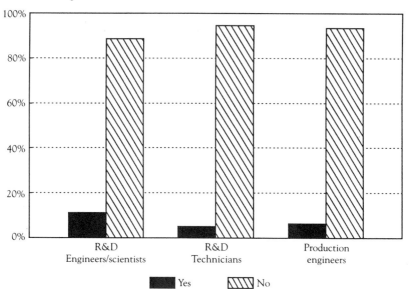

40. *Administer Salaries with Broad Banding Concept:*

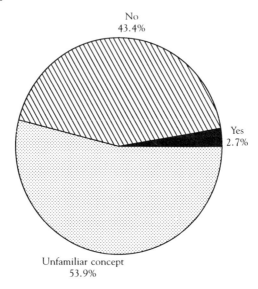

No
43.4%

Yes
2.7%

Unfamiliar concept
53.9%

Section VI: Locality Pay Practices

Over 80 percent of the survey organizations have employees working in more than one location. Of this group, over 70 percent have at least five work locations, with over 20 percent administering salaries at fifty or more locations.

At the clerical and hourly employee level, over half of the respondents administer local salaries within two or more salary structures. For exempt employees, approximatly 75 percent of the organizations use a single salary structure.

For those organizations that use a single salary structure, differences in salaries for employees in essentially the same job would be most likely attributable to geographic pay differences. An alternative to using two or more structures is to assign jobs to salary ranges based on local prevailing pay levels. Thus, in high pay areas, jobs would be assigned to higher salary grades.

The primary reason for maintaining separate salary structures is local pay differentials. At the management and professional level, industry pay differentials are a secondary reason. However, for clerical and hourly employees, local pay differentials are significantly more important than any other reason.

Organizations use a variety of survey sources to monitor prevailing pay levels in relevant labor markets. Significantly, the surveys conducted by the Bureau of Labor Statistics are the least important source of survey data.

If a respondent planned to establish a new work location, and published survey data for clerical and hourly jobs were unavailable, the organization would conduct a formal private survey (or contract for a survey). This suggests strong interest in understanding prevailing pay levels and in setting salaries at levels appropriate to the new work location.

In virtually all of the survey organizations, the human resources staff in either the parent company (67 percent) or in a subsidiary/division (27 percent) is responsible for developing and/or adjusting salary structures. Significantly, line managers are rarely responsible for these decisions.

41a. Locations with 10 or More Employees:

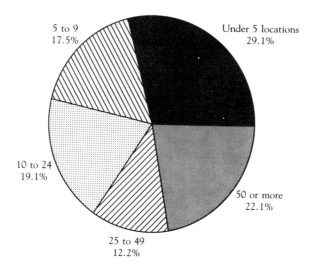

5 to 9
17.5%

Under 5 locations
29.1%

10 to 24
19.1%

50 or more
22.1%

25 to 49
12.2%

41b. States with 100 or More Employees:

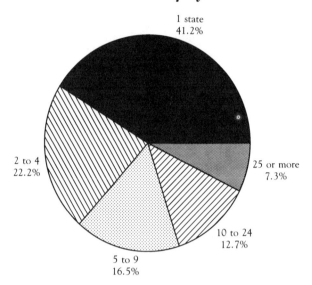

1 state
41.2%

2 to 4
22.2%

25 or more
7.3%

10 to 24
12.7%

5 to 9
16.5%

42. Organizations Maintaining Two or More Different Schedules:

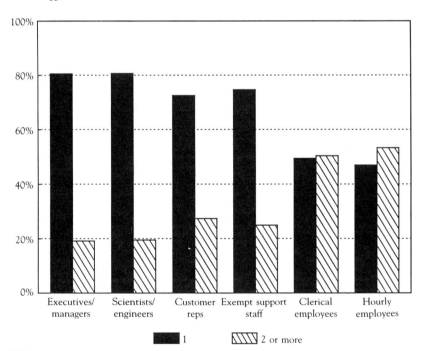

43. Employees in Same Job but at Different Locations Paid at Same Levels:

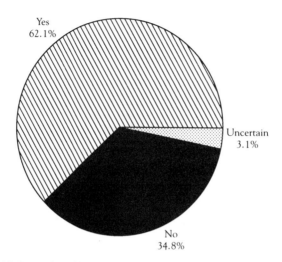

Yes
62.1%

Uncertain
3.1%

No
34.8%

If no, most likely attributable to:

39.9% Individual performance
        differences
2.2   Seniority differences
73.9   Geographic pay
        differences

2.7 Decentralized administrative
     differences
.3   Uncertain

44. Reasons for Maintaining Different Structures/Schedules:

	Local pay differential	Industry pay differential	Business unit profitability	Decentralized administration
Executives/managers	25.3%	14.5%	6.3%	4.7%
Scientists/engineers	20.8	13.5	3.8	3.9
Customer representatives	33.0	10.9	4.7	3.9
Exempt support staff	37.5	16.4	5.1	6.3
Clerical employees	82.8	12.1	5.0	8.2
Hourly employees	63.4	11.8	4.7	8.4

45. How Do You Monitor the Local or Industry Pay Differentials:

40.2%   Survey conducted by the Bureau of Labor Statistics
63.1   Surveys sponsored jointly by other area employers
68.7   Surveys sponsored by industry or professional associations
57.1   Surveys conducted by consultants or private survey organizations
55.4   We conduct our own surveys

46. Responsible for Developing and/or Determining Periodic Adjustments for Exempt Employees:

67.6%   Parent company human resources staff
27.2   Subsidiary/division human resources staff
1.1   Local line managers
.2   Consultant
3.9   Other

47. How Would You Establish Nonexempt Pay Levels for a New Work Location:

74.4%   Conduct a formal private survey (or contract for a survey)
7.8   Rely on the available published data
8.5   "Guesstimate" prevailing pay levels based on a few contacts with other employers
9.4   Utilize a salary structure used in other locations

Section VII: Salary Planning

In a typical year, the most important consideration in developing the salary increase budget is the company's financial performance. As survey data for recent years shows, companies that are experiencing less than satisfactory financial performance often control costs by holding down salary increases or by actually reducing salaries. The next most important consideration is maintaining salaries at competitive levels. The third consideration is the budgeted salary increases of other employers in the same industry.

Significantly, over 95 percent of the respondents plan their salary program to pay salaries for managers and professionals that are at least average (or above) relative to competitors. They tend to use the same compensation strategy for all employees.

The typical participating organization takes part in ten surveys, and sponsors or conducts one survey each year. Some larger organizations participate in over 100 surveys a year.

Surprisingly, given the size of the federal work force, government salaries have either no impact (65 percent) or are not relevant to the work force (22 percent) in administering the respondent's salary program.

48. Most Important Considerations in Developing the Salary Increase Budget:

	Mean ranking
Budget plans of other employers in same geographic area	2.49
Budget plans of other employers in same industry(s)	2.27
Comparison of current salaries relative to competitive levels	1.79
Company's financial performance	1.61

49. Compensation Strategy for Middle Management and Professionals is Generally to Pay Salaries:

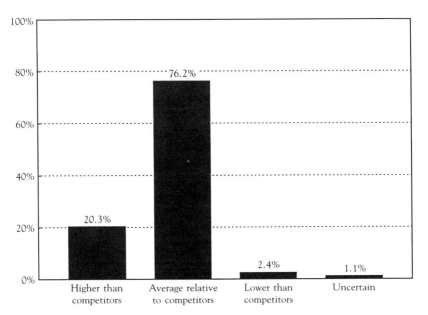

50. *Use of Same Compensation Strategy for Planning Salary Program for Following Groups:*

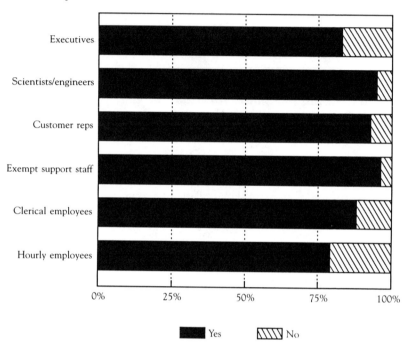

51. *Do You Analyze Payroll Expenditures Relative to Prevailing Levels in Your Industry?*

34.4%   Yes, routinely on a scheduled basis
 9.7   Yes, periodically at management's request
14.7   Yes, on an informal, "roughcut" basis
16.0   No, but we would if better data were available
25.3   No, this has not been an issue in at least the past 3 years

52. Analyze Organization's Productivity Relative to Payroll Expenditure:

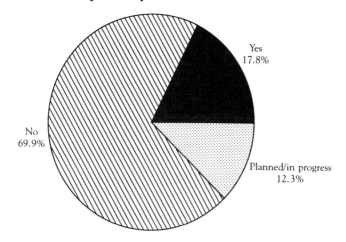

No
69.9%

Yes
17.8%

Planned/in progress
12.3%

53. Salary Surveys That Company Sponsors and/or Conducts Each Year:

Median	1
0	30.5%
1–5	52.8
6–10	9.0
11–25	5.7
Over 25	2.0

54. Participates in Other Organizations' Surveys:

Median	10
0	.3%
1–5	25.4
6–10	30.5
11–25	30.1
Over 25	13.7

55. *Impact of Federal Wage and Salary Levels on Pay in Your Company:*

64.6%   No specific impact
5.0   Government salaries are typically above ours
8.4   Our salaries tend to be higher than government salaries
22.0   Government salaries are not relevant to our work force

---

Section VIII: Program Administration

For respondents with multiple business units (divisions, subsidiaries, or profit centers), almost 70 percent maintain a single job evaluation system, with centralized administration. Another 20 percent maintain a single system, but decentralize its administration.

In over 80 percent of the organizations, a job evaluation committee, personnel manager, or job analyst is responsible for evaluation positions. Only 8 percent of the respondents delegate this responsibility to supervisors.

The job evaluation committees are typically comprised of personnel staff representatives and/or line and staff managers. In less than 5 percent of the organizations are union representatives or professional association representatives included on the committee.

The majority of respondents provide only an informal procedure for appealing job evaluation decisions.

Final approval for salary grade changes is typically retained by the personnel manager. However, the final approval authority for starting salary offers and merit increases is often delegated to the immediate supervisor or to a business unit head. These actions are commonly limited or controlled by policies or budgets.

The supervisor is the primary media or method used to communicate information to employees regarding the salary program. Although other methods, such as employee handbooks or employee meetings, are prevalent for communicating salary program objectives and policies, the supervisor is often the only source of information for individual salary ranges and media pay actions.

56. Best Describes Policy if Company Has Multiple Business Units:

68.1%   Maintain a single job evaluation system, with centralized administration

21.5   Maintain a single job evaluation system, with decentralized administration

10.4   Business units are responsible for selecting and administering job evaluation system

57. Person Responsible for Evaluating Positions in Middle Management:

38.6%	Job evaluation committee	8.1%	Supervisor
27.5	Personnel manager	2.6	Outside consultant
32.5	Job analyst	15.3	Other

58. Job Evaluation Committee Is Comprised Of:

63.9%	Personnel staff representatives	2.4%	Professional association representatives
1.2	Union representatives	43.8	Line managers
30.1	Other	9.6	Employees

59. Procedure for Appealing Job Evaluation Decisions:

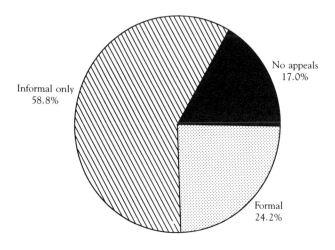

Informal only
58.8%

No appeals
17.0%

Formal
24.2%

60. Person with Final Approval Authority for Salary Actions in Middle Management:

	Immediate supervisor	Business unit head	Personnel manager	Personnel analyst
Salary grade change	28.2%	57.7%	62.7%	21.1%
Merit increase	48.3	70.8	45.5	13.2
Starting salary offer	45.6	53.9	63.8	14.8

61. *Media or Methods Used to Communicate Information to Exempt Employees:*

	Not communicated	*Directed by supervisor*	*Employee handbook*	*Newsletter/ memos*	*Group meetings*
Salary program objectives	17.0%	46.7%	37.8%	22.2%	34.5%
Methods for job evaluation	28.3	36.8	24.3	14.4	28.8
Policy related to competitive practice	28.6	31.7	28.6	15.5	27.3
Individual salary ranges	11.9	72.0	8.6	9.7	7.8
Performance appraisal and merit pay	3.4	85.0	24.9	15.4	19.3

Glossary of Key Terms

accrual of benefits   Refers to rules under ERISA for vesting benefits in an employee's account.

across-the-board increase   A raise in base salary rate, expressed as either a percentage or a lump sum, given to all employees covered by a wage structure.

AFSCME v. State of Washington   A comparable worth case in which plaintiffs charged sex discrimination in pay under Title VII. The state's own job evaluation study found that pay differences between jobs dominated by men and those dominated by women were not due solely to job worth. The state failed to remedy the disparity and the U.S. District Court found the state to be in violation of Title VII.

all-salaried work force   Jobs that are traditionally paid on an hourly wage basis are paid on a salary basis. No distinctions are made between salaried and hourly employees in status.

American Compensation Association (ACA)   The leading U.S. association of compensation professionals whose objective is to improve the design, implementation, and management of employee compensation and benefits programs. ACA also has a program allowing compensation professionals to become certified.

American Society for Personnel Administration (ASPA)   The major general professional organization for human resource managers. The ASPA Foundation sponsors research in personnel areas, including compensation, and offers certification programs.

area wage surveys   Wage surveys conducted by the Bureau of Labor Statistics in local labor markets. These are the basic surveys used by most compensation specialists.

audit   Any review of pay practices for conformance to policies and laws.

award basis   The basis for making pay adjustments (e.g., seniority, performance).

balkanized market   *See* segmented market

base pay   The salary rate associated with an employee's job. It does not vary once it is established, but it may be adjusted upward periodically for seniority or merit.

base wage   The wage earned by an employee before such add-ons as shift differentials, performance bonuses, and overtime.

benchmark job   *See* key job

benefits   Compensation consisting of rewards to employees other than base salary. The three major benefits types are security and health benefits, pay for time not worked, and free or reduced cost services.

benefits policy   Rules regarding the provision of benefits to employees.

benefits survey   Information collected regarding benefits practices among competitors.

bonus   Any direct additional lump-sum payment made on top of a base salary for either individual or group performance.

bottom-up budget   A salary budgeting process by which individual managers consider each employee separately and plan budget requests according to their business plans and needs.

Bureau of Labor Statistics (BLS)   Research area of the U.S. Department of Labor. The BLS develops area wage surveys and a variety of other reports involving wages and salaries.

cafeteria bonus program   A program in which employees have a choice as to the benefits they receive, within a dollar limit. Usually, a common core benefits package is offered (insurance, pension, profit sharing), plus a group of elective programs from which the employee may select a set dollar amount.

cash flow The amount of money that will be spent on compensation during a given period of time.

Certified Compensation Professional A compensation or benefits professional who has successfully completed the certification program of the American Compensation Association.

charitable matching A policy by which the employer matches charitable contributions made by employees.

classification method of job evaluation A whole job, job-to-standard evaluation technique. Generalized classifications are defined in terms of several compensable factors, and a job is placed in whichever classification best describes it.

COLA *See* cost-of-living adjustment

commission A direct performance payment, usually for sales personnel, set as a percentage of gross or net sales. Group commissions for sales teams are allocated among team members on the basis of salary.

comparable worth The idea that jobs have an inherent value, or worth, which can be compared across jobs of very different types (such as nursing versus parking meter maintenance). Jobs of greater inherent value should be paid more, according to adherents of the comparable worth doctrine.

compa ratio The ratio of the actual average salary for a wage grade (numerator) to the midpoint for the grade (denominator). The compa ratio indicates the match between the distribution of actual salaries being paid in a class and the ideal. Generally, a compa ratio of about 1 is considered appropriate.

compensable factor Any factor used to provide a basis for judging a job value in a job evaluation scheme. The most commonly employed compensable factors are responsibility, skill requirements, effort requirements, and working conditions.

compensable performance dimension Performance dimensions that are to be rewarded under a pay for performance system.

compensation The provision of monetary and nonmonetary rewards in return for employment.

compensation planning A forward-oriented process that begins with the establishment of a mission for the compensation program. Compensation practices such as job evaluation, performance appraisal, job pricing, and merit formulae are considered on their merits as strategies to achieve the program's mission. Then policies are established and carried out in the service of these strategies. Finally, the entire process is audited for mission achievement.

compensation system In salary surveys, refers to information about how the pay program is administered (for example, the type of job evaluation system in use).

competitive compa ratio The ratio of the market midpoint rate (numerator) to a company's midpoint rate (denominator). The competitive compa ratio helps the compensation specialist compare an organization's pay structure to the market.

cost-of-living adjustment (COLA) An adjustment in individual wages based on changes in the consumer price index. COLAs are no longer prevalent; they became popular due to union pressure and the misguided notion that organizations had an obligation to keep all wages and salaries growing faster than living costs. Salaries based solely on employee needs are unlikely to meet organizational needs.

cost reduction programs Performance bonus plans in which the emphasis is on increasing profits by reducing labor-related costs such as waste, scrap rates, and machine downtime due to human error.

Davis-Bacon Act of 1931 A law requiring most federal contractors of construction or related contracts to pay wage rates and fringe benefits prevailing in the area.

demand side factors Aspects of the job that create value for the employer because of what is produced. Marginal physical product, completed processes, and time span of discretion are examples of demand-side factors as sources of job value.

Denver Nurses Case *Lemons v. Denver* is a major comparable worth case. Nurses employed by the city and county of Denver, Colorado, argued that even though parking meter repairers and other craft workers were paid more than nurses in external labor markets, it was still unfair for the city to pay nurses less than the crafts workers because the work performed by nurses was at least of comparable worth to the city as the work performed by the craft employees. The court found against the nurses and upheld the criterion of the external market in setting wage rates.

derived demand A term referring to the fact that an employer's demand for labor is in part derived from the demand for the employer's product or service.

Dictionary of Occupational Titles **(DOT)** A reference manual published by the U.S. Department of Labor that provides standard definitions and descriptions for more than 30,000 jobs. Useful in setting up common benchmark jobs in salary surveys. This manual provides the basis for the jobs surveyed in the USDL's area wage surveys.

distributive justice An idea, attributed to George C. Homans, that provides the basis for equity theory. According to the principle of distributive justice, people in an exchange relationship are happiest when the ratios defining outcomes/inputs are equal for everyone in the exchange.

earnings Total wages due an employee including base pay, shift differentials, and bonuses.

earnings at risk The percent of an employee's annual earnings that is at risk and does not fold into base pay (for example, gainsharing bonuses, lump sum bonuses).

Economic Recovery Tax Act (ERTA) of 1981 Provisions of this law make certain benefits, like health and accident insurance, nontaxable.

elasticity of labor demand The proportionate change in a wage that an employer is willing to pay, given the proportionate change in the number of people he wishes to employ.

elasticity of substitution The ease with which an employer can substitute one form of labor or technology for work being done by an employee.

employee benefits *See* benefits

Employee Retirement Income Security Act (ERISA) of 1974 An act regulating employer pension programs.

employee stock ownership plan (ESOP) An employee benefit in which the organization contributes its stock to an employee trust, usually as a form of profit sharing. Variants are the stock bonus plan, the leveraged stock bonus plan (the trust can borrow money to buy more stock), and TRASOP (in which employees match company contributions). ESOPs are useful as tax-deferral devices for employees and as tax deductions for employers.

entitlements Any payments made on the basis of membership in an organization.

Equal Employment Opportunity Commission A commission of the federal government charged with enforcing the provisions of the Civil Rights Act of 1964. In addition, the commission is charged with enforcing the provisions of the Equal Pay Act of 1963 as it pertains to sex discrimination in pay.

Equal Pay Act of 1963   An amendment to the Fair Labor Standards Act prohibiting wage differentials based on gender between men and women employed by the same establishment in jobs that require equal skill, effort, and responsibility, and that are performed under similar working conditions.

equity   Anything of value earned through the provision or investment of something of value. In the case of compensation, an employee earns equity interest through the provision of labor on a job.

equity theory   A theory, most frequently associated with the ideas of J. S. Stacy Adams, proposing that in an exchange relationship (such as employment) the equality of outcome/input ratios between a person and a comparison other will determine fairness or equity. If the ratios diverge from each other, the person will experience reactions of unfairness and inequity (*see* distributive justice).

ERISA   *See* Employee Retirement Income Security Act of 1974

ESOP   *See* employee stock ownership plan

EVALUCOMP   The American Management Association's job evaluation plan for office personnel, technicians, professional and scientific personnel, and management.

exchange rate   Economically defined as the intersect of the labor demand and the labor supply functions in an external market. It constitutes the wage rate both that employers are willing to pay and that labor is willing to accept. From an economic viewpoint, the exchange clears the market. From a compensation viewpoint, the exchange rate defines the criterion of external equity.

exempt job   A job not subject to the provisions of the Fair Labor Standards Act with respect to minimum wage and overtime. Exempt employees include most professionals, administrators, and executives.

expectancy theory   A motivation theory that proposes that the effort an employee puts into his job is a function of his beliefs that he will be able to perform and that his performance will be rewarded, and the value he places on the reward offered.

external equity   A fairness criterion that directs an employer to pay a wage that corresponds to rates prevailing in external markets for an employee's occupation.

external wage structure   The distributions of wage rates across external labor markets. The external wage rate defines the variety of different wage rates an employer faces across different occupations and different labor markets.

factor comparison method of job evaluation A specific-factors (as opposed to whole-job), job-to-job comparison method of job evaluation. It is a complex system and not much used now.

Fair Labor Standards Act of 1938 A federal law governing minimum wage, overtime pay, equal pay for men and women in the same type of job, child labor, and recordkeeping requirements.

Federal Insurance Contributions Act (FICA) The source of social security contributions withholding requirements, known commonly as FICA deduction. The current (1988) FICA tax is 7.51% on the first $45,000 earned. This rate is paid by both employee and employer.

felt fair pay The rate of pay that is fair for a job, determined by shared group norms on the basis of time span of discretion associated with the job.

FICA *See* Federal Insurance Contributions Act

first quartile The value in a set of data below which 25% of the data falls and above which 75% of the data falls. Often used in salary surveys as a measure of the lower end of the market.

flexible benefits program *See* cafeteria bonus program

forced distribution A rule that specifies for each performance rating or ranking category the specific proportions of employees to be rated. Thus, only 5% of the employees are allowed to be rated at the highest level and 10% must receive the lowest rating, for example.

forecasting An analysis in which future events are predicted based on present or past information. Compensation analysts use past salary information to forecast future salary movements.

fringe benefits *See* benefits

gainsharing Unitwide bonus systems designed to reward all members of the unit for improved performance. Gainsharing usually employs some business plan model, often involving productivity measures, to measure improvements. Part of every dollar improvement is shared with employees in the form of a lump-sum bonus payment.

garnishment A court order requiring the employer of a debtor to deduct a portion of the debtor's pay and to deliver it to the creditor.

General Schedule (GS) A system used by the U.S. federal government to grade jobs and specify pay adjustments for time in grade.

general training In human capital theory, any training that contributes marginal revenue product in all employment settings, thereby increasing the value of the trainee to all employers. Learning to weld is an example of general training.

goal setting theory   A body of research that demonstrates the importance of goal setting in motivating behavior. The research indicates that goals will not have motivation value unless they are accepted by the employee. The theory also says that specific monetary goals will be more effective than vaguely stated goals.

green-circle   When a job is reevaluated, and an incumbent is making less than the bottom of the wage range assigned to that job, his salary is *green-circled* to assure that a speeded-up adjustment is made to bring him up to the range.

Gunther v. County of Washington   A landmark case in pay discrimination based on sex. The U.S. Supreme Court ruled that plaintiffs are not prohibited from bringing pay discrimination suits under Title VII of the Civil Rights Act of 1964 by the Equal Pay Act of 1963. It is felt by many that this ruling opens up the courts to increased comparable worth litigation.

Harvard Business Review Syndrome   The adoption of management ideas read about in the prestigious journal with little or no thought to their applicability in a specific or current setting.

Hay system   A point factor job evaluation system that evaluates jobs with respect to "know-how," "problem solving," and "accountability." It is probably the most widely used proprietary job evaluation system.

holidays   Specific days when employees do not work but are paid as if they did. Most companies in the United States give about 10 paid holidays per year.

human capital theory   A branch of labor economic thought proposing that the investment one is willing to make to enter an occupation is related to the returns one will earn over time in the form of compensation. We have used the theory, in this book, as one way of looking at the value a person brings to the job.

independent variables   The x variables in multiple regression, used to explain the impact on some dependent or y variable. In many market pricing studies, compensable factors are the independent variables in the linear regression model.

individual equity   A fairness criterion that directs employers to set wage rates for individual employees (workers on the same job, in the simplest case) according to individual variation in merit.

industry wage surveys   Wage surveys conducted by the Bureau of Labor Statistics in some 70 industries.

internal equity   A fairness criterion that directs an employer to set wage rates that correspond to the relative value of each job to the organization.

Internal Revenue Code   The law concerning the taxation of income.

I.U.E. v. Westinghouse   A pay discrimination suit in which Westinghouse was found guilty of sex discrimination in pay. Westinghouse was found to have segregated women's jobs from men's jobs and established different pay rates for these groups, thereby discriminating against women.

job analysis   A systematic study of the tasks making up a job, employee skills required to do the job, time factors, situation-specific factors such as technology used, physical aspects, information flows, interpersonal and group interactions, and historical traditions associated with the job. Job analysis provides the information needed to do job evaluations.

job description   A document that details and explains task elements, responsibilities, and dynamics for a given job or occupation.

job evaluation   A formal process by which management assigns wage rates or wage grades to jobs according to some preestablished method for judging internal job value to the organization.

job family   A series of jobs clustered for job evaluation and wage and salary administration on the basis of common skills, occupational qualifications, technology, licensing, working conditions, union jurisdictions, work place, career paths, and organizational tradition.

Just Price doctrine   A medieval theory of job value that posited a "just," or equitable, wage for any occupation based on that occupation's place or station in the larger social hierarchy.

Kaiser plan   A cost-reduction program in which specific cost savings due to employee effort are shared with employees.

key job   A sample job used in wage surveys and job evaluation. Key jobs should vary in terms of job requirements, should exist in many organizations, should represent all salary levels in the organization, and should be technologically stable. Also known as benchmark jobs.

Kouba v. Allstate   A sex-discrimination case in which the defendant's practice of setting initial pay rates according to an employee's previous earnings led to women sales agents making less than men.

labor demand   The highest wage an employer or employers are willing to pay for a given level of employment or number of employees. Economists most often consider labor demand to be a function or line of points defining this wage for a series of employment levels.

Labor Management Relations Act (LMRA) of 1947   A federal law covering the conduct of labor relations. It defines unfair labor practices for management and labor unions.

labor market   In labor economic theory, a place where labor is exchanged for wages. In practice, labor markets are identified and defined by some complex combination of the following factors: (1) geography, (2) education and/or technical background required, (3) experience required by the job, (4) licensing or certification requirements, and (5) occupational membership.

labor's capacity value   Value placed on those jobs that rely heavily on general training.

labor's scarcity value   The value one places on labor because it is in short supply in the short run.

labor supply   The minimum wage necessary to attract a given number of employees or level of employment. Economists most often consider labor supply as a function or line of points defining this wage for a series of employment levels.

labor theory of value   A theory that proposes that the labor on a job adds to its value. Thus, the value of a commodity or service is determined by the amount of labor necessary to produce it. Karl Marx took the theory to its logical extreme by averring that labor was the only source of value in production. Thus, returns to capitalists in the form of profit or owners in the form of rent were considered as exploitation by Marx.

labor union   An organization that represents the collective interests of a group of employees. A certified union has the right to be the sole representative of the group in negotiating contracts with management specifying all terms of employment including wages and benefits.

law of effect   A principle in reward theory that says employees will tend to behave and perform in ways that get rewarded and will avoid behaving and performing in ways that do not get rewarded.

lead or lag policy   In annually adjusting wage structures to meet the market, the organization must decide when it will match (or follow or exceed) the market. If it chooses to match the market at the start of the year, it has adopted a lag policy; that is, it will lag behind the market the rest of the year as the market increases. If it chooses to project the market to the end of the year and match that, it has adopted a lead policy; that is, its wages will exceed the market rates during the year.

Lemons v. Denver   *See* Denver Nurses Case

leveraged ESOP   *See* employee stock ownership plan

local labor market   The market for a given type of labor in a local area (for example, the market for secretaries in a given city).

long-term incentive   An incentive that is deferred and may depend upon future performance (for example, a stock option).

lump-sum bonuses   Incentive bonus payments that are separate from base pay and do not fold into base pay.

McNamara-O'Hara Service Contract Act of 1965   A law that requires certain federal contractors providing services to the federal government to pay area prevailing wage rates.

management by objectives (MBO)   A management theory that emphasizes mutual goal setting between managers and their subordinates. According to MBO, motivation to perform is enhanced when employees participate in the goal-setting process and when the goals set are defined as explicitly as possible.

marginal physical product (MPP)   The physical output produced by the last employee hired.

marginal revenue product (MRP)   Technically defined as the product of additional physical product (marginal physical product) generated by the addition of another unit of labor and the price at which the employer can sell the additional physical product. According to economists, the marginal revenue product of labor defines the maximum wage an employer would be willing to pay for additional labor and is used to define an employer's demand for labor.

market pricing   The practice of setting wage rates for jobs directly according to the market price for that job in the external labor market.

maturity curve   Survey data reporting wage or income trends for professionals (for example, engineers, accountants) as a function of time in the profession. Some organizations use maturity curves for pricing jobs rather than relying on job evaluation techniques.

mean, or average   A statistic that is calculated by adding up all the values in a data set and dividing that figure by the number of observations. It is often used in salary surveys as a measure of the middle of the market.

median (second quartile)   The middle value in a set of data: 50% of the values are higher and 50% are lower. It is often used in salary surveys as the measure of the middle of the market.

Medicaid   An insurance program that provides medical benefits for indigent elderly persons.

Medicare   An insurance program under social security that provides medical and hospitalization benefits for covered persons 65 years of age and older.

merit increase   An adjustment to individual salary based on seniority, performance, or some other individual equity basis.

minimum wage   A minimum wage level for the majority of Americans, set by Congress under the Fair Labor Standards Act. Currently (1988) the minimum wage is $3.35.

monopsony   An economic condition in which one large purchaser dominates a market characterized by many small sellers. Monopsinists often find that because of their size relative to the sellers, they must pay increasingly higher prices to attract additional supply. This idea is used to explain why huge employers who dominate a single labor market often face upward-sloping supply functions.

Multiemployer Pension Plan Amendments Act of 1980   Some unionized employers participate in pension programs with other employers. The programs are usually administered by the union. The MPPAA requires an employee, once in such a plan, to assume liabilities for the fund, even on withdrawal from the plan.

multiple correlation coefficient   An index of how well the x variables in a multiple regression model explain variance in the y variable.

multiple linear regression   A statistical technique that allows the analyst to examine the joint impact of several independent variables (xs) on some one dependent variable (y) of interest. The technique is often employed in compensation when market survey wages (y) are regressed on measure of compensable factors (xs) employed in point factor job evaluation.

national, international labor market   A labor market that is truly national, or even international, in scope (for example, the market for nuclear physicists with Ph.D. qualifications).

National Position Evaluation Plan   A point-factor job-evaluation system that can be used to evaluate all jobs in an organization. It was developed from the old NEMA (National Electronic Manufacturers Association) system.

NEMA *See* National Position Evaluation Plan

nonexempt job A job subject to the minimum wage and overtime provisions of the Fair Labor Standards Act (*see* exempt job).

Old Age, Survivors, Disability, and Health Insurance Program (OASDHI) An omnibus federal social bill including retirement, survivors and disability insurance (social security), hospital and medical insurance for the aged and disabled (Medicare/Medicaid), black lung benefits for miners, supplemental security income, unemployment insurance, and public assistance and welfare services.

open pay system A compensation system in which information about wage ranges—at the extreme, even individual wage levels—is made public.

organizational culture The patterns of basic assumptions about what is right and what is wrong that has worked well enough to be taught to new members as the correct way to perceive, think, and feel in relation to each other and the organization.

organizational development (OD) Refers to attempts at improving organizational and individual behavior and performance through training and development efforts. Specific techniques may include group exercises, management by objectives (MBO), sensitivity training, and group discussion. Recently, proponents of organizational development have rediscovered an early principle of scientific management—that pay can be used as a powerful incentive for employees and groups to change their behavior.

organization chart Used in a salary survey to show where a specific benchmark job is located in the respondent's organization.

overlap The percentage overlap between two adjacent pay grades.

overtime Under the Fair Labor Standards Act, nonexempt employees must be paid one and one-half times their normal wage rate for all hours worked in excess of 40 in any work week.

PAQ *See* Position Analysis Questionnaire

pay as a lag system Compensation used to support and sustain performance over time.

pay as a lead system Compensation used to create incentives for people to change. Used in this fashion, pay communicates business plans and management's intentions and gets people's attention focused on business objectives.

pay at risk *See* earnings at risk

pay compression   A wage distribution problem that exists when a number of individuals receive about the same pay even though there are a number of individual and organizational differences that the organization purports to recognize by wage differentials. The worst pay compression problem exists when subordinates make about the same as their boss.

pay for performance   *See* merit increase

pay for time off   Paid time off such as vacation and holidays.

pay policy   Policy regarding placement of individual employee rates with respect to the salary structure.

pay range   *See* wage range

pay satisfaction   An employee's evaluative reaction to pay. Anticipation of pay satisfaction will influence an employee's decisions about his work. Actual rewards influence satisfaction and act as feedback that allows employees to adjust subsequent behavior.

pension   A benefit that defers income to fund retirement. The pension provides income during retirement years.

Pension Benefit Guarantee Corporation (PBGC)   A federal corporation set up in the Labor Department, similar to the Federal Deposit Insurance Corporation (FDIC) which guarantees vested pension rights. Insurance premiums are paid by employers with covered pension programs.

performance appraisal   Any system of determining how well an individual employee has worked during a period of time, frequently as a basis of a merit increase.

performance-based pay   *See* merit increase

perquisite   A benefit tied to a specific job (e.g., a company car for personal use, free meals for kitchen workers). Most perks are reserved for executives: country club memberships, first class travel rather than coach, and expense account entertainment.

piecerate   Direct performance payment based on production by a worker who receives a set amount for each piece produced.

point factor comparison method of job evaluation   The most prevalent form of job evaluation, the point factor method is a specific-factors (as opposed to whole-job), job-to-standards method.

Position Analysis Questionnaire (PAQ)   A job analysis technique that has been adapted to job evaluation by regressing PAQ results against wage survey data to get values of various job attributes.

prevailing wage   The wage in an area for a job said to be standard by the Department of Labor. This is usually the union rate.

process equity   In addition to fairness in pay outcomes (pay level, pay adjustments, job evaluations), employees also react to the fairness of the processes by which pay is administered. Process equity refers to the fairness by which pay programs are administered.

Elements of process equity include openness of the compensation system, communications about pay, employee participation in the compensation system, and grievance/appeal systems.

process issues   *See* process equity

profit sharing   A program in which some portion of profits is given to employees as a reward for performance.

Project 777   A market-based job evaluation system.

range   *See* wage range

range overlap   The degree to which two adjacent pay ranges coincide, important because overlap allows a job evaluated as higher than another (on internal equity grounds) to be paid less (on individual equity grounds).

range spread   The difference between the minimum rate and maximum rate for a pay grade or range. The statistic can be expressed as a percent of the minimum (for example, the maximum is 180% of the minimum) or as a percent above and below the midpoint (for example, the minimum is 20% lower than the midpoint and the maximum is 20% above the midpoint).

ranking method of job evaluation   The simplest form of job evaluation, a whole-job, job-to-job comparison.

red-circle   When a job is reevaluated and an incumbent is making more than the top of the wage range assigned to that job, the incumbent's salary is not lowered, but frozen, or red-circled, until adjustments to the structure bring that salary in line with the structure.

regional labor market   A labor market that extends beyond the confines of a local community, for example, the regional market for managers.

reward theory   A motivation theory that proposes that rewards that are made contingent on desired performance will be more effective than rewards that are distributed on some other basis (for example, paying for time).

Rucker Share of Production plan   A cost reduction program in which specific cost savings due to employee effort are shared with employees.

salary structure   *See* wage structure

Scanlon plan   A cost reduction program in which specific cost savings due to employee effort are shared with employees. The Scanlon plan involves much employee participation, predating quality circles with most of the same techniques but without the hype. Mr. Scanlon was an American union official. Scanlon plans appear to work best in medium-size organizations.

segmented market   A phrase referring to the fact that external labor markets are discontinuous. The market for physicians is different from the market for engineers, and movement from one to the other is restricted. Of most significance in the concept is the fact that labor demand and supply conditions vary across markets and explain much of the external wage variation observed across occupations. Segmented markets are sometimes called *balkanized markets*.

seniority   Length of time an employee has worked in a specific position. Many organizations provide differentials for seniority, rewarding organizational loyalty.

severance pay   Payments made to employees to compensate employment termination.

shift differentials   Extra wages given to employees who work during periods other than Monday through Friday from nine to five.

short-term incentive   An incentive that is paid in the form of current cash or benefit.

sick leave   Paid time for not working due to illness or injury.

skill-based pay (pay for knowledge)   Pay progression is determined by the increasing number of tasks or jobs an employee masters. Replaces a traditional job evaluation program with a few broadly defined positions. Under skill-based pay, employees perform a broad range of duties.

social security   A federal insurance program designed to provide a base income to the retired and disabled. It was not designed as a complete retirement pension: its creators were successful beyond their expectations in achieving this.

specific training   In human capital theory, any training that contributes marginal revenue product only to the employer providing the training and not to other employers. Specific training adds nothing to the marketability of the trainee. Learning to fire a howitzer in the Army is (hopefully) an example of specific training.

stock bonus plan   *See* employee stock ownership plan

structure policy   Policy regarding placement of the salary structure with respect to the external market.

supply-side factors   Aspects of the job that create value because of what the job demands in order to be carried out. Human capital, skills, and labor scarcity are examples of supply-side factors that create value in the job.

take home pay   Earnings less taxes, social security, and other deductions both voluntary and involuntary; the bottom line on the paycheck.

targeted compa ratio   In salary budgeting, the goal the manager seeks by the end of a plan year. Specifically, this goal is the ideal compa ratio for each employee once salary adjustments are made.

Tax Reform Act of 1986 (TEFRA)   Makes certain forms of benefits like health and accident insurance nontaxable.

third quartile   The value in a set of data below which 75% of the data falls and above which 25% of the data falls. Often used in salary surveys as a measure of the upper end of the market.

time span of discretion   The maximum period of time during which the use of discretion is authorized and expected without review of that discretion by a superior. Time span of discretion has been used as a noneconomic definition of job value by Elliott Jacques.

Title VII   A provision of the Civil Rights Act of 1964 that prohibits employers from taking any employment action that discriminates against a person because of race, religion, color, national origin, or sex. Compensation is covered as an employment action under this law.

top-down budget   A salary budgeting process by which the corporation dictates increases for every employee from the top down.

TRASOP (tax reduction stock ownership plan)   *See* employee stock ownership plan

turnover   The rate at which employees in a given job or group leave the organization. Sometimes seen as a symptom of external equity problems.

two-tier pay plan   Creates two tiers of wage rates for each job. New hires, after a certain date, are hired at a lower rate than those hired prior to the date. Creates two classes of employees. Is used as device for removing labor costs while honoring earlier wage commitments.

unemployment insurance   A state-administered, federally authorized, employer supported program designed to provide partial income replacement for a limited period when a worker loses his job through no fault of his own.

union shop agreement   A union security agreement whereby management agrees to require employees to join a union representing its employees as a condition of employment. Usually the provision calls for a new employee to join the union within some period of time (for example one month) after initial employment.

U.S. National War Labor Board (NWLB)   A government agency active in World War II. The board had as its goals the settlement of disputes between management and labor unions. The NWLB was the first federal agency to address wage discrimination between the sexes. It enforced the wage controls that gave the original impetus to the growth of benefits.

vacation pay   Extended period of time not worked but for which pay is received.

variable pay   *See* earnings at risk

vesting   The ownership of accrued pension rights. Vesting is required for ERISA-qualified pension programs. Basically, after 10 years of service, an employee "owns" all contributions made by the employer to the employee's pension plan. Vesting rules also apply to ERISA-qualified ESOPs and TRASOPs.

W-2 form   The form by which employers report employee earnings to the Internal Revenue Service.

Wage and Hour Division   The division of the U.S. Department of Labor charged with enforcing the provisions of the Fair Labor Standards Act.

wage and price controls   A federal program in which wages and prices are occasionally stabilized by government fiat. Most observers note that, historically, wages are easier to control than prices.

wage and salary policies   Salary survey information regarding the rules and procedures by which the pay program is administered.

wage and salary survey   Surveys conducted to develop information on wages and salaries being paid to various jobs in an industry or labor market.

wage contour   A way of considering an external wage structure, developed by labor economist John Dunlop. He defines a wage contour as a stable group of wage-determining units (bargaining units, plants, or firms) that are so linked together by (a) similarity of product markets, (b) resort to similar sources for labor, or (c) common market organization (custom) that they have common wage-making characteristics. As a practical matter, compensation planners must be accurate in correctly defining the contours in which they are hiring and competing.

wage curve A graph showing interconnected midpoints of wage rates. Dollars are shown on the vertical axis, wage ranges are shown on the horizontal axis.

wage differential Any difference in the wage two individuals get. Wage differentials may be due to occupation, industry, geography, company, performance, seniority, sex, race, age, or luck.

wage preference path A concept employed to explain a union's effect on the supply of labor faced by an employer. Indifference analysis is used to derive a union leadership's preferences for various combinations of wage levels and employment levels. The line connecting these preferences for various levels of labor demand is called the wage preference path and defines the wage level the union will seek in bargaining for various levels of employment.

wage range One segment of a wage structure. The range consists of a minimum wage level, a midpoint, and a maximum. Jobs are assigned to wage ranges through the job evaluation process.

wage structure The wage program of an organization composed of several pay grades and classifications. The organization must decide range width, overlap, and midpoint differences.

Walsh-Healy Public Contracts Act of 1936 A federal law requiring certain employers holding federal contracts for the manufacture or provision of materials, supplies, and equipment to pay industry-prevailing wage rates.

workers' compensation State insurance programs designed to provide immediate money for medical care and support to workers who are injured on the job, and to provide support to dependents if the worker is killed. Employers support these programs through specially assessed taxes.

Name Index

415

Subject Index